CULTURAL  ANTHROPOLOGY

Fourth Edition

CULTURAL ANTHROPOLOGY

MARVIN HARRIS
University of Florida

HarperCollinsCollegePublishers

Senior Acquisitions Editor: Alan McClare
Developmental Editor: Susan Messer
Project management, art direction/coordination, text and cover design:
    York Production Services
Art Studio: Dartmouth Publishing, Inc.
Photo Researcher: Carol Parden
Electronic Production Manager: Christine Pearson
Electronic Page Makeup: R.R. Donnelley & Sons Company
Printer and Binder: R.R. Donnelley & Sons Company
Cover Printer: Coral Graphic Services, Inc.

Cultural Anthropology, 4/e

LIBRARY OF CONGRESS CATALOGING-IN-PUBLICATION DATA
Harris, Marvin, 1927–
    Cultural Anthropology / Marvin Harris. — 4th ed.
        p.   cm.
    Includes bibliographical references and index.
    ISBN 0-673-46975-1
    1. Ethnology   I. Title
GN316.H36   1995
306—dc20   94-15639
                                CIP

95 96 97 98 7 6 5 4 3 2 1

BRIEF CONTENTS

CONTENTS

PREFACE

To the Instructor

Anthropology is the pivotal discipline for understanding contemporary multicultural perspectives and ethnic and racial conflict. I have tried to develop these issues in an even-handed manner in this fourth edition of *Cultural Anthropology* by taking pains to expose the errors and dangers of racism whether espoused by whites or African-Americans, and by acknowledging both the positive and the negative features of ethnic cultural politics. I have made several major changes to this end in this edition. Chapter 14, "Ethnicity, Race, and Racism" is new, as is Chapter 6, "Human Sexuality." The topics covered in Chapter 6 were previously scattered in the "Gender and Culture" and "Personality and Culture" chapters. Now they have been brought together and spotlighted as one of the most important interfaces between biological drives and cultural constructions.

I have also added a new feature called America Now Update. Where appropriate, materials that show the relevance of anthropology to the study of contemporary social issues appear in a special format between chapters. There are eleven such Updates:

Mode of Production

Fertility and the World's Most Expensive Children

New Gender Roles and Forms of Sexuality

Emergent Varieties of Capitalism

Matrifocal Families

Future Family

Law and Disorder

Is There a Ruling Class in the United States?

Race, Poverty, Crime, Drugs, and Welfare

A Theory of Gender Hierarchy Change

The Electronic Church

Many chapters contain their own internal references to relevant aspects of the industrial world that supplement the America Now Updates. This is especially true of the new Chapter 14, "Ethnicity, Race, and Racism."

In previous editions the last chapter, "The Anthropology of an Industrial Society" attempted to apply the basic concepts of the preceding chapters to an analysis of the United States, thereby making it clear that anthropology is relevant to contemporary issues found in postindustrial (or hypeindustrial) societies. Unfortunately, this chapter was not only last but it was also the longest. Instructors who used the text reported that they were obliged to hurry through or leave out the chapter in question. The America Now Update feature solves this problem.

Another major focus of changes in this edition is new boxes. There are 21 of them. Like all boxed material, they are intended to illustrate and explain aspects of the main text. And as you can see from the titles they bear, many are also intended to be provocative and a cause for thought and discussion:

A Great Moment in Science (The Original Darwin Wallace Paper)

Kanzi's Accomplishments

Refuting Creationism

Common Features of Black English

Changing Sexist Language in Catholic Prayer

Hero of Alexandria's Steam Engine

The Problems of Measuring Sustainable Yield

Infanticide in Nineteenth-Century Japan

How Many Biological Sexes Are There?

Is Homosexuality Genetic?

The Origin of Destructive Potlatches

Zumbagua Domestic Behavior

Future Family?

How to Choose a Witch

The Invention of Tradition

Why Africa Lags

Taking Care of Baby Among Hunter-Gatherers

No Rites Hurt Too

The Evidence for Aztec Cannibalism

Other Favorable Consequences of the Taboo on the Consumption of Beef

Emics and Etics in a Hospital Bureaucracy

One of my major objectives in writing the fourth edition has been to produce a livelier, more user-friendly volume. Chapter previews have been expanded and restyled to perk up the reader's curiosity. An expanded visual program should also help. There are cartoons and anthropological jokes. And in addition to the numerous illustrations found within each chapter, this edition contains two full-color photo essays that celebrate the visual dimensions of cultural diversity. One essay depicts the limitless imagination that humans everywhere display in adorning their faces and bodies with cloth, feathers, jewelry, paints, and other adornments; the second shows the various aspects of everyday life in a remote Amazonian Indian village.

Finally, as in previous editions, I have endeavored to make this text second to none in reflecting the latest and most authoritative work on the subjects covered. The instructor or student interested in further reading and research will benefit from 140 new citations added to the bibliography.

I would like at this time to express my appreciation to the people at HarperCollins for their assistance in fulfilling my plans for this edition. I thank especially editors Alan McClare and Susan Messer, as well as editorial assistant Margaret Loftus, photo editor Carol Pardon, and editorial assistant Michael Kimball. I also want to thank the anthropologists who reviewed the manuscript: Walter Adams, Kansas State University; Peter Aschoff, University of Mississippi; Bradley A. Blake, New Mexico State University; Anita Cowan, Texas Woman's University; John Fritz, Salt Lake Community College; Richard Furlow, College of DuPage; Geraldine Gambard, University of Massachusetts-Dartmouth; George L. Hicks, Brown University; Joan D. Laxson, Pine Manor College; Barry P. Michrina, Mesa State College; Edward J. Jay, California State University-Hayward; Richard Scaglion, University of Pittsburgh; Gary Shaffer, Scottsdale Community College; Jim Wanner, University of Northern Colorado. These reviews were deeply appreciated, both for their encouragement and their critical insights. Thanks to Bryan Byrne and Christopher Furlow for their help in matters bibliographical. Thanks also, as always, to Madeline Harris.

Marvin Harris

PREFACE

To the Student

Cultural Anthropology provides us with a global and comparative perspective for understanding the origin and prospects of the modern world. In the pages that follow you will learn mostly about the customs and beliefs of people who are alive today or who lived in the recent past—people who inhabit great cities and are citizens of superpowers, as well as people who live in tiny desert bands and remote jungle villages.

You are about to encounter an amazing variety of customs and beliefs. Some may amuse you; others may shock you. But I have not written this book to compete with Ripley's *Believe-It-Or-Not*. My aim is to explain—to the limits of currently known facts and the latest scientific theories—why customs and beliefs differ from one society to another, and why, despite such differences, remarkable similarities exist in the way human beings live in even the most distant parts of the globe.

I have done everything I could think of to make this book as easy to read as possible. Yet the subject matter of cultural anthropology is vast and complex. If we are to have serious explanations of scholarly merit, mental concentration cannot be eliminated. I won't apologize. I think you will get a lot out of reading this book. It will tell you not only what cultural anthropology is all about, but also something more important. It will tell you about your own customs and beliefs—how they originated, why they are maintained, and why they are changing. In other words, it will tell you a good deal about who you are and why you and your relatives, friends, and fellow citizens think and act in certain ways and not in others.

Marvin Harris

Chapter 1

THE BRANCHES OF ANTHROPOLOGY

Why Anthropology?
Why Study Anthropology?
Chapter Summary

Diversity in the U.S.A. Children wearing ethnic clothing.

Anthropology is the study of humankind—of ancient and modern people and their ways of living. Different branches of anthropology focus on different aspects of the human experience. Some branches focus on how our species evolved from earlier species. Others focus on how we came to possess the facility for language, how languages evolved and diversified, and how modern languages serve the needs of human communication. Still other branches focus on the learned traditions of human thought and behavior, how ancient cultures evolved and diversified, and how and why modern cultures change or stay the same.

People from different continents who speak different languages and who possess different values and religions find themselves living closer and closer together in a new global village. To all members of this new community, anthropology offers a unique invitation to examine, explain, and celebrate human diversity. At the same time, anthropology reminds us that, despite our different languages and cultures, we are all members of the same species, and we share a common nature and a common destiny.

Departments of anthropology in the United States offer courses in five major fields of knowledge about humankind: cultural anthropology (sometimes called ethnology or social anthropology), archaeology, anthropological linguistics, physical (or biological) anthropology, and applied anthropology (American Anthropological Association 1993; Givens and Skomal 1993).[1]

Cultural anthropology, the focus of this text, deals with the description and analysis of cultures—the socially learned traditions of past and present ages. It has a subdiscipline, *ethnography*, that describes and interprets present-day cultures. Comparison of these interpretations and descriptions can lead to the formation of hypotheses and theories about the causes of past and present cultural similarities and differences (Fig. 1.1a).

Archaeology and cultural anthropology possess similar goals but differ in the methods they use and the cultures they study. Archaeology examines the material remains of past cultures. Without the findings of archaeology, we would not be able to understand the human past, especially where people have not left any books or other written records (Fig.1.1b).

Anthropological linguistics is the study of the great variety of languages spoken by human beings. Anthropological linguists attempts to trace the history of all known families of languages. They are concerned with the way language influences and is influenced by other aspects of human life, and with the relationship between the evolution of language and the evolution of our species, *Homo sapiens*. They are also concerned with the relationship between the evolution of languages and the evolution of different cultures (Fig. 1.1c).

Physical anthropology (also called *biological anthropology*) connects the other anthropological fields to the study of ani-

mal origins and the biologically determined nature of *Homo sapiens*. Physical anthropologists seek to reconstruct the course of human evolution by studying the fossil remains of ancient humanlike species. Physical anthropologists also seek to describe the distribution of hereditary variations among contemporary populations and to sort out and measure the relative contributions to human life made by heredity, environment, and culture (Fig. 1.1d).

Applied anthropology utilizes the findings of cultural, archaeological, linguistic, and biological studies to solve practical problems affecting the health, education, security, and prosperity of human beings in many different cultural settings.

Why Anthropology?

This book is mainly about cultural anthropology. (See the author's *Culture, People, Nature: An Introduction to General Anthropology*, 6th edition, for a more comprehensive view of the major findings in all five fields.) We will however, touch briefly on certain key concepts and findings of the other fields that underlie the study of culture.

The distinction of anthropology is that it is global and comparative. Other disciplines are concerned with only a particular segment of human experience or a particular time or phase of our cultural or biological development. But anthropologists never base their general theoretical findings on the study of a single population, race, tribe, class, nation, time, or place. Anthropologists insist first and foremost that conclusions based on the study of one particular human group or civilization be checked against the evidence of other groups or civilizations. In this way, anthropologists hope to control the biases of their own sex, class, race, nation, religion, ethnic group, or culture. In anthropological perspective, all peoples and cultures are equally worthy of study. Thus, anthropology is incompatible with the view that a par-

---

[1]*See the first page of the bibliography for an explanation of the system of citations used in this book.*

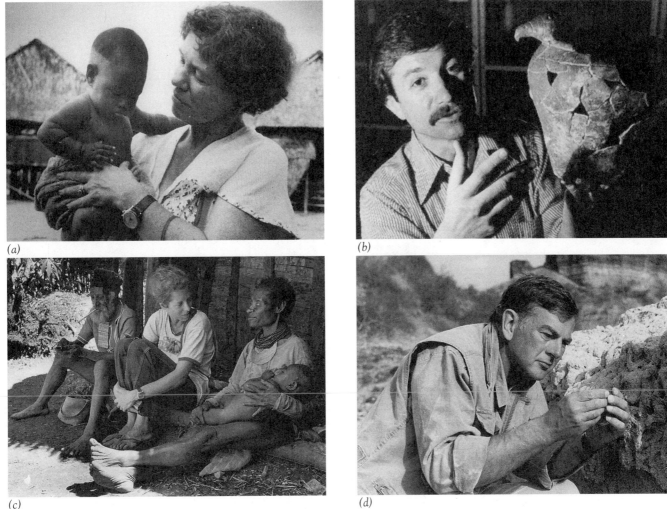

Figure 1.1
Anthropologists at Work
(a) Ethnographer Margaret Mead among the Manus Islanders. (b) Jerald T. Milanich, archaeologist,
Florida Museum of Natural History, with prehistoric (A.D. 200–900) Native-American bird vessel.
(c) Linguist Francesca Merlin with the speakers of a previously unknown language near Mt. Hagen,
New Guinea. (d) Physical anthropologist Donald Johanson fossil hunting at Olduvai Gorge.

ticular group and no one else represents humanity, stands at the pinnacle of progress, or has been chosen by God or history to fashion the world in its own image.

Anthropologists believe that a sound knowledge of humankind can be achieved only by studying distant as well as near lands and ancient as well as modern times. By adopting this broad view of the totality of human experience, perhaps we humans can tear off the blinders put on us by our local lifestyles and see ourselves as we really are.

Because of its biological, archaeological, linguistic, cultural, comparative, and global perspective, anthropology can answer many fundamental questions. In its exploration of our species' animal heritage, it can help us define what is distinctly human about human nature. Furthermore, it is strategically equipped to study the interaction between biological

and cultural differences and holds the key to the origins of social inequality in the form of racism, sexism, exploitation, poverty, and international underdevelopment. Thus anthropology has much to contribute to the understanding of the major issues that divide contemporary society and endanger world peace.

Why Study Anthropology?

Most anthropologists make their living by teaching in universities, colleges, and community colleges, and by carrying out university-based research. But a substantial and increasing proportion of anthropologists find employment in nonacademic settings. Museums, for example—especially

---

Box 1.1

AN ANTHROPOLOGICAL SCORECARD

Anthropologists frequently identify themselves with one or more specialized branches of the five major fields. The following is only a partial listing.

CULTURAL ANTHROPOLOGY

Ethnography—Describe contemporary cultures.

Medical anthropology—Study biological and cultural factors in health, disease, and the treatment of the sick.*

Urban anthropology—Study city life, gangs, drug abuse.*

Development anthropology—Study the causes of underdevelopment and development among the less-developed nations.*

ARCHAEOLOGY

Historic archaeology—Study cultures of the recent past by means of a combination of written records and archaeological excavations.

Industrial archaeology—Historic archaeology that focuses on industrial factories and facilities.

Contract archaeology—Conduct archaeological surveys for environmental impact statements and protection of historic and prehistoric sites.*

PHYSICAL (BIOLOGICAL) ANTHROPOLOGY

Primatology—Study social life and biology of monkeys, great apes, and other primates.

Human paleontology—Search for and study fossil remains of early human species.

Forensic anthropology—Identify victims of murders and accidents.

Establish paternity through genetic analysis.*

Population genetics—Study hereditary differences in human populations.

ANTHROPOLOGICAL LINGUISTICS

Historical linguistics—Reconstruct the origins of specific languages and families of languages.

Descriptive linguistics—Study the grammar and syntax of languages.

Sociolinguistics—Study the actual use of language in the communication behavior of daily life.

APPLIED ANTHROPOLOGY*

Starred items have strong applied focus.

---

museums of natural history, archaeology, and art and folklore—have long relied on the expertise of anthropologists. In recent years, anthropologists have been welcome in a greater variety of public and private positions: in government agencies concerned with welfare, drug abuse, mental health, environmental impact, housing, education, foreign aid, and agricultural development; in the private sector as personnel and ethnic relations consultants and as management consultants for multinational firms; and as staff members of hospitals and foundations (see Box 1.1).

In recognition of the growing importance of these nonacademic roles as a source of employment for anthropologists, many university departments of anthropology have started or expanded programs in applied anthropology. These programs supplement traditional anthropological studies with training in statistics, computer literacy, and other skills suitable for

solving practical problems in human relationships under a variety of natural and cultural conditions.

Despite the expanding opportunities in applied fields, the study of anthropology remains valuable not so much for the opportunities it presents for employment but for its contribution to the basic understanding of human variations and relationships. Just as the majority of students who study mathematics do not become mathematicians, so too the majority of students who study anthropology do not become anthropologists. For human relations fields, such as law, medicine, nursing, education, government, psychology, economics, business administration, and communication media, anthropology has a role to play that is as basic as mathematics. Only by becoming sensitive to the cultural dimensions of human existence and learning to cope with them can one hope to become optimally effective in any of these fields.

Anthropology has much to contribute to the educational philosophy known as *multiculturalism*, which stresses the importance of viewing the world from the perspectives of all the different cultures, races, and ethnic groups present in modern nations. As part of their attempt to broaden the cultural horizons of their students and combat ethnocentrism, many colleges have developed required cultural "diversity" courses. Cultural anthropology is the original multicultural approach to human social life. And it remains by far the most systematic and comprehensive alternative to traditional curriculums that view the world primarily in terms of "dead, white, European males."

Chapter Summary

Anthropology is the study of humankind. Its five major branches are cultural or social anthropology, anthropological linguistics, physical (or biological) anthropology, archaeology, and applied anthropology. Its distinctive approach lies in its global, comparative, and multidimensional perspective. The combined approach of all five fields is known as general anthropology.

"Anthropologists! Anthropologists!"

Chapter 2

THE NATURE OF CULTURE

Tuareg nobility. Among these lords of the Sahara, it is the men who wear the veils.

In this chapter, you will find alternative definitions of culture and of other key concepts such as society and enculturation. You will also encounter certain general processes that help explain why customs, traditions, and behavior are both similar and different around the world. Then we embark on the difficult but necessary task of identifying the principal parts of the system of behaviors and thoughts that constitute human social life—not only the parts but, to complicate matters, the alternative perspectives in which they can be viewed.

Finally, I will try to set forth as simply as possible the particular theoretical viewpoint that has guided my own work as an anthropologist and that underlies the organization of this textbook. It is tempting to spare you such brain-busting concepts as emics and etics or infrastructure, structure, and superstructure, but I think that would greatly diminish the scope and coherence of the explanations offered in the chapters to come.

Definitions of Culture

Culture refers to the learned, socially acquired traditions of thought and behavior found in human societies. (Animals, too, especially primates, have rudimentary forms of culture, as we shall see—p. 29). When anthropologists speak of a human culture, they usually mean the total, socially acquired lifestyle of a group of people, including their patterned, repetitive ways of thinking, feeling, and acting. Note that they do not just mean the literary and artistic achievements and standards of "cultured" elites, for anthropologists, plumbers, and farmers are as "cultured" as art collectors and opera-goers. And studying the lives of ordinary people is just as important as studying the lives of famous and influential people.

The definition of culture as consisting of patterns of acting (behavior) as well as patterns of thought and feeling follows the precedent set by Sir Edward Burnett Tylor, the founder of academic anthropology in the English-speaking world and author of the first general anthropology textbook:

> Culture taken in its wide ethnographic sense is that complex whole which includes knowledge, belief, art, morals, law, custom, and any other capabilities and habits acquired by man as a member of society. The condition of culture among the various societies of mankind, in so far as it is capable of being investigated on general principles, is a subject apt for the study of laws of human thought and action.

[1871: 1]

Many anthropologists, however, prefer to view culture as a purely mental phenomenon consisting of the ideas that people share concerning how one should think and act. As such, culture has been compared to a computer program—to a kind of "software" that tells people what to do under various circumstances. It is implicit in this view that ideas guide and cause behavior. But the relationship between ideas and behavior is much more complex. Behavior can also guide and

cause ideas. This can be seen in times when cultures change rapidly, as is happening today in most of the world. For example, prior to the 1970s, women who had husbands and school-age children in the United States believed that wives should depend on their husbands for family income. Driven by rising prices and a desire to maintain or raise their standard of living, increasing numbers of married women with school-age children violated this "program" and went to work anyway. Today, the majority of married women are in the labor force, with the highest participation rates found among women with school-age children, and it is generally regarded as fitting for women to do this. (See p. 82 for a more detailed look at how and why the program governing marriage and the family in the United States changed.)

Another drawback of viewing culture as a mental program rather than as having both mental and behavioral aspects is that many of the most pressing social problems of our times are not programmed at all. The traffic jam, for example (see p. 13), is a highly patterned cultural phenomenon that occurs despite of the programming that drivers receive to keep moving. Poverty is another example of a whole complex of activities that people are programmed not to do.

Society, Subculture, and Sociocultural System

As used in this book, the term *society* means an organized group of people who share a homeland and who depend on each other for their survival and well-being. Each human society has an overall culture, but all societies contain groups of people who have lifestyles that are not shared by the rest of the society. In referring to patterns of culture characteristics of such groups, anthropologists often use the term *subculture*. Even small societies have subcultures associated with such groups as males and females, or children and adults. In larger and more complex societies, one encounters subcultures associated with, for example, groups based on ethnic, religious, and class distinctions.

Finally, the term *sociocultural* should be noted. This term is short for "social and cultural" and is useful as a reminder that society and culture form a complex system of interacting parts (more about the components of sociocultural systems in a moment).

Enculturation

The culture of a society tends to be similar in many respects from one generation to the next. In part, this continuity in life-ways is maintained by the process known as *enculturation*. Enculturation is a partially conscious and partially unconscious learning experience whereby the older generation invites, induces, and compels the younger generation to adopt traditional ways of thinking and behaving. Thus, Chinese children use chopsticks (Fig. 2.1) instead of forks, speak a tonal ("sing-song") language, and learn to worship their ancestors because they have been enculturated into Chinese culture rather than into the culture of the United States. Enculturation is primarily based on the control that the older generation exercises over the means of rewarding and punishing children. Each generation is programmed to reward thought and behavior that conforms to the patterns of its own enculturation experience and to punish, or at least not to reward, behavior that does not so conform (Fig. 2.2).

The concept of enculturation (despite its limitations, as discussed later) occupies a central position in the distinctive outlook of modern anthropology. Failure to comprehend the role enculturation plays in maintaining each group's patterns of behavior and thought lies at the heart of the phenomenon known as *ethnocentrism*. Ethnocentrism is the belief that one's own patterns of behavior are always natural, good, beautiful, or important, and that strangers, to the extent that they live differently, live by savage, inhuman, disgusting, or irrational standards. People who are intolerant of cultural differences usually ignore the following fact: Had they been enculturated within another group, all those supposedly savage, inhuman, disgusting, and irrational lifestyles would now be their own. Recognizing the fallacy of ethnocentrism leads to tolerance of cultural differences and a desire to learn more about them.

Cultural Relativism

Anthropologists place great emphasis on the viewpoint known as *cultural relativism*. This concept has several meanings. To some anthropologists, cultural relativism means not passing judgment on the moral worth of other peoples' cultures. It means disavowing any absolute, universal moral

(a)

(b)

(c)

Figure 2.1
How, What, and When We Eat: Culture at Work
(a) *Midday meal, Rangoon, Myanmar. Food is good to touch as well as to eat.* (b) *Fast food, America's most notable contribution to world cuisine.* (c) *The correct way to eat in China.*

(a)

Figure 2.2
Passing Culture On
(a) In Bali, a man reads to his grandchildren from a script on narrow bamboo strips. (b) In India, a Sikh father teaches his daughter how to wrap a turban. (c) In Mission Viejo, California, young people learn the culturally approved manner of eating artichokes. (d) Navajo rug makers are made, not born.

(b)

(c)

(d)

standards that can be used to rank cultural beliefs and practices as good or evil. Probably the majority of anthropologists, however, would argue for a more provisional kind of relativism. Namely, they would hold in abeyance any moral judgments until they have learned what the world looks like to people in different cultures. Like everybody else, most anthropologists make ethical judgments about certain kinds of cultural patterns, but they seek to minimize the effect of these preferences and beliefs on the conduct of their research.

Science and the Relativity of Truth

It is important to clarify the distinction between the relativity of values and the *relativity of truth*. The first says there are no universal moral values, whereas the second says objective truth about human thoughts and actions is unobtainable. Objective truth is unobtainable according to some anthropologists because all observers, even those who use scientific methods, are biased by their own enculturation experience and by the values and perspectives associated with their race, nationality, ethnic group, class, and gender. The position that I adopt in this textbook is that anthropologists do not need to reject their values in order to carry out an objective study of cultural phenomena. They can disapprove of pollution, genocide, sexism, racism, poverty, child abuse, and nuclear war and still maintain scientific objectivity about these phenomena. Nor is there anything antiscientific in setting out to study certain cultural patterns because one wants to change them.

Scientific objectivity does not arise from having no biases—everyone is biased—but from taking care not to let one's biases influence the result of research. Indeed, science is a system of knowledge whose most important feature is that it seeks to control the influence of various biases on the conduct of research. Scientists do this by telling one another as clearly as possible what they have done to gather and analyze their data and by formulating coherent theories that can be tested and retested by other researchers. Those who assert that scientific methods cannot be applied to sociocultural phenomena commit a basic error: They assume that objective truth means the absolute, final, unquestioned truth. But science results in something else. It results in temporary and provisional objective truth. Science involves a never-ending process of formulating and testing new and better theories. Just because the final, absolute, objective, certain truth can never be reached does not mean that all truths are equally arbitrary and biased (Collins 1989; Harraway 1989; Lett 1991; Watson 1990).

Limitations of the Enculturation Concept

It is easy to see that enculturation cannot account for a considerable portion of the lifestyles of existing social groups. Clearly, replication of cultural patterns from one generation to the next is never complete (Fig. 2.3). Old patterns are not always faithfully repeated in successive generations, and new patterns are continually being added (Fig. 2.4).

In fact, the rate of innovation and nonreplication in the industrial societies has reached proportions alarming to each successive generation. Margaret Mead was among the first to call attention to the profound worldwide significance of the resulting "generation gap." Her description of the generation gap was written over two decades ago, but her words are as pertinent now as then:

> Today, nowhere in the world are there elders who know what the children know; no matter how remote and simple the societies are in which the children live. In the past there were always some elders who knew more than any children in terms of their experience of having grown up within a cultural system. Today there are none. It is not only that parents are no longer guides, but that there are no guides, whether one seeks them in one's own country or abroad. There are no elders who know what those who have been reared within the last twenty years know about the world into which they were born.

[1970: 77–78]

Enculturation, in other words, can account for the continuity of culture, but it cannot account for the evolution of culture.

Even with respect to the continuity of culture, enculturation has important limitations. As indicated, not every replicated cultural pattern results from the programming that one generation experiences at the hands of another. Many patterns are replicated because successive generations adjust to similar conditions in social life in similar ways. Sometimes the programming received may even be at odds with the actual patterns; people may be enculturated to behave in one way but be obliged by conditions beyond their control to behave in another way. I have already mentioned traffic jams as an example (Fig. 2.5); poverty is another one. As we will see in Chapter 13, many poor people find themselves living in houses, eating food, working at jobs, and raising families according to patterns that replicate their parents' subculture, not because their parents trained them to follow these patterns but because poor children confront educational, political, and economic conditions that perpetuate their poverty.

Diffusion

Whereas enculturation refers to the passing of cultural traits from one generation to the next, *diffusion* refers to the passing of cultural traits from one culture and society to another (Fig. 2.6). This process is so common that the majority of traits found in any society can be said to have originated in some other society. One can say, for example, that much of the government, religion, law, diet, and language of the

(a)

Figure 2.3
Culture, People, and the Sun
The relationship between people and the sun is mediated by culture.
Sunbathing (a) is a modern invention. On the beach at Villerville in
1908 (b), only "mad dogs and Englishmen went out in the midday
sun" without their parasols. As the rising incidence of skin cancer
attests, sunbathing can indeed be hazardous to your health.

(b)

United States was "borrowed" or diffused from other cultures. Thus the Judeo-Christian religions come from the Middle East; parliamentary democracy comes from Western Europe; the food grains in the American diet—rice, wheat, maize—come from Asian, Middle Eastern, and Native American civilizations, respectively; and the English language comes from the amalgam of several different European tongues (see p. 41).

Early in this century (see Appendix), diffusion was regarded by many anthropologists as the most powerful explanation for sociocultural differences and similarities. The lingering effects of this approach can still be seen in popular attempts to explain the similarities among major civilizations as the result of their derivation from each other—Polynesia from Peru, or vice versa; lowland Mesoamerica from highland Mesoamerica (Mesoamerica is roughly Mexico plus Central America), or vice versa; China from Europe, or vice versa; the New World (the Americas) from the Old; and so forth.

In recent years, however, diffusion has lost ground as an explanatory principle. It is true that, in general, the closer two societies are to each other, the greater will be their cultural resemblance. But these resemblances cannot simply be attributed to some automatic tendency for traits to diffuse. Societies close together in space are also likely to occupy similar environments; hence, the similarities between them may be caused by the effects of similar environmental conditions. Moreover, numerous societies in close contact for hundreds of years retain radically different ways of life. For example, the Incas of Peru (see p. 154) had an imperial government,

whereas the nearby forest-dwelling societies lacked centralized leadership of any kind. Other well-known cases are the African Ituri forest hunters and their Bantu agriculturalist neighbors, and the "apartment house" Pueblos and their marauding, nomadic Apache neighbors in the southwest United States. Resistance to diffusion, in other words, is as common as acceptance. If this resistance were absent, there would be no difference between Catholics and Protestants in Northern Ireland; Mexicans would speak English (or U.S. citizens Spanish), and Jews would accept the divinity of Jesus Christ (or Christians would reject it).

Furthermore, even if one accepts diffusion as an explanation, the question still remains of why the diffused item (say, monotheism or agriculture) originated in the first place. Finally, diffusion cannot account for many remarkable instances in which people who are known never to have had any contact with each other invented similar tools and techniques and developed remarkably similar forms of marriage and religious beliefs. The most dramatic examples of such independent inventions consist of discoveries and inventions that not only occur independently but at approximately the same time (see Box 2.1, 2.2).

In sum, diffusion is no more satisfactory than enculturation as a mode of explaining cultural differences and similarities. If only diffusion and enculturation affected social life, then we should expect all cultures to be the same and to stay the same; this is clearly not the case.

It would not be accurate to conclude, however, that diffusion plays no role in sociocultural evolution. The nearness of

(a)

Figure 2.4
The Limitations of Enculturation
(a) Punk grunge was not passed on by (b) Frank Sinatra's generation.

(b)

one culture to another often does influence the rate and direction of change as well as the specific details of sociocultural life, even if it does not shape the general features of the two cultures. For example, tobacco smoking originated among the native peoples of the Western Hemisphere and after 1492 spread to the most remote regions of the globe. This diffusion could not have happened if the Americas had remained cut off from the other continents. (The tobacco plant did not grow outside the Americas.) Yet contact alone obviously does not tell the whole story. Hundreds of other native American practices such as living in wigwams or in matrilocal households (see p. 127) did not diffuse even to the colonists who lived next door to native American peoples.

Fieldwork and the Mental and Behavioral Aspects of Culture

Cultural anthropologists employ many kinds of methods to learn about cultural patterns. These include survey questionnaires, censuses, life histories, genealogies, formal and informal interviews, filming, videotaping and audiotaping, and notetaking (Sanjek 1990; Bernard 1993). The most distinctive anthropological method, however, is *participant observation*. This method involves living for extended periods among a people and participating as much, and as closely, as possible in their daily round of activities, talking, listening, and just plain looking. (I have been a participant observer in two field studies, one in Mozambique and the other in Brazil, and I have used all the other methods at one time or another in my research in Brazil, Mozambique, New York's East Harlem, and India).

The aim of the fieldworker is to obtain knowledge of both the mental and behavioral aspects of a culture. The mental aspects consist of an inner world of thoughts and feelings that exist at various levels of consciousness:

a. People may not be aware of their "body language." For example, they may not be able to state the rules that govern the distance that they maintain between each other while holding a conversation (Fig. 2.7).

b. Other culturally patterned ways of thought exist closer to consciousness, but people express them only when questioned by the fieldworker. Thus, they can usually state the values, norms, and proper codes of conduct for activities such as weaning babies, courting mates, choosing leaders, treating diseases, entertaining guests, categorizing kin, worshiping God, and thousands of additional commonplace behaviors.

Figure 2.5
Traffic Jams
Nobody wants them, but they are a cultural pattern. (a) New York;
(b) Mexico City.

c. There are also numerous, fully conscious, explicit, and formal rules of conduct and statements of values, norms, and goals that people talk about during ordinary conversations, write down in law codes, or announce at public gatherings (rules about littering, making bank deposits, playing football, trespassing, and so on).

d. Finally, to make matters more complex, cultures have rules not only for behavior but also for breaking rules of

behavior, such as when you park your car in front of a sign that says "No Parking" and gamble on not getting a ticket (Fig. 2.8).

But knowledge of this inner world is not the only product of fieldwork. In addition, anthropologists observe, measure, film, and take notes about what people do during their daily, weekly, or annual rounds of activities. They watch births take place, attend funerals, go along on hunting expeditions, watch marriage ceremonies, and attend hundreds of other events and activities as they unfold. These events and activities constitute the behavioral aspect of culture.

Emic and Etic Aspects of Culture

The fieldworker can describe both mental aspects and behavioral events and still not offer a satisfactory description of culture. The problem is that both the thoughts and behavior of the participants can be viewed from two different perspectives: that of the participants themselves and that of the observers. In both instances, scientific, objective accounts of the mental and behavioral fields are possible. In the first instance, the observers use concepts and distinctions that are meaningful and appropriate to the participants; in the second instance, they use concepts and distinctions that are meaningful and appropriate to the observers. The first way of studying culture is called *emics*—pronounced ee-miks—and the second way is called *etics*—pronounced et-iks. (See Chapter 4 for the derivation of these terms from the linguistic concepts "phonemics" and "phonetics.")

The aim of emic descriptions is to produce a view of the world that the native participants accept as real, meaningful, or appropriate. In carrying out emic research, anthropologists attempt to acquire a knowledge of the categories and rules one must know in order to think and act as a native. They attempt to learn, for example, what rule lies behind the use of the same kin term for mother and mother's sister among the Bathonga, or when it is appropriate to shame house guests among the Kwakiutl, or how to ask a boy or a girl out for a date among U.S. teenagers.

The aim of etic descriptions, however, is simply to generate scientific theories about the causes of sociocultural differences and similarities. Rather than employ concepts that are necessarily real, meaningful, and appropriate from the native point of view, the anthropologist interested in the etic aspects of a culture uses categories and rules derived from the vocabulary of science—categories and rules that are often unfamiliar to the native. Thus etic studies may involve the measurement and juxtaposition of activities and events that native informants find inappropriate or meaningless (Headland, Pike, and Harris 1990).

(a)

(b)

(c)

Figure 2.6
Diffusion
Can you reconstruct the diffusionary history of the objects and activities shown in these scenes? (a) Headman in Arnhem, Australia, summoning his clanspeople to a meeting with a portable transmitter; (b) Mongolian metropolis; (c) Brazilian woodsman.

Box 2.1

OLD AND NEW WORLD SIMILARITIES

All items listed were present in both Old and New Worlds prior to 1492.

Technology
Textiles
Purple dye
Prepared from coastal mollusk
Elite connotation of purple
Scarlet dye (cochineal/kermes)
Prepared from plant louse
Resist dyeing
Loom
Cotton
Clothing
Turban
"Nightcap"
Pointed-toe shoes
Long robes
Sash, mantle, sandals, loincloth
Weapons, armor
Kettle-shaped helmet
Sling
Thickened textile armor
Metallurgy
Lost-wax casting
Smelting, alloying, forging, hammering, gilding, etc.
Ceramics highly developed
Paper
Lime sizing of writing surface

Architecture
Colonnade, aqueduct, canal, cement-lined reservoir, highway
Corbelled arch
True arch
Walled city
Fired brick
Pyramids
Mathematics
Place value notation
Zero concept
Zero sign
Astrology
Day names with associations like Eurasian constellations
Writing
Hieroglyph system (ca. 750 signs; use of ideographs, rebus, affixes)
Astronomy
Articulated lunar, solar, stellar calendar counts 360-day plus 5 extra days
Cycle of 7 days
Day measured sunset to sunset
Observatories
Eclipse records

(Box continued on next page)

Emics, Etics, and Cattle Sex Ratios

The following example demonstrates the importance of distinguishing between emics and etics when trying to describe and explain cultural differences and similarities. In the Trivandrum district of the state of Kerala in southern India, farmers told me that they obeyed the Hindu prohibition against the slaughter of cattle and that they never knowingly did anything to shorten the lives of their animals. Yet in Kerala, the mortality rate of male calves is almost twice as high as the mortality rate of female calves. In fact, male cattle 0 to 1 years-of-age are outnumbered by female cattle of the same group in a ratio of 67 to 100. The farmers themselves are aware that male calves are more likely to die than female calves, but they attribute the difference to the relative "weakness" of the males. "The males get sick more often," they said. When I asked them to explain why male calves got sick more

often than females, some farmers suggested that the males eat less than the females. A few farmers even explained that the male calves eat less because they are not allowed to stay at the mother's teats for more than a few seconds. But no one said that male cattle were not as valuable in Kerala as they are in other regions of India, where they are used for plowing dry fields. In Kerala, where rice, the principal crop is grown in postage-stamp fields, oxen are at a disadvantage. They tend to get stuck in the mud and break their legs. Water buffalo have no such problems and are thus preferred over oxen to prepare the fields for planting. The emics of the situation are that every calf has the "right to live" regardless of its sex. But the etics of the situation are that cattle sex ratios are systematically adjusted to the needs of the local ecology and economy through preferential male "bovicide." Although the unwanted calves are not slaughtered, many are more or less starved to death.

Box 2.1

OLD AND NEW WORLD SIMILARITIES *(continued)*

Social Organization

   Merchant class or caste

   Organized trade, "caravans"

   Corvée labor

   Kingship complex

      King concept

      Divine mandate

      Throne

      Canopy

      Umbrella, parasol, sign of dignity, rank

      Sceptre

      Crown or diadem

      Tomb in elevated structure with or without temple atop

      Burial chamber with hidden entry

      "Royal tombs" (conspicuous display)

      Dedicatory sacrifice, subfoundation burial of children

      Gold necklace, sign of office

      Heraldic devices

      Litter

      Deference of bowing, downcast eyes

Religion and Ritual

   Paradise concept

   Underworld, "hell" concept

   Dualism (strongly manifest)

   Earth, air, fire, water as basic elements

   Deluge motif

      Produced by rain

      A few persons saved in a vessel

      Bird sent forth to check drying

Pryamid tower built for safety against deluge

      Destroyed by being blown down by wind

Sacrifice complex

      Animals slain

      Human sacrifice

      Offerings burned on altar in ceremonial area

      Communion in consumption of part of the sacrifice

         Incense mixed with cereal one type of offering

      Parched grain or meal as offering

      Blood offered as sacrifice

      Blood scattered over area and participants

Snake symbolism

      Signifying wisdom, knowledge

      Signifying healing

      Signifying fertility

Incense

      Accompanying most rituals

      For purification

      For offering to gods, sweet, attractive

      Symbolizing prayer

      As route for ascent of soul

Adapted from Riley et al. 1971

The comparison of etic and emic versions of culture gives rise to some of the most important and intriguing problems in anthropology. Of course, emic and etic descriptions need not always differ from each other. And even in this case, if one gets to know Indian farmers very well, some of them may reluctantly discuss the need they feel to cull animals of the unwanted sex. But only an etic perspective can lead one to understand why in Northern India, where different ecological and economic conditions prevail, etic bovicide is practiced more against female than male cattle, resulting in some states in an adult cattle sex ratio of over 200 oxen for every 100 cows. (See Chapter 17 for more discussion on the emics and etics of cattle in India.)

The Universal Pattern

In order to compare one culture with another, the anthropologist has to collect and organize cultural data in relation to cross-culturally recurrent aspects or parts of the sociocultural system. The total inventory of these recurrent aspects or parts is called the *universal pattern*.

Anthropologists agree that every culture has patterns of behavior and thoughts related to making a living from the environment; raising children; organizing the exchange of goods and labor; living in domestic groups and larger communities; and expressing the creative, playful, aesthetic, moral, and intellectual aspects of human life. However,

Box 2.2

SIMULTANEOUS INDEPENDENT INVENTIONS

When the culture process has reached a point where an invention or discovery becomes possible, that invention or discovery becomes inevitable.

The discovery of sun spots was made independently by at least four men in a single year: by Galileo, Fabricius, Scheiner, and Harriott, in 1611. The parallax of a star was first measured by Bessel, Struve, and Henderson, working independently, in 1838. Oxygen was discovered independently by Scheele and Priestly in 1774. The invention of the self-exciting dynamo was claimed by Hjorth, Varley, Siemens, Wheatstone, and Ladd in 1866–67, and by Wilde between 1863–67. The solution of the problem of respiration was made independently by Priestly, Scheele, Lavoisier, Spallanzani, and Davy, in a single year, 1777. Invention of the telescope and the thermometer each is claimed by eight or nine persons independently and at approximately the same time.

"Even the southpole, never before trodden by the foot of human beings, was at last reached twice in one summer." The great work of Mendel in genetics lay unnoticed for many years. But when it was eventually rediscovered, it was done not by one man but by three—de Vries, Correns, and Tschermak—and in a single year, 1900. One could go on indefinitely. When the growing, interactive culture process reaches a certain point, an invention or discovery takes place.

The simultaneity of multiple inventions or discoveries is sometimes striking and remarkable. Accusations of plagiarism are not infrequent; bitter rivalries are waged over priorities. "The right to the monopoly of the manufacture of the telephone was long in litigation; the ultimate decision rested on an interval of hours between the recording of concurrent descriptions by Alexander Bell and Elisha Gray."

White 1949: 208–210.

Figure 2.7
Body Language.
In a Spanish village, the women follow unconcious rules for maintaining a space between them while conversing.

1. Infrastructure

Consists of the technologies and productive and reproductive activities that bear directly on the provision of food and shelter, protection against illness, and the satisfaction of sexual and other basic human needs and drives. Infrastructure also embraces the limitations and opportunities placed on production and reproduction by a society's natural habitat, as well as the means employed to increase or decrease population growth. For example, a sketch of the infrastructure of modern-day Japan might include Japan's electronic computerized and robotized information and manufacturing economy, its dependence on imported raw materials, the effectiveness of its public health system, its reliance on abortions as a means of population regulation, and the extensive damage that has been done to the natural habitat by various forms of industrial pollution and economic growth.

2. Structure

Consists of the groups and organizations present in every society that allocate, regulate, and exchange goods, labor, and information. The primary focus of some groups is on kinship and family relations; others provide the political and economic organization for the whole society; still others provide the organization for religious rituals and various intellectual activities. To continue to use Japan as an example, structural features would include a domestic economy based on small, male wage-earner, urban-dwelling nuclear families (see p. 104); a political econo-

anthropologists do not agree on how many subdivisions of these categories should be recognized or on what priority they should be given when it comes to doing research.

In this book, we will use a universal pattern consisting of three major divisions: infrastructure, structure, and superstructure (Box 2.3).

(a)

(b)

(c)

(d)

Figure 2.8
Rules for Breaking Rules
Cultural behavior cannot be predicted from a knowledge of a simple set
of rules. In (b), a handicapped driver is taking down the license number
of a car that has parked against the rule. (a), (c), and (d) tell their
own sad stories.

my that is characterized by global corporations regulated and assisted by the state; and a moderately democratic parliament. It would also include organizations such as universities, Buddhist temples, and art museums.

Obviously the focus of a given social group may overlap with the focus of another. Multinational corporations, for

example, do more than produce and sell commodities; they also foster or create beliefs about free trade and consumerism. Governments may contribute to the regulation of every aspect of social life; established churches may regulate sexual and reproductive behavior as well as spread religious beliefs. But in order for us to study

---

Box 2.3

COMPONENTS OF THE UNIVERSAL PATTERN*

INFRASTRUCTURE

MODE OF PRODUCTION.

The technology and the practices employed for expanding or limiting basic subsistence production, especially the production of food and other forms of energy, given the restrictions and opportunities provided by a specific technology interacting with a specific habitat. Technology of subsistence. Techno–environmental relationships. Ecosystems. Work patterns.

MODE OF REPRODUCTION.

The technology and the practices employed for expanding, limiting, and maintaining population size. Fertility, natality, mortality. Nurturance of infants. Medical control of demographic patterns. Contraception, abortion, infanticide.

STRUCTURE

DOMESTIC ECONOMY.

The organization of reproduction and basic production, exchange, and consumption within camps, houses, apartments, or other domestic settings. Family structure. Domestic division of labor. Domestic socialization, enculturation, education. Age and gender roles. Domestic discipline, hierarchies, and sanctions.

POLITICAL ECONOMY.

The organization of reproduction, production, exchange, and consumption within and between bands, villages, chiefdoms, states, and empires. Political organizations, factions, clubs, associations, and corporations. Division of labor, taxation, tribute. Political socialization, enculturation, education. Law and order. Class, caste, urban, and rural hierarchies. Discipline, police and military control. War.

SUPERSTRUCTURE

Art, music, dance, literature, advertising. Values. Meaning. Symbols. Religious rituals, myths, and beliefs. Sports, games, hobbies. Science

Remember, each of these components can be viewed from an emic, etic, behavioral, or mental perspective.

---

these connections, we must begin with some preliminary map of a society's structure based on the primary focus of its most important groups.

3. Superstructure

Consists of the behavior and thought devoted to symbolic, ideational, artistic, playful, religious, and intellectual endeavors as well as all the mental and emic aspects of a culture's infrastructure and structure. This would include, in the case of Japan, such features as the Shinto and Buddhist religions; distinctive forms of Japanese painting, theater, and poetry; a penchant for baseball and wrestling; and a belief in teamwork as a source of competitive advantage.

The Diversity of Anthropological Theories

The kinds of research that anthropologists carry out and the kinds of conclusions they stress are greatly influenced by the basic assumptions they make about the causes of cultural evolution. Basic assumptions made by anthropologists of different theoretical persuasions are called *research strategies*, or *paradigms*.

No textbook can conceivably be written so as to represent all the current research strategies with bias toward none and equal coverage for all. In the chapters to come, I have made a conscious effort to include alternative viewpoints on controversial issues. Inevitably, however, my own research strategy dominates the presentation. The point of view followed throughout is known as *cultural materialism*. This research strategy holds that the primary task of cultural anthropology is to give scientific causal explanations for the differences and similarities in thought and behavior found among human groups. Cultural materialism makes the assumption that this task can best be carried out by studying the material constraints and opportunities to which human existence is exposed. These constraints and opportunities arise from the need to produce food, shelter, tools, and machines and to reproduce human populations under conditions set by biology and the environment. They are called material constraints and opportunities in order to distinguish them from constraints or opportunities presented by ideas and other mental or spiritual aspects of a society's superstructure, such as values, religion, and art. For cultural materialists, the most likely causes of variation in the mental or spiritual aspects of human life are the variations in a society's infrastructure.

Thus, infrastructure, structure, and superstructure are not equally effective in determining the retention or extinction of sociocultural innovations. When innovations originate on the infrastructural level (industrial robots, for example), they are likely to be selected for if they enhance the efficiency with which infrastructure satisfies basic human biopsychological needs and drives. Moreover, such infrastructural changes are likely to be selected for, even if they are markedly incompatible with the preexisting structural and superstructural components (unionized, labor-intensive assembly lines; fear that robots will cause unemployment). In other words, any deep incompatibility between an adaptive infrastructural innovation and the structural and superstructural components will usually result in substantial changes in the other components. In contrast, innovations that arise in the structural or superstructural sectors (for example, new religions) are likely to be selected against if they are deeply incompatible with the infrastructure (that is, if they substantially impede the system's ability to satisfy basic human needs and drives).

This does not mean that the mental and spiritual aspects of cultures are somehow less significant or less important than production, reproduction, and ecology. Moral values, religious beliefs, and aesthetic standards are in one sense the most significant and most distinctly human of all of our attributes. Their importance is not an issue. What is an issue is how we can best explain—if we can explain at all—why a particular human population has one set of values, beliefs, and aesthetic standards, whereas others have different sets of values, beliefs, and aesthetic standards. (See the Appendix for a discussion of alternative approaches in anthropology.)

Chapter Summary

A culture consists of the socially acquired ways a particular society's members think and feel. Cultures maintain continu-

ity by means of the process of enculturation. In studying cultural differences, one must guard against the habit of mind called ethnocentrism, which arises from a failure to appreciate the far-reaching effects of enculturation on human life. Enculturation, however, cannot explain how and why cultures change. Moreover, not all cultural recurrences in different generations result from enculturation. Some result from reactions to similar conditions or situations.

Whereas enculturation denotes the process by which culture is transmitted from one generation to the next, diffusion denotes the process by which culture is transmitted from one society to another. Diffusion, like enculturation, is not automatic and cannot stand alone as an explanatory principle. Neighboring societies can have both highly similar as well as highly dissimilar cultures.

Culture, as defined in this book, consists of thoughts that take place inside people's heads as well as the behavior that people engage in. Anthropologists use many kinds of methods for studying cultures, but they are best known for participant observation. Unlike other social animals, which possess only rudimentary cultures, human beings can describe their thoughts and behavior from their own point of view. In studying human cultures, therefore, one must make explicit whether it is the native participant's point of view or the observer's point of view that is being expressed. These are the emic and etic points of view, respectively.

Both mental and behavioral aspects of culture can be approached from either the emic or etic point of view. Emic and etic versions of reality sometimes differ markedly; however, there is usually some degree of correspondence between them. In addition to emic, etic, mental, and behavioral aspects, all cultures share a universal pattern. The universal pattern as defined in this book consists of three main components: infrastructure, structure, and superstructure. These components in turn consist, respectively, of the modes of production and reproduction; the domestic and political economy; and the creative, expressive, aesthetic, and intellectual aspects of human life. Categories such as these are essential for the organization of research and differ according to the research strategy one adopts.

Anthropology encompasses many alternative research strategies; the one followed in this book is cultural materialism. The aim of this strategy is to discover the causes of the differences and similarities in thought and behavior that characterize particular human populations. Cultural materialists regard infrastructure as the key to understanding the evolution of sociocultural systems. This does not mean, however, that structure and superstructure are less important or less essential for human social life.

Chapter 3

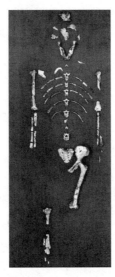

GENES, EVOLUTION, AND CULTURE

"Lucy." An early hominid found at Hadar, Ethiopia.

The human capacity for culture evolved from rudimentary beginnings among our apelike ancestors. Once these ancestors passed certain biological thresholds under the influence of natural selection, cultural behavior underwent its own form of evolution, resulting in an increasingly complex social life and an increasing dependence of human beings on cultural practices for survival. This leads to the question of the extent to which the capacity for culture exists among nonhuman species. We shall examine the evidence for the use of tools and language among chimpanzees and other primates—the species that most resemble humans—in order to answer this question. A point to be emphasized is that the processes that account for biological evolution and those that account for cultural evolution are quite distinct even though it was biological evolution that made cultural "takeoff" possible. The chapter ends with a clarification of the difference between evolutionism and creationism as explanatory principles.

Genes and Natural Selection

The principal process responsible for biological evolution is known as *natural selection*. Natural selection takes place because individual organisms reproduce at different rates and because every species confronts limits on the space, energy, and resources that it needs for reproduction. Natural selection alters the frequency and type of *genes*—the fundamental units of heredity—present in successive generations of a particular species.

This is how it works: During the process by which genes replicate themselves, they are prone to make errors in their chemical code. Most of these errors decrease the fitness of the individuals in whom they occur; others, however, increase their fitness. *Fitness* here means nothing more than the number of offspring in which a particular genetic variant appears in successive generations. Genetic variants that lead to higher fitness are said to be selected for by natural selection; those that lead to lower fitness are said to be selected against by natural selection.

Fitness is associated with many kinds of factors such as the organism's ability to resist disease, to gain or hold space more securely, to obtain energy in larger or more dependable amounts, or to the increased efficiency and dependability of some aspect of the reproductive process itself.

If the rates of reproductive success associated with different *genotypes* (types of genes) are markedly unequal, natural selection can increase the frequency of the favored genotypes in a few tens of generations. The power of natural selection to raise the frequency of a rare gene variant can be seen in the evolution of penicillin-resistant strains of bacteria. The variants conferring resistance are present in normal populations of bacteria but in only a small percentage of individuals. As a result of the differential reproductive success of such individuals in the presence of the antibiotic, however, the resistant genotype soon becomes the most common genotype.

Natural Selection and the "Struggle for Survival"

It was Charles Darwin and Alfred Wallace (Box 3.1) who formulated the basic principles of how organic evolution could result from natural selection. Under the influence of the prevailing philosophy of economic competition, however, both Darwin and Wallace accepted Thomas Malthus's concept of a "struggle for survival" as the main source of selection for reproductive success. Thus, in the nineteenth century, natural selection was pictured incorrectly as the direct struggle between individuals for scarce resources and sexual partners, and even more erroneously as the preying upon and destruction of one another by organisms of the same species. Although within-species killing and competition sometimes do play a role in organic evolution, the factors promoting differential reproductive success do not necessarily relate to an organism's ability to destroy other members of its own population or to prevent them from obtaining nutrients, space, and mates.

Today, biologists recognize that natural selection favors cooperation within species as often as it favors competition. In social species, the perpetuation of an individual's genes often depends as much on the reproductive success of its close relatives as on its own survival and reproduction. Many social insects even have "altruistic" sterile "castes" that assure their own genetic success by rearing the progeny of their fertile siblings.

Natural Selection and Behavior

Natural selection not only shapes anatomy and physiology, it also shapes behavior. Specific genes determine, for example, that some species of fruit flies will fly upward and others downward when they try to avoid a hungry bird, or that some

On the Tendency of Species to form Varieties; and on the Perpetuation of Varieties and Species by Natural Means of Selection. By Charles Darwin, Esq., F.R.S., F.L.S., & F.G.S., and Alfred Wallace, Esq. Communicated by Sir Charles Lyell, F.R.S., F.L.S., and J. D. Hooker, Esq., M.D., V.P.R.S., F.L.S. &c.[*]

[Read July 1st, 1858.]

London, June 30th, 1858.

MY DEAR SIR,—The accompanying papers, which we have the honour of communicating to the Linnean Society, and which all relate to the same subject, viz. the Laws which affect the Production of Varieties, Races, and Species, contain the results of the investigations of two indefatigable naturalists, Mr. Charles Darwin and Mr. Alfred Wallace.

These gentlemen having, independently and unknown to one another, conceived the same very ingenious theory to account for the appearance and perpetuation of varieties and of specific forms on our planet, may both fairly claim the merit of being original thinkers in this important line of inquiry; but neither of them having published his views, though Mr. Darwin has for many years past been repeatedly urged by us to do so, and both authors having now unreservedly placed their papers in our hands, we think it would best promote the interests of science that a selection from them should be laid before the Linnean Society.

[*]*Darwin's friends, Lyell and Hooker, interceded to protect Darwin from being upstaged by Wallace. This is one of the most remarkable cases of simultaneous independent invention (see p. 17).*

Journal of the Proceedings of the Linnean Society—Zoology 3(1859): 45–46.

wasps lay their eggs in a particular species of caterpillar and none other. Genes also directly determine the mating rituals of fish, the web-building of spiders, the feeding of queen bees by workers, and countless other behavioral expressions of drives and instincts characteristic of different animal species. Like all other genetically determined traits, these behaviors evolve as a result of copying errors in the replication of genotypes. The wasp's preference for one species of caterpillar, for example, was an error (a mutation) that was selected for because it increased the wasp's fitness. Thus, a new pattern of behavior based on a new genotype became part of the wasp's instinctual program.

Although it is very useful for organisms to be equipped with a program of detailed behavioral responses encoded in their genes, there is another type of behavior that is not programmed in the genes and that has many advantages. This is behavior that is learned and that is programmed in the organism's neural network and brains. For example, seagulls learn to recognize and to follow fishing boats; they learn the location of fast-food restaurants, town dumps, and other sources of garbage; and they learn all these behaviors without a single change in their genotype. None of this behavior therefore will be encoded in the genes of their offspring. Future generations of seagulls can acquire these behaviors only by learning them on their own.

The ability to acquire new patterns of behavior through learning is a fundamental feature of all multicelled animals. This ability has been widely selected for because it is a more flexible and opportunistic pattern of behavior than genetically controlled responses. Learning enables individuals to adjust to or take advantage of novel opportunities (like fast-food french fries spilled in parking lots) without having to wait for the appearance and selection of genetic errors.

Nonhuman Culture

Selection for increased learning capacity set the stage for the emergence of culture. This capacity has a neurological base; it depended on the evolution of larger and more complex brains and of more intelligent species. The great evolutionary novelty represented by culture is that the capabilities and habits of culture-bearing animals are acquired through *social heredity* rather than through the more ancient process of biological heredity. By social heredity is meant the shaping of a social animal's behavior in conformity with information stored in the brains rather than in the genes of other members of its social community. (It must be stressed, though, that actual cultural responses always depend in part on genetically predetermined capacities and predispositions.)

Many animals possess learned traditions that are passed on from one generation to the next and that can be thought of as rudimentary forms of culture. As we shall see in a moment, chimpanzees and other primates possess rudimentary learned traditions. However, only among the *hominids* (members of the human as opposed to the ape family) has culture become a more important source of adaptive behavior than biological evolution based on changes in gene frequencies. Able to stand and walk erect, their hands freed entirely from locomotor and support functions, the earliest hominids probably manufactured, transported, and made effective use of tools as a primary means of subsistence. Apes, on the other hand, survive nicely with only the barest inventory of such tools.

Hominids, ancient or modern, have probably depended on some form of culture for their very existence.

Tools and Learning

Experimental approaches to behavior show that most birds and mammals and especially monkeys and apes are "intelligent" enough to learn to make and use simple tools under laboratory conditions. Under natural free-ranging conditions, however, the capacity to make and use tools is expressed less frequently because most animals can get along quite effectively without having to resort to artificial aids. Natural selection has adapted them to their particular habitat by providing body parts such as snouts, claws, teeth, hooves, and fangs. Thus, though primates are intelligent enough to make and use tools, their anatomy and normal mode of existence disincline them to develop extensive tool-using repertoires. Among monkeys and apes, the use of the hand for tool use is inhibited by the importance of the forelimbs in walking, running, and climbing. That is probably why the most common tool-using behavior among many different species of monkeys and apes is the repelling of intruders with a barrage of nuts, pinecones, branches, fruits, feces, or stones. Throwing such objects requires only a momentary loss of the ability to run or climb away if danger threatens (Fig. 3.1)

Among free-ranging monkeys and apes, the most accomplished tool user is the chimpanzee. Over a period of many years, Jane Goodall and her associates have studied the behavior of a single population of free-ranging common chimpanzees in the Gombe National Park in Tanzania (Fig. 3.2). They have discovered that the chimpanzees "fish" for ants and termites (Fig. 3.3). Fishing for termites involves first breaking off a twig or a vine, stripping it of leaves and side branches, and then locating a suitable termite nest. Such a nest is as hard as concrete and impenetrable except for certain thinly covered tunnel entrances. The chimpanzee scratches away the thin covering and inserts the twig. The termites inside bite the end of the twig, and the chimpanzee pulls it out and licks off the termites clinging to it. Especially impressive is the fact that the chimpanzees will prepare the twig first and then carry it in their mouths from nest to nest while looking for a suitable tunnel entrance (van Lawick-Goodall 1986).

"Anting" provides an interesting variation on this theme. The Gombe chimps "fish" for a species of aggressive nomadic driver ant that can inflict a painful bite. On finding the temporary subterranean nest of these ants, the chimps make a tool out of a green twig and insert it into the nest entrance. Hundreds of fierce ants swarm up the twig to repel the invader:

> The chimpanzee watches their progress and when the ants have almost reached its hand, the tool is quickly withdrawn.

Figure 3.1
Omo Tools
These stone tools, found at Omo, Ethiopia, may have been manufactured as long as three million years ago.

In a split second the opposite hand rapidly sweeps the length of the tool catching the ants in a jumbled mass between thumb and forefinger. These are then popped into the open, waiting mouth in one bite and chewed furiously.

[McGrew 1979: 278]

Additionally, chimpanzees can manufacture "sponges" for sopping up water from an inaccessible hollow in a tree. They strip a handful of leaves from a twig, put the leaves in their mouth, chew briefly, put the mass of leaves in the water, let them soak, put the leaves to their mouths, and suck the water off. A similar sponge is employed to dry their fur, to wipe off sticky substances, and to clean the bottoms of chimpanzee babies. Gombe chimpanzees also use sticks as levers and digging tools to pry ant nests off trees and to widen the entrance of subterranean beehives.

Observers in other parts of Africa report similar types of behavior—variants of fishing for ants, dipping for termites, and digging up insect nests or prying them loose. They have watched chimpanzees pound or hammer tough-skinned fruit, seeds, and nuts with sticks and stones. The chimps of the Tai forest of the Ivory Coast open the hard shells of the panda

Figure 3.2
Jane Goodall
Making friends with chimps Prof and Pax in Gombe National Park, Tanzania.

nut with rocks that serve as hammers. They search the forest floor for a suitable hammerstone, which may weigh anywhere from 1 to 40 pounds. Then they bring the stones back in the crook of their arm, hobbling on three legs, from as far as 600 feet. They place the nuts on thick tree roots or exposed rock that serve as anvils and pound away (Boesch and Boesch 1984, 1991; Whitesides 1985). In West Senegal, chimps use stone hammers to pound open the fruits of the baobab tree (Bermejo et al. 1989).

Inspired by these feats of chimpanic ingenuity, Nicholas Toth of the University of Indiana has been teaching a chimpanzee named Kanzi how to make stone tools (Gibbons 1991) (Fig. 3.4). Ultimately, Toth hopes that Kanzi will teach his fellow chimps to do the same. (See p. 31 for more about Kanzi.)

Is It Culture?

There appears to be no specific genetic information that is responsible for chimpanzee termiting and anting. True, in order for this behavior to occur, genetically determined capacities for learning, for manipulating objects, and for omnivorous eating must be present in the young chimpanzee. But these general biological capacities and predispositions cannot explain termiting and anting. Given nothing but groups of young chimpanzees, twigs, and termite nests, termiting and anting are unlikely to occur. The missing ingredient is the information about termiting and anting that is stored in the brains of the chimpanzee mothers who display this information to their young. In the Gombe preserve, chimpanzees do not begin termiting until they are 18 to 22 months old. At first their behavior is clumsy and inefficient, and they do not become proficient until they are about 3 years old. Goodall witnessed many instances of infants watching intently as the adults termited. Novices often retrieved discarded termiting sticks and attempted to use them on their own. Anting, with its risk of being bitten, takes longer to learn. The youngest chimp to achieve proficiency was about 4 years old (McGrew 1977: 282).

The conclusion that anting is a cultural trait is strengthened by the fact that chimps at other sites do not exploit driver ants even though the species is widely distributed throughout Africa. At the same time, other groups of chimps do exploit other species of ants and in ways that differ from the Gombe tradition. For example, chimps in the Mahale mountains 170 kilometers south of Gombe insert twigs and

Figure 3.3
Chimpanzee Termiting
A stick carefully stripped of leaves is inserted into the nest. The chimpanzee licks off the termites that cling to the stick when it is withdrawn.

Figure 3.4
Handy Chimp
Pygmy chimp Kanzi fashions a stone tool.

bark into the nests of tree-dwelling ants, which Gombe chimps ignore (Nishida 1987; McGrew 1992).

Extensive studies of nonhuman culture have been carried out with Japanese macaques. Primatologists of the Primate Research Institute of Kyoto University have found a wide variety of customs and institutions based on social learning. They have even observed the process by which behavioral innovations spread from individual to individual and become part of a monkey troop's culture independently of genetic transmission.

To attract monkeys near the shore for easier observation, Kyoto researchers set sweet potatoes on the beach. One day a young female began to wash the sand from the sweet potatoes by plunging them in a small brook that ran through the beach. This washing behavior spread throughout the group. Nine years later, 80 to 90 percent of the animals were washing their sweet potatoes, some in the brook, others in the sea (Fig. 3.5). When wheat was spread on the beach, the mon-

keys of Koshima at first had a hard time separating the kernels from the sand. Soon, however, one of them invented a process for doing so, and this behavior was taken over by others. The solution was to plunge the wheat into the water (Fig. 3.6). The wheat sinks more slowly than the sand (Itani 1961; Itani and Nishimura 1973; Miyadi 1967).

The Evolution of the Hominids

The separation of the ancestral line leading to human beings from the line leading to chimpanzees, our closest nonhuman relatives, probably occurred between five and eight million years ago. By 2.5 million years ago (Ciochon 1987; Johanson and Shreeve 1989; Johanson 1993; Leakey and Lewin 1992), there were at least two kinds of hominids, one called the *Australopithecines,* which had ape-sized brains and became extinct, and the other called *Homo habilis,* which was a remote but direct ancestor of our species (Fig. 3.7). We know that the Australopithecines were hominids because their limbs and bodies were already completely adapted to walking upright—Mary Leakey even found 3-million-year-old australopithecine footprints to prove it (Fig. 3.8)!

Hominids were not initially selected for their braininess but for their peculiar upright gait. Why this mode of getting about, called *bipedalism*, was selected for is still a matter of debate, but it is clear that once hands were no longer needed for walking or running, more use could be made of tools than was possible for monkeys and apes. Bipedal creatures could manufacture and carry tools such as clubs, digging sticks, stone hammers, and knives without lessening their ability to explore, move about, and flee from danger.

Some 1.6 million years ago, *habilis* was succeeded by a larger and brainier human ancestor known as *Homo erectus*. This species appeared first in Africa and then spread to much of the rest of the Old World. Despite its considerably bigger brain, however, erectus does not appear to have had a markedly advanced capacity for complex mental tasks. For almost 1.3 million years, the tools manufactured by erectus changed very little while its brain size increased only slightly or not at all. Then about 200 thousand years ago, archaic forms of *H. sapiens* began to replace erectus in Europe, Asia, and Africa. In Europe and the Middle East, these archaic forms of sapiens are called *Neanderthals*. Much controversy surrounds what happened next. One theory, called the "out of Africa" or single origin theory, is that modern humans

Figure 3.5
Japanese Monkey Culture
A female monkey of Koshima troop washing a sweet potato.

Figure 3.6
Japanese Monkeys Washing Wheat
(a) Members of Koshima troop separating wheat from sand by placing mixture in water. (b) Central figure carrying the mixture in its left hand. Two monkeys in foreground are floating the wheat and picking it up.

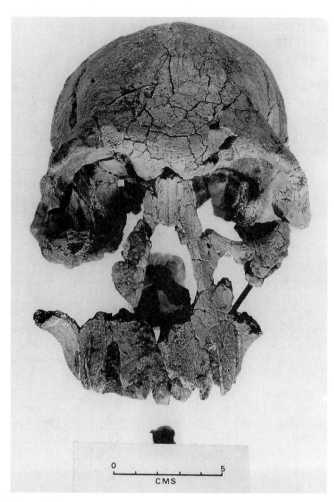 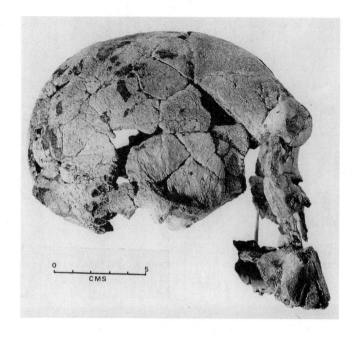

Figure 3.7
Homo Habilis (KNM-ER 1470)
This skull may be 2.0 million years old, and its volume is greater than that of the australopithecines living at the same time. Front view (left); side view (right).

evolved out of archaic humans between 150,000 and 100,000 years ago in Africa and from there spread out to the rest of the Old World, replacing the local archaic populations (Stringer 1992). The other theory, known as "the multiple origins theory" (Frayer et al. 1993) is that local archaic sapiens evolved into modern sapiens in parallel sequences that occurred at more or less the same time in several different regions of the Old World, between 150,000 and 100,000 years ago.

Cultural Takeoff

At about 45,000 years ago, culture entered a period of "takeoff."

Between 40,000 and 45,000 years ago the material culture of Western Eurasia changed more than it had during the previous million years. This efflorescence of technological and artistic creativity signifies the emergence of the first culture that observers today would recognize as distinctly human, marked as it was by unceasing invention and variety.

[Bar-Yosef and Vandermeersch 1993: 94]

Prior to this time, cultural and biological evolution occurred at comparable rates, and cultural and biological changes were closely tied together. After cultural takeoff, the rate of cultural evolution increased dramatically without any concurrent increase in the rate of human biological evolution. The occurrence of cultural takeoff justifies the contention of most anthropologists that to understand the last 40,000 years of the evolution of culture, primary emphasis must be given to cultural rather than biological processes. Natural selection and organic evolution lie at the base of culture, but once the capacity for culture became fully developed, a vast number of cultural differences and similarities could arise and disappear entirely independently of changes in genotypes.

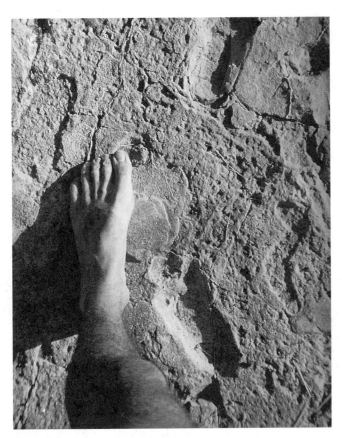

My Ambition in Life Is to Become Part of the Fossil Record

Figure 3.8
Earliest Hominid Footprints
These footprints were discovered at Laetoli by Mary Leakey. Human foot is shown for comparison.

Closely linked with the capacity for cultural behavior is the uniquely human capacity for language and for language-assisted systems of thought. Although other primates use complex signal systems to facilitate social life, modern human languages are qualitatively different from all other animal communication systems. The unique features of modern human languages (to be discussed in Chapter 4) undoubtedly arise from genetic adaptations related to an increasing dependence on social cooperation and on culturally acquired modes of subsistence. Modern human infants are born with the kind of neural circuitry that makes learning to talk as natural for them as learning to walk (Bickerton 1990). This circuitry in turn represents the kind of mental "wiring" useful for a species that needs to acquire and transmit large amounts of new information during its lifetime. Note, however, that no one knows for sure when fully modern forms of languages were acquired by our hominid ancestors.

One way to sum up the special characteristics of human language is to say that we have achieved "semantic universality" (Greenberg 1968). A communication system that has semantic universality can convey information about aspects, domains, properties, places, or events in the past, present, or future, whether actual or possible, real or imaginary, near or far.

Apes and Language

In recent years, a revolutionary series of studies has revealed that the gap between human and ape language capacities is not as great as had previously been supposed. Yet these same experiments have shown that innate species-specific factors prevent this gap from being closed. Many futile attempts had been made to teach chimpanzees to speak in human fashion before it was found that the vocal tract of apes cannot make the sounds necessary for human speech. Attention then shifted toward trying to teach apes to use sign languages and to read and write (Fig. 3.9).

Experiments with a chimpanzee named Washoe soon demonstrated that apes could learn to communicate in Ameslan (American Sign Language). Washoe used sign language productively; that is, she combined the signs in novel ways to send many different messages. For example, she first learned how to sign the request "open" with a particular closed door and later spontaneously extended its use beyond the initial training context to all closed doors, then to closed containers such as the refrigerator, cupboards, drawers, briefcases, boxes, and jars. When Susan, a research assistant, stepped on Washoe's doll, Washoe had many ways to tell her what was on her mind: "Up Susan; Susan up; mine please up; gimme baby; please shoe; more mine; up please; please up; more up; baby down; shoe up; baby up; please move up" (Gardner and Gardner 1971, 1975).

Figure 3.9
Nim Chimpsky Signing "Me Hat" To Herbert Terrace

Figure 3.11
Kanzi

Both Washoe and Lucy, a chimpanzee raised by Roger Fouts, learned to generalize the sign for "dirty" from the sign for "feces." Lucy applied it to Fouts when he refused her requests! Lucy also invented the combinations "cry hurt food" to name radishes and "candy fruit" for watermelon.

Koko, a female gorilla trained by Francine Patterson, has acquired a vocabulary of 300 Ameslan words (Fig. 3.10). Koko signed "finger bracelet" for ring, "white tiger" for zebra, and "eye hat" for mask. Koko also learned to talk about her inner feelings, signaling happiness, sadness, fear, and shame (Hill 1978: 98–99).

A remarkable achievement of more recent studies is the demonstration that signing chimpanzees can pass on their signing skills as a cultural tradition to nonsigning chimpanzees without human mediation. Loulis, a 10-month-old chimp whose mother had been incapacitated by a medical experiment, was presented to Washoe, whose baby had died. Washoe adopted the infant and promptly began to sign to him. By 36 months, Loulis was using twenty-eight signs that he had learned from Washoe. After about 5 years of learning to sign from Washoe and two other signing chimps, but not from humans, Loulis had acquired the use of fifty-five signs. Washoe, Loulis, and other signing chimps regularly used their sign language to communicate with each other even when humans were not present. These "conversations," as recorded on remote videotape, occurred from 118 to 659 times a month (Fouts and Fouts 1985, 1989: 301).

But it is Kanzi, the pygmy chimpanzee genius who has learned to make stone tools (p. 26), who has captured everybody's attention. Without training, Kanzi has developed a true comprehension of 150 spoken English words (see Fig. 3.11). Like a human child, Kanzi acquired his comprehension of spoken words merely by listening to the conversations that surrounded him from infancy on (Rambaugh et al. 1990: 247ff.). With the help of a keyboard and voice synthesizer, Kanzi can carry on extensive conversations in English. Every precaution has been taken in testing Kanzi's comprehension of symbols to make sure that no unconscious prompting or scoring bias has been introduced by his guardian teachers (see Box 3.2).

Clearly, however, a vast gap still remains between the language performances of humans and apes. Despite all the effort being expended on teaching apes to communicate, none has acquired the linguistic skills we take for granted in 3-year-old children. Still, what all these experiments have shown is that natural selection could easily have given rise to the human capacity for semantic universality by selecting for intellectual skills already present in rudimentary form among our ape-like hominid ancestors (Lieberman 1991; Parker 1985: 622; Savage-Rumbaugh 1987; Snowdon 1990).

Figure 3.10
Koko and Francine Patterson

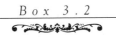

Box 3.2

KANZI'S ACCOMPLISHMENTS

Kanzi's comprehension of spoken English has led to a variety of tests of his understanding of vocabulary and syntax. In a vocabulary test, Kanzi listened to words presented over earphones and had to pick one of three lexigrams presented to him. The person testing him could neither hear the word nor see the lexigrams that were presented. He responded correctly at 75 percent or better performance to 149 of the 194 words presented with natural speech and 103 of 150 words produced by a speech synthesizer that had no intonation. When 24 pairs of similarly sounding words were presented (Orange-Onion or Shot-Shirt), Kanzi correctly discriminated among 21 of the pairs. In a recent comprehension test, Kanzi was presented with more than 700 novel commands asking him to do things with objects or people in a way he had never done before. These novel sentences were presented by an experimenter who was out of sight, and the responses were evaluated by observers wearing headphones playing music so that they could not hear the commands. Kanzi responded correctly on more than 90 percent of these trials, indicating an ability to understand the symbolic referents of the words and the way in which the relationship between words was encoded by syntax. Because each sentence was novel, there is no possibility of rote learning accounting for the results.

Snowden, 1990: 221–222.

Creationist Explanations

Anthropology's attempt to study human physical and cultural origins from an evolutionary perspective, and in terms of natural causes, has been challenged by creationists who believe in the literal truth of the Old Testament. Perhaps I should explain why this textbook does not present the creationist alternative to the evolutionary approach. The aim of the creationists is to compel the public schools either to stop teaching evolutionism or to give equal time to their views. They seek to achieve this aim by labeling evolutionism as "theory, not fact."

This label contains a grain of truth. All scientific "facts," "theories," and "laws" are held provisionally and are subject to being overturned by new evidence, so it cannot be denied that evolutionism is theory, not fact. But the theories that scientists teach are those that have withstood rigorous testing and are supported by the greatest amount of evidence available. Creationist theory is not acceptable as science because it has not withstood rigorous testing and is contradicted by an enormous amount of evidence (see Box 3.3). No student should be prevented from reading about scientifically discredited theories, but no teacher should be compelled to teach every theory that has ever been proposed. There are still people who believe that the earth is flat (Berra 1990; Spuhler 1985; Numbers 1993).

Chapter Summary

The human capacity for culture is a product of natural selection. Natural selection alters genotypes through differential reproductive success but is not synonymous with a struggle for survival between individuals. Fitness in humans results as often from cooperation and altruism as from struggle and competition. Both anatomical and behavioral traits can be shaped by natural selection and encoded in the genes. However, learning is a process of behavioral change that is entirely different from the behavioral change induced by natural selection. Learning permits organisms to adjust to or take advantage of novel contingencies and opportunities independently of genetic changes and is the basis of cultural traditions. Although the capacity for acquiring traditions is shaped by natural selection and took off only with the evolution of brainier species, culture is encoded in the brain, not in the genes. Cultural behavior such as toolmaking and tool use occurs in many nonhuman species, especially monkeys and great apes. Yet even among monkeys and great apes, tool-using traditions remain rudimentary. One reason for this is that monkeys and apes use their forelimbs for walking and hence cannot readily carry tools.

Early hominids such as the Australopithecines had ape-sized brains but upright posture. The evolution of the human foot thus set the pattern for further evolution of the human brain and the unique degree of human dependence on culture. The increasing braininess of *Homo erectus* and *Homo sapiens* resulted in an increasing reliance on culture. This process accelerated dramatically about 45,000 years ago when culture "took-off" and vast numbers of traditions began to evolve at a rapid rate without any significant changes in the size of the brain.

A vital ingredient in this takeoff was the development of the human capacity for semantic universality. As shown by numerous experiments, chimpanzees and gorillas can be taught to use signs. Compared with 3-year-old children, however, apes have only rudimentary capabilities for language.

The theories of creationism are not acceptable alternatives to evolutionism. They are either untestable or contradicted by the available evidence. In contrast, evolutionary theories have been vigorously tested and found to be compatible with the available evidence.

Box 3.3

REFUTING CREATIONISM

Scientific creationists propose that before the flood, everyone spoke the same language; afterward, each group suddenly began to speak in mutually unintelligible languages. This unintelligibility in turn caused people to emigrate from their homeland to distant parts of the globe. But no evidence supports such an event, and in fact, it is contradicted by all that is known about the history of languages. As we shall see (p. 40), the science of historical linguistics has patiently reconstructed the ancestral forms of the major linguistic families of the globe. The languages we speak today evolved gradually from these ancestral protolanguages. The evolution of new languages did not provoke the migration and separation of ancient populations; rather, it was the migrations and separations of ancient populations that led to the evolution of new languages. Creationists claim that the Old Stone Age lasted not the 2 million years (or more) that archaeologists contend but only 3,000 years, from the dispersal caused by the Tower of Babel to the reappearance of advanced civilizations outside the Middle East. Their reasoning goes like this: If the Old Stone Age had lasted for two million years, the population of the earth would be much greater than it is today. But as we shall see (p. 62), a substantial anthropological literature demonstrates that prehistoric peoples maintained very low rates of population increase by means of abstinence, abortion, prolonged nursing, and direct and indirect forms of infanticide.

Furthermore, the creationist theory that all civilizations can be traced to the Middle East ignores the most important archaeological discoveries of the twentieth century—that pre-Columbian state societies in Mexico and Peru evolved from a hunter–gatherer base independently of significant Old World influences. Archaeologists have found step-by-step evidence for the processes by which Native-American plants and animals unknown in the Old World—such as llamas, alpacas, guinea pigs, potatoes, manioc, maize, and amaranth—were domesticated and integrated into prehistoric Native-American cultures. These plants and animals furnished the food–energy base for the evolution of bands into villages, villages into chiefdoms, chiefdoms into states, and states into empires in pre-Columbian America.

Chapter 4

LANGUAGE AND CULTURE

Spectators in the Royal enclosure at Ascot, England. Their speech is as distinctive as their dress.

This chapter contains a brief introduction to anthropological linguistics. We begin with the basic analytic concepts that are employed in formal linguistics. Then we move on rapidly to such questions as the relative value and efficiency of different languages, the effect of language on culture, the relationship between language and gender, and the extent to which different languages are associated with different ways of seeing and understanding the world. Another issue to be discussed is the universal occurrence of change in a language's features. Ultimately, all languages are "corruptions" of parent languages, as we shall see from an examination of the processes responsible for linguistic change. A remarkable feature of languages is that they maintain their structural coherence through centuries of change without native speakers being aware of the changes taking place.

Phonemes

Language consists of sounds. But the sounds used by one language can be very different from the sounds used by another language. The sounds that native speakers of a particular language perceive as being distinct—that is, as contrasting with other sounds in their language—are called *phonemes*. Phonemes are meaningless in isolation, but when combined into prescribed sequences, they convey a definite meaning. Here are three phonemes in English: [a], [t], [c]. By themselves they mean nothing, but combined in the utterance "cat" they mean a small animal; reversing the order, they mean a small nail or a sailing maneuver. Thus the phonemes combine and recombine to form different messages.

Theoretically, a language could function with only two phonemes. This is actually the case in the dots and dashes of Morse Code and in the binary 0 and 1 of digital computers. But a natural language having only two phonemes would require a much longer string of phonemes per average message than one having several phonemes. The smallest number of phonemes known in a natural language is thirteen, in Hawaiian. English has between thirty-five and forty. Once a language has more than ten or so phonemes, there is no need to produce exceptionally long strings per message. A repertory of 10 phonemes, for example, can be combined to produce 10,000 different words consisting of 4 phonemes each. Let us now take a closer look at how phonemes can be identified and at how they are combined to form meaningful utterances.

Phonemic Systems

Phonemes consist of etic sounds called *phones*. To convey information effectively, the phones of a language must be clearly distinguishable, or contrastive with respect to each other. But all sounds share some elements. Therefore, no two phones "naturally" contrast with each other. If we are able to distinguish one phoneme from another, it is only because as native speakers we have learned to accept and recognize certain phones and not others as being clearly distinguishable and contrastive. For example, speakers of English automatically regard the [t] in "ten" and the [d] in "den" as contrastive sounds. Yet these two sounds actually have many acoustical phonetic features in common. It is culture, not nature, that makes them significantly different.

What is the critical difference between [t] and [d] for speakers of English? Let us examine the articulatory features—that is, the manner in which they are produced by the vocal tract (Fig. 4.1). Notice that when you produce either sound, the tip of your tongue presses against the alveolar ridge just behind the top of your teeth. Notice also that when you made either sound, the flow of the column of air coming from the lungs is momentarily interrupted and then released. In what way, then, are they different? The major articulatory difference between [t] and [d] consists of the way the column of air passes through the vocal chords. The vibration of the vocal chords produces a *voiced* effect in the case of [d] but not in the case of [t]. Both [t] and [d] are described phonetically as alveolar stops, but [d] is a voiced alveolar stop, whereas [t] is an unvoiced alveolar stop. The use of a voiced and unvoiced alveolar stop to distinguish utterances such as "ten"–"den," "tock"–"dock," "to"–"do," or "train"–"drain" is an entirely arbitrary device that is characteristic of English but is absent in many other languages. The phonemic system of a given language thus consists of sets of phones that are arbitrarily but habitually perceived by the speakers as contrastive.

The structure of a given language's phonemic system—its system of sound contrasts—is discovered by testing observed phonetic variations within the context of pairs of words that sound alike in all but one respect. The testing consists in part of asking native speakers whether they detect a change in meaning between, for example, "ten" and "den." By asking native speakers to compare similar pairs of words, we can detect most of the phonemic contrasts in English. Another

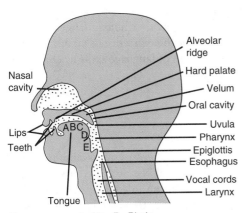

Tongue areas A. Tip B. Blade
C. Center D. Dorsum E. Root

Figure 4.1
Parts of Oral Passage

instance in which voicing sets up a phonemic contrast is found in "bat"–"pat." Here the initial sounds are also stops, but this time the speaker makes them by pressing both lips together, and thus they are called bilabial stops. Again one of the stops, [b], is voiced, whereas the other, [p], is unvoiced. It is only the fact that these phones are contrastive from the native speaker's point of view that validates the classification of these two sounds as different phonemes. This is the fact that is generalized when the terms *emic* from phonemic and *etic* from phonetic are applied to other domains of culture (Headland, Pike, and Harris 1990, and see p. 13).

To the linguist's trained ear, many sound differences that escape the notice of the native speaker will appear as possible contenders for phonemic status. For example, the removal of the labial obstruction in the utterance "pat" is accompanied by a slight puff of air that is not found in the word "spat." This phonetic feature is known as aspiration and can easily be detected by placing your hand close to your lips and pronouncing first "pat" and then "spat" several times in succession. A more precise phonetic description of the [p] in "pat," therefore, is that it is an aspirated bilabial unvoiced stop, for which the phonetic symbol is [ph].

Do [p] and [ph] constitute separate phonemes in English? The answer is no, because there are no meaningful English utterances in which the substitution of [p] for [ph], or vice versa, alters the meaning of the utterance. Closely resemblant but nondistinctive sounds like [p] and [ph] are called *allophones*.

Phones that regularly occur in one language may not occur at all in another. Good examples are the "clicks" that occur in several languages spoken in Africa and the sing-song tones of Chinese. Furthermore, when the same phone does occur in two languages, it may be phonemic in one but not the other. For example, the difference between a v-sound and a b-sound in English is phonemic, as in "bat" versus "vat." In Spanish,

however, the capital of Cuba (Havana) sounds the same to native speakers of Spanish if you pronounce it with a b-sound or a v-sound in the middle. In English, the difference between an aspirated and unaspirated k-sound is nonphonemic, but in Hindi the difference is phonemic. Thus khii means "parched grain," whereas kii means "nail" (Akmajian et al. 1992: 80).

In English the initial sound difference in "rot" and "luck" is phonemic, whereas in Chinese it is not (in an initial position). Hence "rots of ruck" sounds the same as "lots of luck" to a Chinese learning English.

Morphemes

The smallest part of an utterance that has a definite meaning is called a *morpheme*. A morpheme may consist of single phonemes or of strings of phonemes in different combinations and permutations. Some morphemes can occur as isolates, whereas some can occur only in conjunction with other morphemes. "Hello," "stop," and "sheep" are free morphemes because they can constitute the entirety of a well-formed message. ("Are those goats or sheep?" "Sheep.") But the past-forming /-ed/ of "talked" or "looked" and the /-er/ of "speaker" or "singer" are bound morphemes because they can never constitute well-formed messages on their own. Languages vary widely in their reliance on free or bound morphemes. Chinese, for example, has many free morphemes, whereas Turkish has many bound morphemes. Words are free morphemes or combinations of morphemes that can constitute well-formed messages.

Grammar

MORPHOLOGY

Grammar has two facets: the rules for combining phonemes into morphemes (morphology) and the rules for combining morphemes into words and sentences (syntax). The existence of rules governing the formation of permitted sequences of phonemes can be seen in the reaction of speakers of English to common names in Polish such as Zbigniew Brzezinski. English, unlike Polish, does not permit sound combinations such as zb and brz. Similarly, speakers of English know by unconscious rule that the words "btop" and "ndak" cannot exist in English since they involve prohibited sound combinations.

SYNTAX

Similar unconscious rules govern the combination of morphemes into sentences. This branch of grammar is called *syntax*. Native speakers can distinguish between grammatical and ungrammatical sentences even when they have never heard particular combinations before. Here is a classic example:

a. Colorless green ideas sleep furiously.
b. Furiously sleep ideas green colorless.

Most speakers of English will recognize sentence (a) as a grammatical utterance but reject (b) as ungrammatical even when both seem equally nonsensical.

Native speakers can seldom state the rules governing the production of grammatical utterances. Even the difference between singular and plural nouns is hard to formulate as a conscious rule. Adding an s converts "cat" into "cats," "slap" into "slaps," and "fat" into "fats"; but something else happens in "house"–"houses," "rose"–"roses," "nose"–"noses"; and something else again in "crag"–"crags," "flag"–"flags," and "hand"–"hands." What *is* happening here? Three different variations of the same morphene called *allomorphs*—/-s/, /-ez/, and /-z/—are employed according to a complex rule that most native speakers of English cannot put into words.

The set of unconscious structural rules and the sharing of these rules by the members of a speech community make it possible for human beings to produce and interpret a potentially infinite number of messages, none of which need precisely replicate any other previous message. Noam Chomsky described this behavior as follows:

> Normal linguistic behavior as speaker or reader or hearer, is quite generally with novel utterances, with utterances that have no physical or formal similarity to any of the utterances that have ever been produced in the past experience of the hearer or, for that matter, in the history of the language, as far as anyone knows.

[1973: 118]

Deep Structure

How is it possible for us to create so many different messages and still be understood? No one is quite sure of the answer to this question. One of the most popular theories is that proposed by Chomsky. According to Chomsky, every utterance has a surface structure and a deep structure. Surface structures may appear dissimilar, yet deep structure may be identical. For example, "Meat and gravy are loved by lions" is superficially different from the sentence "Lions love meat and gravy." Yet both sentences take as their model a third sentence: "Lions love meat and lions love gravy." This third sentence more closely reflects the deep structure, which can be transformed into various superficially different variations.

An essential feature of Chomsky's notion of grammar is that at the deepest levels, all human languages share an inborn species-specific structure. It is the existence of this inborn structure that makes it possible for children to learn to speak at an early age and that makes it possible to translate any human language into any other human language. Other authorities, however, doubt the existence of inborn grammar and attribute the acquisition of language skills by children to ordinary learning processes.

Are There Superior and Inferior Languages?

Linguists of the nineteenth century were convinced that the languages of the world could be arranged in a hierarchical order. Europeans invariably awarded the prize for efficiency, elegance, and beauty to Latin, the mastery of whose grammar was long a precondition for scholarly success in the West. Beginning with the study of Native American languages, however, anthropological linguists, led by Franz Boas, showed that the belief in the superiority of "civilized" grammars was untenable. In fact, grammatical rules run the full gamut from simple to complex systems among peoples on all levels of technological and political development. The conclusion of the great anthropological linguist Edward Sapir (1921: 234) stands unchallenged: "When it comes to linguistic form, Plato walks with the Macedonian swineherd, Confucius with the headhunting savages of Assam."

Other kinds of language differences used to be cited as evidence that one language was more "primitive" than another. For example, there are numerous words for different types of parrots in native Brazilian Tupi languages, yet no term for parrots in general. This was considered evidence of the inferiority of Tupi. On the other hand, some languages lack specific terms. For example, there are languages that have no specific words for numbers higher than five. Larger quantities are simply referred to as "many." This was once also interpreted as evidence of linguistic inferiority.

These evaluations failed to take into account a simple fact. The extent to which discourse is specific or general reflects the culturally defined need to be specific or general, not the capacity of one's language to transmit messages about specific or general phenomena. A Brazilian Indian has little need to distinguish parrots in general from other birds but must be able to distinguish one parrot from another since each type is valued for its plumage. The ordinary individual in a small-scale society can name and identify 500 to 1,000 separate plant species, but the ordinary modern urbanite can usually name only 50 to 100 such species. Paradoxically, urbanites usually have a more complex set of general terms, such as plant, tree, shrub, and vine, than band and village peoples, for whom such generalities are of little practical use (Witowski and Brown 1978: 445–446).

English, which has terms for many special vehicles—cart, stretcher, auto, sled, snowmobile—lacks a general term for wheeled vehicles. Yet this does not prevent communication about wheeled vehicles as distinguished from sleds and helicopters when the need arises. Similarly, the absence of higher-number terms usually means that a culture has few occasions in which it is useful to specify precisely large quantities. When these occasions become more common, any language can cope with the problem of numeration by repeating the largest term or by inventing new ones.

Similarly, many languages use one term to designate "hand" and "arm" and one term for "leg" and "foot." It has been found that this lack of distinction correlates with languages spoken by peoples who live in the tropics and wear little clothing. Among peoples who live in colder climates and who wear special garments (gloves, boots, sleeves, pants, and so on) for different parts of the body, the parts of the limbs tend to be designated by distinctive terms (Witowski and Brown 1985).

These differences, in any event, are necessarily superficial. When the social need arises, terms appropriate to industrial civilization can be developed by any language. This can be done either through the direct borrowing of the words of one language by another (sputnik, blitzkrieg, garage) or by the creation of new words based on new combinations of the existing stock of morphemes (radiometric, railroad, newspaper). No culture is ever at a loss for words—not for long, that is.

Language, Social Class, and Ethnicity

Another basis for claiming language superiority is associated with the dialect variations characteristic of stratified societies (see p. 152). Members of elite strata often assert that the dialects of ordinary people are "substandard." This judgment has no basis in linguistic science. Labeling a dialect spoken by a segment of a larger speech community substandard is a political rather than a linguistic phenomenon (Gal 1989). The demotion of dialects to inferior status can be understood only as part of the general process by which ruling groups attempt to maintain their superordinate position (see Chapter 13). Linguistically, the phonology and grammar of the poor and uneducated classes are as efficient as those of the rich, educated, and powerful classes.

This point should not be confused with the problem of functional vocabulary differences. Exploited and deprived groups often lack key specialized and technical words and concepts as a result of their limited educational experience. This lack constitutes a real handicap in competing for jobs but has nothing to do with the question of the adequacy of the phonological and grammatical systems of working-class and ethnic dialects (Fig. 4.2).

A TALL TALE FROM THE SOUTH SEAS

An anthropology student and his instructor landed on a small island in the Pacific Ocean to do fieldwork. The instructor, who had several other students to watch over on some neighboring islands, didn't get off the plane.

"I'm sorry to have to leave you alone," she said, "but I'll be back to see how you're doing in a few days. In the meantime you should start learning their language."

"How?" the student asked.

"It's easy. Just point at things and say 'ilya lya' which means 'What's that?'."

As soon as the plane took off the student pointed to the ocean and said to the people who had gathered around him, "Ilya lya."

"Weena," they answered.

Next he pointed to the sky. "Ilya lya."

"Weena."

When he pointed to a dog, he got the same answer.

No matter what he pointed to, whether a house, a tree or a child, their only response was "weena." Could it be that this language had one word for all objects! "This will make a great thesis," he thought. "I'll be famous!"

Two days later the instructor returned. As soon as she got off the plane, the student recounted his experience.

"What does 'weena' mean?" he asked.

"Index finger," she replied.

(a)   (b)

Figure 4.2
Class and Accent
The language spoken by these youths in London (a) is
as distinct from that spoken by the royal guests at the
Ascot horse races (b) as the clothes worn by each class.

Well-intentioned educators often claim that poor inner-city children are reared in a "linguistically deprived" environment. In a detailed study of the speech behavior of blacks in northern ghettos, William Labov (1972) has shown that this belief reflects the ethnocentric prejudices of middle-class teachers and researchers rather than any deficit in the grammar or logical structure of the ghetto dialect. The nonstandard English of the black ghetto, black vernacular English, contains certain forms that are unacceptable in white, middle-class settings. Yet the use of these forms in no way prevents or inhibits the expression of complex thoughts in concise and logically consistent patterns (Box 4.1 and Box 4.2). The grammatical properties of nonstandard language are not haphazard and arbitrary variations. On the contrary, they conform to rules that produce regular differences with respect to the standard grammar. All the dialects of English possess equivalent means for expressing the same logical content.

Language, Thought, and Causality

For many years, linguists have investigated the extent to which different word categories and grammars produce habitually incompatible modes of thought (Kay and Kempton 1984). At the center of this controversy is the comparison made by the anthropological linguist Benjamin Whorf between Native-American languages and the Indo-European family of languages, a group that includes English, many of the languages of Europe, Hindi, Persian, and others (see p. 41). According to Whorf, when two language systems differ radically in their vocabularies and grammars, their speakers live in wholly different thought-worlds. Even such fundamental categories as space and time are said to be experienced differently as a result of the linguistic "molds" that constrain thought (Box 4.3).

According to Whorf, English sentences are constructed in such a way as to indicate that some substance or matter is part of an event that is located at a definite time and place. Both time and space can be measured and divided into units. In Hopi sentences, however, events are not located with reference to time but, rather, to the categories of "being" as opposed to "becoming." English encourages one to think of time as a divisible rod that starts in the past, passes through the present, and continues into the future—hence, the English language's past, present, and future tenses. Hopi

---

Box 4.1

COMMON FEATURES OF BLACK ENGLISH

negative inversion	"don't nobody know"
negative concord	"you ain't goin' to no heaven"
invariant "be"	"when they be sayin"
dummy "it" for "there"	"it ain't no heaven"
copula deletion	"if you bad"

Labov, 1972

Box 4.2

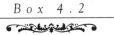

BLACK ENGLISH AND LOGICAL THOUGHT

Soon as you die, your spirit leaves you. (And where does the spirit go?) Well, it all depends. (On what?) You know, like some people say if you're good an' shit, your spirit goin' t'heaven 'm' if you bad, your spirit goin' to hell. Well, bullshit! Your spirit goin' to hell anyway, good or bad. (Why?) Why? I'll tell you why. 'Cause, you see, doesn' no body really know that it's a God, y'know, 'cause, I mean I have seen black gods, pink gods, white gods, all color gods, and don't nobody know it's really a God. An' when they be saying if you good, you goin' t'heaven, tha's bullshit, 'cause you ain't goin' to no heaven. 'Cause it ain't no heaven for you to go to.

Labov 1972: 214–215.

Box 4.3

WHORF'S HYPOTHESIS

The forms of a person's thoughts are controlled by inexorable laws of pattern of which he is unconscious. These patterns are the unperceived intricate systematizations of his own language—shown readily enough by a candid comparison and contrast with other languages, especially those of a different linguistic family. His thinking itself is in a language—in English, in Sanskrit, in Chinese. And every language is a vast pattern-system, different from others, in which are culturally ordained the forms and categories by which the personality not only communicates, but also analyzes nature, notices or neglects types of relationships and phenomena, channels his reasoning, and builds the house of his consciousness.

Whorf 1956: 252.

---

grammar, however, merely distinguishes all events that have already become manifest from all those still in the process of becoming manifest; it has no equivalent of past, present, and future tenses. Does this mean that a Hopi cannot indicate that an event happened last month or that it is happening right now or that it will happen tomorrow? Of course not. But Whorf's point is that the English tense system makes it easier to measure time, and he postulated some type of connection between the tense system of Indo-European languages and the inclination of Euro-Americans to read timetables, make time payments, and punch time clocks.

Whorf's point of view, however, implicitly distorts the fundamental causal relationships between language and culture. No one would deny that the absence of calendars, clocks, and timetables must have given preindustrial societies like the Hopi an orientation to time very different from that of industrial-age societies. But we have no evidence to support the view that one kind of grammar rather than another facilitated or caused industrialization.

An interest in calendars and other time-reckoning devices is a recurrent feature of social and political development associated with peoples whose languages are as diverse as those of the Egyptians and the Mayans. Indeed, the Chinese contributed as much to the invention of modern mechanical clocks as did the Europeans. On the other hand, a lack of concern with counting time is a characteristic of preindustrial peoples in general, from Patagonia to Baffin Land and from New Guinea to the Kalahari desert, among peoples who speak a thousand different tongues.

Color Categories

Whorf's idea that people who speak different languages see the world in fundamentally different ways has been tested in the domain of color categories. Some languages have separate terms only for brightness contrasts, such as those designated by black and white. Others have up to a dozen basic color terms. This difference would seem to indicate a highly relativistic or culture-specific form of color perception. Yet there is considerable evidence that even when their language contains only two or three basic terms, people actually tend to see the same parts of the color spectrum as those whose languages contain many color terms. Moreover, color terms tend to be added in a definite sequence. If a language is to have more than two basic categories, the third term will be red. If there is a fourth category, it will be either green or yellow; then yellow or green; then blue; then brown; and finally purple, pink, or orange (Berlin and Kay, 1991). Unfortunately, we can find exceptions to this scheme, and the basic question of why different cultures have color terms remains unresolved. (Witowski and Brown 1978; Hewes 1992; Maclaury 1992; but see Agar 1994).

Is a language that has only two or three color terms at a disadvantage with respect to those that have a dozen or more? It seems unlikely because one can always refer to additional colors by saying it is the color of some familiar object. Orange in English, for example, was initially distinguished as that color found on the skin of oranges.

Obligatory Sexism

Languages differ in having certain obligatory categories built into their grammatical rules. English requires us to specify number. Speakers of the Romance languages must indicate the sex (gender) of all nouns. Certain Native-American languages (for example, Kwakiutl) must indicate whether an object is near or far from the speaker and whether it is visible or invisible. These obligatory categories do not necessarily indicate any active psychological tendency to be obsessed with numbers, sex, or the location of people or objects. Still, grammatical conventions are not necessarily trivial either. Whorf's general hypothesis is correct when applied to some features of grammar. For example, certain obligatory categories in standard English seem to reflect a pervasive social bias in favor of male-centered viewpoints and activities. Many nouns and pronouns that refer to human beings lack gender—child, everybody, everyone, person, citizen, American, human. However, teachers of standard English once prescribed masculine rather than feminine pronouns to refer to these words. Thus it was once considered "correct" to say: "Everyone must do his homework," even though the group being addressed consisted of both males and females. Newspaper columnists were fond of writing: "The average American is in love with his car." And high school grammars used to insist that one must say: "All the boys and girls were puzzled, but no one was willing to raise his hand." Obviously, a perfectly intelligible and sexually unbiased substitute is readily available in the plural possessive pronoun *their*. In fact, nowadays almost everybody uses the word *their* in their [sic] everyday conversation (Hill and Manheim 1992; Lakoff, R. T. 1990).

Other male-centered conventions of the English language cannot be regarded as benign or trivial. The use of him and he as pronouns for God reflects the fact that men are the traditional priests of Judaism and Christianity. Feminists within the Catholic Church regard the dominance of male gender categories in the Catholic liturgy as a major obstacle in their struggle to have women ordained as priests (Box 4.4). Yet it would be a mistake to blame the exclusion of women from the priesthood on obligatory linguistic categories; obligatory sexism in language is the consequence rather than the cause of male-biased religions.

Linguistic Change

Like all other parts of culture, language is constantly undergoing change. These changes result from slight phonological, morphemic, or grammatical variations. They are often identifiable at first as "dialect" differences, such as those that distinguish the speech of American Southerners from the speech of New Englanders. If New Englanders and Southerners were to move off to separate islands and lose all linguistic contact with each other and their homelands (no TV or radios), their speech would eventually cease to be mutually intelligible. The longer the separation, the less resemblances the languages would have.

Dialect formation and geographical isolation are responsible for much of the great diversity of languages. Many mutually unintelligible languages of today are "daughter" languages of a common "parent" language. This can be seen by the regular resemblances that languages display in their phonological features. For example, English t corresponds to German z, as in the following pairs of words:

tail	Zagel	tin	Zinn
tame	zahm	to	zu
tap	zapfen	toe	Zehe
ten	zehn	tooth	Zahn

Box 4.4

CHANGING SEXIST LANGUAGE IN CATHOLIC PRAYER

The Gloria.

Glory to God in the highest, and peace to all {his people} on earth.

Holy God, loving God {Lord God, heavenly king}

Almighty God, Creator {and Father}

We worship you, we give you thanks

We praise you for your glory

Jesus Christ, Son of God, Lamb of God, our Savior {Lord Jesus Christ, only Son of the Father}.

Excised words in brackets: his, Lord, Father, king.

From "Cleaning Up Sexist Language," 8th Day Center for Justice.

These correspondences result from the fact that both English and German have a common parent language known as Proto-West Germanic.

In the 2,000 years that have elapsed since the Roman conquest of Western Europe, Latin has evolved into an entire family of languages, of which French, Italian, Portuguese, Rumanian, and Spanish are the principal representatives. If linguists did not know of the existence of Latin through the historical records, they would be obliged to postulate its existence on the basis of the sound correspondences among the Romance languages.

The anthropological linguist can see clearly that every contemporary spoken language is a transformed version of a dialect of an earlier language, and that even in the absence of written records, languages can be grouped together on the basis of their derivation from a common predecessor. Thus, in a more remote period, Proto-West Germanic was undifferentiated from a large number of languages, including the earliest forms of Latin, Hindi, Persian, Greek, Russian, and Gaelic, each of which is a member of the Indo-European family of languages. Inferences based on the similarities among the Indo-European languages have led linguists to reconstruct the sound system of the parent language from which

they all ultimately derive. This language is called Proto-Indo-European (Fig. 4.3).

Many non-Indo-European languages spoken in Asia, Africa, and the Americas have also been shown to belong to linguistic superfamilies that originated in a single language thousands of years ago and were taken to their current territories by migrants (Renfrew 1994). The question that is now being debated among linguists is whether these protolanguages can in turn be traced to a small number of still more ancient tongues—perhaps even to just one—the original language of the first anatomically modern humans (Ross 1991).

Languages may also change without any geographical separation of portions of a speech community. For example, within 1,000 years, English changed from Old English to its modern form as a result of shifts in pronunciation and the borrowing of words from other languages. The two languages today are mutually unintelligible (see Box 4.5). As these changes illustrate, Modern English can be regarded as a "corruption" of Old English. Indeed, all modern languages are corruptions of older ones. This does not prevent people from forming committees to save the "King's English" or to protect the "purity" of French.

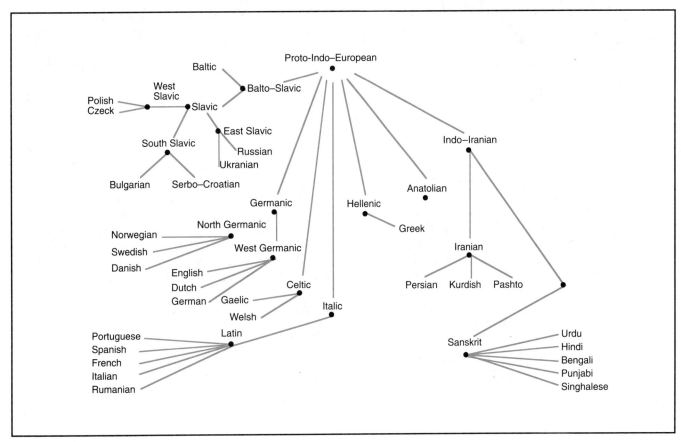

Figure 4.3
Indo-European Family of Languages

THE KING'S ENGLISH A.D. 1066

Figure 4.4
King Harold

On bissum eare. be he cyning waes, he for ut mid scrip-here to eanes Willelme; and ba hwile com Tosti eorl into Humbran mid 60 scripum. Eadwine eorl com mid land-fierde and darf hine ut; and ba butse-carlas hine forsocon, and he for to Scotlande mid 12 snaccum, and hine emette Harald se Norrena cyning mid 300 scipum, and Totsi him tobeag. And man cyode Harolde cyning hu hit waes baer edon and eworden, and he com mid miclum here Engliscra manna and emette hine aet Staengfordes brycge and hine of slog, and bone eorl Tosti, and eallne bone here ehtlice ofercom.

In this year when he [Harold] was king, he went out with a fleet against William; and meanwhile Earl Tosti came into the Humber with sixty ships. Earl Edwin came with a land force and drove him out; and then the sailors forsook him [Tosti], and he went to Scotland with twelve small boats, and Harald, the Norwegian king, met him with three hundred ships, and Tosti submitted to him. And they told King Harold (Fig. 4.4) what had been done and had befallen there, and he came with a large army of Englishmen and met him [the Norwegian king] at Starnford Bridge and slew him and Earl Tosti, and coura-geously overcame the whole army.

The Anglo-Saxon Chronicle

Language and Consciousness

Language and language change illustrate the remarkable forms that can emerge in human culture without the conscious design of the participants. As pointed out by Alfred Kroeber:

> The unceasing processes of change in language are mainly unconscious or covert, or at least implicit. The results of the change may come to be recognized by speakers of the changing languages; the gradual act of change, and especially the causes, mostly happen without the speaker being aware of them. When a change has begun to creep in, it may be tacitly accepted or it may be observed and consciously resisted on the ground of being incorrect or vulgar or foreign. But the underlying motives of the objectors and the impulses of the innovator are likely to be equally unknown to themselves.
>
> [1948: 245]

Chapter Summary

Languages are based on etic sounds known as phones. Phonemes, the basic code elements, consist of phones that are emically contrastive. Different languages have widely different repertoires of phones, and phonemes, neither of which conveys meaning in itself. The smallest units of meaningful sounds are called morphemes.

The ability to send and receive messages in a human language depends on the sharing of rules of grammar. There are two different aspects of grammar: morphology or rules for combining phonemes into morphemes and syntax or rules for combining morphemes into words and sentences. Knowledge of the rules of grammar makes it possible to produce completely novel utterances and yet be understood. A theory that accounts for this property of grammar states that all languages have a deep structure to which various superficially dissimilar utterances can be reduced. Novel sentences are transformations of these deep structures and can be understood by tracing them to their underlying components.

All human languages are mutually translatable, and no one language has a more efficient grammar than the others. Grammars and vocabularies differ widely, but these differences do not indicate any inherent defect in a language or any intellectual inferiority of the speakers. General and specific categorizations—as with numbers, plant classifications, and color terms—reflect the practical need for making general or specific distinctions under particular cultural and natural conditions. Moreover, the view that certain dialects of standard languages are "inferior" forms of speech reflects class and ethnic biases. Dialects such as black vernacular English do not in and of themselves inhibit clear and logical thought.

Attempts to show that linguistic differences determine how people think and behave in different cultures have not been successful. All humans, for example, probably have a similar set of perceptions of time and color differences despite the different ways in which their languages indicate time and color differences. Few, if any, correlations other than vocabulary can be shown between language and the major forms of demographic, technological, economic, ecological, domestic, political, and religious aspects of sociocultural systems.

However, obligatory linguistic categories such as those concerned with gender may play a role in the maintenance of various forms of hierarchical relationships.

Languages, like all other aspects of culture, are constantly being changed as a result of both internal and external processes. Thus, all languages are "corruptions" of earlier parent languages.

The study of language change, as well as the study of the other aspects of linguistics, offers a glimpse into the unconscious processes that shape sociocultural systems.

Chapter 5

PRODUCTION

Rice harvest in Bali, Indonesia.

To provide a coherent framework for understanding the causes of sociocultural differences and similarities, we focus first on the principal varieties of infrastructures. It is in the interaction between the technological, economic, demographic, and ecological aspects of human social life that the basic sources of both diversity and similarity are to be found. In this chapter, we will be considering primarily the aspects of infrastructure that make up a society's mode of production. Moreover, the focus is on different modes of food production such as hunting and gathering, pastoralism, and preindustrial and industrial forms of agriculture. Cultures engage in many kinds of production besides food production (handicrafts, mining, manufacturing, and the like), but food production systems have been the main focus of productive effort throughout history and prehistory.

Using energy as a measure of input and output, we will look at the interaction between technology and the environment. Although the intensification of production can lead to diminishing returns, diminishing returns can lead to new and more productive technologies. What, then, is the long-range result of technological innovation? The answer may surprise you.

Evolution of Energy Production

Human life and culture cannot exist unless societies appropriate and transform the energy available in the environment for the production of goods and services. The amount of energy produced and the method of production depend in turn on an interaction between the energy-producing technology that a society possesses at a given time and environmental variables such as sunlight, soils, forests, rainfall, or mineral deposits. Since neither technology nor the features of the environment can be changed rapidly or limitlessly, a society's mode of energy production provides a powerful set of constraints and opportunities with regard to a people's entire way of life (Moran 1982).

During the time of the earliest hominids, all the energy used for the conduct of social life stemmed from food. The first great step in the evolution of energy production was the use of fire. We do not know exactly when hominids began to use fire. Erectus may have achieved partial control over fire, but full control may not have been achieved before the appearance of modern sapiens (see p. 28). Certainly by the time of cultural takeoff 40,000 years ago, fire was being used for cooking, warmth, protection against carnivores, driving game animals over cliffs or into ambushes, and possibly for favoring the growth of desired plant species (Goudsblom 1992).

By 10,000 years ago, animals began to provide energy in the form of muscle power harnessed first to sleds and then to plows and wheeled vehicles. At about the same time, humans began to use high-temperature charcoal fires, first for making ceramics and later for smelting and casting metals. We do not know with certainty when wind power was first used (probably to propel small canoes), but modern humans were sailing in large ships by the time the earliest states arose. Not until the medieval period in Europe was the energy in falling water

tapped extensively. And only in the last 200 or 300 years have fossil fuels—coal, oil, and gas—come to dominate production.

New sources of energy have followed each other in a logical progression, with the mastery of later forms dependent on the mastery of earlier ones. For example, in both the Old World and the New World, the sequence of inventions that led to metallurgy depended on the prior achievement of high-temperature wood-fire ovens and furnaces for baking ceramics. In turn, the development of this technique depended on learning how to make and control wood fires in cooking. Low-temperature metallurgical experience with copper and tin almost of necessity had to precede the use of iron and steel. Mastery of iron and steel, in turn, had to precede the development of the mining machines that made the use of coal, oil, and gas feasible. Finally, the use of these fossil fuels spawned the Industrial Revolution, from which the technology for today's nuclear energy derives (Fig. 5.1).

The dependence of later forms of technology on earlier forms acts as a powerful constraint on the evolution of sociocultural systems. This is not to say that all technological change has to occur in a single definite sequence throughout the world (Pfaffenberger 1992). The earliest known ceramics, for example, were figurines fired in special kilns 27,000 years ago in Dolni Vestonice, Czechoslovakia. Presumably, the artisans who made these small statues possessed sufficient knowledge to make pots. But ceramic pots are too heavy to be lugged from one campsite to another. Hence the full development of ceramic technology was put on hold until more sedentary villages developed toward the end of the last Ice Age. Similarly, the wheel was, invented in pre-Columbian Mexico, but was used only as a toy, given the absence of appropriate domesticated traction animals and the prevalence of steep and rocky trails that were better managed by human bearers (Box 5.1)

Figure 5.1
Chernobyl Nuclear Explosion
Explosion of reactor near Kiev contaminated meat and milk as far away as Sweden. Here technicians try to determine level of radioactivity from a helicopter. Nuclear energy may yet turn out to be the least efficient mode of energy production ever created.

Hunting and Gathering

Hunting and gathering was the only mode of food production from the time of the first humans to about 12,000 years ago. Most of the living hunter-gatherers who have been studied by anthropologists or who are known through historical documents occupy regions that are unsuited for agriculture: the lands close to the Arctic Circle or deserts like the interior of Australia. Most of these hunter-gatherers are organized into small groups called bands, numbering from about twenty to fifty people. Bands consist of individual families who make camp together for periods ranging from a few days to several years before moving on to other campsites. Band life is essentially migratory; shelters are temporary and possessions are few.

One must be careful, however, not to overgeneralize about hunter-gatherers and their environments. Even in recent

In the first century A.D., Hero of Alexandria designed the first steam engine (Fig 5.2). It was based on the principle of the reaction turbine. Hero's engine had no practical application because it appeared at a moment in the history of technology when the technology needed to make pipes, screws, and gears out of iron did not exist (Drachmann 1963: 206). Hence, Hero's turbine just went round and round, and the age of steam did not dawn for another 1,700 years.

Figure 5.2
Hero's Steam Turbine

times, some hunter-gatherers lived in lush environments that provided the infrastructural basis for sociocultural systems that were more complex than those of hunter-gatherers who inhabited less bountiful regions (Box 5.2). The hunter-gatherers who inhabited the coastal zones of the Pacific Northwest, an environment rich in fish, wild plants, and sea mammals, lived in permanent villages. Moreover, there is much archaeological evidence, from both the Old and New Worlds, that in favored environments complex, sedentary villagelike settlements long preceded the appearance of domesticated plants and animals. Thus anthropologists gen-

Box 5.2

NOT ALL HUNTER-GATHERERS ARE ALIKE

There are two main varieties of hunter-gatherer societies: simple and complex. The !Kung are an example of the simple variety, and the Kwakiutl (see p. 000) are an example of the complex variety. Complex hunter-gatherers share many features in common with sedentary agricultural peoples. The major differences between the two varieties of hunter-gatherers are these:

Simple:
> Low-population density
> Not dependent on stored foods
> Live in temporary camps most of the year
> Weak distinctions of rank
> Sharing ethic
> No ownership of resources

Complex:
High-population density
Dependent on stored foods
Live in villages most of the year
Strong distinctions of rank
Sharing ethic weak
Family ownership of resources

Hayden 1992; Keely 1988; Testart 1982; Woodburn 1982a and b.

Figure 5.3
Planting in a Swidden (A Slash-and-Burn Garden)
This Amahuaca woman from eastern Peru is using a digging stick to plant corn in a recently burned garden.

erally agree that recent band-organized hunter-gatherers cannot be regarded as typical of hunter-gatherers of the remote past, when no agriculturalists or pastoralists existed anywhere, and when every kind of habitat, dry or wet, cold or hot, bountiful or sparse, was available for occupation by hunter-gatherer peoples.

Agriculture

Agricultural peoples tend to live in more permanent settlements than hunter-gatherers. But again, not all agricultural societies are alike. Many groups depend on a mixture of hunting and gathering and farming or stockraising. And, of course, many kinds of farming and stockraising exist, each with its own ecological and cultural implications. *Rainfall agriculture*, for example, utilizes naturally occurring showers as a source of moisture; *irrigation agriculture* depends on artificially constructed dams and ditches to bring water to the fields.

Several varieties of rainfall agriculture and irrigation agriculture, each with its own ecological and cultural implications, must also be distinguished. For example, if rainfall agriculture is to be practiced, the problem of replenishing the nutrients taken from the soil by successive crops must be solved. One of the most ancient methods for solving this problem, still widely practiced to this day, is known as *slash-and-burn*. A patch of forest is cut down and left to dry. Then the slash is set on fire; later the ashes, which contain a rich supply of nutrients, are spread over the area to be planted (Fig. 5.3). In regions of heavy rainfall, a slash-and-burn garden cannot be replanted for more than two or three seasons before the nutrients in the ashes become depleted. A new patch of forest is then cleared and burned. Slash-and-burn thus requires large amounts of land in fallow awaiting the regrowth of vegetation suitable for burning.

A totally different solution to the problem of maintaining soil fertility is to raise animals as well as crops and to use the animal's manure as fertilizer. This system, known as *mixed farming*, was once characteristic of the European and American small family farm. With the advent of the industrial era, soil fertility came to depend primarily on chemical fertilizers, eliminating the need for raising animals and crops on the same farm (but introducing a whole new set of problems associated with the toxic effects of the chemicals employed).

In irrigation agriculture, soil fertility is a lesser problem since the irrigation water often contains silt and nutrients that are automatically deposited on the fields. But irrigation agriculture varies greatly in type and in scale (Hunt 1988; D. Price 1993). Some irrigation systems are confined to terraces on the walls of mountain valleys, as in the Philippines; others embrace the flood plains of great rivers such as the Nile and the Yellow River (Fig. 5.4).

Another form of irrigation involves mounding: Mud is scooped from shallow lakes and piled up to form ridges in which crops are planted, as in the misnomered "floating gardens" of Mexico. Throughout much of India, irrigation water is pulled up by oxen from deep brick-lined wells. More recently, India and other Third World nations have begun to rely on water that is pumped up by electric or gasoline-powered pumps through tube wells.

The Influence of the Environment

In recent decades, scientists and technicians have altered their assessment of the ability of technology to dominate the environment. Increasingly, we have seen that industrial modes of production have not liberated human social life from the constraints of nature. For example, we now realize that we have ignored or silently passed on many costs of industrial production to generations yet unborn. Specifically, we have depleted irreplaceable resources and polluted air and water in many parts of the world (Fig. 5.5).

Efforts are now under way in many industrial nations to reduce air and water pollution and to prevent the depletion and poisoning of the environment. The costs of these efforts testify to the continuing importance of the interaction between technology and environment. These costs will continue to mount, for this is only the very beginning of the industrial era. In the centuries to come, the inhabitants of specific regions may pay for industrialization in ways as yet uncalculated.

Carrying Capacity and the Law of Diminishing Returns

The abundance of game, quality of soils, amounts of rainfall, and extent of forests, in combination with a particular form of technology, set an upper limit on the production of food and hence on the number of human beings who can live in a particular environment. This upper limit on production and population is called the environment's *carrying capacity*. Though carrying capacity sets the upper limit to production

and reproduction, most societies maintain their production and population below that limit. To understand why this gap between carrying capacity and the actual level of food production and population occurs, we must identify another critical feature of food production called the *point of diminishing returns*[1] (Fig. 5.6). This is the point at which the amount of food produced per unit of effort begins to fall. Slash-and-burn farmers, for example, bring on diminishing returns as they increase the number of years they consecutively plant in the same garden.

The reason most food production systems maintain themselves below carrying capacity is that diminishing returns set in before carrying capacity is reached. When their system of production reaches the point of diminishing returns, people find themselves working harder and harder to maintain their level of production and population. In some cases, this will result in an attempt to relieve the pressure on resources by reducing productive effort. No one willingly wants to work more for less. As a result, production and population will remain below carrying capacity.

However, unless population growth is also regulated, the temptation to maintain or even increase production will be very great (see p. 50). This can be done by *intensification*, that is, by increasing the time and energy devoted to production. Through intensification, a mode of production can be pushed far beyond the point of diminishing returns all the way to and beyond carrying capacity, thereby irreversibly damaging the resource base.

The present condition of the ocean fisheries in many parts of the world illustrates what happens when production passes the point of diminishing returns. In general, the rate of return per unit of fishing effort has declined by almost half. And some local fisheries such as haddock in the Gulf of Maine have been completely destroyed (Royce 1987; Brown et al. 1991). Between 1950 and 1989, the annual world fish harvest increased from 22 to 100 million tons. This rise was made possible by intensifying fish production through the use of bigger boats, better electronic gear, bigger nets, spotter airplanes, and other technological advances. Since 1989, however, total production has leveled off, and production per capita has started to decline. Additional fisheries will soon collapse if these trends continue (Browin 1994; Weber 1994).

Maximum Sustainable Yield

In seeking to avoid depletions, environmentalists must consider the importance of maintaining production at a high level in order to feed and provide incomes for a particular population. This requirement has led to the concept of *max-*

---

[1]*Point of diminishing returns is defined differently by economists.*

Figure 5.4

Irrigation Agriculture

This form of agriculture occurs in many varieties, each with a special influence on social life.
(a) Massive Chinese water works. (b) Terraces cover much of Javanese croplands.
(c) Ifuago, Philippines, where terraces are constructed on steep mountain slopes and are among
the engineering wonders of the world. (d) Tube well in Africa.

(a)

(b)

Figure 5.5
The Hidden Costs of the Industrial Mode of Production
(a) Abandoned hazardous waste dump. Pit is 5 feet deep and covers
34,000 square feet. (b) Times Beach, Missouri. Floodwaters spread
soil contaminated with dioxin, previously concentrated near highways,
all over residential neighborhoods. Cleanup crews collect samples for
analysis.

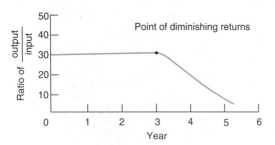

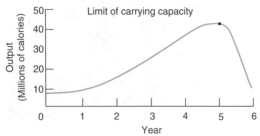

Figure 5.6
Production, Carrying Capacity, and Diminishing Returns
Point of diminishing return is reached in year 3, but limit of
carrying capacity is reached in year 5. Production is intensi-
fied and continues to increase until year 5, then crashes.

imum sustainable yield, which may be defined as a level of production immediately prior to the point of diminishing return
(National Research Council 1992; Costanza 1991). No one
has yet demonstrated that maximum sustainable yield is a
realistic goal for resource management. Indeed, some environmentalists flatly deny that scientists can reach a scientific consensus on the maximum sustainable yield of any
resource and assert that resources throughout history and prehistory have always been overexploited (Ludwig, Hilborn,
and Walters 1993: 17; see Box 5.3).

Depletion and New Modes of Production

What happens to a society when its modes of production
are pushed beyond diminishing returns and into environmental collapse? Various scenarios may unfold: The people
may migrate to a new habitat; or they may die off through
hunger and disease. In the past, environmental depletions
have sometimes stimulated the adoption of new modes of
production. As suggested in the work of Ester Boserup
(1965), when hunters and gatherers deplete their animals
and plants, they are likely to begin to adopt a mode of production based on the domestication of animals and plants.
When slash-and-burn peoples deplete their forests, they may
begin to cultivate permanent fields using animal fertilizer.
And when rainfall agriculturalists using permanent fields

SELF ADORNMENT

Samburu youth, Kenya.

Body painting. The body is the canvas of the Masai.

A Masai "prom," a ceremony marking the transition to adulthood.

Finland. Lazo throwing competition to celebrate the traditional reindeer hunting economy of Lapland.

Cuna India woman from Panama. Her adornments and dress design combine European and Native American elements. (Roosters are not native to the new world.)

New Guinea man. "High fashion" among the Samo.

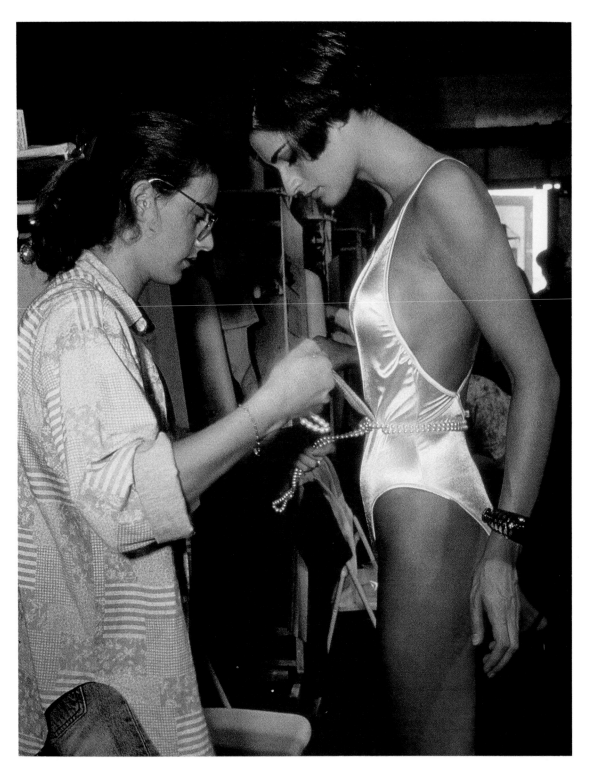

"High fashion" in France. Getting ready for a showing at Chanel, Paris.

*Padang, Myanmar woman. The more rings, the longer the neck,
the higher the status.*

India. Rajasthani women dressed for a visit from their relatives.

Native Americans, Hollywood USA. These modern Native Americans combine elements of dress and adornment from many different tribal heritages.

Box 5.3

THE PROBLEMS OF MEASURING SUSTAINABLE YIELD

a. Large levels of natural variability in the abundance of species mask the effects of human predation.
b. Scientists are unable to carry out laboratory experiments to determine if a given level of production is sustainable.
c. Even if scientists reach a consensus, the prospect of immediate wealth generates political power that is used to promote unlimited exploitation of resources.

Adapted from Ludwig, Hilborn, and Walters 1993.

---

deplete their soils, they may shift to irrigation agriculture. The shift from preindustrial to industrial and petrochemical forms of agriculture can also be seen as a response to depletions.

The depletion of ocean fish stocks provides another example: Aquaculture—the raising of fish in nets and ponds—is rapidly overtaking fishing in some parts of the world as a mode of fish production just as agriculture and animal husbandry once replaced the hunting and gathering of terrestrial plants and animals. We have reasons to believe, therefore, that if we deplete additional natural components of the industrial mode of production, new and still more productive infrastructures may yet arise.

However, technology alone will never provide a long-term guarantee of high levels of production and consumption for the majority of human beings. No matter what the next mode of production may be, its increased efficiency will soon be strained to the limits if population growth is not checked. Ocean fisheries again provide an example of what I mean. Even though production increased from 22 to 100 million tons from 1950 to 1990, world population has been growing so fast that per capita production has actually begun to decline (Brown 1994: 181).

Indeed, one might argue that the wisest course for humanity to follow in pursuit of affluence for all would be to not only prevent further growth of world population through family planning but to promote gradual global population reduction by limiting each couple to one child. But how to impose so great a restriction on individual liberty without violating democratic principles remains an unsolved dilemma.

Hunter–Gatherer Ecology

The !Kung San (! designates a click sound; see p. 35) are a hunter–gatherer people who live in the Kalahari Desert on both sides of the border between Botswana and Namibia in southern Africa. With two qualifications, they may be taken to represent the "simple" band-organized, mobile hunter-gatherers identified in Box 5.2. The first qualification is that the description that follows pertains to the way the !Kung lived in the 1960s. Since then, they have changed greatly and become involved in new commercial and political relationships. Although I will use the present tense, it should be understood as referring to what anthropologists call the "ethnographic present"—how things were when the ethnographers did their field work.

The second qualification is that even before the 1960s, the !Kung had intermittently been more or less intensely involved with nearby groups of cattle-herding peoples with whom they traded and for whom they sometimes worked. Nonetheless, the !Kung of the 1960s practiced a way of life that was quite distinct from the cultures of their nearest neighbors in almost every respect (Soloway and Lee 1990; Wilson and Denbow 1990; Lee and Guenther 1991).

Like most hunter-gatherers who inhabit sparse environments, the !Kung San move about a great deal from one camp to another in search of water, game, and wild plant foods. They build only temporary shelters and have few possessions, yet they are well nourished and moderately long-lived. As occurs almost universally (see p. 97), !Kung San men specialize in hunting and the !Kung San women specialize in gathering although, on occasion, women will bring a small

Figure 5.7
!Kung Women Returning to Camp
They have been out gathering wild vegetables and are carrying digging sticks.

animal back to camp and men will help carry heavy loads of nuts (Fig. 5.7).

The number of people in a !Kung camp varies from twenty-three to forty, with an average camp size of thirty-one (twenty adults and eleven children). During a 4-week study period, Richard Lee calculated that twenty adults put in an average 2.4 days per week in hunting and gathering. On any particular day, the number of people hunting or gathering varied from zero to sixteen. About 71 percent of the calories consumed by a !Kung camp are provided by women's gathering activities. Women range widely throughout the countryside, walking about 2 to 12 miles a day round-trip for a total of about 1,500 miles a year each. On an average trip, each woman brings back from 15 to 33 pounds of nuts, berries, fruits, leafy greens, and roots, whose proportions vary from season to season.

Men hunt on the average only every 3 or 4 days and are successful only about 23 percent of the time they hunt. Hunting is therefore not an efficient source of energy for the !Kung. For every calorie (above basal metabolism) expended on hunting, only about 3 calories worth of meat was produced. Of the average total of about 2,355 calories consumed per person per day, meat provides about 29 percent, nuts and vegetables the rest. One nut in particular, the mongongo, alone accounts for about 58 percent of the !Kung caloric intake and a large share of protein as well.

Studies of the !Kung and similar band-organized hunter-gatherers have dispelled the notion that the hunting–gathering way of life, even in adverse environments, necessarily condemns people to a miserable hand-to-mouth existence, with starvation avoided only by dint of unremitting daily effort. About 10 percent of the !Kung are over 60 years of age (compared with 5 percent in countries such as Brazil and India), and medical examination shows them to be in good health. Judged by the large quantity of meat and other sources of protein in their diet, their sound physical condition, and their abundant leisure, the !Kung San have a relatively high standard of living. The key to this situation is that their population is low in relation to the resources they exploit. They have fewer than one person per square mile on their land, and their production effort remains far below carrying capacity, with no appreciable intensification (except where they have become involved in raising livestock).

Optimal Foraging Theory

Despite their dependence on wild plants and animals, hunters and gatherers do not eat every edible species in their habitat. They pass up many edible plants and animals even when they encounter them while searching for food. Of some 262 species of animals known to the !Kung San, for example, only about 80 are eaten (Lee 1979: 226). This pickiness also occurs among animals that, like human hunter-gatherers, must forage (search) for their food. To account for this selective behavior, ecologists have developed a set of principles known as *optimal foraging theory* (Box 5.4).

This theory predicts that hunters or collectors will pursue or harvest only those species that give them the maximum energy return for the time spent foraging. At least one species will always be taken on encounter, namely, the one with the highest rate of energy return for each hour of "handling time"—time spent in pursuing, killing, collecting, carrying, preparing, and cooking the species after it is encountered. The foragers will take a second, third, or fourth species when they encounter it only if by doing so it raises the rate of caloric return for their total effort (Hawkes, Hill, and O'Connell 1982; Hawkes and O'Connell 1992; Smith and Winterhalder 1992). Of course, foragers do not actually measure how many calories they expend or obtain. But through repeated trial and error, they achieve a rather precise knowledge of whether it is worth their while to take a particular species. (If lions and wolves can develop this selective behavior, so can humans!)

In other words, optimal foraging theory predicts that foragers will continue to add items to their diets only as long as each new item increases (or does not diminish) the overall efficiency of their foraging activities. This prediction is especially interesting with regard to the question of how the abundance of a food item—such as an insect species—influences its position on or off the optimal diet list. Items that lower the overall rate of energy return will not be added to the list no matter how abundant they become. Only the abundance of the higher-ranked items influences the breadth of the list. As a high-ranking item becomes scarce, items previously too inefficient to be on the list get added. The reason for this is that the scarcity of the top-rated item means that

Box 5.4

An Intuitive Explanation of Optimal Foraging

Imagine that you are in a forest in which some trees have a $1 bill and other trees have a $20 bill hanging from the topmost branches. Should you climb every money tree you come across, or should you climb only the $20 trees? The answer depends on how many $20 money trees there are. If there are a lot of them, it would be a mistake to climb $1 trees. On the other hand, no matter how scarce $20 trees might be, if you happened to find one, you would always stop to climb it.

more time must be spent before it is encountered. Therefore, the average rate of return for the whole list shifts downward so that it is no longer a waste of energy to stop for items that have a lower rate of caloric return (Hawkes, Hill, and O'Connell 1982).

Optimal foraging theory helps explain why people on skimpy diets may nonetheless pass up items that are very abundant in their habitats, such as insects and earthworms. It is not the commonness or rarity of a food item that predicts whether it will be in the diet, but its contribution to the overall efficiency of food production. A word of caution is needed here. Energetic efficiency is not the only factor determining the diet of human hunter-gatherers. Many other factors, such as the protein, fat, mineral, and vitamin composition of foods, may also determine which species are favored. But energetic efficiency is always an important consideration and is the factor that has thus far been measured most successfully by anthropologists (Fig. 5.8).

Slash-and-Burn Food Energy Systems

Roy Rappaport (1968, 1984) made a careful study of the food energy system of the Tsembaga Maring, a clan living in semipermanent villages on the northern slopes of the central highlands of New Guinea. The Tsembaga, who number about 204, plant taro, yams, sweet potatoes, manioc, sugar cane, and several other crops in small gardens cleared and fertilized by the slash-and-burn method (Fig. 5.9). Slash-and-burn is a more efficient method of meeting caloric needs than hunting, yielding 18 calories of output for every 1 calorie of input. Thus, the Tsembaga are able to satisfy their caloric needs with a remarkably small investment of working time—only 380 hours per year per food producer is spent on raising crops.

At the same time, the Tsembaga manage to feed almost ten times as many people as the !Kung and to live in the same house for several years. But tropical slash-and-burn modes of production are constrained by environmental limits. First, there is the problem of forest regeneration. Because of leaching by heavy rains and because of the invasion of insects and weeds, the productivity of slash-and-burn gardens drops rapidly after 2 or 3 years of use, and additional land must be cleared to avoid diminishing returns (Johnson and Earle 1987: 67ff.). Optimum productivity is achieved when gardens are cleared from a substantial secondary growth of large trees. If gardens are cleared when the secondary growth is very immature, only a small amount of wood-ash fertilizer will be produced by burning. On the other hand, if the trees revert to maximum size, they will be very difficult to cut down.

Figure 5.8
Aché Hunters

(a) Drawing bow. (b) Returning from hunt with slain peccary. This Paraguayan group has been shown to maintain an optimal foraging diet.

Figure 5.9
"Cooking" the Garden

A Tsembaga Maring woman during the burning phase of swidden cycle

Optimum regeneration may take anywhere from 10 to 20 years or more, depending on local soils and climates.

Thus, in the long run, slash-and-burn ecosystems use up a considerable amount of forest per capita, but in any particular year, only 5 percent of the total territory may actually be in production (Boserup 1965: 31). The Tsembaga, for example, plant only 42 acres in a given year. Nonetheless, over the years they have gardened a total of 864 acres. This is about the amount of forest that the Tsembaga need if their population remains at about 200 people and if they burn secondary-growth garden sites every twenty years.

Rappaport estimates that the Tsembaga had at their disposal an amount of forest land sufficient to support another eighty-four people without permanently damaging the regenerative capacities of the trees. However, the bulk of this land lies above or below the optimum altitude levels for their major crops and thus would probably somewhat diminish efficiency if put into use. All slash-and-burn peoples confront the ultimate specter of "eating up their forest" (Condominas 1977) by shortening the fallow period to a point where grasses and weeds replace trees. In some parts of highland New Guinea permanent grasslands have replaced forests (Sorenson 1972; Sorenson and Kenmore 1974).

The Problem of Animal Food

Another problem with tropical slash-and-burn modes of production is the vulnerability to depletion of animal species. This problem is especially acute where the main staples are protein- and fat-deficient root crops such as sweet potatoes, plantains, yams, manioc, and taro. Natural tropical forests produce a vast amount of plant biomass per hectare, but they are very poor producers of animal species that human hunters can exploit (Bailey 1989; Bailey and Meadland 1991). The animals that inhabit tropical forests tend to be small, furtive, and arboreal. As human population density rises, these animals quickly become very scarce and hard to find.

The total animal biomass—the weight of all the spiders, insects, worms, snakes, mammals, and so on—in a hectare of central Amazon rain forest is 45 kilograms. This compares with 304 kilograms in a dry East Africa thorn forest. In East African savannah grasslands, 627 kilograms of large herbivores are found per hectare, far outweighing all the large and small animals found per hectare in the Amazon (Fittkau and Klinge 1973: 8). In fact, some anthropologists believe that the natural productivity of tropical forests may be too low for hunter-gatherers to have subsisted within them for any length of time without practicing agriculture (Bailey and Headland 1991). Although plant foods can provide nutritionally adequate diets if eaten in variety and in large quantities, meat is a more efficient source of essential nutrients than plant food, kilo for kilo. Hence, one of the most important limiting factors in the growth of slash-and-burn energy systems is thought to be the availability of animal food (Gross 1975, 1981; Harris 1984; Good 1989; but see Collinvaux and Bush 1991).

The Tsembaga, like virtually every other human group, highly prize animal food, especially in the form of fatty meat. (Vegetarians who abstain from meat usually prize animal foods in the form of milk and yogurt.) The Tsembaga, whose population density is sixty-seven persons per square mile, compared with less than one per square mile among the !Kung San, have depleted the wild animals in their territory. Among the Tsembaga, the flesh eaten on the majority of days ranges from nothing at all to less than 1 ounce. Fruits and vegetables constitute approximately 99 percent by weight of the usual daily intake. These figures do not include the sometimes considerable amount of meat that the Tsembaga consume on special festive occasions (Rappaport 1984: 448).

The Tsembaga have compensated for the scarcity of game animals by stocking their land with a domesticated animal—the pig. The Tsembaga's pigs root for themselves during the day but come home to a meal of sweet potatoes and food scraps in the evening. An average Tsembaga pig weighs as much as an average Tsembaga human, and Rappaport estimates that each pig consumes almost as much garden produce as each person. When the Tsembaga pig herd is at its maxi-

Figure 5.10
Dispatching a Pig Among the Maring

Pigs have a great ritual significance throughout New Guinea and Melanesia. The people in this scene are Fungai Maring, neighbors of the Tsembaga Maring.

mum, almost as much time and energy are devoted to feeding pigs as to feeding people. Like many New Guinea cultures, the Tsembaga allow their pig population to increase over a number of years, slaughtering them only on ceremonial occasions (Watson 1977). When the effort needed to care for pigs becomes excessive, a pig feast is held, resulting in a sharp decline in the pig population (Fig. 5.10). This feast may be related to the cycle of reforestation in the Tsembaga's gardens and the regulation of war and peace between the Tsembaga and their neighbors (Morren 1984: 173).

Irrigation Agriculture

Under favorable conditions, irrigation agriculture yields more calories per calorie of effort than any other preindustrial mode of food production. And among irrigation farmers, the Chinese have excelled for thousands of years. A detailed study of the labor inputs and weight yield of agricultural production in pre-Communist times was carried out by the anthropologists Fei Hsiao-t'ung and Chang Chih-I (1947) in the village of Luts'un, Yunnan Province. There, the villagers obtained over 50 calories for each calorie of effort they expended in the fields. The principal crops were rice (which accounted for 75 percent of the total), soybeans, corn, manioc, and potatoes. Because of the efficiency of their agriculture, the 700 people of Luts'un produced five times more food than they consumed. What happened to the surplus? The villagers exchanged it via markets and money for nonfarm goods

and services; they used it to pay taxes and rent; and they used it to raise large numbers of children and to sustain a high rate of population increase. The high population density in the irrigated parts of China is characteristic of societies that practice large-scale irrigation agriculture. It results from the fact that if the amount of water sent to the fields is increased, more labor can be applied to production without diminishing returns.

Energy and Pastoralism

If one feeds grain (wheat, barley, or maize) to animals rather than to people and then eats the meat, much of the energy available in the grains will be lost. Thus, for cattle in feedlots, it takes about 7 kilograms of grain to add 1 kilogram of live weight (Brown 1994: 192). The loss in efficiency associated with the processing of plant food through the gut of domesticated animals accounts for the relatively infrequent occurrence of cultures whose mode of food production is that called *pastoralism*. Pastoralists are peoples who raise domesticated animals and who do not depend on hunting, gathering, or the planting of their own crops for a significant portion of their diets. Pastoralists typically occupy arid grasslands and steppes where precipitation is too sparse or irregular to support rainfall agriculture and where water for irrigation is not available.

There are two basic types of pastoralists. The first type consists of those who move their livestock in a regular seasonal pattern in relation to seasonal changes in the available pasture. This strategy is called *transhumance*. Transhumant groups move their camps and animals to higher and cooler mountain pastures during the heat of the summer and then reverse their steps to return to the lower elevations during winter. In some transhumant adaptations, as formerly practiced in the Swiss Alps, for example, only a small number of herders take the animals to the high pastures. In other cases, such as the Basseri of Iran (Barth 1961), people and animals stay close together during the entire migration (Fig. 5.11).

The second major type of pastoralism does not involve movement back and forth along a traditional migration route. Instead, people and animals try to find the best pastures wherever they may be located. This strategy is called *nomadic pastoralism,* an adaptation that is often associated with migrations over vast distances of pastoral peoples such as the Mongols and Huns.

Pastoral peoples are not nutritionally self-sufficient. They need to supplement milk, cheese, blood, and meat (the last always being a relatively small part of the daily fare) with plant foods that they obtain through trade with their sedentary farming neighbors. Pastoralists frequently attempt to improve their bargaining position by raiding the sedentary villagers and carrying off the grain harvest without paying for

Figure 5.11
Pastoral Nomadism
Basseri of Iran on the move.

it. They can often do this with impunity since their possession of animals such as camels and horses makes them highly mobile and militarily effective. Continued success in raiding may force the farming population to acknowledge the pastoralists as their overlords. Repeatedly in the history of the Old World, relatively small groups of pastoral nomads—the Mongols and the Arabs being the two most famous examples—have succeeded in gaining control of the large agricultural empires on their borders. The inevitable outcome of these conquests, however, was that the conquerors were absorbed by the agricultural system as they attempted to feed the huge populations that had fallen under their control (Khazanov 1984; Galaty and Johnson 1990).

Energy and the Evolution of Culture

According to anthropologist Leslie White (1949: 368–369), a basic law governs the evolution of cultures: "Other factors remaining constant, culture evolves as the amount of energy harnessed per year is increased, or as the efficiency of the means of putting energy to work is increased." The first part of this law seems to be supported by the per capita output of Chinese irrigation agriculture and the per capita output of the !Kung and Tsembaga, as Table 5.1 shows.

The second part of White's law is not so clear. If one considers only human labor inputs, the ratio of output to input rises from 11:1 for the !Kung to 18:1 for the Tsembaga to 54:1 for Luts'un. But these figures do not include the energy that the Tsembaga use in the combustion of trees to make their gardens, nor the considerable amount of energy that the Tsembaga "waste" in converting vegetable foods to pork. Nor

do the numbers for Luts'un include the considerable energetic cost of milling and cooking rice. As Timothy Bayliss-Smith (1977) has shown in an attempt to test White's law, South Sea communities drawn into participating in aspects of modern industrial modes of production produce much more food energy per capita, but their efficiency in terms of energy output to input shows no clear upward trend. In fact, if we consider the total energy inputs and outputs of food production in advanced industrial societies, the trend in efficiency of putting energy to work runs counter to White's prediction.

Industrial Food Energy Systems

Estimating the input–output ratio of industrial agriculture (see Barlett 1989) is difficult because the amount of indirect labor put into food production exceeds the amount of direct labor (Fig. 5.12). An Iowa corn farmer, for example, can produce 81 bushels of corn in 9 hours with an energy equivalent of 8 million calories (Pimentel et al. 1973). This gives a nominal ratio of 5,000 calories of output for every calorie of input! But enormous amounts of indirect human labor are embodied in the tractors, trucks, combines, oil and gas, pesticides, herbicides, and fertilizers used by the Iowa corn farmer.

In the United States, 15 tons of machinery, 22 gallons of gasoline, 203 pounds of fertilizer, and 2 pounds of chemical insecticides and pesticides are invested per acre per year. This represents a cost of 2,890,000 calories of nonfood energy per acre per year (Pimentel et al. 1975), a cost that has increased steadily since the beginning of the century. Before 1910, more calories were obtained from agriculture than were invested in it. By 1970, it took 8 calories in the form of fossil fuels to produce 1 calorie of food. Today, vast quantities of energy are used simply to process and package food (Box 5.5). If the people of India were to emulate the U.S. system of food production, their entire energy budget would have to be devoted to nothing but agriculture (Steinhart and Steinhart 1974).

Chapter Summary

In the comparative study of modes of production, we consider the quantitative and qualitative aspects of energy production and of ecological relationships. Most of the energy flowing through preindustrial energy systems consists of food energy. Moreover, the technology of energy production cannot be altered by whim. It has evolved through successive stages of technical competence, in which the mastery of one set of tools and machines has been built on the mastery of an earlier set. Through technological advance, the energy available per capita has steadily increased. However, technology never exists in the abstract but only in the particular

Table 5.1

PER CAPITA ENERGY PRODUCTION

	TOTAL OUTPUT IN CALORIES (IN THOUSANDS)	POPULATION	PER CAPITA OUTPUT IN CALORIES (IN THOUSANDS)
!Kung	23,400	35	670
Tsembaga	150,000	204	735
Luts'un	3,790,000	700	5,411

instances where it interacts with a specific environment. There is no such thing as technology dominating or controlling the natural environment. Even in the most advanced industrial ecosystems, depletion and pollution of habitats add unavoidable costs to energy production and consumption.

Technology, interacting with environment, determines carrying capacity, which is the upper limit of production and consequently the upper limit of human population size and density as well. When a population exceeds its environment's carrying capacity, production will decline precipitously. The fact that a food energy system is operating below carrying capacity, however, does not mean that ecological restraints are absent. Production may be cut back after reaching the point of diminishing returns. But it may also be increased by intensifying the production inputs. Still, intensification if continued without technological change will result in irreversible damage to the habitat.

Figure 5.12
Industrial Farming
Rice harvest near Yuba City, California. Are these farmers or engineers?

A common human cultural response to declining efficiency brought about by intensification is to alter technology and thereby adopt new modes of production.

Hunting and gathering was the universal mode of food production until the end of the Stone Age. Depending on the kind of technology and the environmental conditions, several types of hunter-gatherers can be distinguished. The !Kung San are an example of the simple, band-organized, mobile variety found in less favored habitats. Their output-to-input efficiency is low, especially for the male-dominated activity of hunting. However, by maintaining low population densities and avoiding intensification, they enjoy a relatively high standard of living (good diets, unpolluted environments, and lots of leisure time). Energetic efficiency plays an important role in the selection of the species that hunter-gatherers use for food. According to optimal foraging theory, foragers stop to take only those species whose handling time adds to or does not decrease the overall efficiency of their foraging effort.

Slash-and-burn agriculturalists such as the Tsembaga Maring satisfy their caloric needs with greater efficiency than the !Kung San, but they have depleted the game animals in their habitat and must rely on costly domesticated pigs for their animal proteins and fats.

By using irrigation agriculture, the people of Luts'un produce a large surplus. Their output–input ratio for human effort is three times higher than the output–input ratio of the Tsembaga.

Pastoralism, another preindustrial mode of food production, is practiced only in areas unsuitable for agriculture because feeding plant food to domesticated animals rather than consuming crops directly results in a 90 percent reduction in the efficiency of converting sunlight to human food. As Leslie White predicted, the amount of energy harnessed per capita in the long run has steadily increased. Energy efficiency has also increased as measured by the return for human labor input. But when other sources of energy are included in the calculation of efficiency, advances in technology have resulted in decreased efficiency of food production, as demonstrated by the enormous energy inputs that characterize industrial agricultural systems.

Box 5.5

ENERGY INPUT IN PACKAGING AND PROCESSING INDUSTRIAL FOOD

ENERGY REQUIRED TO PRODUCE VARIOUS FOOD PACKAGES:

Package	kcal
Wooden berry basket	69
Styrofoam tray (size 6)	215
Molded paper tray (size 6)	384
Polyethylene pouch (16 oz)	559
Steel can, aluminum top (12oz)	568
Small paper set-up box	722
Steel can, steel top (16 oz)	1,006
Glass jar (16 oz)	1,023
Coca-Cola bottle, returnable (16 oz)	1,471
Aluminum TV-dinner container	1,496
Aluminum can, pop-top (12 oz)	1,643
Plastic milk container, disposable (½ gal)	2,159
Coca-Cola bottle, nonreturnable (16 oz)	2,451
Polyethylene bottle (1 qt)	2,494
Polypropylene bottle (1 qt)	2,752
Glass milk container, returnable (½ gal)	4,455

ENERGY REQUIRED TO PROCESS VARIOUS PRODUCTS:

Product	kcal/kg
Instant coffee	18,948
Chocolate	18,591
Breakfast cereals	15,675
Beet sugar (assumes 17% sugar in beets)	5,660
Dehydrated foods (freeze-dried)	3,542
Cane sugar (assumes 20% sugar in cane)	3,380
Fruit and vegetables (frozen)	1,815
Fish (frozen)	1,815
Baked goods	1,485
Meat	1,206
Ice cream	880
Fruit and vegetables (canned)	575
Flour (includes blending of flour)	484
Milk	354

Adapted from Pimentel and Pimentel 1985: 38–39.

AMERICA NOW UPDATE

Mode of Production

The mode of production in the United States is an advanced, increasingly high-tech form of industrialism. Industrialism denotes the mass production of goods, services, and information by means of a highly detailed division of labor in which workers use electronic and other kinds of machines in routinized, repetitive ways. Detailed division of labor refers to the separation of production tasks into many tiny steps carried out by different workers. The United States remains the top-ranking industrial manufacturing country in the world. Nonetheless, three quarters of all employees produce information and services rather than tangible objects (Howe and Parks 1989: 6). Most employed adult Americans work in offices, stores, restaurants, schools, clinics, and moving vehicles rather than on factory assembly lines. They wait on customers; repair broken machines; keep accounts; write letters; transfer funds; and provide grooming, schooling, training, information, counseling, and therapy to students, clients, customers, and patients. Farming, which once accounted for the vast majority of American workers, now occupies only 3 percent of the work force.

The rise of the service and information sectors has led to the characterization of the United States as a postindustrial society (Bell 1973). It would seem more appropriate, however, to call the United States and other advanced industrial societies, such as Germany and Japan, "hyperindustrial" (hyper means "extra strong") rather than postindustrial since the shift to services and information processing has merely resulted in extending the detailed division of labor and the use of mass-production machines—office computers, word processors, duplicators, supermarket bar-code scanners, electronic mail, automatic dialing machines—into additional kinds of production (Harris 1987; Sanderson 1988: 451). Offices are factories whose product is information, blurring the distinction between blue-collar and white-collar workers (Fig. 5.13). Here is a description of the work patterns of customer service operators in the "back office" of a large oil company:

> The pace is strenuous (an average of 160 calls per day) and automatically set by the computer's automatic call distributor; tasks are repetitive, and workers are isolated in carrels on duty, while their movement is restricted by their headsets and the necessary concentration on the VDT [video display

Figure 5.13
Information Factory
Collections department of telephone company. Note the
predominance of women.

terminal] screen. Machine-measured performance statistics are the basis for promotion: for each operator the computer measures the number of calls taken, the length of each call, the number of callers who "abandoned" before being answered, and the amount of time spent off the telephone or away from the work station. In order to monitor performance, supervisors listen in on 10% of each operator's daily call volume (approximately 16 calls) each month, using a telephone pickup that cannot be heard by the operator. More than three errors places the operator below the shop standard for "accuracy." One supervisor and former operator observed, "You can tell when they've been working the phones too long; their voices on the phone get louder and louder without their noticing it."

[Nelson 1986: 158]

Chapter 6

REPRODUCTION

Parents and infant among the San of the Kalahari Desert.

We will now focus on the reproductive aspect of infrastructure. Given the potential that human beings have to increase population, how is population brought into balance with modes of production and carrying capacity? We will see that preindustrial societies have employed a variety of means that have the effect of regulating population growth, including prolonged nursing, abortion, and direct and indirect infanticide. But why do people in poverty-stricken parts of the world persist in having large families while people in rich industrial countries have fewer and fewer children? We will see that the key to answering this question and to understanding rates of population growth is not the possession of contraceptives or abortifacients but the costs and benefits of raising children under different modes of production. What are the implications of this approach for the abortion debate? If people regulate reproduction not only before but after birth, when does human life really begin?

The Relation Between Production and Reproduction

Reproduction is a form of production—the "product" being new human beings. Under optimal conditions, women can have between twenty and twenty-five live births during their fertile years (which last roughly from age 15 to 45). In all human societies, women on the average have far fewer children than that. The record, 8.97 children per woman, is held by the Hutterites, a communitarian sect in western Canada (Lang and Gohlen 1985). If all children born live to reproduce, any number of births greater than two per woman would potentially result in population increase (holding death rates constant and without emigration). Even small rates of increase can result in enormous populations in a few generations. The !Kung, for example, have a growth rate of 0.5 percent per year. If the world had started 10,000 years ago with a population of 2, and if that population had grown at 0.5 percent per year, the world population would now be 604,436,000,000,000,000,000,000. No such growth has occurred because, through various combinations of cultural and natural factors, reproduction has been kept within limits imposed by systems of production.

Much controversy surrounds the nature of the relationship between production and reproduction. Followers of Thomas Malthus, the founder of the science of demography (the science of population phenomena), have long held the view that the level of population is determined by the amount of food produced. According to the Malthusians, population would always rise to the limit of production; in fact, it would tend to rise faster than any conceivable rise in productivity, thereby dooming a large portion of humanity to perpetual poverty, hunger, and misery. However, from the evidence showing that many nonindustrial societies maintain their levels of production well below carrying capacity (see Chapter 5), Malthus was clearly wrong in at least one crucial

respect. Moreover, we could turn Malthus upside down and see the amount of food produced as being determined by the level of population growth. In this view, which has been advocated most forcefully by Ester Boserup (see p. 50), food production tends to rise to the level demanded by population growth. As population expands, and the point of diminishing returns is reached, people invent or adopt new and more efficient modes of food production.

In light of modern anthropological research, the position that seems most correct is that production and reproduction are equally important in shaping the course of sociocultural evolution, and that to an equal extent, each is the cause of the other. Reproduction generates *population pressure* (physiological and psychological costs such as malnutrition and illness). Population pressure often leads to intensification, diminishing returns, and irreversible environmental depletions. Depletions, as we have seen (p. 50), often lead, in turn, to new technologies and to new modes of production.

Population Pressure

Population pressure and population growth are not the same thing. Under favorable environmental conditions, population size and density can increase, at least temporarily, without lowering a people's standard of living. During the nineteenth century, for example, the settling of the American West was accompanied by high *fertility* rates, rapidly rising population, and a rising standard of living among pioneer farm families.

Moreover, population pressures may exist even if population is not growing. To prevent the erosion of their standard of living, people often limit population growth by using physically and emotionally costly means of reproductive controls, such as infanticide and nonmedical abortion. For example, Arctic hunter-gatherers had very low population densities and virtually zero rates of population growth. Yet they experienced population pressure because their standard of living was maintained only by practicing a considerable amount of infanticide. Population pressure might even exist among people who are experiencing a population decline. Many Native-American peoples who live in the Amazon, for example, are declining in numbers at the same time that they find it increasingly difficult to maintain their standards of health and well-being (Isaac1991; Turner 1991).

Perhaps the best way to envision population pressure is to regard it as present with varying intensity among virtually all societies (the exception being societies that are expanding into uninhabited frontiers). Even in high-tech industrial countries where completed fertility rates have fallen below replacement levels (see p. 69), largely through the use of modern antireproductive technologies, population pressure has a role to play in phenomena such as unemployment, crime, homelessness, child abuse, and pollution. Although each of these problems is partly the result of the inequitable distribution of wealth, each is also made worse by the increase in human numbers. This relationship is certainly clear in the case of energy consumption and pollution. "At any given level of per capita pollution, more people means more pollution" (Brown 1991: 16). The earth's rivers, oceans, forests, and atmosphere have a limited ability to absorb industrial waste. Similarly, given the finite nature of our capacity to produce energy, population growth can only drive up the price of energy and the goods and services energy makes possible. At best, population pressure is a destabilizing force. It interacts with natural sources of instability, such as changes in climate, to bring about both small- and large-scale shifts in modes of production. Thus, though production limits population growth, population pressure provides a perpetual motivation for overcoming such limits (Johnson and Earle 1987; Keeley 1988; Graber 1991, 1992).

Preindustrial Population-Regulating Practices

Contrary to the Malthusian view, much evidence supports the conclusion that preindustrial cultures reduced or controlled population pressure by lowering reproductive rates. How did they do this in the absence of condoms, diaphragms, pills, spermicides, effective abortion drugs (Riddle and Estes 1992), or knowledge of the human ovulatory cycle? Four categories of practices have had the effect of regulating population growth: (1) care and treatment of fetuses, infants, and children; (2) care and treatment of girls and women (and to a lesser extent of boys and men); (3) intensity and duration of lactation (the period of breast feeding); and (4) variations in the frequency of coital intercourse.

Before describing these practices, I should point out that many anthropologists and demographers regard only conscious attempts to limit reproduction to a targeted number of children as evidence of population regulation (Wood 1990).

True, presence or absence of a conscious reproductive goal results in different patterns of birthing for women. But the point here is that effective limitation of rates of population growth can be achieved in the absence of family planning.

TREATMENT OF FETUSES AND CHILDREN

Maltreatment of fetuses, infants, and young children is a common means of lowering reproductivity. A subtle gradation leads from active attempts to avoid fetal death (abortion), infant death, and child death to active efforts to promote fetal death, infant death, and child death. Full support of the fetus involves supplementing the diets of pregnant women and reducing their work loads (MacCormack 1982: 8). Indirect abortion begins when heavy work loads and meager diets are imposed on pregnant women. Direct abortion occurs with starvation diets for pregnant women and often involves trauma caused by squeezing the mother's abdomen with tight bands, jumping on her, or having her ingest toxic substances (Riddle and Estes 1992). In a study of 350 preindustrial societies, George Devereux (1967: 98) found that direct abortion was "an absolutely universal phenomenon."

Some forms of infanticide are as widely practiced as abortion. Again, a subtle gradation leads from indirect to direct methods. Full support of the life of a newborn infant requires that it be fed to gain weight rapidly and that it be protected against extremes of temperature and from falls, burns, and other accidents. Indirect infanticide begins with inadequate feeding and careless and indifferent handling, especially when the infant is sick. Direct infanticide involves more or less rapid starvation, dehydration, exposure to the elements, suffocation, or blows to the head (S. Scrimshaw 1983). Often no sharp distinction exists between abortion and infanticide. The Yanomamo (see p. 143), for example, induce labor during the sixth or seventh month of pregnancy and kill the fetus if it shows signs of life after expulsion. Similarly, there is often no clear distinction between infanticide and the direct or indirect removal of unwanted children 2 or 3 years old by more or less rapid starvation and neglect during illness. In this connection, it should be pointed out that many cultures do not regard children as human until certain ceremonies, such as naming or hair cutting, are performed. Infanticide and the induced death of small children seldom take place after such ceremonies have been performed (Minturn and Stashak 1982). Hence, in emic perspective, such deaths are rarely seen as homicides.

TREATMENT OF WOMEN

The treatment of women can raise or lower the age at which women begin to be capable of bearing children and the age at which they can no longer conceive. It can also affect the total number of pregnancies women are capable of sustaining. Women who are nutritionally deprived are not as fertile as women whose diets are adequate, although considerable controversy exists over how severe the deprivations must be before significant declines in fertility occur. Still, severe, famine-level nutritional deprivation can reduce fertility by 50 percent (Bongaarts 1980: 568). Rose Frisch (1984: 184), however, maintains that even a 10 to 15 percent weight loss is sufficient to delay menarche and to disrupt the menstrual cycle. Others assign less significance to the role of body fat in fertility (Wood 1990: 234).

Other effects of malnutrition on mother, fetus, and infant are well-established. Poor maternal nutrition increases the risk of premature births and of low birth weights, both of which increase fetal and infant mortality; poor maternal nutrition also diminishes the quantity if not the quality of breast milk, thus lowering the chances of infant survival still further (Hamilton et al. 1984: 388). In turn, women who become pregnant and who recurrently provide mother's milk from a nutritionally depleted body also have elevated mortality rates (Lunn 1988; Adair and Popkin 1992; Kusin et al. 1993). These nutritional effects will all vary in interaction with the amount of psychological and physical stress imposed on pregnant and lactating women. In addition, life expectancy can be affected by exposure to toxic, body-shock techniques of abortion, again in interaction with general nutritional status.

Extreme malnutrition and physical and mental stress can also affect male *fecundity* (see Box 6.1) by reducing *libido* (sexual desire) and sperm count. However, the abundance of sperm as compared with the ova and the female's birthing and nursing physiology renders the treatment of women far more important than the treatment of males in regulating reproduction. High sickness and mortality rates among males are readily counterbalanced by the widespread practice of *polygyny* (one husband with several wives; see p. 106) and by the fact that one male can impregnate dozens of females.

LACTATION

Amenorrhea (disruption of the menstrual cycle) is a typical accompaniment of breast feeding. The effect is associated with the production of prolactin, a hormone that regulates mammary activity. Prolactin, in turn, inhibits the production of the hormones that regulate the ovulatory cycle. Several biocultural factors appear to control the duration of lactation amenorrhea. To begin with, there is the state of the mother's health and her diet. Additional variables include the intensity of suckling as determined by the age at which the infant is fed supplemental soft foods and by the scheduling of suckling episodes.

Although the relative importance of these factors remains controversial, under favorable conditions, prolonged nursing can clearly result in birth-spacing intervals of three or more years, with a degree of reliability comparable to that of modern mechanical and chemical contraceptives (Short 1984: 36). But one must be on guard against the notion that any social group is free to adjust its fertility rate upward or downward merely by intensifying and prolonging lactation (Fig. 6.1). Prolonged lactation cannot take place without suitably nourished mothers. Moreover, because human breast milk is deficient in iron, its use as the sole source of nourishment much beyond the age of 6 months will cause anemia in the infant.

Box 6.1

SOME BASIC DEMOGRAPHIC CONCEPTS

Crude Birth Rate
  The number of births per thousand people, in a given year.
Crude Death Rate
  The number of deaths per thousand people, in a given year.
Fertility Rate
  The number of live births per thousand women ages 15 to 44, in a given year.
Completed Fertility Rate
  The average number of children born to women who have completed their reproductive years.
Fecundity
  The physiological capacity to produce a live child.
Mortality
  Death as a factor in population stability or change.

Figure 6.1
Breastfeeding Older Children
San women breastfeed their children for 4 or 5 years per child.

COITAL FREQUENCY AND SCHEDULING

Coital abstinence can be sustained long enough to reduce pregnancies, and delays in the onset of coital behavior can shorten the female's reproductive span (Nag 1983). A mother can reinforce the effects of lactational amenorrhea with coital abstinence while continuing to nurse her child. And various forms of nonreproductive sex can influence fertility rates: Homosexuality, masturbation, *coitus interruptus* (withdrawal before ejaculation), and noncoital heterosexual techniques for achieving orgasm can all play a role in regulating fertility. Age of marriage is another important population-regulating variable, but its significance depends on the existence of a taboo on extramarital sex and unwed motherhood.

As we shall see (p. 112), many societies do not regard couples as being married until they have children (Wilmsen 1982: 4).

Type of marriage is also relevant to fertility. Polygyny (see p. 106), for example, assures that almost all females will engage in reproductive sex (in the absence of contraception). But polygyny is also effective in prolonging female sexual abstinence and the latter's reinforcing effect on lactational amenorrhea. In addition, polygyny probably results in lower rates of coital intercourse per wife as husbands grow older (Bongaarts et al. 1984: 521–522; Hern 1992). And for reasons not thoroughly understood, women whose husbands are polygynous tend to have a lower ratio of male to female children than those whose husbands are monogamous (Whiting 1993).

Clearly preindustrial societies have never lacked means for regulating their reproductive rates in response to the limits and possibilities of their modes of production.

The Influence of Disease and Other Natural Factors

Most of the great lethal epidemic diseases—smallpox, typhoid fever, influenza, bubonic plague, and cholera—are primarily associated with dense urbanized populations rather than with dispersed hunter-gatherers or small village cultures. Even diseases like malaria and yellow fever were probably less important among low-density populations that could avoid swampy mosquito breeding grounds. (Knowledge of the association between swamps and disease is very ancient even though mosquitoes were not recognized as disease carriers.) Other diseases such as dysentery, measles, tuberculosis, whooping cough, scarlet fever, and the common cold were also probably less significant among hunter-gatherers and early farmers (Armelagos 1990; Armelagos et al. 1994). Furthermore, the ability to recuperate from these infections is closely related to the general level of bodily health, which in turn is heavily influenced by the level of calories and protein consumption. Thus among many preindustrial societies, the role of disease as a long-term regulator of human population is to some extent a consequence of the success or failure of other population-regulating mechanisms. Only if these other mechanisms are ineffective and population density rises, productive efficiency drops, and diet deteriorates will some diseases figure as an important check on preindustrial population growth (Post 1985).

Some evidence indicates that Stone Age hunter-gatherers were healthier than early farmers and the peasants of preindustrial state societies. Exactly when and where a deterioration occurred is the focus of much continuing research (Cohen 1987; Cohen and Armelagos 1984). For much of the late Stone Age "artificial" population controls rather than sickness were probably the principal factors governing rates of population growth (Handwerker 1983: 20).

Obviously, a component in human birth and death rates reflects "natural" causes over which cultural practices have little influence. In addition to lethal diseases, natural catastrophes such as droughts, floods, and earthquakes may raise death rates and lower birth rates in a manner that leaves little room for cultural intervention. And of course, biology constrains the number of children a human female can have, as well as the length of human life.

The Costs and Benefits of Rearing Children

"Population pressure" implies that people are affected by the costs and benefits entailed in the process of reproduction. Costs of rearing children include the extra food consumed during pregnancy; the work forgone by pregnant women; the expenses involved in providing mother's milk and other foods during infancy and childhood; the burden of carrying infants and children from one place to another; and in more complex societies, expenditures for clothing, housing, medical care, and education. In addition, the birth process itself is dangerous and often places the life of the mother at risk.

Benefits of reproduction include the contributions that children make to food production, to family income in general, and to the care and economic security of their parents. Children are also widely valued for their role in marital exchanges and intergroup alliances (see pp. 116 and 112); that is, in many cultures, groups exchange sons and daughters in order to obtain husbands and wives. These exchanges are used to arrange alliances against aggressors. Hence, where chronic warfare exists, larger groups are safer than smaller ones; they have more alliances as well as greater military strength. All this, of course, is not to deny that people have children for sentimental reasons as well (see Box 6.2).

Humans may have a genetically controlled propensity, shared with other primates, to find infants emotionally appealing and to derive emotional satisfaction from holding and fondling them and from watching and helping them play and learn. As children grow older, their respect and love for their parents may also be highly valued. But this appreciation of infants and children, if it is innate, can be modified by culture so completely as to allow most people to have fewer children than they are biologically capable of producing and to enable others, such as monks, priests, nuns, and even some modern-day "yuppies," to have none at all.

Much recent evidence suggests that the rate at which the parental generation has children is largely determined by the extent to which having each additional child results in a net gain of benefits over costs for the average couple (Caldwell 1982; Harris and Ross 1987; Nardi 1983). Among band-organized hunter-gatherers, the number of children is limited by the burden that infants present to mothers who must carry them hundreds of miles each year on their forag-ing expeditions. According to Richard Lee, !Kung San mothers try to avoid having one child close on another in order to escape the burden of carrying two children at once. The benefits of additional children are further reduced among hunter-gatherers by the vulnerability of wild species of plants and animals to depletion. As band size increases, per capita food production tends to decline since hunter-gatherers have no effective way of creating a concomitant increase in the population of the wild plants and animals they use for food. Finally, the children of hunter-gatherers do not produce more than they consume until relatively late in childhood. For these reasons, population densities among simple hunter-gatherers seldom rise above one person per square mile.

If contemporary hunter-gatherers are at all representative of prehistoric times, *Homo sapiens* must have been a very rare creature during the early Stone Age. Perhaps only 5 million people lived in the entire world in those times (Dumond 1975; Hassan 1978: 78); certainly no more than 15 million (M. Cohen 1977: 54), compared with 5 billion today. Whether one takes the upper or lower estimate, for tens of thousands of years, the rate of growth of the human population was undoubtedly very slow (see Table 6.1).

Fertility is generally higher among sedentary complex hunter-gatherers and agriculturalists (Roth 1985). Children no longer have to be carried about over long distances; they can perform many useful economic chores at an early age; and since the rate of reproduction of domesticated plants and animals can be controlled, a considerable amount of intensification and hence population growth could be achieved without a decline in per capita output. After weaning, children in many agricultural societies rapidly begin to "pay for themselves." They contribute to the production of their own food, clothing, and housing, and under favorable conditions, they may begin to produce surpluses above their own subsistence needs as early as 6 years of age. This transition is hastened with successive births since senior siblings and other children assume much of the costs of grooming and caring for their juniors.

Measuring the Costs and Benefits of Rearing Children

A number of attempts have been made to measure the economic value of children in contemporary peasant communities. For example, in village Java, boys of 12 to 14 years contribute 33 hours of economically valuable work per week, and girls 9 to 11 contribute about 38 hours a week of the same. Altogether, children contribute about half of all work performed by household members (Fig. 6.2). Much household labor involves making handicrafts, working in petty trade, and processing various foods for sale. Similar

---

B o x   6 . 2

THE ECONOMY OF PARENTAL LOVE

Children fulfill a need for close, affectionate, emotional relationships with supportive, concerned, trustworthy, and approving beings. We need children because we need to be loved. In the support parents lavish on children there is a culturally instructed expectation that a balance will be struck with the love and affection that children can be so good at giving in return.

Even in their least giving mood, babies respond with warm, wet sucking and mouthing; they grasp your fingers and try to put their arms around you. Already you can anticipate the ardent hugs and kisses of early childhood, the tot who clings to your neck, the 4-year-old tucked in bed, whispering "I love you," the 6-year-old breathless at the door or running down the path as you come home from work. And with a little more imagination, you can see all the way to a grateful son or daughter, dressed in cap and gown, saying, "Thanks, Mom and Dad. I owe it all to you."

The fact that many of the sentimental rewards of parenthood are delayed does not mean that dreams rule the economy of love. As in every other kind of exchange, mere expectation of a return flow will not sustain the bonds indefinitely. The family sanctuary is a fragile temple. People will not forever marry and have children no matter how far the actual experience departs from expectation.

Adapted from Harris 1989: 230ff.

---

findings are reported for Nepal (White 1976; Nag et al. 1978).

Costs are more difficult to measure, but Javanese children themselves do most of the work needed to rear and maintain their siblings, freeing mothers for income-producing tasks. In any event, larger households are more efficient income-producing units than smaller households in rural Java because in large households a smaller proportion of each individual's total labor time is required for maintenance. Given these conditions, women have about five births and four surviving children, which "seems an entirely appropriate response" (White 1982: 605). (It is nonetheless a response that yields an alarming 2 percent per annum increase in Java's population.)

T a b l e   6 . 1

RATE OF GROWTH OF THE HUMAN POPULATION

PERIOD	WORLD POPULATION AT END OF PERIOD	PERCENTAGE ANNUAL RATE OF GROWTH DURING PERIOD
Paleolithic	5,000,000	0.0015
Mesolithic	8,500,000	0.0330
Neolithic	75,000,000	0.1000
Ancient empires	225,000,000	0.5000

Sources: Spengler 1974; Hassan 1978.

Figure 6.2
Child Worker
A Javanese boy earning his
keep.

Figure 6.3
Child Workers, Bangladesh

Meade Cain (1977: 225) quantified both benefits and costs for male children in a rural Bangladesh village (Fig. 6.3). Cain describes his findings:

> Male children become net producers at the latest by the age of 12. Furthermore, male children work long enough hours at high enough rates of productivity to compensate for consumption during their earlier periods of dependence by the age of 15. Therefore, in general parents realize a net economic return on male children for the period when they are subordinate members of the parental household.

Thus, the popular perception that people in less-developed countries have large numbers of children simply because they do not know how to avoid conception does not hold up. Much evidence tells us that more children and larger households mean a higher, not a lower, standard of living in the short run. In explaining why they did not wish to join any family-planning programs, the men of Manupur village in the Punjab explained: "Why pay 2,500 rupees for an extra hand? Why not have a son?" (Mamdani 1973: 77). Still, high fertility may simply give large families a more favorable standard of living relative to that of smaller families if the average standard of living for the whole farming sector is stagnant or even deteriorating (Weil 1986).

With the expansion of urban, industrial, technical, and white-collar employment opportunities, the net return from child rearing can be increased by investing in fewer but better-educated offspring. In Rampur village, close to the Indian capital of New Delhi, the number of children per woman declined as wage opportunities increased outside the village (Das Gupta 1978). Tractors, tube wells, and pumps reduced the demand for child labor. In addition, parents wanted their children to get more education to prepare for higher-quality jobs in New Delhi. Similarly, in Sri Lanka (Tilakaratne 1978), employers of wage labor have come to prefer adult males over children who can work only part time because they attend school. Furthermore, white-collar jobs are becoming available for which children are unsuited because they have not achieved the required levels of literacy and mathematical skills. Even families headed by manual workers desire to have children participate in white-collar, high-status jobs and to give them more schooling. Getting married to an educated and well-employed person has become the ideal, and this can be done only by postponing marriage, which in turn decreases the number of children per woman.

In Indian villages located near the city of Bangalore, three factors accounted for the trend against child labor: (1) Land holdings had become fragmented and too small to absorb the

Figure 6.4
Manupur, Punjab, India

Collection of cow dung by children to make cow-dung cakes for use as cooking fuel is becoming less important as families become more prosperous and the land is farmed more intensively.

labor of additional children in agriculture; (2) new nonfarm employment opportunities requiring arithmetic skills and literacy had opened up; and (3) educational facilities had been introduced or improved within the villages (Caldwell et al. 1983). Similarly, on returning to the village of Manupur in the Punjab (see p. 67), Nag and Kak (1984) found a sharp increase in the number of couples practicing contraception and a sharp reduction in the number of sons regarded as desirable (Fig. 6.4). These changes resulted from shifts in the mode of production, which lowered the demand for child labor.

Shortening or eliminating fallow, for example, has led to the disappearance of grazing land within the village so that young boys can no longer make themselves useful tending cattle. The loss of cattle and the increased reliance on chemical fuels and fertilizers have also done away with the childhood task of collecting cow dung to be used for fertilizer and

fuel (see p. 242). With the introduction of industrial herbicides, children are no longer needed for weeding. Furthermore, the proportion of Manupur workers employed in industrial, commercial, and government sectors has risen substantially. Meanwhile, the mechanization of farm operations, the expanded use of credit, and the need to keep account books have made Manupur parents consciously eager to expand their children's educational horizons. Secondary school enrollment increased in a decade from 63 to 81 percent for boys and from 29 to 63 percent for girls. Parents now want at least one son to have a white-collar job so that the family will not be entirely dependent on agriculture; many parents want both sons and daughters to attend college.

The Contraception, Abortion, and Infanticide Debate

If powerful cultural practices for raising or lowering fertility and mortality rates exist, it implies that human reproduction is much more than an act that takes place at a specific instant, such as the moment when an ovum and sperm unite. It implies that human reproduction is a social process that begins long before conception and that continues long after birth. For human reproduction to take place, prospective parents must have adequate material and psychological support; the pregnant woman and her fetus must be nourished and protected; the nursing mother and her infant must be fed and cared for; and a commitment must be made by the parents, relatives, and other supportive individuals and institutions to find the resources necessary to rear the newborn from infancy and childhood to adulthood.

As we have just seen, the decision to make the social effort necessary to give birth to and rear children is heavily influenced by the balance of costs and benefits confronting prospective parents. This means that when the balance is adverse, some form of birth or death control will be activated at some point in the reproductive process. When and how birth- or death-control measures will be taken vary from one culture to another. To a degree that is shocking to Western sensibilities, most preindustrial and underdeveloped societies employ reproduction-regulating measures that achieve their effect after children are born (see Box 6.3) That is, they practice some form of direct or indirect infanticide.

The existence of postpartum reproduction-regulating practices can be obscured by the failure to distinguish between emic and etic viewpoints. Yet the recognition of postpartum etic death-control practices is essential to understanding the controversy concerning contraception and abortion. Much evidence exists that if reproduction is not limited before or during pregnancy, then it will be limited after pregnancy by direct or indirect infanticide or pedicide (the killing of young children). Attempts to discourage contraception, medical abortion, and other modern prepartum reproductive controls

---

Box 6.3

INFANTICIDE IN NINETEENTH-CENTURY JAPAN

Japan's country folk were at one time the world's most efficient managers of human reproduction. During the nineteenth century, Japanese farm couples precisely fitted the size and sexual composition of their broods to the size and fertility of their land holdings. The small-holder's ideal was two children, one boy and one girl; people with larger holdings aimed for two boys and one or two girls. But the Japanese did not stop there! As expressed in a still-popular saying, "first a girl, then a boy," they tried to rear a daughter first and a son second. According to G. William Skinner, this ideal reflected the practice of assigning much of the task of rearing firstborn sons to an older sister. It also reflected the expectation that the firstborn son would replace his father as the farm's manager at an age when the father was ready to retire, and the son was not yet so old as to have grown surly while waiting to take over. A further complexity was the age at which couples got married. An older man would not dare to delay having a son, and so, if the firstborn was a male, he would count himself fortunate. Since the parents had no way of telling the sex of a child before birth, they were able to achieve these precise reproductive goals only by practicing systematic infanticide.

Skinner 1993.

---

may inadvertently increase reliance on postpartum homicidal practices. With this possibility in mind, we next present the case of indirect infanticide in Northeast Brazil.

Indirect Infanticide in Northeast Brazil

Northeast Brazil is a region subjected to periodic droughts, chronic malnutrition, and widespread poverty. Its infant mortality rate is about 200 deaths per 1,000 births in the first year of life (compared with a rate of less than 10 in developed countries). Nancy Scheper-Hughes has carried out a study of reproductive processes over a period of 25 years in a shanty town called Alto do Cruzeiro located in this region. Out of a total of 688 pregnancies (an average of 9.5 per woman!), there were 579 live births. Only 308 of these infants survived to age 5, an average of 3.6 infant and child deaths per woman (Scheper-Hughes 1992: 307). From circumstantial evidence, it is clear that many of these deaths are best described as forms of indirect infanticide.

Scheper-Hughes found that Alto do Cruzeiro mothers often withdraw support from a particular infant whom they perceived as lacking in "readiness or fitness for life." Mothers expressed a preference for "quick, sharp, active, verbal, and developmentally precocious children." Children with the opposite traits were not given medical assistance when they became ill, and they were not fed as well as their sisters and brothers. Mothers spoke of children who "wanted to die," whose will and drive toward life were not "sufficiently strong or developed." These unwanted children tend to die during one of the crises of childhood: infections of the umbilical cord, infant diarrhea, or teething. The women regard some childhood diseases as incurable, but the diagnostic symptoms of these diseases are so broad that almost any childhood disorder can be interpreted as a sign that the child is doomed to die: fits and convulsions, lethargy and passivity, retarded verbal or motor function, or a "ghost-like" or "animal-like" appearance (Fig. 6.5).

When a child marked with one of these fatal diseases dies, mothers do not display grief: They say there was no remedy, that even if you treat the disease, the child "will never be right," that it is "best to leave them to die," and that no one wants to take care of such a child. "It was a blessing that God decided to take them in their infancy" (Scheper-Hughes 1984: 539).

Scheper-Hughes (1992: 365) estimates that 43 percent of child deaths were attributable to the withdrawal of support from infants and children. The implication for the abortion

Figure 6.5
Doomed Infants, Northeast Brazil
(a) Mother said that her 16-month-old son has an "aversion" to life and will not live much longer. The color of his hair and lack of teeth show that he is suffering from advanced protein-calorie malnutrition. But 5 years later, Scheper-Hughes (1992: 389) found him still alive. (b) Baby has anemia and is listless and malnourished. The mother says she is conforming to God's will that the child will soon be an angel.

and contraception debate is this: If people are deprived of the means of preventing unwanted conceptions and births, this does not mean that they will support the unwanted child after it is born.

An important source of motivation for indirect infanticide is the belief that after babies and infants die, they become angels. The little corpses are placed in cardboard coffins and escorted to shallow graves by a smiling and laughing throng of children. Mothers do not weep when one of their babies becomes an angel (1992: 429).

As Scheper-Hughes emphasizes, to the extent that mothers practice indirect (or direct) infanticide through neglect, they are reacting to life-threatening conditions that are not of their own making: shortage of food, contaminated water supplies, unchecked infectious diseases, lack of day care, absence of affordable medical care, and the other stigmas and penalties of extreme poverty. While recognizing that mothers hasten the deaths of their unwanted children by rationing infant and child care, we must not fall into the trap of "blaming the victims." These women do not have access to modern forms of contraception or to medical abortion, and they are themselves too poorly nourished to limit their pregnancies by prolonging lactation. Moreover, coital abstinence is difficult for them because of their need to attract male support and companionship. In Scheper-Hughes's words, because of the indignities and inhumanities forced on them, these women must at times "make choices and decisions that no woman and mother should have to make" (1984: 541).

We must also guard against the impression that high rates of infanticide occur only in Brazil. Selective neglect of female infants accounts for the lopsided sex ratios found in many societies, including India and China (George, Able, and Miller 1993). Both indirect and direct infanticide were widely practiced in Europe in previous centuries (Kertzer 1993). In Japan, perhaps more than elsewhere, direct infanticide was used as a conscious means of family planning during the nineteenth century (Box 6.3).

Industrial Modes of Reproduction

Shifts in the costs and benefits of rearing children may explain the "demographic transition" that took place in Europe, the United States, and Japan during the nineteenth century. This transition involved a drop in both birth rates and death rates and a slowing of the rate of population growth (Fig. 6.6).

With industrialization, the cost of rearing children rose rapidly, especially after the introduction of child labor laws and compulsory education statutes. The skills required to earn a living took longer to acquire; hence parents had to wait longer before they could receive any economic benefits from their children. At the same time, the whole pattern of how people earned their livings changed. Work ceased to be something done by family members on the family farm or in the family shop; rather, people earned wages as individuals in factories and offices. What the family did together was to consume; its only product was children. The return flow of benefits from rearing children came to hinge more and more

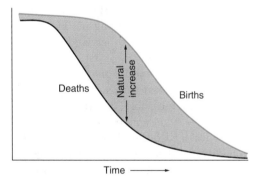

Figure 6.6
Demographic Transition
Rapid fall in death rate followed by slower fall of birth rate causes temporary increase in population growth until demographic transition is completed.

on their willingness to help out in the medical and financial crises that beset older people. But longer life spans and spiraling medical costs make it increasingly unrealistic for parents to expect such help from their children. Thus, the industrial nations have been obliged to substitute old-age and medical insurance and old-age homes for the preindustrial system in which children took care of their aged parents.

To meet the rise in the cost of rearing children in industrial societies, wives as well as husbands must participate in the wage-earning labor force. As long as this situation continues, more and more men and women will decide to have only one child or none, and more and more individuals will find that the traditional forms of marriage, family, sex, and emotional togetherness are incompatible with the maintenance of middle-class status (Harris and Ross 1987; see also America Now Update).

Chapter Summary

Production sets limits to reproduction. Contrary to the position advocated by Thomas Malthus, populations do not normally rise to the maximum limit of production, nor are they usually checked by starvation and other catastrophes. Instead, they are usually maintained well below carrying capacity. Reproduction leads to population pressure, which leads to intensification, depletions, and changes in the modes of production. This can be seen in the sequence leading from big-game hunting to agriculture.

Variations in reproductive rates cannot be explained by the universal desire to have children. Rather, reproductive rates reflect the variable costs and benefits of rearing children under different modes of production. Band-organized hunter–gatherer reproduction rates are influenced by the need for women to avoid carrying more than one infant at a time over long distances, as well as by the limited intensifiability of the hunter–gatherer mode of production. Sedentary agriculturalists rear more children because agriculture can be intensified, the burden of carrying infants and toddlers is reduced, children more rapidly "pay for themselves," and senior children can take care of juniors.

Findings from contemporary peasant societies lend support to the cost–benefit approach to reproductive rates. In Java, children contribute about half of all the wealth of household members. In Bangladesh, male children by age 12 produce more than they consume, and in 3 more years make up for all previous expenses incurred on their behalf. Moreover, contrary to the popular impression that the poorest peasant households have the most children, we often see a positive correlation between large numbers of children and wealthier families.

With the expansion of urban, industrial, technical, and white-collar employment, the benefits of raising fewer but "costlier" children outweigh the advantages of rearing many but "cheaper" children. In India and Sri Lanka, the number of children per woman has declined as children cease to have important roles in agriculture and as the offspring of peasants find advancement through white-collar jobs and business opportunities that require high levels of education. These shifts in the costs of rearing children in relation to new modes of production are similar to the shifts that brought about the demographic transition in nineteenth-century Europe and the United States.

Thus, again contrary to Malthusian theory, preindustrial cultures regulated the sizes of their families so as to minimize the costs and maximize the benefits of reproduction. Although they lacked a modern technology of contraception or abortion, they were nonetheless never at a loss for means of controlling birth and death rates. Four principal categories of practices were used: care and treatment of fetuses, infants, and children; care and treatment of girls and women; intensity and duration of lactation; and variations in the frequency of heterosexual coitus. Subtle gradations exist from abortion to infanticide to induced child mortality. Family planning in nineteenth-century rural Japan is an example of how direct infanticide was used to maximize the benefits provided by children to farm households.

Much controversy surrounds the question of whether poor nutrition reduces the ability of women to conceive, but poor nutrition clearly jeopardizes the life of mother, fetus, and child. The amenorrhea associated with lactation is a more benign form of fertility regulation widely practiced by preindustrial people. Finally, various forms of nonreproductive sex and degree of sexual abstinence can raise or lower reproductive rates.

Though human death rates have a "natural" component, the influence of natural variables is always conditioned to some extent by cultural practices. Moreover, the influence of disease on death rates in small-scale band and village societies should not be exaggerated. To a surprising extent, even when people are faced with epidemics, droughts, famine, and other natural catastrophes, cultural practices influence demographic outcomes.

A vivid example of such practices can be seen in Northeast Brazil: Impoverished mothers who lack access to modern contraception or medical abortion contribute to the extremely high rates of infant and child mortality through the selective neglect and indirect infanticide of their unwanted offspring. These findings have important implications for the definition of the beginning of a new human life and the ban on medical abortions and modern contraception. Care must be taken not to blame the victims. Lacking the means of rearing all of their children, these mothers have no way to avoid a tragic choice. It also should be remembered that direct and indirect infanticide were commonly practiced in Europe in previous centuries.

AMERICA NOW UPDATE

Fertility and the World's Most Expensive Children

After World War II, fertility rates in the United States rose rapidly, producing the phenomenon of the "baby boom." But after peaking in 1957, the fertility rates fell a full 50 percent from 3.69 to 1.81 (Newitt 1985; Westoff 1986; U.S. Statistical Abstract 1994).

A common misunderstanding of this decline is that it was caused by the introduction of birth control pills. This is incorrect since the decline began in 1957, and it was not until 1963–1964 that the pill was widely adopted. Beyond that, many contraceptive devices and practices were available in the 1930s, as demonstrated by the fact that the current fertility rate was much lower than it became immediately after World War II. Moreover, as we have seen (p. 62), even preindustrial populations have effective means of limiting family size.

The key to understanding the fall in fertility rates in America (and in other hyperindustrial societies) lies in the increased costs and lowered benefits of raising children. The U.S. Department of Agriculture's Family Economics Research Group projects that the cumulative cost of raising a child who will be 17 years old in 2007 will be $151,170 for low-income families, $210,070 for middle-income families, and $293,400 for high-income families (Exter 1991). Add between $50,000 and $100,000 for 4 years of college, and the cost of raising an upper-middle-class child to adulthood will easily reach half a million dollars. And the more the economy shifts toward services, information, and high-tech jobs, the greater the amount of schooling needed to achieve or maintain middle-class status. In other words, "higher-quality" children cost more.

The average U.S. family cannot rear more than one or two costly high-quality children without a second income, and wives are generally incapable of providing that second income if they have to raise more than one or two children (given the absence of adequate subsidized day-care facilities). There is a positive feedback effect (p. 152) between working in the labor force, staying in it, and paying the cost of rearing children. The more a woman puts into a job, the more she earns and the more it costs her in the form of "forgone income" to give it up. As forgone income increases, so does the cost of staying home to rear children—and the likelihood that fewer children will be born.

At the same time, children in hyperindustrial societies provide fewer benefits for parents. The counterflow of economic benefits from children to parents has steadily decreased. Children now work apart from parents, establish separate households, and are no longer capable of paying the medical and housing costs of their aged fathers and mothers.

Thus, the current balance of the costs and benefits of rearing children represents the climax of the long-term shift from agricultural to industrial modes of production and from rural to urban ways of life associated with the demographic transition.

Chapter 7

HUMAN SEXUALITY

❦

Yam Harvest Dance, Losuia, Trobriand Islands.

There is no single pattern of human sexuality. As in all other domains of human life, the definition of what is normal or natural sex varies drastically from one culture to another. Categories such as "gay" and "straight," as defined in Western cultures, are not meaningful elsewhere. Homosexual behavior occurs to some extent in every society, but is as variegated as heterosexual behavior. This chapter is not intended either to change or to reinforce anyone's sexual preferences and practices. However, when we begin to see that our own preferences and activities seem strange to others, perhaps we will be more tolerant of those who seem strange to us.

Sex Versus Gender

The etic sexual identity of human beings can be established by examining an individual's chromosomes, interior and exterior sex organs, and secondary sexual characteristics such as body build, size of breasts, and fat deposits (see Box 7.1). Although all societies recognize a distinction between male and female based on some of these features, the emic definition of being male or female, or some other gender, varies considerably from one society to another. Anthropologists use the term *gender* to denote the variable emic meanings associated with culturally defined sex-based identities (Ortner and Whitehead 1981; Errington and Gewertz 1987; Jacobs and Roberts 1989; Gilmore 1990). In this chapter, we will be concerned with both the etic and emic views of sexual behavior and sexual identity.

Human Sexuality

The quest for sexual pleasure motivates much of human behavior and should be seen as an aspect of infrastructure. Sexual acts do not necessarily lead to pregnancy, but pregnancy does not occur without coitus (except for recent "test tube" and uterus-for-hire-inseminations and embryo implants). Needless to say, a society's mode of reproduction depends very much on the biological givens of human sexuality. The fact that it takes a male and a female to have sex that results in reproduction should not be taken lightly. Imagine the effects on social life that might occur if only one individual were needed. Or suppose it took three individuals instead of two to make babies. Surely the structural and organizational features of social life would be vastly different from anything that we know of here on earth.

Homo sapiens is capable of being the sexiest species in the animal kingdom. The human penis is longer and thicker than that of any other primates, and the testes are heavier than in the gorilla or orang. Moreover, we are capable of spending more time in precopulatory courtship and in copulatory sessions than other primates. The capacity for female orgasm, though not unique to humans as once thought, can be highly developed. So can the frequency of copulatory behavior. The peculiarly human nocturnal emissions from males—wet dreams—convey some notion of the strength of the human sex drive. Rates of masturbation among both human males and females are matched only in primates kept in zoos or laboratories. Further, the human male's psychological preoccupation with sex seems to have no parallel in other species. American adolescents aged 12 to 19 report thinking about sex on average every 5 minutes during their waking hours, and even at age 50, American males think about sex several times a day. And humans have no innate breeding season; they can be ready for sex any hour of any day of any month.

Notice, however, that all interspecific comparisons of sexual performance can be expressed only as potentials. Because of the pervasive effects of culture, humans can be the least instead of the most sexy of primates. All aspects of sexual relationships, from infantile experiences through courtship and marriage, exhibit an immense amount of cultural variation (Frayser 1985; Gregersen 1982, 1986; Suggs and Miracle, 1993). For example, consider the modes of sexuality found among the Mangaians of Polynesia as compared with those of Hindu India.

Sex in Mangaia

According to Donald Marshall (1971), Mangaian boys and girls never hold hands in public, nor do Mangaian husbands and wives embrace in public. Brothers and sisters must never be seen together. Mothers and daughters and fathers and sons do not discuss sexual matters with one another. And yet both sexes engage in intercourse well before puberty. After puberty, both sexes enjoy an intense premarital sex life. Girls receive varied nightly suitors in the parents' house, and boys compete with their rivals to see how many orgasms they can achieve. Mangaian girls are not interested in romantic protestations, extensive petting, or foreplay. Sex is not a

---

B o x 7 . 1

HOW MANY BIOLOGICAL SEXES ARE THERE?

According to Anne Fausto-Sterling (1993:24), there are at least five:

1. Hermaphrodites: Individuals born with one testis and one ovary and a mixture of male and female genitalia.
2. Male pseudo-hermaphrodites: Individuals who have two testes and a mixture of male and female genitalia but no ovaries.
3. Female pseudo-hermaphrodites: Individuals who have two ovaries and a mixture of male and female genitalia but no testes.
4. Females: Individuals born with two ovaries and female genitalia.
5. Males: Individuals born with two testes and male genitalia.

Some hermaphrodites have a large penis and a vagina and enjoy sex with either male or female partners. Fausto-Sterling questions the practice of using surgery and hormones to "correct" hermaphroditic conditions: "Why should we care if there are people whose biological equipment enables them to have sex 'naturally' with both men and women? . . . Society mandates the control of intersexual bodies because they blur and bridge the great divide: they challenge traditional beliefs about sexual difference."

---

reward for masculine affection; rather, affection is the reward for sexual fulfillment:

> Sexual intimacy is not achieved by first demonstrating personal affection; the reverse is true. The Mangaian girl takes an immediate demonstration of sexual virility and masculinity as the first test of her partner's desire for her and as the reflection of her own desirability. Personal affection may or may not result from acts of sexual intimacy, but the latter are requisite to the former—exactly the reverse of the ideals of Western society.
>
> [Marshall 1971: 181]

According to a consensus of Marshall's informants, males sought to reach orgasm at least once every night, and women expected each episode to last at least 15 minutes. Males agreed

---

A NOT SO GREAT MOMENT IN SCIENCE

Margaret Mead was the head anthropologist on the first starship voyage to the planet Pluto, which is inhabited by culturally advanced life forms. After learning the language, she found a willing informant and began to enquire about the sex life of the Plutonians. Her informant didn't seem to understand what she was talking about. So like any good anthropologist, she decided to set the Plutonian at ease by describing her own culture. As she began to explain how men and women made babies back on Earth, the Plutonian's eyes opened wider and wider: "Holy Pluto! That's how we make automobiles!"

on the data presented in Table 7.1 as indicative of typical male sexual activity.

Sex in India

A very different attitude toward sexual activity appears to characterize Hindu India. There, Hindu men widely believe, as do men in other societies (see p. 79), that semen is a source of strength and that it should not be squandered.

> Everyone knew that semen was not easily found; it takes forty days and forty drops of blood to make one drop of semen. Everyone was agreed that the semen is ultimately stored in a reservoir in the head, whose capacity is twenty tolas (6.8 ounces). Celibacy was the first requirement of true fitness, because every sexual orgasm meant the loss of a quantity of semen, laboriously formed.
>
> [Carstairs 1967; quoted in Nag 1972: 235]

Contrary to popular stereotypes concerning Hindu eroticism (Fig. 7.1), evidence indicates that coital frequency among Hindus is considerably less than among U.S. whites in comparable age groups. Moni Nag gives a summary (Table 7.2) of average weekly coital frequency for Hindu women and for white U.S. women. Clearly, again contrary to popular impressions, India's high level of fertility and population growth are not the result of sexual overindulgence caused by "not having anything else to do for entertainment at night."

Sex in Inis Beag

The extreme opposite of sex in Mangaia, but still different from sex in Hindu India, is practiced in Inis Beag, an island off the coast of Ireland. Regarding sex as a duty they must perform for their husbands, women remain entirely passive during coitus. They engage in little foreplay, and husbands reach orgasm as quickly as they can on the assumption that women have no interest in prolonging intercourse. Husband and wife keep their underwear on during intercourse and turn off the lights even though they are not visible to anyone but themselves (Messenger 1971).

Figure 7.1
Hindu Erotic Art: Temple of Kajuraho
Erotic themes are common in the sacred art of India.

Table 7.1

MANGAIAN MALE SEXUALITY

APPROXIMATE AGE	AVERAGE NUMBER OF ORGASMS PER NIGHT	AVERAGE NUMBER OF NIGHTS PER WEEK
18	3	7
28	2	5–6
38	1	3–4
48	1	2–3

Source: Marshall 1971: 123.

Table 7.2

AMERICAN AND HINDU FEMALE COITAL FREQUENCY

AGE GROUP	WHITE U.S. AVERAGE WEEKLY	HINDU AVERAGE WEEKLY
10–14	—	0.4
15–19	3.7	1.5
20–24	2.6	1.8
25–29	2.3	1.1
35–39	2.0	0.7
40–44	1.7	0.2
Over 44	1.3	0.3

Source: Nag 1972.

Heterosexuality

Despite a high level of curiosity, very little is known about the actual forms of coitus in different societies. The major reason is that sex is performed in private in virtually every society that has ever been studied. Anthropologists, therefore, have had to rely on accounts of sexual behavior elicited from informants rather than on actual observation. (Ethical issues inhibit discussion of participatory sexual observations, if any, by anthropologists during fieldwork.)

Bronislaw Malinowski's account of lovemaking in the Trobriands, although told from the male perspective, remains one of the best descriptions of non-Western sexual performance. We find the young couple on their way to a secluded spot in the jungle. They spread their mat, and lie down side by side. When they are sure they are not being observed, pubic leaf and grass skirt are removed. They run their fingers through each other's hair and catch and eat each other's lice. They entwine their arms and legs and talk for a long time about their love for each other with endearing phrases. They rub noses, cheek against cheek, mouth against mouth. Their caresses become more passionate, tongue is rubbed against tongue, and they suck and bite the lower lip until blood comes; they bite each others cheeks, noses, and especially their eyelashes. They scratch their backs with their fingernails, inflicting deep lacerations.

> The woman lies on her back, the legs spread and raised, and the knees flexed. The man kneels against her buttocks, her legs resting on his hips. The more usual position, however, is for the man to squat in front of the woman and, with his hands resting on the ground, to move towards her, or, taking hold of her legs, to pull her towards him. When the sexual organs are close together the insertion takes place. Again the woman may stretch her legs and place them directly on the man's hips, with his arms outside them, but the far more usual position is with her legs embracing the man's arms and resting on the elbows. As the act proceeds, the man . . . waits until the woman is ready for orgasm. Then he presses his face to the woman's, embraces her body and raises it toward him, she putting her arms around him at the same time and, as a rule, digging her nails into his skin"

[1929: 334ff].

According to Malinowski, the Trobrianders reject the "missionary position" (woman on back, legs spread with man on top facing her). Many other cultures also reject this position. But even making allowance for Western influence, it is probably the most common position worldwide. Rear entry is reported as the preferred position in a small number of cultures in South America and Africa. Intercourse performed standing is the most common position depicted in Hindu Temple erotic art, but it was probably associated with temple prostitutes and was not otherwise in common use.

As for noncoital heterosexual practices, kissing is widespread among state-organized societies, but it is unknown among many other cultures. (Despite the importance of mouth-to-mouth contact among the Trobrianders, kissing is not part of their lovemaking.) Data on the frequency of heterosexual oral sex are scarce, but if cunnilingus is present, fellatio is also likely to occur. Masturbation occurs worldwide and is generally considered normal adolescent behavior, but when practiced by adults, it is almost universally condemned (Gregersen 1986: 91).

This survey can claim to depict only a tiny portion of the immensely variegated forms of heterosexuality. For the most part, our information identifies only the statistically most frequent techniques found in a particular culture. A vast amount of individual variation in sexual preferences and avoidances remains. And on top of that, the picture is further complicated by the widespread occurrence of homosexual preferences and avoidances and various culturally constructed combinations of homosexuality and heterosexuality.

Male Homosexuality

Attitudes toward homosexuality range from horror to chauvinistic enthusiasm. Given the many ways in which humans separate sexual pleasure from unwanted reproduction, the widespread occurrence of homosexual behavior should come as no surprise. More surprising are the many people who masturbate themselves or their partners, who take birth control pills, use condoms and spermicidal jellies, have abortions, and practice various gymnastic forms of noncoital heterosexuality but who condemn and ridicule homosexual behavior on the grounds that it is "unnatural." Nor does the linkage between homosexual behavior and AIDS render the fierce prejudices against those who find pleasure in homophile or lesbian relationships any less irrational. Were it not for medical advances, good clean "natural" heterosexual men and women would still be dying in vast numbers from syphilis.

To say that homosexuality is as natural as heterosexuality is not to say that the majority of men and women find same-sex individuals to be as arousing and erotically satisfying as members of the opposite sex. But we have no evidence that people predisposed to prefer opposite-sex relationships are also predisposed to loathe and avoid same-sex relationships. And this holds the other way as well. That is, it is doubtful that the small numbers of humans who are genetically predisposed to prefer same-sex relationships are born with phobic tendencies toward the opposite sex (see Box 7.3)

It takes a great deal of training and conditioning, parental disapproval, social ridicule, threats of fiery hell, repressive legislation, and now, the threat of AIDS to convert our kind's bountiful sexual endowment into an aversion against even the mere thought of homosexual congress. Most societies—about 64 percent, according to one survey—don't make the effort to create this aversion and either tolerate or actually encourage some degree of same-sex along with opposite-sex erotic behavior. If one includes clandestine and noninstitutionalized practices, then it is safe to say that homosexual behavior occurs to some extent in every human population.

Homosexual behavior in different cultural contexts is as variegated as heterosexual behavior. For example, several cultures studied by anthropologists incorporate male homosexuality into their systems for developing masculine male personalities. Thus among Native Americans of the Great Plains, certain men donned a combination of male and female attire and dedicated themselves to providing sexual favors to great warriors. These homosexuals were regarded as a separate gender and were honored in turn (Fig. 7.2). For a warrior to be served by one of them was proof of manliness (Callender and Kochems 1983; Williams 1986; Fulton and Anderson 1992).

Similarly, among the Azande of the Sudan, also renowned for their prowess in warfare, the unmarried warrior-age males, who lived apart from women for several years, had homosexual relations with the boys of the age grade of warrior apprentices (Fig. 7.3). After their experiences with "boy-wives," the warriors graduated to the next age status, got married, and had children (Evans-Pritchard 1970).

Box 7.3

IS HOMOSEXUALITY GENETIC?

There is some evidence that at least one gene may be involved in predisposing men to develop homosexual preferences. It has long been known that in the United States brothers of gay men tend to be gay at a higher rate than men in the general population (which has been estimated to be as low as 2 percent and as high as 10 percent). Since brothers tend to share the same environment, these data carry little weight. However, a study carried out by Dean Hammer and associates at the National Cancer Institute (Hammer et al. 1993) further found more homosexual males on the mother's side than on the father's side, specifically among the maternal uncles and sons of maternal uncles. This indicates that if a gene for male homosexuality does exist, it is located on the X-chromosome, which is inherited exclusively through women. Hammer compared the X-chromosomes of the gay men in the study and found that most had the same set of genetic markers at the tip of the long arm of the X-chromosome but as yet the gene itself has not been found. Note, however, that even if the gene actually exists, its presence will not be able to account for the very high rates of homosexuality found in many societies known to anthropologists, nor for the shift from homosexuality to heterosexuality as men in these societies grow up and get married.

Male homosexuality was highly ritualized in many New Guinea and Melanesian societies. It was ideologically justified in a manner that has no equivalent in Western notions of sexuality. It was not viewed as a matter of individual preference but as a social obligation. Men were not classifiable as homosexual, heterosexual, or bisexual. All men were obliged to be bisexual as a matter of sacred duty and practical necessity. For example, among the Etoro, who live on the slopes of the central Papua, New Guinea highlands, the emics of homosexuality revolve around the belief that semen is the source not only of babies but of manhood as well. Like the men of Hindu India, the Etoro believe that each man has only a limited supply of semen. When the supply is exhausted, a man dies. Although coitus with their wives is necessary to prevent the population from becoming too small, husbands stay away from wives most of the time. Indeed, sex is taboo between husband and wife for over 200 days of the year. The Etoro males regard wives who want to break this taboo as witches. To complicate matters, the supply of semen

Figure 7.2
Finds-Them-and-Kills-Them, a Crow male homosexual "man-woman"
or "two-spirit.'

Figure 7.3
Azande

is not something that a man is born with. Semen can be acquired only from another male. Etoro boys get their supplies by having oral intercourse with older men. But it is forbidden for young boys to have intercourse with each other and, like the oversexed wife, the oversexed adolescent boy is regarded as a witch and condemned for robbing his age-mates of their semen supply. Such wayward youths can be identified by the fact that they grow faster than ordinary boys (Kelly 1976).

Among the Sambia of the southeastern highlands of New Guinea, boys are allowed to play with girls only until age 4 or 5. Subsequently, they are strictly regulated, and all heterosexual play is forcefully punished. It is normal for young boys to hold hands with each other. But Sambia males and females never kiss, hold hands, or hug each other in public. Late in childhood, boys are initiated into the men's secret society and are taught how to act as warriors. Obedience to the male elders is rigidly enforced. Younger men, as among the Etoro, obtain the gift of semen from their seniors. Males must con-

tinue to avoid any heterosexual contact until they are married (Herdt 1987).

Homosexuality in New Guinea and Melanesia is closely associated with a heightened level of male–female sexual antagonism, fear of menstrual blood, and exclusive male rituals and dwellings. Obligatory homosexuality and intense warfare in New Guinea are also strongly associated. Warfare justified and rationalized an ethos of masculine prowess that placed men above women as desirable sexual partners (Herdt 1984a: 169). As in other patrilocal warlike village societies (see p. 145), their juvenile sex ratios show a marked imbalance favoring males over females, attaining ratios as high as 140:100 (Herdt 1984b: 57).

It is difficult to avoid the conclusion, therefore, that ritual homosexuality in New Guinea and Melanesia is part of a population-regulating system. As Dennis Werner (1979) has shown, societies that are strongly antinatalist (against having large numbers of children) tend to accept or encourage homosexual and other nonreproductive forms of sex. In addition, Melvin Ember (1982) has demonstrated that warfare in New Guinea is correlated with competition for scarce or depleted resources, which implies a high level of population pressure. However, much controversy surrounds these relationships.

Whatever the explanation for obligatory male homosexuality may be, its existence should serve as a warning against equating one's own culturally determined expressions of sexuality with human nature.

Female Homosexuality

Less is known about female homosexuality than about male homosexuality because of the predominance of male-biased ethnographies (see Chapter 15). Unlike males, females seldom seem to be subjected to initiation rituals that entail homosexual relationships. It is reported, however, that among the Dahomey of West Africa, adolescent girls prepared for marriage by attending all-female initiation schools where they learned how to "thicken their genitalia" and engaged in sexual intercourse (Blackwood 1986).

Since women seldom bear the brunt of military combat, they have little opportunity to use same-sex erotic apprenticeships to form close-knit teams of warriors. Similarly, enforced absence from the classical Greek academies precluded women's participation in homosexual philosophical apprenticeships, and since men controlled women's sexual behavior, the incidence of overt lesbian behavior between women of high rank and slave girls or other social inferiors was probably never very high.

More commonly, women do adopt socially sanctioned "not-man-not-woman" gender roles: dressing like men; performing manly duties such as hunting, trapping, and going to war; and using their in-between gender status to establish their credibility as shamans. Thirty-three Native-American societies are reported to have accepted gender transformations in women (Albers 1989: 135). Among several western Native-American tribes, female not-men-not-women entered into enduring lesbian relationships with women, whom they formally "married" (Blackwood 1984).

Several reported cases of institutionalized lesbianism are related to the migration of males in search of work. On the Caribbean island of Carriacou, where migrant husbands stay away from home for most of the year, older married women bring younger single women into their households and share the absent husband's remittances in exchange for sexual favors and emotional support. A similar pattern exists in South Africa, where it is known as the "mummy–baby game" (Gay 1986).

One of the most interesting forms of institutionalized lesbianism occurred in mid-nineteenth-century to early twentieth-century China in several of the silk-growing districts of the Pearl River Delta region in southern Kwangtung. There, single women provided virtually all the labor for the silkworm factories. Although poorly paid, they were better off than their prospective husbands. Rather than accept the subordinate status that marriage imposed on Chinese women, the silk workers formed antimarriage sisterhoods that provided economic and emotional support. Though not all the 100,000 sisters formed lesbian relationships, enduring lesbian marriages involving two and sometimes three women were common (Sankar 1986).

Even when allowance is made for blind spots in the ethnographic reports of male observers, there appear to be fewer forms of institutionalized female than of male homosexuality. Does this mean that females engage in homosexual behavior less often than males? Probably not. More likely, most female homosexuality has simply been driven underground or has been expressed in noninstitutionalized contexts that escape observation. Although seldom reported, adolescence is probably an occasion for a considerable amount of female homosexual experimentation the world over. Only recently, for example, has it come to light that among the Kalahari !Kung, young girls engage in sexual play with other girls before they do so with boys (Shostak 1981: 114).

Polygynous marriage (see p. 106) is another context in which lesbian relationships probably flourish. The practice seems to have been common in West Africa among the Nupe, Haussa, and Dahomey, and among the Azande and Nyakusa in East Africa. In Middle Eastern harems, where co-wives seldom saw their husbands, many women entered into lesbian relationships despite the dire punishment such male-defying behavior could bring (Blackwood 1986; Lockard 1986).

We will return to the subject of human sexuality with an emphasis on gender roles and gender hierarchies in Chapter 15.

Chapter Summary

Cross-cultural variations in gender roles prevent any single culture from serving as the model for what is natural in the realm of sex. Mangaian heterosexual standards and practices contrast with those of Hindu India, Inis Beag, and contemporary industrial societies. Homosexuality also defies neat stereotyping, as can be seen in the examples of the Crow and the Azande. Ritual male homosexuality, as among the Etoro, Sambia, and other New Guinea and Melanesian societies, is an elaborate, compulsory form of sexuality that has no equivalent in Western societies. It was probably selected for by the need to rear male warriors under conditions of environmental stress and intense intersocietal competition.

Female homosexuality is less frequently reported, possibly as a result of male bias among ethnographers and the suppression of female liberties by dominant males.

AMERICA NOW UPDATE

New Gender Roles and Forms of Sexuality

A profound change has taken place in the United States regarding attitudes toward premarital and extramarital intercourse. The number of adults who in response to questionnaire surveys say that they sanction or accept premarital and extramarital intercourse rose from 20 percent of adults to over 50 percent in the period from 1960 to 1980. During the same period, the number of unmarried couples who say they are living together increased almost as fast as the number of female-headed families (Herbers 1985). Considerable evidence points to an increase in premarital sexual activity among unwed juveniles and young adults. Planned Parenthood studies show that one-half of the teenagers graduating from high school have an active sex life. Given the wide resistance to intensive, publicly supported contraceptive programs for teenagers (New York City is an exception), it is not surprising that the rate of teenage pregnancies has doubled since 1965 and that the United States now finds itself with the highest rate in the industrial world. This distinction is partially attributable to the very high rate of pregnancies among U.S. black teenagers, but the rate for white teenagers (93 per 1,000) is double that of England and quadruple that of the Netherlands (Brozan 1985, Hacker 1992: 77). Four out of ten American women will have become pregnant by the time they reach 20 years. With the spread of AIDS, condoms have become the first line of defense against teenage pregnancies ending with the birth of AIDS-infected infants.

The basic shift in U.S. attitudes toward sexuality can be described in terms of an ever-widening separation of the hedonistic from the reproductive aspects of sexual relations. One derivative of this trend is the increased production and consumption of pornographic materials, including "adult" books and magazines such as *Playboy, Hustler,* and *Penthouse* (Fig. 7.4). Pornographic videocassettes make up a substantial percent of the rental volume of stores that rent cassettes to home users. "What would have been off-limits even in a red-light district a few years ago is now available for people to see in their living rooms" (Lindsey 1985: 9).

Much controversy surrounds the questions of how much of what seems to be a trend toward greater sexual activity of all

Figure 7.4
Porn
Making money out of sex is a big industry in the United States.

sorts is really taking place. According to one study (Laumann et al. 1994), Americans age 18 to 59 fall into three groups: one third have sex twice a week or more; one third have sex just a few times a month; and the rest have sex just a few times a year or not at all.

The relaxation of U.S. laws against homosexuality can also be viewed as an expression of the same trend. As we have seen (p. 80), societies that interdict homosexuality are strongly pronatalist and tend to condemn all forms of sex that do not lead to childbirth and parenting. Heterosexual couples committed to the separation of sex from reproduc-tion do not differ from homosexual couples in this regard. The increase in the numbers of self-identified homosexuals testifies to the general liberalization of sexual rules of con-duct since World War II (Fig. 7.5). It remains to be seen, however, how far the AID's epidemic will lead to a return to more conservative patterns. Sexual promiscuity among both homosexuals and heterosexuals appears to be declining (Laumann, et al. 1994). If no vaccine or cure for AIDS is found, marriage rates or long-term, living-together arrange-ments may increase substantially. Fertility rates, however, will probably remain unaffected.

Figure 7.5
Out of the Closet
A gay rights march in Washington, D.C.

Chapter 8

ECONOMIC ORGANIZATION

Market day in Paipa, Highland Colombia.

In this chapter, our concern is not with the type of production process, such as hunting and gathering, pastoralism, or industrial manufacturing, but with the way in which labor is organized and how access to resources, goods, and services is regulated or controlled. At this point, in other words, our focus will shift from the infrastructural to the structural aspects of society and culture. This will enable us to study the extent to which the organizational features of production can be explained by the evolution of particular kinds of infrastructures.

Economies differ according to their characteristic modes of control over production and exchange. We will identify the principal kinds of exchange and explore their relationship to infrastructural conditions. We will see that many societies organize their economic activities without the use of money and that money itself comes in many specialized forms in addition to the all-purpose money with which we are familiar. The subject of money leads to the question of whether capitalist economies can be found among nonstate societies. The chapter also takes up the question of whether people work harder in industrial than in hunter–gatherer societies.

Definition of Economy

In a narrow sense, economy refers to the kinds of decisions people make when they have only limited resources or wealth, and there are unlimited goods and services they would like to acquire or use. Most professional economists hold that in making such decisions, human beings in general tend to economize, that is, to maximize the achievement of ends while minimizing the expenditure of means (or to maximize benefits while minimizing costs; Plattner 1989: 13). For most anthropologists, however, an economy refers to the activities people engage in to produce and obtain goods and services (setting aside the question of whether they are "economizing"):

> An economy is a set of institutionalized activities which combine natural resources, human labor, and technology to acquire, produce, and distribute material goods and specialist services in a structured, repetitive fashion.

[Dalton 1969: 97]

These two definitions of economy are not incompatible. Anthropologists stress the fact that the specific motivations for producing, exchanging, and consuming goods and services are shaped by cultural traditions. Different cultures value different goods and services and tolerate or prohibit different kinds of relationships among the people who produce, exchange, and consume. Some cultures emphasize economic cooperation; others emphasize competition. Some emphasize communal property; others place great importance on private property. In other words, if "economizing" takes place, its premises and consequences differ from culture to culture.

Exchange

Most of what human labor produces is distributed by means of exchange. (The exceptions consist of instances of direct consumption by the producers themselves.) *Exchange* refers to the practice of giving and receiving valued objects and services. This practice is more highly developed in our species than in any other. Human beings could not survive infancy without receiving valuable objects and services from their parents. However, patterns of exchange differ markedly from one culture to another. Following the work of the economist Karl Polanyi, anthropologists have come to distinguish three main types of exchange: reciprocal, redistributive, and market.

Reciprocal Exchange

One of the most striking features of the economic life of simple hunter-gatherers and small-scale agricultural societies is the prominence of exchanges conducted according to the principle known as reciprocity. In *reciprocal exchanges*, the flow of products and services is not contingent on any definite counterflow. The partners in the exchange take according to need and give back according to no set rules of time or quantity (Fig. 8.1). (As we shall see in Chapter 11, reciprocity is characteristic of relatively egalitarian societies.)

Richard Lee has written a succinct description of reciprocity as it occurs among the !Kung: In the morning, anywhere from one to sixteen of the twenty adults in the !Kung band leave camp to spend the day collecting or hunting. They return in the evening with whatever food they have managed to find. Everything brought back to camp is shared equally,

Figure 8.1 Reciprocity.
Hunter-gatherers of the Kalahari exchange the day's catch.

regardless of whether the recipients have spent the day sleeping or hunting. Eventually all the adults will have gathered or hunted and given as well as received food. But wide discrepancies in the balance of giving and receiving may exist among individuals over a long period without becoming the subject of any special talk or action.

Some form of reciprocal exchange occurs in all cultures, especially among relatives and friends. In the United States and Canada, for example, husbands and wives, friends, and sisters and brothers, and other kin regulate and adjust their economic lives to a minor degree according to informal, uncalculated, give-and-take transactions. Teenagers do not pay cash for their meals at home or the use of the family car. Wives do not bill their husbands for cooking a meal. Friends give each other birthday gifts and Christmas presents. These exchanges, however, constitute only a small portion of the total acts of exchange among North Americans. The great majority of exchanges in modern cultures involve rigidly defined counterflows that must take place by a certain time (as anyone who has forgotten to pay the electric bill can tell you).

Reciprocity and the Freeloader

As we know from the experience of taking from parents or from giving a birthday or holiday gift and not receiving one in return, the failure of an individual to reciprocate in some degree will eventually lead to bad feelings, even between close relatives and friends or spouses. No one likes a "freeloader" ("moocher" or "sponge"). In economies dominated by

reciprocity, a grossly asymmetrical exchange does not go unnoticed. Some individuals will come to enjoy reputations as diligent gatherers or outstanding hunters, whereas others acquire reputations as shirkers or malingerers. No specific mechanisms exist for obliging the debtors to even up the score, yet subtle sanctions discourage one from becoming a complete freeloader. Such behavior generates a steady undercurrent of disapproval. Eventually freeloaders may meet with violence because they are suspected of being bewitched or of bewitching others through the practice of sorcery (see p. 137).

What is distinctive about reciprocal exchange, therefore, is not that products and services are simply given away without any thought or expectation of return but rather that there is (1) no need for immediate return, (2) no systematic calculation of the value of the services and products exchanged, and (3) an overt denial that a balance is being calculated or that the balance must come out even.

No culture can rely exclusively on purely altruistic sentiments to get its goods and services produced and distributed. But in simple band and prestate village societies, goods and services are produced and reciprocally exchanged in such a way as to avoid the notion of material balance, debt, or obligation. This system works because reciprocal exchanges are expressed as kinship obligations. These kinship obligations (see Chapter 10) establish reciprocal expectations with respect to food, clothing, shelter, and other goods.

Kinship-embedded reciprocal exchanges constitute only a small portion of modern exchange systems, whereas among hunter-gatherers and small-scale agriculturalists, almost all exchanges take place among kin, for whom the giving, taking, and using of goods have sentimental and personal meaning.

Reciprocity and Trade

Even hunters and gatherers, however, want valuables such as salt, flint, obsidian, red ochre, reeds, and honey that are produced or controlled by groups with whom they have no kinship ties. Economic dealings among nonkin are based on the assumption that every "stranger" will try to get the best of an exchange through cheating or stealing. As a result, trading expeditions are likely to be hazardous and to bear a resemblance to war parties.

One interesting mechanism for facilitating trade between distant groups is known as *silent trade*. The objects to be exchanged are set out in a clearing, and the first group retreats out of sight. The other group comes out of hiding, inspects the wares, lays down what it regards as a fair exchange of its own products, and retreats again. The first group returns and, if satisfied, removes the traded objects. If not, it leaves the wares untouched as a signal that the balance

Figure 8.2 New Guinea Market
Man at left is giving fish in exchange for yams at right.

Figure 8.3 Kapauku of Western New Guinea
The men (wearing penis sheaths) are counting shell money.

is not yet even. In this fashion, the Mbuti of the Ituri Forest used to trade meat for bananas with Bantu agriculturalists, and the Vedda of Sri Lanka traded honey for iron tools with the Sinhalese. Silent trade should not be seen as the most primitive stage in an evolutionary sequence. It usually took place between traders sent out by chiefdoms or state-level societies who periodically encountered hunter–gatherer bands living in remote regions (Price 1980).

More developed trade relations occur between agricultural villages. Conditions for the develoment of trade markets seem to have been especially favorable in Melanesia. In New Guinea, people regularly trade fish for pigs and vegetables (Fig. 8.2). Among the Kapauku of western New Guinea (today, West Irian, Indonesia), full-fledged price markets involving shell and limited-purpose bead money may have existed before the arrival of European or Indonesian merchants (Fig. 8.3). Generally speaking, however, trade based on marketing and all-purpose money is associated with the evolution of the state (see Chapter 12) and with the use of soldiers and market police to enforce peaceful relations between buyers and sellers.

Perhaps the most common solution to the problem of trading with strangers in the absence of state-supervised markets is the establishment of special *trade partnerships*. In this arrangement, members of different bands or villages regard one another as metaphorical kin. The members of trading expeditions deal exclusively with their trade partners, who greet them as "brothers" and give them food and shelter. Trade partners try to deal with one another in conformity with the principle of reciprocity. They deny an interest in getting the best of the bargain and offer wares as if they were gifts.

The Kula

A classic example of trade partnerships is described in Bronislaw Malinowski's *Argonauts of the Western Pacific*. The argonauts in question are the Trobriand Islanders, who trade with neighboring islands by means of daring canoe voyages

Figure 8.4 Kula Canoe
These large canoes are used by the Trobrianders for long-distance voyages.

across the open sea (Fig. 8.4). The entire complex associated with this trade is known as the Kula. According to the men who take these risky voyages, the purpose of the Kula trade is to exchange shell ornaments with their trade partners. The ornaments, known to the Trobrianders as "vaygu'a," consist of armbands and necklaces. In trading with the Dobuans, who live to the southeast, the Trobrianders give armbands and receive necklaces. In trading with the people who live to the southwest, the Trobrianders give necklaces and receive armbands in return. The armbands and necklaces are then traded in opposite directions from island to island, returning again and again to their points of origin.

Participation in the Kula trade is a major ambition of youth and a consuming passion of senior men. The vaygu'a have been compared with heirlooms or crown jewels. The older they are and the more complex their history, the more valuable they become in the eyes of the Trobrianders. Like many

other examples of special-purpose exchange media (see p. 95), Kula valuables are seldom used to "buy" anything. They are, however, given as gifts in marriage and as rewards to canoe builders (Scoditti 1983). Most of the time, the ornaments are simply used for the purpose of obtaining other armbands and necklaces. To trade vaygu'a, men establish more or less permanent partnerships with each other on distant islands. These partnerships are usually handed down from one kinsman to another, and young men are given a start in the Kula trade by inheriting or receiving an armband or a necklace from a relative.

When the expedition reaches shore, the trade partners greet one another and exchange preliminary gifts. Later, the Trobrianders deliver the precious ornaments, accompanied by ritual speeches and formal acts concerned with establishing the honorable, giftlike character of the exchange. As in the case of reciprocal transactions within the family, the trade partner may not immediately be able to provide a shell whose value is equivalent to the one just received. Although the voyager may have to return home empty-handed except for some preliminary gifts, he does not complain. He expects his trade partner to work hard to make up for the delay by presenting him with even more valuable shells at their next meeting.

Why all this effort in order to obtain a few baubles of sentimental or aesthetic value? As is often the case, the etic aspects of the Kula are different from the emic aspects. The boats that take part in the Kula expedition carry trade items of great practical value in the life of the various island peoples who participate in the Kula ring. While the trade partners fondle and admire their priceless heirlooms, members of the expedition trade for practical items: coconuts, sago palm flour, fish, yams, baskets, mats, wooden swords and clubs, green stone for tools, mussel shells for knives, creepers and lianas for lashings. These items can be bargained over with impunity. Although Trobrianders deny it, the vaygu'a are valuable not only for their qualities as heirlooms but also for their truly priceless gift of trade (Irwin 1983: 71ff; Scoditti 1983: 265).

Kula is also better understood as part of the Trobriand and the neighboring island's system of achieving or validating political rank. Those who come into possession of the most valuable shells are usually extremely able leaders who are accomplished navigators and, in former times, bold warriors (Campbell 1983: 203). Thus in modern times, Kula has persisted even though fewer practical items are traded.

Redistributive Exchange

As we shall see in Chapter 12, the evolution of economic and political systems is in large degree a consequence of the development of coercive forms of exchange that supplement or almost entirely replace reciprocal exchange. Coercive forms of exchange did not appear in sudden full-blown opposition to reciprocal forms. Rather, they probably first arose through what seemed to be merely an extension of familiar reciprocal forms.

The exchange system known as redistribution can best be understood as such an extension. In *redistribution exchange,* the labor products of several different individuals are brought to a central place, sorted by type, counted, and then given away to producers and nonproducers alike. Considerable organizational effort is required if large quantities of goods are to be brought to the same place at the same time and given away in definite shares. This coordination is usually achieved by individuals who act as redistributors. Typically, redistributors consciously attempt to increase and to intensify production, for which they gain prestige in the eyes of their peers.

Egalitarian and stratified forms of redistribution must be distinguished. As an egalitarian system of exchange, redistribution is carried out by a redistributor who (1) works harder than anyone else producing the items to be given away, (2) takes the smallest portion or none at all, and (3) is left with no greater material wealth than anyone else. In its egalitarian form, therefore, redistribution appears to be merely an extreme example of reciprocity; the generous provider gives everything away and for the moment gets nothing in return, except the admiration of those who benefit from the transaction. In the stratified form, however, the redistributor (1) lets others do most of the work, (2) retains the largest share, and (3) ends up with more material wealth than anyone else.

Redistributive exchange, like reciprocal exchange, is usually embedded in a complex set of kinship relations and rituals that may obscure the etic significance of the exchange behavior. Redistribution often involves a feast held to celebrate some important event such as a harvest, the end of a ritual taboo, the construction of a house, a death, a birth, or a marriage. A common feature of Melanesian redistributive feasts is that the guests gorge themselves with food, stagger off into the bush, stick their fingers down their throats, vomit, and then return to eating with renewed zest. Another common feature of redistributive feasting is the boastful and competitive attitude of the redistributors and their kin with respect to other individuals or groups who have given feasts. This contrasts markedly with reciprocal exchange. Let us take a closer look at this contrast.

Reciprocity Versus Redistribution

Boastfulness and acknowledgment of generosity are incompatible with the basic etiquette of reciprocal exchanges. Among the Semai of Central Malaya, no one even says "thank you" for the meat received from another hunter (Fig. 8.5). Having struggled all day to lug the carcass of a pig home through the jungle heat, the hunter allows his prize to be cut up into exactly equal portions, which are then given away to the entire group. As Robert Dentan explains, to express gratitude for the portion received indicates that you are the kind of ungenerous person who calculates how much you give and take:

> In this context saying thank you is very rude, for it suggests first that one has calculated the amount of a gift and second, that one did not expect the donor to be so generous. To call attention to one's generosity is to indicate that others are in debt to you and that you expect them to repay you. It is repugnant to many egalitarian peoples even to suggest that they have been treated generously.

[1968: 491]

Richard Lee tells how he learned about this aspect of reciprocity through a revealing incident. To please the !Kung with whom he was staying, he decided to buy a large ox and have it slaughtered as a Christmas present. He spent days

Figure 8.5 Semai Hunter
Among the Semai, reciprocity prevails.

Yes, when a young man kills much meat he comes to think of himself as a chief or a big man, and he thinks of the rest of us as his servants or inferiors. We can't accept this, we refuse one who boasts, for someday his pride will make him kill somebody. So we always speak of his meat as worthless. This way we cool his heart and make him gentle.

Richard Lee 1968: 62.

Patterns of Culture, the Kwakiutl redistributor seems like a virtual megalomaniac (see Box 8.2).

In the potlatch, the guests behaved somewhat like Lee's !Kung. They grumbled and complained and never appeared satisfied or impressed. Nonetheless, in public they carefully counted all the gifts displayed and distributed (Fig. 8.7). Both hosts and guests believed that the only way to throw off the obligations incurred in accepting these gifts was to hold a counter potlatch in which the tables were reversed (Jonaitas 1991).

I am the great chief who makes people ashamed.
I am the great chief who makes people ashamed.
Our chief brings shame to the faces.
Our chief brings jealousy to the faces.
Our chief makes people cover their faces by what he is continually doing in this world.
Giving again and again, [fish] oil feasts to all the tribes.
I am the only great tree, I the chief!
I am the only great tree, I the chief!
You are my subordinates, tribes.
You sit in the middle of the rear of the house, tribes.
I am the first to give you property, tribes.
I am your Eagle, tribes!
Bring your counter of property, tribes, that he may try in vain to count the property that is to be given away by the great copper maker, the chief.

Benedict 1960.

searching the neighboring Bantu agricultural villages looking for the largest and fattest ox in the region. Finally, he bought what appeared to be a perfect specimen. But one !Kung after another took him aside and assured him that he had been duped into buying an absolutely worthless animal. "Of course, we will eat it," they said, "but it won't fill us up—we will eat and go home to bed with stomachs rumbling." Yet when Lee's ox was slaughtered, it turned out to be covered with a thick layer of fat. Lee eventually succeeded in getting his informants to explain why they had claimed that his gift was valueless even though they certainly knew better than he did what lay under the animal's skin (Box 8.1).

In flagrant violation of these prescriptions for modesty in reciprocal exchanges, redistributive exchange systems involve public proclamations that the host is a generous person and a great provider. This boasting is one of the most conspicuous features of the potlatches (Jonaitas 1991) that were once engaged in by the Native Americans who inhabit the northwest coast of the United States and Canada (Fig. 8.6). In descriptions made famous by Ruth Benedict in

Figure 8.6 *Kwakiutl of the Pacific Northwest*
The signs over the doors read "Boston. He is the Head chief of Arweete. He is true Indian. Honest. He don't owe no trouble to white man" and "Cheap. He is one of the head chief of all tribes in this country. White man can get information." Photo was taken about 1901–1902.

The Infrastructural Basis of Redistribution and Reciprocity

Why do the !Kung esteem hunters who never draw attention to their own generosity, whereas the Kwakiutl and other redistributor societies esteemed leaders who could boast about how much they gave away? One theory is that reciprocity reflects an adjustment to modes of production in which intensification would rapidly lead to diminishing returns and environmental depletions. Simple hunters and gatherers seldom have an opportunity to intensify production without rapidly reaching the point of diminishing returns. Intensification poses a grave threat to such peoples in the form of faunal overkills. To encourage the !Kung hunter to be boastful is to endanger the group's survival. In addition, reciprocity is advantageous for most hunter-gatherers because individuals and families experience a great deal of variation in their success from one day to the next. "The greater the

degree of risk, the greater the extent of sharing" (Gould 1982: 76). Sharing spreads the risk over many hunters like commercial insurance policies spread the risk over many subscribers (Cashdan 1989: 37).

In contrast, the Kwakiutl derived most of their food from the annual upriver runs of salmon and candlefish. Using aboriginal dip nets, the Kwakiutl and their neighbors could not affect the overall rate of reproduction of these species. Hence, their mode of production was highly intensifiable. Moreover, though the migrations of fish varied from one year to the next (Langdon 1979), there were plenty of fish for everybody from day to day. Thus, it was ecologically feasible for the Kwakiutl to try to intensify production by using prestige and the privilege of boasting to reward those who worked harder or who got others to work harder (Isaac 1988; Mitchell and Donald 1988; Hayden 1992: 534; Ames 1994).

When an impoverished and unprestigious group could no longer hold its own potlatches, the people abandoned their

(a)

Figure 8.7 Potlatch
(a) Spokesman for Kwakiutl chief making speech next to blankets about to be given away. (b) Cash is redistributed in modern version of potlatch.

(b)

defeated redistributor-chief and took up residence among relatives in more productive villages. Thus the boasting and the giving away and displaying of wealth led to the recruitment of additional labor power to the work force gathered about a particularly effective redistributor. This system also helps explain why Northwest Coast peoples lavished so much effort on the production of their world-famous totem poles. These poles bore the redistributor-chief's "crests" in the guise of carved mythic figures; title to the crests was claimed on the basis of outstanding potlatch achievements. The larger the pole, the greater the potlatch power and the more the members of poor villages would be tempted to change their residence and gather around another chief (Fig. 8.8)

Before the coming of the Europeans, Kwakiutl potlatch feasts were probably less destructive (Box 8.3) and more like Melanesian competitive feasts (see p. 149). With the coming of the Europeans, however, there was a shift toward more destructive forms of redistribution. The impact of European diseases had reduced the population of the Kwakiutl from about 10,000 in 1836 to about 2,000 by the end of the century. At the same time, the trading companies, canneries, lumber mills, and gold-mining camps pumped an unprecedented amount of wealth into the aboriginal economy. The

Figure 8.8 Totem Poles
The height of the pole and skill of the carvings and the animal ancestors shown validated the claim of chiefly rank.

Box 8.3

THE ORIGIN OF DESTRUCTIVE POTLATCHES

Potlatching came under scientific scrutiny long after the people of the Pacific Northwest had entered into trade and wage–labor relations with Russian, English, Canadian, and American nationals. Declining populations and a sudden influx of wealth had combined to make the potlatches increasingly competitive and destructive by the time Franz Boas began to study them in the 1880s (Rohner 1969). At this period, the entire tribe was in residence at the Fort Rupert trading station of the Hudson's Bay Company, and the attempt on the part of one potlatch giver to outdo another had become an all-consuming passion. Blankets, boxes of fish oil, and other valuables were deliberately being destroyed by burning or by throwing them into the sea. On one occasion, a house almost burnt to the ground when the roof caught fire from too much fish oil poured on the fire (Benedict 1960: 177). Potlatches that ended in this fashion were regarded as great victories for the potlatch givers.

percentage of people available to celebrate the glory of the potlatcher dropped. Many villages were abandoned; rivalry intensified for the allegiance of the survivors.

A final and perhaps the most important factor in the development of destructive potlatches was the change in the technology and intensity of warfare. The earliest contacts in the late eighteenth century between the Europeans and the Native Americans of the Northwest Pacific Coast centered on the fur trade. In return for sea-otter skins, the Europeans gave guns to the Kwakiutl and to the Kwakiutl's traditional enemies. This trade had a double effect. On the one hand, warfare became more deadly; on the other hand, it forced local groups to fight one another for control of trade in order to get the ammunition on which success in warfare now depended. Small wonder, therefore, that as population declined, the potlatch chiefs were willing to throw away or destroy wealth that was militarily unimportant in order to attract manpower for warfare and fur trade (Ferguson 1984).

Stratified Redistribution

A subtle line separates egalitarian from stratified forms of redistribution. In the egalitarian form, contributions to the central pool are voluntary, and the workers either get back all or most of what they put into it or they receive items of comparable value. In the stratified form, the workers must contribute to the central pool or suffer penalties, and they may not get back anything. Again, in the egalitarian form, the redistributor lacks the power to coerce followers to intensify production and must depend on their goodwill; in the stratified form, the redistributor has that power, and the workers must depend on that person's goodwill. The processes responsible for the evolution of one form of redistribution to another will be discussed in Chapter 12. Here, we will note only that fully developed forms of stratified redistribution imply the existence of a class of rulers who have the power to compel others to do their bidding. The expression of this power in the realm of production and exchange results in the political subordination of the labor force and in its partial or total loss of control over access to natural resources, technology, and the place, time, and hours of work.

Figure 8.9 Hunting and Gathering in a hyper-industrial hyper-store in France.

Price–Market Exchange: Buying and Selling

Marketplaces occur in rudimentary form wherever groups of strangers assemble and trade one item for another. Among hunter-gatherers and simple agriculturalists, marketplace trading usually involves the barter of one valuable consumable item for another: fish for yams, coconuts for axes, and so forth. In this type of market, before the development of all-purpose money (see the next section), only a limited range of goods or services is exchanged. The great bulk of exchange transactions takes place outside the marketplace and continues to involve various forms of reciprocity and redistribution. With the development of all-purpose money, however, *price–market exchanges* came to dominate all other forms of exchange.

In a price market, the price of the goods and services exchanged is determined by buyers competing with buyers and sellers competing with sellers. Virtually everything that is produced or consumed soon comes to have a price, and buying and selling becomes a major cultural preoccupation or even an obsession (Fig. 8.9).

One can engage in reciprocal exchange using money, as when a friend gives you a loan and does not specify when it must be repaid. Redistributive exchange can also be carried out with money, as in the collection of taxes and the disbursement of welfare payments. Buying and selling on a price market, however, is a distinctive mode of exchange since it involves the specification of the precise time, quantity, and type of payment. Furthermore, unlike either reciprocity or redistribution, once the money payment is concluded, no further obligation or responsibility exists between buyer and seller. They can walk away from each other and never meet again.

Price–market exchanges, therefore, are noteworthy for the anonymity and impersonality of the exchange process, and they stand in contrast to the personal and kin-based exchanges of reciprocal and redistributive economies. Now let us take a closer look at the nature of that strange entity we call money.

Money

The use of certain objects to symbolize and measure the social value of other objects occurs almost universally. And people widely exchange such standard-of-value "stuffs" for goods and services. Throughout much of East Africa, for example, cattle are a standard of value that can be used for measuring the value of a wife. A young man gives cattle to his father-in-law and gets a wife in return (see p. 112). In many parts of Melanesia, shells are exchanged for stone implements, pottery, and other valuable artifacts (Fig. 8.10). Elsewhere, beads, feathers, shark teeth, dog teeth, or pig tusks are exchanged for other valuable items and are given as compensation for death or injury and for personal services rendered by magicians, canoe builders, and other specialists. Although these standards of value possess some of the characteristics of modern coins or paper currency, they all lack one or more of the major characteristics of money found in societies that have price–market economies. In price–market economies, *money* has the following characteristics:

1. Portability. It comes in sizes and shapes convenient for being carried about from one transaction to the next.
2. Divisibility. Its various forms and values are explicit multiples of each other.

3. Convertibility. A transaction completed by a higher-valued unit can be made as well by its lower-valued multiples.
4. Generality. Virtually all goods and services have a money value.
5. Anonymity. For most purchases, anyone with enough money to pay the market price can conclude a transaction.
6. Legality. The nature and quantity of money in circulation is controlled by a government.

By these criteria, cattle exchanged for wives are not money. Being neither very portable nor readily divisible, they would not be welcome at the supermarket checkout counter. As employed in bride-price (see p. 112), cattle are frequently not convertible; that is, a large, beautiful, fat bull with a local reputation cannot readily be substituted for by two small and undistinguished animals. Furthermore, cattle lack generality since only wives can be "purchased" with them, and they lack anonymity because any stranger who shows up with the right amount of cattle will find that he cannot simply leave the animals and take off with the bride. Cattle are exchanged for women only between kinship groups who have an interest in establishing or reinforcing preexisting social relationships.

Figure 8.10 Shell Money
Cowrie and Rongo shells are used as money in the Solomon Islands.

Finally, cattle are put into circulation by each individual household as a result of productive effort that is unregulated by any central authority.

Capitalism

Where reciprocity, egalitarian redistribution, and trade-partner relations are the dominant modes of exchange, modern dollar and cents types of money do not and cannot exist. The development of price-markets accompanied the evolution of the first states. And they reach their highest development as part of the political economy known as *capitalism*. In capitalist societies, buying and selling by means of all-purpose money extends to land, resources, and housing. Labor has a price called wages, and money itself has a price called interest.

Of course, there is no such thing as a completely free market in which price is set wholly by supply and demand and in which everything can be sold. By comparison with other forms of political economy, however, capitalism is aptly described as a system in which money can buy anything. This being so, everyone tries to acquire as much money as possible, and the object of production itself is not merely to provide valuable goods and services but to increase one's possession of money, that is, to make a profit and accumulate capital (Fig. 8.11).

The rate of capitalist production depends on the rate at which profits can be made, and this in turn depends on the rate at which people purchase, use, wear out, and destroy goods and services. Hence, an enormous effort is expended on extolling the virtues and benefits of products in order to convince consumers that they should make additional purchases. Prestige is awarded not to the person who works hardest or gives away the greatest amount of wealth but rather to the person who has the most possessions and who consumes at the highest rate. Capitalism inevitably leads to marked inequalities in wealth based on differential access to capital, technology, and resources. As in all stratified political–economic systems, the rich use soldiers and police forces to prevent the poor from confiscating their wealth and privileges.

"Primitive Capitalism"? The Kapauku Case

In general, band and village societies lack the essential features of capitalism because, as we have seen, their exchange systems are based on reciprocal and redistributive exchanges rather than on price–market exchanges. In some cases, however, egalitarian, reciprocal, and redistributive systems may have certain features strongly reminiscent of contemporary capitalism.

Figure 8.11 Tokyo Stock Exchange
The public sale and purchase of shares in companies and corporations is a fundamental feature of cap-
italist economies.

The Kapauku Papuans of West Irian, Indonesia, are a case in point (see Fig. 8.3). According to Leopold Pospisil (1963), the Kapauku have an economy that is best described as "primitive capitalism." All Kapauku agricultural land is said to be owned individually; money sales are the regular means of exchange; money in the form of shells and glass beads can be used to buy food, domesticated animals, crops, and land; money can also be used as payment for labor. Rent for leased land and interest on loans are also said to occur.

A closer look at the land ownership, however, reveals fundamental differences. To begin with, access to land is controlled by kinship groups known as sublineages (see p. 123). No individual is without membership in such a group. These sublineages control communal tracts of land. Only with regard to sublineage tracts may one speak of private titles to land, and the economic significance of these titles is minimal on several counts: (1) The price of land is so cheap that all the gardens under production have a market value in shell money less than the value of ten female pigs. (2) Prohibition against trespass does not apply to sublineage kin. (3) Although even brothers will ask each other for land payments, credit is freely extended among all sublineage members. The most common form of credit with respect to land consists merely of giving land on loan and in expectation that the favor will shortly be returned. (4) Each sublineage is under the leadership of a headman (see Chapter 10) whose authority depends on his generosity, especially toward the members of his own sublineage. A rich headman does not refuse to lend his kinsmen whatever they need to gain access to the environment since "a selfish individual who hoards money and fails to be generous never sees the time when his word is taken seriously and his advice and decisions followed, no matter how rich he may become" (Pospisil 1963: 49).

Obviously, therefore, the wealth of the headman does not bestow the power associated with capitalist ownership. In Brazil or India, landlords can bar their tenants or sharecroppers from access to land and water regardless of the landlord's reputation. In the United States, under the rules of capitalist landownership, it is of no significance to the sheriff and the police officers when they evict farmers that the bank is being "selfish."

Pospisil states that differences in wealth correlate with striking differences in consumption of food and that Kapauku children from poor homes are undernourished, whereas neighbors are well fed. However, the neighbors are not members of the same sublineage. As Pospisil notes, sublineage kinsmen "exhibit mutual affection and a strong sense of belonging and unity" and "any kind of friction within the group is regarded as deplorable" (1963: 39). It is true that certain sublineages are poorer than others. Sickness and misfortune of various sorts frequently lead to inequalities in physical well-being among kinship units, but such misfortunes do not lead to the formation of a poverty class as they do under capitalism. Without central political controls, marked economic inequalities cannot be perpetuated for long because the rich cannot defend themselves against the demand of the poor that they be given credit, money, land, or whatever is necessary to end their poverty. Under aboriginal conditions, some Kapauku villagers might have starved while neighbors ate well, but it is extremely unlikely that those who starved did so because they lacked access to land, money, or credit.

A stingy egalitarian redistributor is a contradiction in terms, for the simple reason that no police exist to protect such people from the murderous intentions of those whom they refuse to help. As Pospisil tells it:

> Selfish and greedy individuals, who have amassed huge personal properties, but who have failed to comply with the Kapauku requirement of "generosity" toward their less fortunate tribesmen, may be, and actually frequently are, put to death. Even in regions such as the Kamu Valley, where such an execution is not a penalty for greediness, a nongenerous wealthy man is ostracized, reprimanded, and thereby finally induced to change his ways.

[1963: 49]

The Division of Labor

One of the most important organizational features of every economy is the assignment of different tasks to different people. This arrangement is called the *division of labor*. All economies, for example, assign different kinds of work to children and adults and to males and females. In most hunting and simple agricultural economies, men hunt large animals, fish, collect honey, and burn and clear forests. Women and children collect shellfish, plants, and small animals; they weed, harvest, and process grains and tubers. Men do most of the craft work in hard materials such as stone, wood, and metals; women spin fibers, weave cloth, and make pottery and baskets. In more advanced economies, men usually do the plowing and the herding of large animals. In almost all societies, women do most of the cooking of plant foods, water carrying, cleaning, and other household chores, as well as taking care of infants and small children. In general, in preindustrial societies, men perform the activities that require greater muscular effort and freedom of movement (Murdock and Provost 1973; Burton and White 1987).

The division between male and female tasks in hunter–gatherer and simple agricultural economies probably adds to the efficiency of food production. Because of their heavier musculature, men can bend stronger bows, hurl spears farther, and wield bigger clubs (see p. 198). Training men rather than women in the use of these weapons has another advantage: Since the weapons of war are essentially the weapons of the hunt, investment in the training of men

to be hunters simultaneously trains them to be warriors. In hunter–gatherer and simple agricultural societies, women are seldom trained to be warriors (see p. 198). It is consistent with this pattern, therefore, that men also specialize in craft production involving stone, metal, and wood since these are the materials out of which the weapons of war and the hunt are fashioned (Murdock and Provost 1973).

Although the muscle-strength differences between men and women can be reduced by training, the remaining advantage for males—20 to 30 percent—is sufficient to make the difference between life and death in certain kinds of economies. In India, for example, every ounce of human muscle power is needed to carry out plowing operations with oxen and crude plows. Males carry out the most physically demanding tasks not to keep women down but to keep production up (Maclachlan 1983).

The impact of the division of labor on sex and gender roles will be discussed in Chapter 15. Little of this explanation applies to the division of labor by gender in industrial societies, where the use of machines cancels out most of the muscular advantage that men have over women (see p. 202).

Patterns of Work

Among hunter–gatherer and simple agricultural societies, one finds very little specialization. Each man does the same kind of work as other men; each woman does the same kind of work as other women. But each adult performs many different tasks from day to day, in contrast to the standardized routines of contemporary factory or office employees. Moreover, the decision to switch from one task to another—from setting traps to making arrows or collecting honey, for example—is largely voluntary and arrived at either individually or by group consensus. Therefore, people in small-scale, nonstate societies probably do not experience work as a tedious aspect of life. Indeed, recent experimental reforms of factory work patterns are designed to let industrial workers do many jobs instead of just one and to include them in "quality circles" that make decisions about how tasks are performed. These experiments represent attempts to recapture some of the enviable characteristics of work in small-scale, unspecialized economies.

In societies with hunter–gatherer and simple agricultural infrastructures, people do not spend as much time at work as they do in intensive agriculture societies. The !Kung San, for example, put in an average of only about 20 hours per week in hunting. The basic reason for this is that their mode of production is not intensifiable. If they worked more hours per week, they would not only find it progressively more difficult to capture their prey, they would also run the risk of depleting the animal population below the point of recovery. In a sense, the !Kung San benefit from being at the mercy of the natural rates of increase of the plants and animals in their habitat; their mode of production obliges them to work less than intensive agriculturalists or modern factory workers.

In Table 8.1, the amount of time spent on work among the !Kung is compared with that in two other societies: the Machiguenga, slash-and-burn agriculturalists of the eastern Andes in Peru (Fig. 8.12), and Kali Loro, an irrigation rice-growing peasant village of Java. The average work time is considerably greater for both sexes in Kali Loro, the society that has the most advanced technology. The basic reason for this is that, as previously discussed, irrigation agriculture is highly intensifiable (see p. 55). In addition, Kali Loro is part of a stratified state society with political and economic controls such as taxation, rent, and price markets, which compel or induce people to work more hours than would be necessary if they could keep for their own use the value of all the goods and services they produce.

Work occupies an ever greater part of daily life among industrial wage earners. To the basic 8-hour day, add 1 hour for commuting, a half hour for shopping for food and other items (including transportation), a half hour for cooking, a half hour for housework and repairs, and a half hour for child care (including transportation of children and babysitters). These are minimal estimates; for many modern-day Americans, the time devoted to each activity could be more than doubled (Gross 1984). The minimal total—11 hours—is on a par with the work time of the Javanese peasant women. (True, this schedule is kept only on workdays. But on the weekend, the time devoted to all the other forms of work greatly increases, and many people have second jobs, as well.) When labor leaders and employers boast about how much progress has been made in obtaining leisure for the working class, they have in mind the standard established in nineteenth-century Europe, when factory workers put in 12 hours a day or more, rather than the standards observed by the Machiguenga or the !Kung (Figs. 8.13 and 8.14).

Chapter Summary

All societies have an economy—a set of institutions that combines technology, labor, and natural resources to produce and distribute goods and services. The organizational aspects of economy are distinguished from its infrastructural aspects in order to explore the relationship between infrastructure and structure. Selection for different modes of exchange reflects differing degrees of intensifiability and population growth. Exchange is an integral part of all economies, but the flow of goods and services from producers to consumers can be organized in several different ways.

Modern-day price markets and buying and selling are not universal traits. The idea that money can buy everything (or almost everything) has been alien to most of the human beings who have ever lived. Two other modes of exchange— reciprocity and redistribution—once played a more important economic role than price markets.

In reciprocal exchange, the time and quantity of the counterflow is not specified. This kind of exchange can be effective only when it is embedded in kinship or close personal relationships. Daily food distribution among the !Kung San is an example of reciprocal exchange. Control over the counterflow in reciprocal exchange is achieved by communal pressure against freeloaders and shirkers. Reciprocity lingers on in price–market societies within kinship groups and is familiar to many of us as gift giving to relatives and friends.

In the absence of price markets and police or military supervision, trade poses a special problem to people accustomed to reciprocal exchange. Silent barter is one solution. Another is to create trading partners who treat each other as kin. The Kula is a classic example of how barter for necessities is carried out under the cloak of reciprocal exchanges.

Redistributive exchange involves the collection of goods in a central place and its disbursement by a redistributor to the producers. In the transition from egalitarian to stratified

Table 8.1

HOURS OF WORK PER DAY

	!KUNG		MACHIGUENGA		KALI LORO	
	MEN	WOMEN	MEN	WOMEN	MEN	WOMEN
Food production and preparation	3.09	1.80	4.60	4.20	5.49	4.70
Crafts	1.07	0.73	1.40	2.10	0.50	2.32
Trade and wage work	0.00	0.00	0.00	0.00	1.88	1.88
Housework and child care	2.20	3.20	0.00	1.10	0.50	2.07
Total	6.36	5.73	6.00	7.40	8.37	10.97

Sources: Johnson 1975; White 1976; Lee 1979; Carlstein 1983.

Figure 8.12 Machiguenga at Work
As in most slash-and-burn economies, Machiguenga men do the heavy work of felling trees and clearing the forest for new plantings. Here, a Machiguenga uses the felled trees to build a house.

Figure 8.13 All Work and No Play in a Japanese Camera Factory
Workers get 10 minutes per day for exercise and 10 minutes per day for a "tea break."

forms of redistribution, production and exchange cross the line separating voluntary from coerced forms of economic behavior. In its egalitarian form, the redistributor depends on the goodwill of the producers; in the stratified form, the producers depend on the goodwill of the redistributor.

Redistribution is characterized by the counting of shares contributed and shares disbursed. Unlike reciprocity, redistribution leads to boasting and overt competition for the prestigious status of being a great provider. The Kwakiutl potlatch is a classic example of the relationships between redistribution and bragging behavior. The predominance of redistribution over reciprocity is related to the intensifiability of various modes of production. Where production can be intensified without depletions, rivalrous redistributions may serve adaptive ecological functions, such as providing an extra margin of safety in lean years and equalizing regional production. The development of destructive potlatches among the Kwakiutl may have been caused by factors stemming from contact with Europeans, such as the intensification of warfare, trade for guns and ammunition, and depopulation.

Price–market exchange depends on the development of all-purpose money as defined by the criteria of portability, divisibility, convertibility, generality, anonymity, and legality. Although some of these features are possessed by limited-purpose standards of value, all-purpose money and price markets imply the existence of state forms of control.

The greatest development of the price–market mode of exchange is associated with the political economy of capitalism, in which virtually all goods and services can be bought and sold. Since capitalist production depends on consumerism, prestige is awarded to those who own or consume the greatest amount of goods and services. Price–market exchanges are embedded in a political economy of control made necessary by the inequalities in access to resources and the conflict between the poor and the wealthy. The Kapauku illustrate why price–market institutions and capitalism cannot exist in the absence of such controls.

The division of labor is a hallmark of human social life. Gender and age are universally used to assign different economic tasks. In preindustrial societies, men carry out activities that require greater strength. Their monopoly over the weapons of the hunt is also probably related to their role as combatants in warfare. Women in preindustrial societies spe-

Figure 8.14 Labor-Saving Devices That Don't Save Work
The first assembly line. Ford's Highland Park, Michigan, magneto assembly line saved
15 minutes per unit and initiated the era of mass production in 1913—but the workers
worked harder than ever.

cialize in tasks centered on food gathering and child care. The infrastructural basis for this widespread sexual division of labor, however, ceases to exist in industrial societies.

Simple hunter-gatherers and village peoples have no full-time specialists. Except for the division of labor based on sex, everyone does the same things. Parallel with an increase in specialization, work becomes less voluntary, less spontaneous, and more coerced and routinized. Paradoxically, advanced agriculturalists and factory and office workers labor longer hours than people like the !Kung or the Machiguenga.

AMERICA NOW UPDATE

Emergent Varieties of Capitalism

Although Americans think of the United States as being a capitalist country, its political economy is actually best characterized as a mixture of capitalism and democratic state socialism—the same mixture that to varying degrees constitutes the political economies of Western Europe and Japan. Some 17 million people are directly employed by federal, state, and local governments. Another 36.7 million depend largely on government social security payments. Other forms of state, local, and federal pensions support an additional 5.2 million people. Welfare in the form of aid to dependent children, home relief, and aid to the handicapped supports about 14 million people. Two million people are in the armed forces, and 2.3 million are receiving unemployment benefits. At least 1 million farm families depend on government subsidies. Then an estimated 6 million people have jobs in private industry that depend on government purchases of military equipment, construction contracts, government "bailout" loans to companies on the verge of bankruptcy, and assorted forms of government subsidies. Adding the dependents of these workers raises the total in this category to at least 10 million. By conservative estimate, therefore, over 80 million U.S. citizens depend on the redistribution of tax money rather than a share of profits made as a result of capitalist free enterprise.

The United States has other political–economic features that depart from a pure capitalist model. The essence of capitalist enterprise is the freedom to buy and sell in competitive price-making markets. Price-making markets exist where there are enough buyers and sellers to enable buyers to compete with buyers, buyers to compete with sellers, and sellers to compete with sellers for the prices that best suit their respective interests. It has long been recognized that in order to preserve the free enterprise system, limitations must be placed on the ability of small groups of powerful buyers or sellers to gain control over a market to the extent that the prices they offer effectively determine the price that must be paid by anyone who wants a particular product or service.

Early in this century, the U.S. Congress passed laws against the formation of monopolies and actively pursued the breakup of companies that then dominated the railroad, meat-packing, and petroleum industries. The antimonopoly laws stopped short, however, of prohibiting the formation of semimonopolies or oligopolies—that is, companies that control not all but a major share of the market for a particular product. The trend toward oligopoly was already well advanced in the earlier part of this century. But after the end of World War II, the pace of acquisitions and expansions quickened. As a result, by 1980, the 50 largest U.S. manufacturing corporations owned 42 percent of all assets used in manufacturing, whereas the top 500 owned 72 percent of these assets (Silk 1985). In 1988, 3,487 mergers worth $227 billion occurred among corporations worth more than $1 million (U.S. Bureau of the Census 1990: 534).

The most important trend in capitalism in the 1990s is the emergence of *multinational, transnational,* and *supranational* corporations. Multinationals have their headquarters and do most of their business in one country but have markets and facilities around the globe. Transnationals also have headquarters in one country but depend on their international divisions for the bulk of their production and sales. When threatened by unions or government regulators, they move their operations from one country to another. Supranationals have multiple or mobile headquarters. Their managers are multiethnic and multilingual and feel no particular need to identify with a particular government or labor force. It seems likely that in the next decade, the power of the transnationals—some of which already have budgets equal to that of large countries—will expand at the expense of the power of national states.

Chapter 9

DOMESTIC LIFE

Interior of an Iban Long House, Borneo, Indonesia.

In this chapter, we continue the comparative study of structural features, focusing on the variety of family groups and their relation to aspects of infrastructure. We catch our first glimpse of the astonishing variety of human family forms and of mating arrangements: monogamy, polygyny, and polyandry, secondary marriages and preferred-cousin marriages, to mention only a few. Although this chapter is primarily descriptive, it takes up some perennially interesting questions. Is the nuclear family universal? What is marriage? Can marriage take place between partners of the same sex? Are there marriages in which husband and wife never live together? Why do some types of marriages require a gift to the bride's family, whereas others require a gift to the groom's family? Why does every culture have a taboo against incest? Is the taboo based on instinctual sexual aversions, or is it a cultural adaptation? One important conclusion: There is no single natural way to organize domestic life.

The Domestic Sphere of Culture

All societies have a domestic sphere of life. The focus of the domestic sphere is a dwelling space, shelter, residence, or household, in which certain universally recurrent activities take place. It is not possible to give a simple checklist of what these activities are (Netting, Wilk, and Arnould 1984). In many cultures, domestic activities include preparation and consumption of food; cleaning, grooming, teaching, and disciplining the young; sleeping; and adult sexual intercourse. However, in no culture are these activities carried out exclusively within domestic settings.

In the case of modern industrial cultures, this pattern is evident with respect to enculturation and education. Enculturation and education in contemporary life are increasingly carried out in special nondomestic buildings (schools) under the auspices of specialists (teachers) who live in separate households. Many village and band societies also separate their children and adolescents from the entire domestic scene in order to teach them the lore and ritual of the ancestors, sexual competence, or the military arts. Among the Nyakyusa of southern Tanzania, for example, at age 6 or 7, boys begin to put up reed shelters or playhouses on the outskirts of their villages. The boys gradually improve and enlarge these playhouses, eventually constructing a whole new village. Between the ages of 5 and 11, Nyakyusa boys sleep in their parents' house. But during adolescence, they are permitted to visit only during daylight hours and must sleep in the new village although their mothers still cook for them. The founding of a new Nyakyusa village is complete when the young men take wives who cook for them and begin to give birth to the next generation (M. Wilson 1963).

Another famous variation on this pattern is found among the Masai of East Africa, where unmarried men of the same age-set, or ritually defined generation (see p. 138), establish special villages or camps from which they launch war parties and cattle-stealing raids. It is the mothers and sisters of these men who cook and keep house for them (Fig. 9.1).

In many societies, married men spend a good deal of time in special men's houses. Food is handed in to them by wives and children, who are themselves forbidden to enter. Men also sleep and work in these "club-houses" although they may on occasion bed down with their wives and children. Among the Fur of the Sudan, for example, husbands usually sleep apart from their wives in houses of their own and take their meals at an exclusive men's mess. One of the most interesting cases of the separation of cooking and eating occurs among the Ashanti of West Africa. Ashanti men eat their meals with their sisters, mothers, and maternal nephews and nieces, not with their wives and children. But it is the wives who do the cooking. Every evening in Ashanti land one sees a steady traffic of children taking their mother's cooking to their father's sister's house (see Barnes 1960; Bender 1967).

Among the Zumbagua peasants of the Peruvian Andes (Fig. 9.2), households undergo a regular cycle of growth in which varieties of domestic behavior are gradually added to everyday life. During courtship, couples have sex in the fields at a distance from the houses where they eat and sleep. When they get married, they build a small windowless hut that lacks any source of heating for warmth or cooking. This hut adjoins the house of the groom's or bride's parents. Now they sleep and have sex together under one roof, but they continue to cook and eat in the kitchen (Box 9.1) of their parents. Their first children are brought up and cared for by the couple's parents. With the birth of additional children, the couple adds a kitchen of their own to their hut, which becomes a storeroom, and they gradually begin to sleep, cook, eat, have sex, and nurture their offspring around their new hearth (Weismantel 1989).

Figure 9.1   Masai Warrior Age-Set

The Nuclear Family

Many anthropologists believe that at the center of all domestic organization is a group known as the *nuclear family,* which consists of husband, wife, and children (Fig. 9.3). Ralph Linton held the view that the unit of father, mother, and child is the "bedrock underlying all other family structures," and he predicted that "the last man will spend his last hours searching for his wife and child" (1959: 52). George Peter Murdock found the nuclear family in every one of a sample of 250 societies. He concluded that it occurs universally because it fulfills vital functions that cannot be fulfilled as efficiently by other groups. The functions identified by Murdock are sex, reproduction, education, and subsistence. Today, most anthropologists do not believe that these functions are necessarily carried out more efficiently by nuclear families than by other kinds of domestic and nondomestic groups.

Figure 9.2   Zumbagua Peasants of the Peruvian Andes

Box 9.1

ZUMBAGUA DOMESTIC BEHAVIOR

The existence of a [Zumbagua] household is defined by the presence of a kitchen. The word "kitchen" in itself implies much more than a room where food is prepared. It is here that meals are made and eaten, male and female heads of households sleep and live, baths are taken, the family meets, guests are entertained, decisions made, wakes held, babies born and the sick nursed back to health. In addition, only kitchens are warm: the hearth is the only source of heat in Zambagua homes. Cats, guinea pigs, and convalescent sheep demonstrate their innate grasp of the role of the kitchen in the Zambagua household by their refusal to live in any other building, while chickens and dogs, less privileged, spend most of their lives attempting to join the circle around the kitchen hearth.

Weismantel 1989: 57.

Figure 9.3 Japanese Nuclear Families
All dressed up for a day at a shrine in the Meiji area of Tokyo.

Even though nuclear families can be found in the overwhelming majority of human cultures, every culture also has alternative forms of domestic organization, and these arrangements frequently are more important, involving a higher proportion of the population, than the nuclear family. Moreover, people can readily carry out the four functions listed in the context of alternative institutions that may lie entirely outside the domestic sphere.

Polygamy and the Nuclear Family

Next we must consider whether the combination father-mother-child has the same functional significance where either father or mother is married to and is living with more than one spouse at a time. This question is important because *polygamy* (plural marriage) occurs to some extent in at least 90 percent of all cultures (Box 9.2). In one form, called *polygyny* (Fig. 9.4), several wives share a husband; in another, a much less common form called *polyandry* (Fig. 9.5), several husbands share a wife.

Do people who have polygamous families also have nuclear families? G. P. Murdock suggested that nuclear families do exist in such situations. The man or woman simply belongs to more than one nuclear family at a time. But Murdock overlooked the fact that plural marriages create domestic situations that differ significantly from those created by *monogamous* (one husband, one wife) marriages.

Polygamous sexual arrangements, for example, imply a more relaxed attitude toward sharing sexual partners than one expects in monogamous marriages. The mode of repro-

---

Box 9.2

PRINCIPAL FORMS OF HUMAN MARRIAGE

Monogamy
Marriage with one spouse exclusively and for life.
Serial Monogamy
Marriage with one spouse at a time but with remarriage after death or divorce.
Polygamy
Marriage with more than one spouse at a time.
Polygyny
Marriage with more than one wife at a time.
Polyandry
Marriage with more than one husband at a time.

---

duction is also different, especially with polygyny, because the spacing of births is easier to regulate through abstinence (see p. 64).

Further, distinctive patterns of nursing and infant care arise when the mother sleeps alone with her children while the father sleeps with a different wife each night (see p. 209). From the point of view of child rearing, special psychological effects are associated with a father who divides his time among several mothers. The monogamous nuclear family places the focus of adult attention on a small group of full siblings. In a polygynous household, a dozen or more half-siblings must share the affection of the same man. Furthermore, the presence of co-wives or co-husbands changes the burden of child care a particular parent must bear. Industrial-age parents are troubled by the question of what to do with children when both parents go to work or visit friends. Polygynous families, however, have a built-in solution to the babysitting problem in the form of co-wives. From a first wife's point of view, additional wives are welcome because they help spread the work load and increase the productivity and prestige of the household.

The Extended Family

In a majority of the societies studied by anthropologists, domestic life is dominated by groupings larger than simple nuclear or polygamous families. Some form of extended family is especially common. An extended family is a domestic group consisting of siblings, their spouses and their children, or parents and married children (Fig. 9.6). Extended families may also be polygynous. A common form of extended family in Africa, for example, consists of two or more brothers, each

(a)

(b)

Figure 9.4   Polygyny

(a) Polygynous household, Senegal. Islamic law permits this man to take one more wife to fill his quota of four, providing he can take good care of her. (b) Sitting Bull. This famous Sioux chief is shown with two of his wives and three of his children. Polygyny was widespread among native American peoples. This photo was taken in 1882 at Fort Randall, South Dakota.

Figure 9.5   Polyandry
This Tibetan woman (wearing the veil) is being married to the two men on the left, who are brothers.

with two or three wives, living with their adult sons, each of whom has one or two wives.

The domestic life of the Bathonga of southern Mozambique, among whom I carried out fieldwork, was controlled by the senior males of the polygynous extended family's senior generation. These prestigious and powerful men in effect formed a board of directors of a family-style corporation. They made decisions about the domestic group's holdings in land, cattle, and buildings; they also organized the subsistence effort of the coresident labor force—especially of the women and children—by assigning fields, crops, and seasonal work tasks. They tried to increase the size of their cattle herds and supplies of food and beer, obtain more wives, and increase the size and strength of the entire unit. The younger brothers, sons, and grandsons in Bathonga extended families could not reach adulthood, marry, build a hut, carry out subsistence tasks, or have children unless they accepted the policies and priorities established by the senior males. Within the Bathonga polygynous extended-family households, nuclear families existed only in the interval during which a man had only one wife.

In traditional Chinese extended families, marriage is usually monogamous (Fig. 9.7). A senior couple manages the domestic labor force and arranges marriages. Women brought into the household as wives for the senior couple's sons are placed under the direct control of their mother-in-law. She supervises them as they clean, cook, and raise the children. When a family has several daughters-in-law, cooking chores are often rotated so that on any given day a maximum contingent of the domestic labor force can be sent to work in the family's fields (M. Cohen 1976). The degree to which the nuclear family is submerged and effaced by these arrangements is brought out by a custom formerly found in certain Taiwanese households: "Adopt a daughter; marry a sister." To obtain control over their son's wife, the senior couple adopts a daughter, usually someone whose parents are very poor. They bring the girl into the household at a very early age and train her to be hardworking and obedient. Later, they oblige their son to marry this stepsister, thereby preventing the formation of an economically independent nuclear family within their midst while conforming to the socially imposed incest prohibitions (see p. 113).

Among the Rajputs of northern India, extended families take similar stern measures to maintain the subordination of

Figure 9.6   Extended Family, United States
The demand for labor was high on this Minnesota farm in 1895.

Figure 9.7   Taiwan Marriage
Groom's extended family assemble for wedding ceremony.

each married pair. A young man and his wife are even forbidden to talk to each other in the presence of senior persons, meaning in effect that they "may converse only surreptitiously at night" (Minturn and Hitchcock 1963: 241). Here the husband is not supposed to show an open concern for his wife's welfare; if she is ill, that is a matter for her mother-in-law or father-in-law to take care of: "The mother feeds her son even after he is married [and] runs the family as long as she wishes to assume the responsibility" (Minturn and Hitchcock 1963: 241).

As a final brief example of how extended families modify or efface the nuclear family, we have Max Gluckman's (1955: 60) wry comment on the Barotse of Zambia: "If a man becomes too devoted to his wife he is assumed to be the victim of witchcraft."

Why do so many societies have extended families? Probably because nuclear families frequently lack sufficient manpower and womanpower to carry out both domestic and subsistence tasks effectively. Extended families provide a larger labor pool and can carry out a greater variety of simultaneous activities (Pasternak, Ember, and Ember 1976).

One-Parent Domestic Groups

Millions of children throughout the world are reared in domestic groups in which only one parent is present. This arrangement may result from divorce or death of one of the parents. But it also may result from inability or unwillingness to marry. In the most common form of one-parent domestic arrangement, the mother is present and the father is absent. Such households are called *matrifocal*. The mother accepts a

series of men as mates, usually one at a time, but sometimes several at a time (which is a form of nonresident polyandry). The man and woman usually reside together for brief periods, but over the years, the mother may spend long intervals without a resident mate (Box 9.3).

At one extreme, associated with very rich or very poor women, mother and children may live alone. At the other extreme, mother and her children may live together with her sisters and her mother and constitute a large extended family in which adult males play only temporary roles as visitors or lovers.

Matrifocal households are best known from studies carried out in the West Indies, Latin America, and U.S. inner cities (Stack 1974; Safa 1986; R. T. Smith 1990). But this form of household occurs throughout the world (Folbre 1991). Its incidence has been obscured by the tendency to regard such domestic units as aberrant or pathological (Moynihan 1965). In describing domestic groups, social scientists frequently concentrate on the emically preferred form and neglect etic and behavioral actualities. Mother–child domestic groups often result from poverty and hence are associated with many social ills and are regarded as undesirable. But we have no evidence that such domestic arrangements are inherently any more or less pathological, unstable, or contrary to "human nature" than the nuclear family.

What Is Marriage?

The concept of "marriage" is a basic part of the definition of nuclear, polygamous, and extended families and other forms of domestic organization. So far, I have been using the

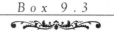

Box 9.3

THE CAUSES OF MATRIFOCALITY

Matrifocal familes form under a variety of conditions. For example, early marriage of girls to men considerably older than themselves leads to high rates of widowhood while children are still young. Remarriage may be difficult or prohibited as among upper caste Hindus in India. High rates of youthful widowhood and matrifocality may also be produced by warfare and political unrest. (Mencher and Okongwu 1993). Dehavenon (1993: 55) offers a more general account of the conditions that underlie most cases of matrifocality in the modern world as follows:

1. The mother has greater access to sources of income than the biological father.
2. Father's access to sources of wealth and income depends on migration or absence from home for extended periods.
3. Mother has greater access to housing.
4. Migration or higher mortality of males leads to a shortage of males available for marriage.

All these conditions underlie the high frequency of matrifocal households in the United States. (See "America Now Update" at the end of this chapter.)

---

word as if everyone agrees on what it means. Although anthropologists are convinced that marriage occurs in every culture, we encounter great difficulty in coming up with a definition that can be applied universally. A famous definition proposed by Kathleen Gough (1968) can serve as a starting point for our discussion. It makes the following points:

1. Marriage is a relationship established between a woman and one or more persons.
2. This relationship assures that a child born to the woman is accorded full birth rights common to normal members of his or her society, provided that
3. The child is conceived and born under certain approved circumstances.

According to Gough, for most if not all societies, this definition identifies a relationship "distinguished by the people themselves from all other kinds of relationships." Yet Gough's definition seems oddly at variance with English dictionary and native Western notions of marriage. First of all, it makes no reference to rights and duties of sexual access or to sexual performance.

In omitting reference to sex as a necessary part of matrimonial relationships, Gough was influenced by her research among the Nayar caste of Southern India (Fig. 9.8). In order to bear children in a socially acceptable way, pubescent Nayar girls had to go through a 4-day ceremony that linked them with a "ritual husband." Sexual relations were not a necessary component of this ceremony, and after it was over, the ritual husband and his wife did not live together or have sex together. Instead, the woman lived with her sisters, her mother, and her mother's brother and had sex with a series of men to whom she was not married and who visited her at her home. The children born from these unions stayed with their mother and were brought up by her. (This makes the Nayar another example of a group that lacks the nuclear family.) Paternity was established by having one of the visiting lovers bestow gifts on the newborn; no further obligations were incurred. Gough regarded the existence of the ritual husbands as proof of the universality of marriage (although not of the nuclear family) since only ritually married Nayar women could have sexual relations with their male visitors.

Besides lacking any reference to sexual access, Gough's definition of marriage is also remarkable in another way. It does not necessarily involve a relationship between males and females since it merely refers to a woman and "one or more" other persons of unspecified sex. What can be the reason for defining marriage as a relationship between a woman and "persons" rather than between "women and men"? The answer is that in a number of cultures such as the Dahomey of West Africa, women "marry" women. There, a woman, who herself is usually already married to a man, pays bride-

Figure 9.8   Nayar of Kerala

price (see p. 112) for a bride. The female bride-price payer becomes a "female husband." She starts a family of her own by letting her "wife" become pregnant through relationships with designated males. The offspring of these unions fall under the control of the "female father" rather than of the biological genitors (see p. 120). Note that this is also another instance of "marriage" that does not involve sexual relations.

Wide as it is, Gough's definition ignores certain mating relationships that take place between males. For example, among the Kwakiutl, a man who desires to acquire the privileges associated with a particular chief can "marry" the chief's male heir. If the chief has no heirs, a man may "marry" the chief's right or left side, or a leg or an arm.

In contemporary European and American cultures, enduring mating relationships between coresident homosexual men or between coresident homosexual women are also often spoken of as marriage. It has thus been suggested that all reference to the gender of the people involved in the relationship should be omitted in the definition of marriage in order to accommodate such cases (Dillingham and Isaac 1975).

The task of understanding varieties of domestic organization is made more difficult when all these forms of mating are crammed into the single concept of marriage. Part of the problem is that when matings in Western culture are denied the designation "marriage," we tend to regard them as less honorable or less authentic relationships, and to impose legal penalties, as is the case with gay couples who are denied access to a spouse's health insurance and sick leave benefits. And so anthropologists are reluctant to stigmatize woman–woman or man–man matings, or Nayar or matrifocal visiting-mate arrangements, by saying they are not marriages.

There is a simple way out of this dilemma. First, let us define marriage as the behavior, sentiments, and rules concerned with coresident heterosexual mating and reproduction in domestic contexts. Second, to avoid offending people by using marriage exclusively for coresident heterosexual domestic mates, let such other relationships be designated as noncoresident marriages, man–man marriages, woman–woman marriages, or by any other appropriate specific nomenclature. Clearly each form of mating has different ecological, demographic, economic, and ideological implications, so nothing is to be gained by arguing about whether they are or are not "real" marriages.

Legitimacy

The essence of the marital relationship, according to some anthropologists, is embodied in that portion of Gough's definition dealing with the assignment of "birth rights" over children. As Bronislaw Malinowski put it, "Marriage is the licensing of parenthood."

It is true that women are universally discouraged from attempting to rear or dispose of their newborn infants according to their own whims, but most societies have several sets of rules defining permissible modes of conception and child rearing. For example, among the people who live in the small Brazilian towns that I have studied, four kinds of relationships occur between a man and a woman, all of which provide children with full birth rights: church marriage, civil marriage, simultaneous church and civil marriage, and consensual marriage. For a Brazilian woman, the most esteemed way to have children is through simultaneous church and civil marriage. This mode legally entitles her to a portion of her husband's property on his death. It also provides the added security of knowing that her husband cannot desert her and enter into a civil or religious marriage elsewhere. The least desirable mode is the consensual marriage because the woman can make no property claims against her consort, nor can she readily prevent him from deserting her. Yet as long as the father acknowledges paternity, the children of a consensual arrangement can make property claims against both father and mother while suffering no deprivation of birth rights in the form of legal disadvantages or social disapproval.

Among the Dahomey, Herskovits (1938) reported thirteen kinds of marriage, determined largely by bride-price arrangements. Children enjoyed different birth rights depending on the type of marriage. In some marriages, the child was placed under the control of the father's domestic group, and in others, under the control of a domestic group headed by a female "father." The point is not that a child is legitimate or illegitimate but rather that specific types of rights, obligations, and groupings emanate from different modes of sexual and reproductive relations. Few of the world's people are concerned with the question of whether a child is legitimate. Instead, the question concerns who will have the right of controlling the child's future. No society grants women complete "freedom of conception," but the restrictions placed on motherhood and the occasions for punishment and disapproval vary enormously.

Where the domestic scene is dominated by large extended families and where there are no strong restrictions on premarital sex, the pregnancy of a young unmarried woman is rarely the occasion for much concern. Under certain circumstances, an "unwed mother" may even be congratulated rather than condemned. Among the Kadar of northern Nigeria, as reported by M. G. Smith (1968), most marriages result from infant betrothals. These matches are arranged by the fathers of the bride and groom when the girl is 3 to 6 years old. Ten years or more may elapse before the bride goes to live with her betrothed. During this time, a Kadar girl may become pregnant. This will disturb no one, even if the biological father is a man other than her future husband:

> Kadar set no value on premarital chastity. It is fairly common for unmarried girls to be impregnated or to give birth to children by youths other than their betrothed. Offspring of such premarital pregnancies are members of the patrilineage . . . of the girl's betrothed and are welcomed as proof of the bride's fertility.

[113]

The absence of concern about legitimacy in many non-Western cultures stands in stark contrast to the persecution of unwed mothers and their "bastard" children, which dominated domestic life in Europe and the Americas as recently as the last century (Kertzer 1993). In industrial countries today, the legal and moral basis for discriminating against unwed mothers and their children is giving way to a growing acceptance of a woman's right to control her reproductive destiny with or without being married (see p. 202).

Every society has rules that define the conditions under which sexual relations, pregnancy, birth, and child rearing may take place, and that allocate privileges and duties in connection with these conditions. And every society has its own, sometimes unique combination of rules and rules for breaking rules in this domain. It would be futile to define marriage by any one ingredient in these rules—such as legitimation of children—even if such an ingredient could be shown to be universal.

Marriage in Extended Families

Extended families collectively maintain an interest in the productive, reproductive, and sexual functions of their members. Individuals serve the interests of the group, and marriage must be seen primarily in the context of group interests.

Figure 9.9   Bride-Price
Among the Kapauku, the bride-price consists of shell money.

If a member of one extended family goes to live in the spouse's family, the spouse-givers expect something in return. The simplest form of such transactions is sister exchange in which the groom's sister is given in marriage to her brother-in-law.

In a sample of 1,267 societies (Gaulin and Bostar 1990: 994), more than half expressed their collective interests are through the institution known as *bride-price* (Fig. 9.9) In bride-price, the wife-receivers give valuable items to the wife-givers. As stated earlier (p. 95), bride-price is not equivalent to the selling and buying of automobiles or refrigerators in capitalist price–market societies. The wife-receivers do not "own" their woman in any total sense; they must take good care of her, or her family will demand that she be returned to them. The amount of bride-price is not fixed; it fluctuates from one marriage to another. (In much of Africa, the traditional measure of bride-wealth was cattle although other valuables such as iron tools were also used. Nowadays, cash

payments are the rule.) Among the Bathonga, a family that had many daughter-sisters was in a favorable position. The family would receive many cattle when the daughter-sisters got married. These cattle would then be used as bride-price for the women's brothers: the more cattle, the more mother-wives; the more mother-wives, the larger the reproductive and productive labor force and the greater the material welfare and influence of the family.

Sometimes the transfer of wealth from one group to another is carried out in installments: so much on initial agreement, more when the woman goes to live with her husband, and another, usually final, payment when she has her first child. Failure to have a child often voids the marriage; the woman goes home to her brothers and father, and the husband's family gets its bride-price back. A common alternative to bride-price is known as bride-service (sometimes called suitor-service). The groom or husband compensates his in-laws by working for them for several months or years before taking his bride away to live and work with him and his extended family.

Dowry

Bride-price and bride-service tend to occur where land is plentiful and the labor of additional women and children can result in additional wealth and well-being for the corporate group (Goody 1976). Where women's productive and reproductive powers are not valued because land is scarce and women's labor cannot be used to intensify production, wives may be regarded as an economic burden. Instead of paying bride-price to the family of the bride, the groom's family may demand a reverse payment, called *dowry* (Fig. 9.10). When this payment consists of money or movable property instead of land, it is usually associated with a low or oppressed status for women (Schlegel and Barry 1986: 145; Bossen 1988; Schlegel and Eloul 1988). Dowry is much rarer than bride-price, occurring in only 3 percent of a sample of 1,267 societies (Gaulin and Boster 1990: 994). However, the societies that have dowry are concentrated in the extremely populous states of Mediterranean Europe and southern Asia. Throughout this region, land is scarce and there is a form of intensive agriculture involving animal-drawn plows guided by men, whereas women's work is largely confined to the domestic scene. As we shall see (p. 197), dowry is closely associated in this region with the subordination of women and a marked preference for male children.

The opposite of bride-price is not dowry but *groom-price,* in which the groom goes to live and work with the bride's family, and the bride's family compensates the groom's family for the loss of his productive and reproductive powers. This form of marriage compensation is extremely rare—only one well-documented case is known (the Nagovisi, see Nash 1974).

Figure 9.10   Dowry
This Arab bride is exhibiting her wealth.

Domestic Groups and the Avoidance of Incest

All these exchanges point to the existence of a profound paradox in the way human beings find mates. Marriage between members of the same domestic group is widely prohibited. Husband and wife must come from separate domestic groups. The members of the domestic group must "marry out," that is, marry exogamously; they cannot "marry in," that is, marry endogamously.

Certain forms of endogamy are universally prohibited. No culture tolerates father–daughter and mother–son marriages. Sister–brother marriage is also widely prohibited, but we know of several important exceptions such as the ruling classes of the Inca, ancient Egypt, ancient China, and Hawaii (Bixler 1982). Most of these marriages were between half-siblings, but some were between full siblings. Moreover, in Egypt during Roman times (approximately from 30 B.C. to A.D. 600), commoners also practiced brother–sister marriage. Such marriages, according to historian Keith Hopkins

(1980), were regarded as perfectly normal relationships, openly mentioned in documents concerning inheritance, business affairs, lawsuits, and petitions to officials.

In the emics of Western civilization, sister–brother, father–daughter, and mother–son sex relations and marriages are called *incest*. Why are these sex relations and marriages so widely prohibited? Explanations of nuclear family incest prohibition fall into two major types: those that stress an instinctual component and those that emphasize the social and cultural advantages of exogamy.

INSTINCT

Advocates of genetic theories of incest avoidance long ago recognized that genes were not likely to contain definite instructions for shutting down sex drives in the presence of siblings, children, and parents. Following the lead of Edward Westermark (1894), they proposed, instead, that members of the opposite sex have an innate tendency to find each other sexually uninspiring if they have been brought up in close physical proximity to each other during infancy and childhood (Spiro 1954; Shepher 1983). Westermark's principle is much in favor among sociobiologists because it provides a way out of the dilemma posed by brother–sister incest among royalty (Fig. 9.11). If brother and sister were brought up apart from each other in different houses or by different nurses and caretakers, then, according to the Westermark principle, they might very well find each other sexually attractive enough to mate (Wilson 1978: 38–39; Bixler 1982).

Behind the Westermark theory and other genetic explanations of incest avoidance is another assumption: Close inbreeding increases the likelihood that individuals who carry defective genes will mate with each other and give birth to children who suffer from pathological conditions that lower their rate of reproduction. Another argument asserts that, simply by lowering the amount of genetic diversity in a population, inbreeding might adversely affect the population's ability to adapt to new diseases or other novel environmental hazards. So, those individuals who find themselves "turned off" through the Westermark effect would have avoided inbreeding, reproduced at a higher rate, and gradually replaced those who were "turned on" by their close kin (Leavitt 1990, 1992; cf. Uhlman 1992; Schields 1994).

There are several soft spots in this part of the argument. It is true that in large modern populations, incest leads to a high rate of stillbirths and congenitally diseased and impaired children (Thornhill 1993). But the same results need not occur from close inbreeding practiced in small preagricultural societies. Inbreeding in small preagricultural societies leads to the gradual elimination of harmful recessive genes because such societies have little tolerance for infants and children who are congenitally handicapped and impaired. Lack of support for such children eliminates the harmful genetic variations

Figure 9.11   Cleopatra
Not bad for eleven generations of brother–sister marriage.

heavily on two famous case studies that allegedly demonstrate the predicted loss of sexual ardor. The first of these concerns Taiwanese adopt-a-daughter-marry-a-sister marriage (see p. 107). Studies have shown that these marriages, in which husband and wife grow up together at close quarters, lead to fewer children, greater adultery, and higher divorce rates than normal marriages, in which future wives and husbands grow up in separate households (Wolf and Haung 1980). But these observations scarcely confirm Westermark's theory. The Taiwanese explicitly recognize that adopt-a-daughter-marry-a-sister is an inferior, even humiliating, form of marriage. Normally, to seal a marriage bond, the families of a bride and groom exchange considerable wealth as a sign of their support for the newlyweds. But these exchanges are smaller or absent altogether in adopt-a-daughter-marry-a-sister. This difference makes it impossible to prove that sexual disinterest rather than chagrin and disappointment over being treated like second-class citizens is the source of the couple's infertility.

The second case used to confirm Westermark's theory concerns an alleged lack of sexual interest displayed by boys and girls who attended the same classes from nursery school to age 6 in the Israeli cooperative community known as a kibbutz. Allegedly these boys and girls were so thoroughly "turned off" that among marriages contracted by people who were reared in a kibbutz, not one involved men or women who had been reared together from birth to age 6 (Shepher 1983). This seems impressive, but anthropologist John Hartung has discovered a fatal flaw in the statistics. Out of a total of 2,516 marriages, there were 200 in which both partners were reared in the same kibbutz although they were not in the same class for their first 6 years of school. Since all kibbutz youth were inducted into the army and commingled with tens of thousands of potential mates from outside their kibbutz before they got married, the rate of 200 marriages from within the same kibbutz is far more than could be expected by chance. One must now ask, of the 200 marriages from within the same kibbutz, what was the chance that not a single one would be between a boy and a girl who had attended the same classes? Since girls were generally 3 years younger than the boys they married, only a very few marriages between people who were reared for 6 years in the same class could be expected. Actually, as Hartung points out, five marriages did occur between boys and girls who had been reared together for part of the first 6 years of their lives (Fig. 9.12). Since Westermark's theory does not predict how long it takes for reared-together boys and girls to lose their interest in each other, these five marriages actually disconfirm the theory (Hartung 1985).

The proposal that an instinctual sexual aversion occurs within the nuclear family is also contradicted by evidence of strong sexual attraction between father and daughter and between mother and son. Freudian psychoanalysis indicates

from future generations and results in populations that carry a much smaller "load" of harmful gene variants than modern populations (Livingstone 1969, 1982).

To test the Westermark theory, one cannot point to the mere occurrence of incest avoidance. One has to show that sexual ardor cools when people grow up together, independent of any existing norms that call for incest avoidance. Since this cannot be done experimentally without controlling the lives of human subjects, advocates of the theory lean

Figure 9.12   Kibbutz Boys and Girls
Does childhood familiarity lead to sexual avoidance?

that children and parents of the opposite sex have a strong desire to have sexual encounters with each other. Indeed, in the case of the father–daughter relationship, at least, these wishes are acted on more frequently than is popularly believed. For example, social workers estimate that tens of thousands of cases of incest occur in the United States annually, of which the great majority involves fathers imposing on young daughters (Glaser and Frosh 1988; Cicchetti and Carlson 1989).

Finally, the instinct theory of incest avoidance is hard to reconcile with the widespread occurrence of endogamous practices that are carried out simultaneously and in support of exogamic arrangements. Members of exogamous extended families, for example, frequently are involved in marriage systems that encourage them to mate with one kind of first cousin (cross cousin) but not another (parallel cousin; see p. 121). The difference between these two forms of inbreeding cannot be explained satisfactorily by natural selection (cf. Alexander 1977). Furthermore, the widespread preference for some form of cousin marriage itself weighs against the conclusion that exogamy expresses an instinct established by the harmful effects of inbreeding (cf. Bittles et al. 1991).

The possibility that incest avoidance is genetically programmed in *Homo sapiens* has received some support from field studies of monkey and ape mating behavior. As among humans, father–daughter, mother–son, and brother–sister matings are uncommon among our nearest animal relatives, but they do occur. The avoidance of sex between these closely related pairs can be explained in terms of gender and age dominance patterns and sexual competition. In the wild, there are far more cases of group endogamy involving matings between closely related primates than there are exogamous matings, and no experimental evidence suggests an aversion

to incest per se among monkeys and apes (Leavitt 1990). Moreover, even if such an instinctual aversion were found to exist among nonhuman primates, its significance for human nature would be dubious. After all, not only mates get exchanged between human groups but a vast array of goods and services are exchanged as well. Are we to believe that humans instinctually avoid keeping food, tools, and labor within the nuclear family?

SOCIAL AND CULTURAL ADVANTAGES OF EXOGAMY

Nuclear family incest avoidance and other forms of exogamy among domestic groups can be explained quite effectively in terms of demographic, economic, and ecological advantages (Leavitt 1989). These advantages are not necessarily the same for all societies. For example, band societies rely on marriage exchanges to establish long-distance networks of kinspeople. Bands that formed a completely closed breeding unit would be denied the mobility and territorial flexibility essential to their subsistence strategy. Territorially restricted, endogamous bands of twenty to thirty people would also run a high risk of extinction as a result of gender imbalances caused by an unlucky run of male births and adult female deaths, which would place the burden for the group's reproduction on one or two aging females. Exogamy is thus essential if a small population is to effectively utilize its productive and reproductive potential. Once a band begins to obtain mates from other bands, the prevalence of reciprocal exchange demands a counter flow of mates and other valuables. Receivers must become givers. The taboos on mother–son, father–daughter, and brother–sister marriages can therefore be interpreted as a defense of reciprocal exchange relationships against the ever-present temptation for parents to keep their children for themselves or for brothers and sisters to keep each other for themselves.

Another factor favoring nuclear family exogamy is the institution of marriage itself. Most marriages (despite the exceptions previously discussed such as the Nayar) limit the sexual freedom of the marriage partners. Thus the great majority of societies prohibit one or both spouses from having extramarital sex, that is, from committing adultery. Illicit sexual encounters between father and daughter and mother and son constitute a form of adultery. Mother–son incest is an especially threatening variety of adultery in the many societies that have strong male supremacist institutions (see Ch.15). Not only is the wife "double-dealing" against her husband but the son is also "double-dealing" against his father. This may explain why the least common and emically most feared and abhorred form of incest is that between mother and son. It follows that father–daughter incest will be somewhat more common since husbands enjoy double standards of sexual behavior more often than wives and are less vulnerable to punishment for adultery. Finally, the same consideration suggests an explanation for the relatively high frequency of brother–sister matings and their legitimizations as marriages in elite classes—they do not conflict with the adultery rules for fathers and mothers.

After the evolution of the state, exogamic alliances between domestic groups continued to have important infrastructural consequences. Among peasants, exogamy also increases the total productive and reproductive strength of the intermarried groups. It permits the exploitation of resources over a larger area than the nuclear or extended families could manage on an individual basis, it facilitates trade, and it raises the upper limit of the size of groups that can be formed to carry out seasonal activities requiring large labor inputs (communal game drives, harvests, and so on). Furthermore, where intergroup warfare poses a threat to group survival, the ability to mobilize large numbers of warriors is decisive. Hence, in militaristic, highly male-centered village cultures, sisters and daughters are frequently used as pawns in the establishment of alliances. These alliances do not necessarily eliminate warfare between intermarrying groups, but they make it less common, as might be expected from the presence of sisters and daughters in the enemy's ranks (Tefft 1975; Kang 1979; Podolefsky 1984).

In cultures with classes and castes, endogamy often combines with extended family exogamy to maintain wealth and power within the ruling circles (see Ch. 13). But as already noted, even the nuclear family may become endogamous when there is an extreme concentration of political, economic, and military power. With the evolution of price–market forms of exchange, the extended family tends to be replaced by nuclear family domestic units. Domestic group alliances lose some of their previous adaptive importance, and the traditional functions of incest avoidance lose their force. Incest has been decriminalized in Sweden, for example, and there is an effort to do as much in the United States (Y. Cohen 1978; De Mott 1980). Some anthropologists predict that nuclear family incest prohibitions will eventually disappear because modern states have so many alternative ways of establishing intergroup relationships, such as price markets and compulsory universal public education (Leavitt 1989). However, given the scientific knowledge that nuclear family incest is genetically risky in populations carrying a heavy load of harmful recessive genes, the complete repeal of antiincest legislation seems unlikely and unwise.

Preferential Marriages

The widespread occurrence of exogamy implies that the corporate interests of domestic groups must be protected by rules that stipulate who is to marry whom. Having given a woman away in marriage, most groups expect either materi-

al wealth or women in exchange. Consider two domestic groups, A and B, each with a core of resident brothers. If A gives a woman to B, B may immediately reciprocate by giving a woman to A. This reciprocity is often achieved by a direct exchange of the groom's sister. But the reciprocity may take a more indirect form. B may return a daughter of the union between the B man and the A woman. The bride in such a marriage will be her husband's father's sister's daughter, and the groom will be his wife's mother's brother's son. (The same result would be achieved by a marriage between a man and his mother's brother's daughter.) Bride and groom are each other's cross cousins (see p. 121). If A and B have a rule that such marriages are to occur whenever possible, then they are said to have preferential cross cousin marriage.

Reciprocity in marriage is sometimes achieved by several intermarrying domestic groups that exchange women in cycles and are called *circulating connubia*. For example, A → B → C → A; or A → B and C → D in one generation and A → D and B → C in the next, and then back to A → B and C → D. These exchanges are enforced by preferential marriage with appropriate kinds of cousins, nephews, nieces, and other kin.

Another common expression of collective familial interest in marriage is the practice of supplying replacements for inmarrying women who die prematurely. To maintain reciprocity or to fulfill a marriage contract for which bride-price has been paid, the brother of a deceased woman may permit the widower to marry one or more of the deceased wife's sisters. This custom is known as the *sororate* (a deceased woman is replaced in marriage by her sister). Closely related to this practice is the preferential marriage known as the *levirate*, in which the services of a man's widow are retained within the domestic unit by having her marry one of his brothers (a deceased husband is replaced in marriage by his brother). If the widows are old, the services rendered by the remarried widow may be minimal, and the levirate then functions to provide security for women who would otherwise not be able to remarry. Thus, the organization of domestic life everywhere reflects the fact that husbands and wives usually originate in different domestic groups that continue to maintain a sentimental and practical interest in the marriage partners and their children.

Chapter Summary

The structural level of sociocultural systems is made up in part of interrelated domestic groups. Such groups can usually be identified by their attachment to a living space or domicile in which activities such as eating, sleeping, marital sex, and the nurturance and discipline of the young take place. However, there is no single or minimal pattern of domestic activities. Similarly, the nuclear family cannot be regarded as the minimal building block of all domestic groups. Although nuclear families occur in almost every society, they are not always the dominant domestic group, and their sexual, reproductive, and productive functions can readily be satisfied by alternative domestic and nondomestic institutions. In polygamous and extended families, for example, the father–mother–child subset may not enjoy any practical existence apart from the set of other relatives and their multiple spouses. And there are many instances of domestic groups that lack a coresident husband-father. Although children need to be nurtured and protected, no one knows the limits within which human domestic arrangements must be confined in order to satisfy human nature. One of the most important facts about human domestic arrangements is that no single pattern can be shown to be more "natural" than any other.

Human mating patterns also exhibit an enormous degree of variation. Though something similar to what is called marriage occurs all over the world, it is difficult to specify the mental and behavioral essence of the marital relationship. Man–man, woman–woman, female–father, and childless marriages make it difficult to give a minimal definition of marriage without offending someone. Even coresidence may not be essential, as the Nayar and other single-parent households demonstrate. And if we restrict the definition of marriage to coresident heterosexual matings that result in reproduction, we still find a staggering variety of rights and duties associated with the sexual and reproductive functions of the marriage partners and their offspring.

To understand coresident heterosexual reproductive marriage in extended families, marriage must be seen as a relationship between corporate groups as much as between cohabiting mates. The divergent interests of these corporate groups are reconciled by means of reciprocal exchanges that take the form of sister exchange, bride-price, suitor-service, dowry, and groom-price. Except for dowry, the common principle underlying these exchanges is that in giving a man or woman away to another extended family, the domestic corporation does not renounce its interest in the offspring of the mated pair and expects compensation for the loss of a productively and reproductively valuable person.

Most domestic groups are exogamous. This can be seen as a result of either instinctual programming or social and cultural adaptation. The discussion of exogamy necessarily centers on the incest prohibitions within the nuclear family. Father–daughter, sister–brother, and mother–son matings and marriages are almost universally forbidden. The chief exception is brother–sister marriages, which occur in several highly stratified societies among the ruling elites and among Egyptian commoners in Roman times. The instinct theory of incest avoidance stresses evidence from Taiwan and Israel, which suggests that children reared together develop a sexual aversion to each other. This aversion is seen as genetically determined since it reduces the risk of harmful genes. Other interpretations of the Taiwan and Israel studies can be made,

however. A purely cultural theory of incest avoidance can be built out of the need for domestic groups to defend their capacity to engage in reciprocal marriage exchanges by preventing parents from keeping their children for themselves. In the future, the perpetuation of the incest taboos may be related exclusively to the increasing genetic dangers associated with close inbreeding in populations carrying a large load of harmful genes.

Exogamy and incest avoidance form only a small part of the spectrum of preferred and prohibited marriages that reflect the pervasive corporate interests of domestic groups. Preferences for certain kinds of marriage exchanges create circulating connubia in which reciprocity between domestic groups may be direct or indirect. Such preferences may be expressed as a rule requiring marriage with a particular kind of cousin. Preferential marriage rules such as the levirate and sororate also exemplify the corporate nature of the marriage bond.

AMERICA NOW UPDATE

Matrifocal Families

In 1965, with the release of a report by Daniel P. Moynihan, then U.S. Assistant Secretary of Labor, matrifocality received official recognition as the prime cause of the perpetuation of poverty among blacks in the United States. According to Moynihan, black youths are not properly motivated to take jobs that are actually available because of the absence of a male father figure in their family. Adult males drift in and out of these households, and thus black youths grow up without the aid and inspiration of a stable male figure who holds a steady job and who provides comfort and security for wife and children. Moynihan proposed that matrifocality was a cause not only of poverty but of crime and drug addiction as well. Explanations of poverty that appeal to enculturation experience within matrifocal households don't explain very much because the phenomenon of matrifocality is itself a response to poverty. Setting aside the relatively small number of matrifocal familes headed by middle- and upper-class professional women, the majority of matrifocal families in the United States fits the explanation offered on page 109. Poverty-class women in the United States do have greater access to sources of income than poverty-class men. Unemployment among poor minority males exceeds unemployment among poor minority women. More important, poor women have access to welfare support for themselves and their children, whereas poor males are seldom favored with aid for dependent children. At the same time, it is women who have access to pub-

Figure 9.13   Children of the Flats Area of Carol Stack's study.

lic housing and to housing subsidies. Poor women thus have little incentive to marry men who would be an economic burden to them. Lacking steady employment, males gravitate toward making money in illegal enterprises, especially the drug trade. Many of them are in prison much of the time, a situation that is scarcely conducive to the formation of patrifocal or nuclear family households. Higher rates of mortality among marriage-age males further reduces the pool of potential mates for poor women (Dehavenon 1994).

In her study of the Flats, a black ghetto in a midwestern U.S. city (Fig. 9.13), anthropologist Carol Stack (1974) pro-

vides an account of the strategies that poverty-level families follow in attempting to maximize their security and well-being in the face of the inadequate wages of the unskilled male. Nuclear families do not exist in the Flats because the material conditions necessary for such families do not exist. Instead, the people of the Flats are organized into large female-centered networks of relatives and neighbors. The members of these networks engage in reciprocal economic exchanges, take care of one another's children, provide emergency shelter, and help one another in many ways not characteristic of middle-class domestic groups. In the Flats, the most important factor that affects interpersonal relationships between men and women is unemployment and the difficulty that men have in finding secure jobs. Losing a job, or being unemployed month after month, debilitates one's self-importance and independence and, for men, necessitates that they sacrifice their role in the economic support of their families. Then they become unable to assume the traditional father role as defined by American society. Ironically, as Stack points out, attempts by women on welfare to form nuclear families are efficiently discouraged by welfare policy. "Women come to realize that welfare benefits and ties with kin networks provide greater security for them and their children" (Stack 1974: 113).

Fifty-four percent of black children and 27 percent of Hispanic children live with their mothers only. But the trend toward matrifocal households is also present among whites: Seventeen percent of white children under the age of 18 live with mothers only, up from 8 percent in 1970. What's more, the great majority of matrifocal white households are headed by poor, nonprofessional women, not by TV sitcom Murphy Browns (U.S. Bureau of the Census 1994).

Chapter 10

DESCENT, LOCALITY, AND KINSHIP

Caroline Island kin group.

We continue with domestic organization. We examine the principal mental and emic components of domestic groups, namely, the concept of kinship through marriage and descent. Then we relate different varieties of kinship concepts to particular kinds of domestic groups and to the influence of infrastructural conditions. To top this off, we briefly explore the wonders of kinship terminologies—systems for classifying relatives. Parts of this chapter may require an extra dose of concentration, but the study of varieties of kinship arrangements is one of the oldest interests of anthropology. Like language, kinship studies demonstrate the power of culture to form systems of thought and behavior on the level of groups rather than on the level of individuals. No one individual, for example, ever decided that our mother's sister and our father's sister should both be called by the single term *aunt* instead of two different terms, as is true in other cultures. I hope you give this chapter a try. You may even enjoy it.

Kinship

The study of hundreds of cultures all over the world has led anthropologists to conclude that two principles are expressed in the organization of domestic life everywhere. The first is relatedness through *descent* or parentage. The second is relatedness through marriage or *affinity*. People who are related to each other through descent or a combination of affinity and descent are relatives, or kin. And the domain of ideas constituted by the beliefs and expectations kin share about one another is called *kinship*.

Kinship should not be confused with biological mating or biological descent. Kinship is an emic, culturally constructed concept; biologic matings and biological descent are etic concepts. As discussed previously (p. 109), marriage may emically establish "parentage" with respect to children who are biologically unrelated to their culturally defined "father." Even where a culture insists that descent must be based on actual biological fatherhood, domestic arrangements may make it difficult to identify the biological father. For these reasons, anthropologists distinguish between the culturally defined "father" and the *genitor*, the actual biological father. A similar distinction is necessary in the case of "mother." Although the culturally defined mother is usually the *genetrix*, the widespread practice of adoption also creates many discrepancies between emic and etic motherhood.

Descent

Descent is the belief that certain persons play an important role in the creation, birth, and nurturance of certain children. Theories of descent vary from culture to culture, but so far as we know, no human society is without such a theory (Scheffler 1973: 749). Descent implies the preservation of some aspect of the substance or spirit of people in future gen-

erations and thus is a symbolic form of immortality (Craig 1979). Perhaps that is why every society believes in one form or another of descent.

In Western folk traditions, parents are linked to children by the belief that children have the same kind of "blood" as their parents. Each child's veins are thought of as being filled with blood obtained from mother and father in equal amounts. As a result of this imagery, "blood relatives" are distinguished from relatives who are linked only through marriage. This imagery led nineteenth-century anthropologists to use the ethnocentric term *consanguine* (of the same blood) to denote relations of descent. Westerners (including college professors) persist in talking about blood relatives even though we know that closely related individuals may have different blood types, distantly or unrelated individuals may have the same blood type, and the closeness of a relationship is measured by the proportion of shared DNA and not by shared blood.

Descent need not depend on the idea of blood inheritance, nor need it involve equal contributions from both father and mother:

- The Ashanti of West Africa believe that blood is contributed only by the mother and that it determines only a child's physical characteristics, whereas a child's spiritual disposition and temperament are the product of the father's semen.
- The Alorese of Indonesia believe that the child is formed by a mixture of seminal and menstrual fluids, which accumulate for two months before beginning to solidify. Many other cultures share this idea of a slowly growing fetus nourished by repeated additions of semen during pregnancy.
- The Innuit believe that pregnancy results when a spirit child climbs up a woman's bootstraps, enters the womb, and is nourished by semen.

- The Seri of Sonora, Mexico, believe that a woman has a small pouch inside the womb. Repeated intercourse fills the sack with semen. A spirit child, a tiny winged figure, enters the woman's body (Moser 1982).
- The Trobrianders contend that semen does not play any procreative role. Here also, a woman becomes pregnant when a spirit child enters her vagina. The only procreative function of the Trobriand "father" is to widen the passageway into the womb. The Trobriand "father," nonetheless, has an essential social role since no self-respecting spirit child would chose a Trobriand girl who was not married and opened up by intercourse. (Although the Trobrianders practiced premarital sex, girls were married by the time that they were capable of becoming pregnant. So they had no evidence to refute the belief that conception did not require semen.)

A similar denial of the male's procreative role occurs throughout Australia:

- The Murngin believed that the spirit children live deep below the surface of certain sacred waterholes. For conception to take place, one of these spirits appears in the future father's dreams. In the dream, the spirit child introduces itself and asks its father to point out the woman who is to become its mother. Later, when this woman passes near the sacred waterhole, the spirit child swims out in the form of a fish and enters her womb.
- The Aranda believed that a totemic ancestor initiates a woman's pregnancy by throwing a small sacred object called a churinga (see p. 228) that pierces her body. Only married women are targeted (Strehlow 1947: 87).
- The Tiwi (see p. 133) believe that there is an invisible world inhabited by little beings. A married man sees one of the spirit children in a dream and tells it who his wife is. The spirit child enters the wife's womb through her vagina and goes into a little egg in the placenta and starts to grow. If no one dreams a particular spirit child, it will grow up, marry, and have a life of its own in the spirit world (Goodale 1971).

Despite the many theories about the nature of procreative roles, all cultures affirm the existence of some special contribution made by both husband and wife to the reproductive process although they may contribute quite unevenly and with vastly different expectations concerning rights and obligations.

Descent Rules

By reckoning their descent relationships, individuals are apportioned different duties, rights, and privileges in regard to many different aspects of social life. Descent may be used to determine a person's name, family, residence, rank, property, ethnicity, nationality, and many other statuses (Fig. 10.1).

Anthropologists distinguish two great classes of descent rules: the cognatic and the unilineal. *Cognatic descent rules* are those in which both male and female parentage are used to establish any of the abovementioned duties, rights, and privileges. *Unilineal descent rules*, on the other hand, restrict parental links exclusively to males or exclusively to females.

The most common form of cognatic rule is *bilateral descent*, the reckoning of kinship evenly and symmetrically along maternal and paternal links in ascending and descending generations through individuals of both sexes (Figs. 10.2 and 10.3).

The second main variety of cognatic rule is called *ambilineal descent* (Fig. 10.4). Here the descent lines traced by ego (Box 10.1) ignore the gender of the parental links, but the links do not lead in all directions evenly. As in bilateral descent, ego traces descent through males and females, but the links twist back and forth, including some female ancestors or descendants but excluding others, and including some male ancestors or descendants and excluding others. In other words, ego does not reckon descent simultaneously and equally through mothers, fathers, and grandparents.

Moving on now to unilineal descent, we find two main varieties: patrilineality and matrilineality. When descent is reckoned *patrilineally*, ego follows the ascending and descending genealogical links through males only (Fig. 10.5). Note that this does not mean that the descent-related individuals are only males; in each generation, ego has relatives of both genders. However, in the passage from one generation to another, only the male links are relevant; children of females are dropped from the descent reckoning.

When descent is reckoned *matrilineally*, ego follows the ascending and descending links through females only (Fig. 10.6). Once again, note that males as well as females can be related matrilineally; only in the passage from one generation to another are the children of males dropped from the descent reckoning.

One of the most important logical consequences of unilineal descent is that it segregates the children of siblings of the opposite sex into distinct categories. This effect is especially important in the case of cousins. Note that with patrilineal descent, ego's father's sister's son and daughter do not share common descent with ego, whereas ego's father's brother's son and daughter do share common descent with ego. In the case of matrilineal descent, the same kind of distinction results with respect to ego's "cousins" on the mother's side. Children whose parents are related to each other as brother and sister are known as *cross cousins*; children whose parents are related to each other as brother and brother or sister and sister are known as *parallel* cousins (Fig. 10.7).

Figure 10.1   American Kindred
Thanksgiving is an occasion for both siblings and cousins to get together.

Anthropologists distinguish an additional variety of descent rule called *double descent*, in which ego simultaneously reckons descent matrilineally through mother and patrilineally through father. This differs from unilineal descent, in which descent is reckoned only through males or only through females but not both together.

Each of these descent rules provides the logical basis for mentally aligning people into emic kinship groups. These groups exert great influence on the way people think and behave in both domestic and extradomestic situations. An

important point to bear in mind about kinship groups is that they need not consist of coresident relatives; members of the same lineages and clans, for example, may be found in different households and different villages. We proceed now to a description of the principal varieties of kinship groups.

Cognatic Descent Groups: Bilateral Variety

Bilateral descent applied to an indefinitely wide span of kin and to an indefinite number of generations leads to the concept of groups known as *kindreds* (Fig. 10.8). When modern-day Americans and Europeans use the word *family* and have in mind more than just their nuclear families, they are referring to their kindreds. The main characteristic of the kindred is that the span and depth of bilateral reckoning are open-ended. Relatives within ego's kindred can be judged as "near" or "far," depending on the number of genealogical links that separate them, but there is no definite or uniform principle for making such judgments or for terminating the extension of the kinship circle. An important consequence of this feature, as shown in Figure 10.8, is that egos and their siblings

△   Male

○   Female

=   Is married to

| Is descended from

⊓   Is the sibling of

◒   Ego whose genealogy is being shown

Figure 10.2   How to Read Kinship Diagrams

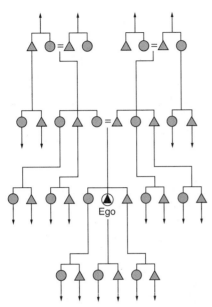

Figure 10.3 *Bilateral Descent*
Everyone on the diagram has a descent relationship with ego.

have a kindred whose membership cannot be the same for any other persons (except for ego's double cousins—cousins whose parents are two brothers who have exchanged sisters). This means that it is impossible for coresident domestic groups to consist of kindreds and very difficult for kindreds to maintain corporate interests in land and people.

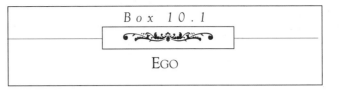

Cognatic Descent Groups: Ambilineal Variety

The open-ended, ego-centered characteristics of the bilateral kindred can be overcome by specifying one or more apical (topmost) ancestors from whom descent is traced through males or females. The resultant group logically has a membership that is the same regardless of which ego carries out the reckoning. This is the *cognatic lineage* (the terms *ramage* and *sept* are also used as synonyms) (Fig. 10.9).

Members of cognatic lineages may not be able to demonstrate the precise genealogical links relating them to the apical lineage founder. For example, people who share the same name as the apical ancestor can claim membership in the cognatic lineages of Scotland (misnomered "clans"; see Neville 1979).

Unilineal Descent Groups

All the people who trace descent patrilineally from a particular male ancestor form a *patrilineage* (Fig. 10.10); whereas all the people who trace descent matrilineally from a particular female ancestress form a *matrilineage*. These kin groups contain the same set of people from any ego's viewpoint. This feature makes them ideally suited to be coresident domestic groups and to hold joint interests in persons and property. Because of exogamy, however, both sexes cannot remain coresident beyond childhood. Some lineages include all the generations and collateral descendants of the first ancestor. These are *maximal lineages*. Lineages may contain sublineages. Those that consist of only three generations are *minimal lineages* (Fig. 10.10).

When unilineal descent from a specific ancestor is not based on demonstrated genealogical links, the group that results is known as either a *patriclan* or a *matriclan* (the terms *patrisib* and *matrisib* are also in use). There are many borderline cases, however, in which it is difficult to decide whether one is dealing with a unilineal lineage or a unilineal clan.

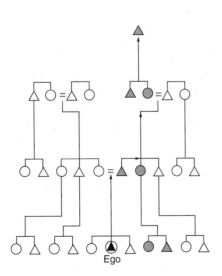

Figure 10.4 *Ambilineal Descent*
Ego traces descent through both males and females, but not equally and not simultaneously.

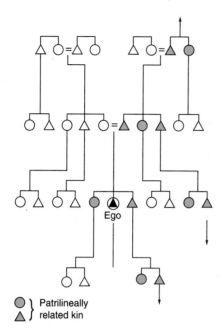

Figure 10.5 *Patrilineal Descent*

Descent is traced exclusively through males.

○ } Patrilineally
△ } related kin

Postmarital Locality Patterns

To understand the processes responsible for the evolution of different varieties of domestic groups and different ideologies of descent, we must discuss one additional aspect of domestic organization: *postmarital residence* (where a newly

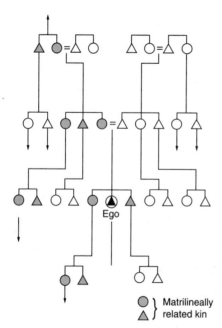

Figure 10.6 *Matrilineal Descent*

Descent is traced exclusively through females.

○ } Matrilineally
△ } related kin

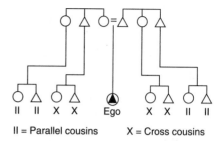

II = Parallel cousins   X = Cross cousins

Figure 10.7 *Cross Cousins and Parallel Cousins*

married couple goes to live). Table 10.1 describes the principal postmarital residence practices.

Postmarital residence practices influence descent rules because they determine who will enter, leave, or stay in a domestic group (Murdock 1949; Naroll 1973). They thus provide domestic groups with distinctive cores of people related by descent and marriage.

But what determines a culture's residence rules? In many cases, residence rules reflect a society's basic patterns of production and reproduction because they are a means of organizing and justifying the structure of domestic groups in relation to particular infrastructural constraints and opportunities.

Causes of Bilateral Descent

Bilateral descent is associated with various combinations of neolocality, ambilocality, and bilocality (see Table 10.1 for definitions of locality patterns). These locality practices in turn usually reflect a high degree of mobility and flexibility among nuclear families. Mobility and flexibility, as we have seen in Chapter 5, are useful for simple hunters and gatherers, and are an intrinsic feature of band organization. The !Kung San, for example, are primarily bilateral, and this reflects in turn a predominant, bilocal, postmarital residence pattern. !Kung San camps contain a core of adult siblings of both sexes, plus their spouses and children and an assortment of more distant bilateral and affinal kin. Each year, in addition to much short-time visiting, about 13 percent of the population makes a more or less permanent residential shift from one camp to another, and about 35 percent divide their time equally among two or three different camps (Lee 1979: 54). This mobility and flexibility is advantageous for people who must rely on hunting and gathering for their livelihood.

In industrial societies, bilaterality is associated with a similar flexibility and mobility of nuclear families. (In the United States, about 20 percent of domestic groups change their residence each year.) Bilaterality in this case reflects a neolocal pattern that is advantageous with respect to wage–labor opportunities and the substitution of price–market money exchanges for kinship-mediated forms of exchange. Whereas the !Kung San always live with relatives

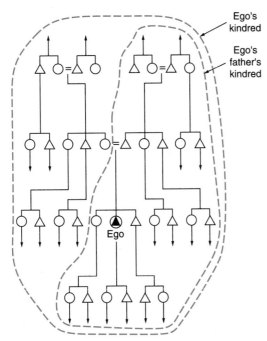

Figure 10.8   Kindreds
Children have kindreds that are different from those of either parent.

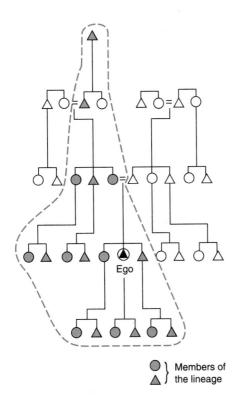

Figure 10.9   Cognatic Lineage
Descent is traced to an apical ancestor through males and/or females.

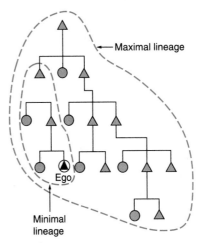

Figure 10.10   Patrilineages
Everyone on the diagram belongs to the same maximal lineage.

and depend on kindreds and extended families for their sub-sistence, industrial-age nuclear families often live far away from any relatives whatsoever and interact with their kindreds primarily at holidays, weddings, and funerals.

Determinants of Cognatic Lineages and Clans

Cognatic lineages and cognatic clans are associated with *ambilocality*. In this form of postmarital residence, the married couple elects to stay on a relatively permanent basis with either the wife's or the husband's domestic group. *Bilocality* differs from ambilocality only in implying rather short intervals between shifts of residence between wife's kin and husband's kin. *Neolocality* differs from both bilocality and ambilocality in not establishing residence with kin groups at all.

Ambilocality differs from the bilocality of simple hunting-and-gathering societies in that the lower frequency of residence change that accompanies ambilocality implies a relatively more sedentary form of village life and a somewhat greater potential for developing exclusive "corporate" interests in people and property. Yet all cognatic descent groups, whether bilateral or ambilineal, have less potential for corporate unity than unilineal descent groups, a point to which we return in a moment.

One example of how cognatic lineages work has already been discussed. Such lineages occurred among the Pacific Northwest Coast potlatchers (see Chapter 8). There, the Kwakiutl potlatch chiefs sought to attract and hold as large a labor force as they possibly could. (The more people a village put to work during a salmon run, the more fish they could catch.)

The core of each village consisted of a chieftain and his followers, usually demonstrably related to him through ambilineal descent and constituting a cognatic lineage known as a

Table 10.1
PRINCIPLE VARIETIES OF POSTMARITAL RESIDENCE

NAME OF PATTERN	PLACE WHERE MARRIED COUPLE RESIDES
Neolocality	Apart from either husband's or wife's kin
Bilocality	Alternately shifting from husband's kin to wife's kin
Ambilocality	Some couples with husband's kin, others with wife's kin
Patrilocality	With husband's father
Matrilocality	With wife's mother
Avunculocality	With husband's mother's brother
Amitalocality	With wife's father's sister
Uxorilocality	With the wife's kin (several of the above may be combined with uxorilocality)
Virilocality	With the husband's kin (several of the above may be combined with virilocality)

numaym. The chieftain claimed hereditary privileges and noble rank on the basis of ambilineal reckoning from his noble forebears. Validation of this status depended on his ability to recruit and hold an adequate following in the face of competition from like-minded neighbor chieftain competitors. The importance placed on individual choice and the uncertainty surrounding the group's corporate estate are typical of cognatic lineages in other cultures as well.

Determinants of Unilineal Lineages and Clans

Although there is no basis for reviving nineteenth-century notions of universal stages in the evolution of kinship (see Appendix), certain well-substantiated, general evolutionary trends do exist. For example, simple hunting-and-gathering societies tend to have cognatic descent groups or bilocal residence because their basic ecological adjustment demands that local groups remain open, flexible, and nonterritorial. With the development of horticulture and more settled village life, the identification between domestic groups or villages and definite territories increased and became more exclusive. Population density increased and warfare became more intense, for reasons to be discussed in Chapter 11, contributing to the need for emphasizing exclusive group unity and solidarity (Ember, Ember, and Pasternak 1974). Under these conditions, unilineal descent groups with well-defined localized membership cores, a heightened sense of solidarity, and an ideology of exclusive rights over resources and people became the predominant form of kinship group.

Using a sample of 797 agricultural societies, Michael Harner (1970) found that a very close statistical association exists between an increased reliance on agriculture as opposed to hunting and gathering and the replacement of cognatic descent groups by unilineal descent groups. Horticultural village societies that are organized unilineally outnumber those that are organized cognatically 380 to 111

in Harner's sample. Moreover, almost all the unilineal societies display signs of increased population pressure, as indicated by the depletion of wild plant and food resources. Unilineal descent groups are closely associated with one or the other variety of unilocal residence—that is, patrilineality with patrilocality and matrilineality with matrilocality. In addition, there is a close correlation between avunculocality and matrilineality.

With *patrilocality*, fathers, brothers, and sons form the core of the domestic group; whereas with *matrilocality*, mothers, sisters, and daughters form the core of the domestic group. But what about avunculocality? (Here things start to get a little rough but hold on!)

With *avunculocality*, mother's brothers and sister's sons form the core of the domestic unit. Sister's son is born in her husband's mother's brother's household, but as a juvenile or adult, sister's son leaves this household and takes up residence with his own mother's brother (Fig. 10.11). The way in which avunculocality works and the reason for its association with matrilineality will become clearer in a moment, as we examine the infrastructural causes of matrilocality and patrilocality.

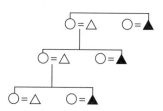

Figure 10.11 Avunculocality
All the males in the shaded area are related to each other as mother's brothers or sister's sons. (Tracing the lines across and up and down with your finger may help.)

Causes of Patrilocality

The overwhelming majority of known societies have male-centered residence and descent patterns. Seventy-one percent of 1,179 societies classified by George Murdock (1967) are either patrilocal or virilocal (Table 10.2); in the same sample, societies that have patrilineal kin groups outnumber societies that have matrilineal kin groups 588 to 164. Patrilocality and patrilineality are thus the statistically "normal" mode of domestic organization. They predominated not only in societies that have plows and draft animals or that practice pastoral nomadism, as was once thought, but also in simple horticultural and slash-and-burn societies (Divale 1974).

It is difficult to escape the conclusion that patrilocality among village societies prevails because cooperation among males is more often crucial than cooperation among females. Specifically, men are more effective in hand-to-hand combat than women, and women are less mobile than men during pregnancy and when nursing infants. As a consequence, men generally monopolize the weapons of war and the hunt, leading to male control over trade and politics. The practice of intense small-scale warfare between neighboring villages may be a crucial factor in promoting a widespread complex of male-centered and male-dominated institutions (Divale and Harris 1976). We will return to the issue of sex and gender hierarchies in Chapter 15.

Causes of Matrilocality

Why matrilocality? One theory holds that when women's role in food production became more important, as in horticultural societies, domestic groups tended to be structured around a core of females. This theory, however, must be rejected because there is no greater association between hor-ticulture and matrilocality than between horticulture and patrilocality (Ember and Ember 1971; Divale 1974). Moreover, why would field labor require a degree of cooperation so high that only women from the same domestic groups could carry it out efficiently? And why would it require all brothers and sons to be expelled from the natal domestic group (Burton and White 1987)?

The question we must ask concerning the origin of matrilocality is this: Under what conditions would the male specialties of warfare, hunting, and trade benefit from a shift to matrilocality (keeping in mind the clear advantage a shift from patrilocality to matrilocality offers to women)? The most likely answer is that when warfare, hunting, and trade change from quick, short-distance forays to long-distance expeditions lasting several months, matrilocality is more advantageous than patrilocality. When patrilocal males leave a village for extended periods, they leave behind their patrilineal kin group's corporate interests in property and people to be looked after solely by their wives. The allegiance of their wives, however, lies with another patrilineal kin group. A patrilocal group's women are drawn from different kin groups and have little incentive to cooperate among themselves in the absence of the male managers of the corporate domestic units into which they have married. No one is home "to mind the store," so to speak. Matrilocality solves this problem because it structures the domestic unit around a permanent core of resident mothers, daughters, and sisters who have been trained to cooperate with each other from birth and who identify the "minding of the store" with their own material and sentimental interests. Thus, matrilocal domestic groups are less likely to be disrupted by the prolonged absence of their adult males.

Furthermore, the ability to launch and successfully complete long-distance expeditions implies that neighboring villages will not attack each other when the men are away. Peace back home is best assured by forming the expeditions

Table 10.2

RELATIONSHIP BETWEEN RESIDENCE AND DESCENT
IN THE ETHNOGRAPHIC ATLAS

POSTMARITAL RESIDENCE

KIN GROUPS	MATRILOCAL OR UXORILOCAL	AVUNCULOCAL	PATRILOCAL OR VIRILOCAL	OTHER	TOTAL
Patrilineal	1	0	563	25	588
Matrilineal	53	62	30	19	164

Sources: Murdock 1967; Divale and Harris 1976.

around a core of males drawn from several neighboring villages or different households within a given village.

Among patrilocal, patrilineal villages, the belligerent territorial teams consist of patrilineally related kin who constitute competitive "fraternal interest groups." These groups make shifting alliances with neighboring villages, exchange sisters, and raid each other. Most combat takes place between villages that are about a day's walk from each other. Matrilocal, matrilineal cultures, on the other hand, are bonded not by the exchange of women but by the inmarrying of males from different domestic groups. Scattering fathers and brothers into several different households in different villages prevents the formation of competitive and disruptive fraternal interest groups.

Thus, matrilocal, matrilineal societies like the Iroquois of New York and the Huron of Ontario enjoy a high degree of internal peace. But most matrilineal societies, like the Iroquois and the Huron, also have a history of intense warfare directed outward against powerful enemies (Gramby 1977; Trigger 1978). The matrilineal Nayar, to cite another example, were a soldier caste in the service of the kings of Malabar. Also among the matrilocal Mundurucu of the Amazon, conflict between villages was unheard of, and interpersonal aggression was suppressed. But the Mundurucu launched raids against enemies hundreds of miles away, and unrelenting hostility and violence characterized their relations with the "outside world" (Murphy 1956). We will encounter other examples of warlike matrilineal societies in Chapter 12.

Causes of Avunculocality

In matrilocal, matrilineal societies, males reluctantly relinquish control over their own sons to the members of their wives' kin groups, and they are not easily reconciled to the fact that it is their sons rather than their daughters who must move away from them at marriage. One way to solve this problem is to loosen the male's marital obligations (already weak in matrilocal societies) to the point where he need not live with his wife at all. This is the path followed by the Nayar. Nayar men, you may recall (p. 109), had no home other than their natal domestic unit; they were not responsible for what happened to their children—whom they were scarcely able to identify—and they had no difficulty keeping their sisters and their nephews and nieces under fraternal and avuncular control.

But a more common solution to the tension between male interests and matrilineality is the development of avunculocal patterns of residence. It is a remarkable fact that more matrilineal groups are avunculocal than are matrilocal (Table 10.2).

Under avunculocality, a male eventually goes to live with his mother's brothers in their matrilineal domestic unit; his wife joins him there. At maturity, a male ego's son will in turn depart for ego's wife's brother's domestic unit. (Ego's daughter, however, may remain resident if she marries her father's sister's son.) Thus, the male core of an avunculocal domestic unit consists of a group of brothers and their sister's sons. The function of this arrangement seems to be to maintain a male fraternal interest group in the residential core of the matrilineal descent group. Avunculocality thus provides the best of two worlds for males who aspire to military and political leadership. They can influence and receive support from their sisters' sons and daughters, and at the same time, they can influence their own unmarried sons and daughters. Avunculocality is thus ideally suited for and correlated with the emergence of bellicose chiefdoms (Keegan and Maclachlan 1989).

The logical opposite of avunculocality is called *amitalocality* (amita means "aunt"). It exists where father's sisters reside in a patrilineal descent group along with the males of their patrilineage. This seems like an improbable arrangement, but it follows automatically if the male members of the patrilineage practice matrilateral cross cousin marriage (male ego marries mother's brother's daughter; female ego marries father's sister's son). Such groups contain male ego's paternal aunts. The combination of patrilineal descent and matrilateral cross cousin marriage does in fact occur in a number of societies. But the incidence of its occurrence both within and among the world's patrilineal societies is surrounded by uncertainties. Future research may demonstrate that amitalocality occurs as frequently as avunculocality. (cf. Ottenheimer 1984; personal communication 1993).

After a society has adopted matrilocality and developed matrilineal descent groups, changes in the original conditions may lead to a restoration of the patrilocal, patrilineal pattern. At any given moment, many societies are probably in a transitional state between one form of residence and another and one form of kinship ideology and another. Since the changes in residence and descent may not proceed in perfect tandem at any particular moment—that is, descent changes may lag behind residence changes—one should expect to encounter combinations of residence with the "wrong" descent rule. For example, a few patrilocal societies and quite a large number of virilocal societies have matrilineal descent, and one or two uxorilocal societies have patrilineal descent (Table 10.1). But evidence indicates a very powerful strain toward consistency in the alignment among domestic groups; their ecological, military, and economic adaptations; and their ideologies of descent.

Kinship Terminologies

Another aspect of domestic ideology that participates in the same strain toward functional consistency is *kinship terminology*. Every culture has a special set of terms (such as father, mother, cousin) for designating types of kin. The terms plus the rules for using them constitute a culture's kin terminological system.

Lewis Henry Morgan was the first anthropologist to realize that despite the thousands of languages on earth, and despite the immense number of kinship terms in these languages, there are only a handful of basic types of kin terminological systems. These systems can best be defined by the way terms are applied to a small set of kin on ego's own and ego's parent generation. Here we will examine three well-known systems in order to illustrate the nature of the causal and functional relationships that link alternative kinship terminologies to the other aspects of domestic organizations. (These are basic terminological types, actual instances often vary in details.)

ESKIMO TERMINOLOGY

The kin terminological system with which most North Americans are familiar is known as Eskimo, shown in Figure 10.12. This system has two important features: First, none of the terms applied to ego's nuclear relatives—1, 2, 6, 5—is applied outside the nuclear family, and second, there is no distinction between maternal and paternal links. This means that there is no distinction between cross and parallel cousins or between cross and parallel aunts or uncles. These features reflect the fact that societies using Eskimo terminology generally lack corporate descent groups. In the absence of such groups, the nuclear family tends to stand out as a separate and functionally dominant productive and reproductive unit. For this reason, its members are given a terminological identity separate from all other kin types. On the other hand, the lumping of all cousins under a single term (7) reflects the strength of bilateral as opposed to unilineal descent. The influence of bilateral descent is also reflected in the failure to distinguish terminologically between aunts and uncles on the mother's side and those on the father's side.

The theoretical predictions concerning Eskimo terminology are strongly confirmed by the tabulations of G. P. Murdock's *Ethnographic Atlas* (1967). Of the seventy-one societies having Eskimo terminology, only four have large extended families, and only thirteen have unilineal descent groups. In fifty-four of the seventy-one Eskimo terminology societies, descent groups are entirely absent or are represented only by kindreds.

As the name implies, "Eskimo" is frequently found among simple hunters and gatherers. As we have seen, simple hunting-and-gathering groups must remain mobile to cope with the movements of game and the seasonal fluctuations in the availability of plant foods. In industrial societies, the same terminological pattern reflects the high level of wage-induced social and geographic mobility.

HAWAIIAN TERMINOLOGY

Another common kin terminological system is known as Hawaiian. This system is easiest to portray since it has the fewest number of terms (Fig. 10.13). In some versions, even the distinction between the sexes is dropped, leaving one term for the members of ego's generation and another for the members of ego's parents' generation. The most remarkable feature of Hawaiian terminology, as compared with Eskimo, is the application of the same terms to people inside and outside the nuclear family. Hawaiian is thus compatible with situations where the nuclear family is submerged within a domestic context dominated by extended families and other corporate descent groups. In Murdock's *Ethnographic Atlas*, 21 percent of the Hawaiian terminology societies do indeed have large extended families. In addition, well over 50 percent of Hawaiian terminology societies have some form of corporate descent group other than extended families.

Theoretically, most of these descent groups should be cognatic rather than unilineal. The reason for this prediction is that the merging of relatives on the maternal side with those on the paternal side indicates an indifference toward unilineality, and an indifference toward unilineality is logically consistent with ambilineal or bilateral descent. However, data from Murdock's ethnographic sample only partially support this prediction. Indeed, many more Hawaiian terminology societies have cognatic as opposed to unilineal descent, but there are also many exceptions for which as yet no generally accepted explanation is available.

IROQUOIS TERMINOLOGY

In the presence of unilineal kin groups, we find a worldwide tendency to distinguish parallel from cross cousins, as previously noted. This pattern is widely associated with a

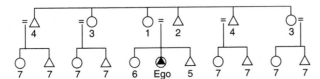

Figure 10.12   Eskimo Terminology

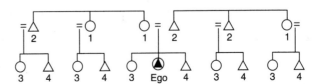

Figure 10.13   Hawaiian Terminology

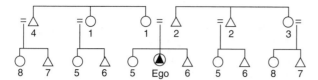

Figure 10.14   Iroquois Terminology

similar distinction in the first ascending generation, whereby father's brothers are distinguished from mother's brothers and father's sisters are distinguished from mother's sisters.

An Iroquois terminology exists where—in addition to these distinctions between cross and parallel cousins and cross and parallel aunts and uncles—mother's sister is terminologically merged with mother, father's brother is terminologically merged with father, and parallel cousins are terminologically merged with ego's brothers and sisters (Fig. 10.14). This pattern of merging occurs largely as a result of the shared membership of siblings in corporate unilineal descent groups and of the marriage alliances based on cross cousin marriage between such groups. In Murdock's ethnographic sample, 166 societies have Iroquois terminology. Of these, 119 have some form of unilineal descent group (70 percent).

We have only skimmed the surface of a few of the many fascinating and important problems in the field of kinship terminology (Fig. 10.15). But perhaps enough has been said to establish at least one point: Kin terminological systems possess a remarkable logical coherence. Yet like so many other aspects of culture, kin terminological systems are never

the planned product of any inventive genius. Most people are unaware that such systems even exist. Clearly, the major features of these systems represent recurrent unconscious adjustments to the prevailing conditions of domestic life. Yet many details of kin terminologies, as well as of other kinship phenomena, still are not well understood.

Chapter Summary

To study kinship is to study the ideologies that justify and normalize the corporate structure of domestic groups. The basis of kinship is the tracing of relationships through marriage and descent. Descent is the belief that certain persons play a special role in the conception, birth, or nurturance of certain children. Many folk theories of descent exist, none of which corresponds precisely to modern-day scientific understandings of procreation and reproduction.

The principal varieties of cognatic descent rules are the bilateral and the ambilineal; these are associated, respectively, with kindreds on the one hand, and with cognatic lineages and clans on the other. The principal varieties of unilineal descent are matrilineality and patrilineality. These are associated, respectively, with patri- and matrilineages or patri- and matriclans.

An important key to understanding alternative modes of descent and domestic organization is the pattern of postmarital residence. Bilateral descent and bilateral descent groups are associated with neolocality, bilocality, and ambilocality.

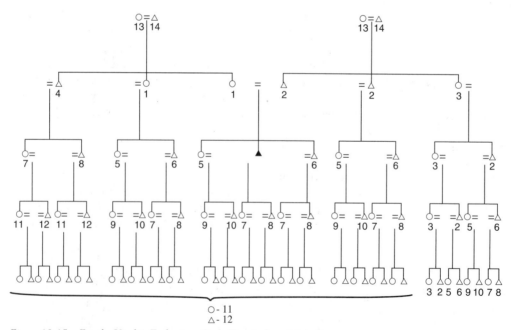

Figure 10.15   For the Kinship Enthusiast: Crow Terminology, Male Ego

More specifically, the flexible and mobile forms of band organization are facilitated by bilocality, whereas the greater isolation of nuclear families in price–market economies gives rise to neolocality. Cognatic lineages and clans, on the other hand, give functional expression to ambilocality.

Unilineal domestic groups reflect unilocal patterns of residence. These patterns in turn imply well-defined membership cores and an emphasis on exclusive rights over resources and people. A strong correlation exists between patrilocality and patrilineality on the one hand, and among matrilineality, matrilocality, and avunculocality on the other. Patrilocal and patrilineal groups are far more common than matrilocal, matrilineal, or avunculocal groups. A reason for this is that warfare, hunting, and trading activities among village societies are monopolized by males. These activities, in turn, are facilitated by stressing the coresidence of fathers, brothers, and sons and the formation of fraternal interest groups.

Under conditions of increasing population density and pressure on resources, local groups may find it adaptive to engage in long-distance war–trade–hunting expeditions. Such expeditions are facilitated by breaking up the fraternal interest groups and structuring domestic life around a residential core of mothers, sisters, and daughters or, in other words, by developing a matrilocal, matrilineal organization. Since males in matrilineal, matrilocal societies continue to dominate military and political institutions, they are inclined to reinject the patrilineal principle into domestic life and to reassert control over their sons and daughters. This tendency accounts for the fact that as many matrilineal societies are avunculocal as are matrilocal.

Thus, the principal function of alternative rules of descent and postmarital residence may be described as the establishment and maintenance of networks of cooperative and interdependent kinspeople aggregated into ecologically effective and militarily secure domestic production and reproduction units. For such units to act effectively and reliably, they must share an organizational ideology that interprets and validates the structure of the group and the behavior of its members. Kinship is that shared organizational ideology.

This interpretation of descent and postmarital residence rules can also be applied to the principal varieties of kin terminological systems. Such systems tend to classify relatives in conformity with the major features of domestic organization, locality practices, and descent rules. Eskimo terminology, for example, is functionally associated with domestic organizations in which nuclear families tend to be mobile and isolated; Hawaiian terminology is functionally associated with cognatic lineages and cognatic clans; and Iroquois terminology, with its emphasis on the distinction between cross and parallel cousins, is functionally associated with unilinear descent groups.

AMERICA NOW UPDATE

Future Family

At the beginning of the century, most marriages in the United States were entered into for life, and families were headed by male breadwinners. Each married pair had on the average three or more children, and the children were brought up by their natural parents unless the marriage was terminated through death. Today, matrifocal domestic groups are the fastest-growing form of family, up by 80 percent since 1960. Largely as a result of divorce, separation, and growth of female-headed families, 45 percent of all children born today in the United States can expect to live with only one parent for some period before they reach the age of 18.

Very little is known as yet about how parents, stepparents, stepsiblings, children, and stepchildren are dealing with each other—what kinds of bonds they form, what kinds of responsibilities they accept, and what kinds of conflicts they experience (Weitzman 1985; Stacey 1990; Box 10.2). It seems likely, however, that higher divorce rates for second and third marriages are linked to the strains of coping with the nation's 6.5 million stepchildren under age 18 (Collins 1985: 15).

Box 10.2

FUTURE FAMILY?

Chapter 11

LAW, ORDER, AND WAR IN NONSTATE SOCIETIES

Cheyenne warriors.

As we continue with the structural aspect of sociocultural systems, the focus shifts from the structure of domestic groups to the regulation of interpersonal relationships and the maintenance of political cohesion and law and order within and between band and village societies. These societies enjoy a high degree of personal security without having written laws, police officers, jails, or any of the other parts of modern criminal justice systems. How do they do it? This is not to say that band and village societies have no violence. On the contrary, feuds and warfare do occur even among hunter-gatherers and small village societies that have very low population densities. Why do they do it? Some anthropologists argue that the propensity to engage in armed combat is part of human nature. Others, however, point out that low population density does not mean that there are no scarce resources worth fighting over. In one important case, at least, a scarce resource seems to be game animals. War, as we shall see, springs no more from human nature than peace.

Law and Order in Band and Village Societies

In every society, people have conflicting interests (Fig. 11.1). Even in band-level societies, old and young, sick and healthy, men and women do not want the same thing at the same time. Moreover, in every society people want something that others possess and are reluctant to give away. Every culture, therefore, must have structural provisions for resolving conflicts of interest in an orderly fashion and for preventing conflicts from escalating into disruptive confrontations. Band and village societies however, have distinctive conflicting interests and distinctive methods for preventing disruptive confrontations.

Simple hunter–gatherer societies such as the Innuit, the !Kung San, or native Australians enjoy a high degree of personal security without having any rulers or law-and-order specialists. They have no kings, queens, dictators, presidents, governors, or mayors; police forces, soldiers, sailors, or marines; CIA, FBI, treasury agents, or federal marshals. They have no written law codes and no formal law courts; no lawyers, bailiffs, judges, district attorneys, juries, or court clerks; and no patrol cars, paddy wagons, jails, or penitentiaries. This is also true of many village societies. How do people get along without law enforcement specialists and facilities, and why are modern societies so dependent on them?

The basic reasons for the differences are: (1) the small size of the bands and villages; (2) the central importance of domestic groups and kinship in their social organization; and (3) the absence of marked inequalities in access to technology and resources. Small size means that everyone knows everyone else personally; therefore, the group can identify stingy, aggressive, and disruptive individuals and expose them to the pressure of public opinion. The centrality of domestic group and kinship relations means that reciprocity can be the

chief mode of exchange and that the collective interests of the domestic unit can be recognized by all its members. Finally, equality of access to technology and natural resources means that food and other forms of wealth cannot be withheld by a wealthy few while others endure shortages and hardships.

Primitive Communism?

Among small band and village societies, all adults usually have access to the rivers, lakes, beaches, and oceans; to all the plants and animals; and to the soil and the subsoil. Insofar as these are basic to the extraction of life-sustaining energy and materials, they are communal property (Lee 1990).

Among the !Kung San, waterholes and hunting-and-gathering territories are said to be "owned" by the residential core of particular bands. But since neighboring bands contain many intermarried kin, they commonly share access to resources as a result of mutual visiting. Neighbors who ask for permission to visit and exploit the resources of a particular camp are seldom refused. Even people who come from distant bands and who lack close kin ties with the hosts are usually given permission to stay, especially for short periods, since all parties understand that the hosts may return the visit at some future date (Lee 1979: 337).

The prevalence of communal ownership of land, however, does not mean that simple hunter-gatherers lack private property altogether. There is little support for the theory of "primitive communism," which describes a universal stage in the development of culture marked by the complete absence of private property. Many material objects are effectively controlled ("owned") by specific individuals in band-level societies, especially items the user has produced. The members of

Figure 11.1   Yanomami Club Fight
Egalitarian societies are not without problems of law and order.

even the most egalitarian societies usually believe that weapons, clothing, containers, ornaments, tools, and other "personal effects" ought not to be taken away or used without the consent of the "owner." However, the chance is remote that theft or misappropriation of such objects will lead to serious conflict (Woodburn 1982a). Why not?

First, the accumulation of material possessions is rigidly limited by the recurrent need to break camp and travel long distances on foot. In addition, most utilitarian items may be borrowed without difficulty when the owner is not using them. If there are not enough such items to go around (arrows, projectile points, nets, bark or gourd containers), easy access to the raw materials and mastery of the requisite skills provide the have-nots with the chance of making their own. Moreover, among societies having no more than a few hundred people, thieves cannot be anonymous. If stealing becomes habitual, a coalition of the injured parties will eventually take action. If you want something, better to ask for it openly. Most such requests are readily obliged since reciprocity is the prevailing mode of exchange. Finally, contrary to the experience of the successful modern bank robber, no one can make a living from stealing bows and arrows or feather headdresses since band-level societies have no regular market at which such items can be exchanged for food (see Chapter 8).

Mobilizing Public Opinion

Control of disputes in small egalitarian societies depends on the actions of the disputants' kin groups. As long as the disputants feel they have the backing of their kin groups, they will continue to press their claims and counterclaims. The members of their kin groups, however, are not eager to be caught in a situation in which they are opposed by a majority of people.

Public opinion influences the support disputants can expect from their kin. Often, what matters is not so much who is morally right or wrong, or who is lying or telling the truth; the important thing is to mobilize public opinion on one side or the other decisively enough to prevent the outbreak of large-scale feuding.

A classic example of how such mobilization can be achieved independently of abstract principles of justice is the song contest of the central and eastern Innuit (Fig. 11.2). Here, it is common for one man to claim that another has stolen his wife. The counterclaim is that she was not stolen but left voluntarily because her husband "was not man enough" to take good care of her. The issue is settled at a large public meeting that might be likened to a court. But no testimony is taken in support of either of the two versions of why the wife has left her husband. Instead, the disputants

Figure 11.2   Song Contest
Innuit "disputants" in "court" in eastern Greenland.

take turns singing insulting songs at each other. The "court" responds to each performance with different degrees of laughter. Eventually one of the singers gets flustered, and the hooting and hollering raised against him become total—even his relatives have a hard time not laughing (Box 11.1).

The Innuit have no police–military specialists to see to it that the "decision" is enforced. Yet, chances are that the man who has lost the song duel will give in since he can no longer count on anyone to back him up if he chooses to escalate the dispute. Nonetheless, the defeated man may decide to go it alone, and wife stealing does occasionally lead to murder. When this happens, the man who has lost public support may survive on the strength of his own vigilance and fighting skill. He will probably have to kill again, however, and with each transgression, the coalition against him becomes larger and more determined, until finally they kill him in an ambush.

Shamans and Public Opinion

In small, egalitarian societies, part-time magico-religious specialists known as *shamans* play an important role in mobilizing public opinion and in eliminating persistent sources of conflict. Most cultures reject the idea that misfortune results from "natural" causes. If animals suddenly become scarce or if several people fall sick, they assume that somebody is practicing witchcraft. It is the shaman's job to identify the culprit. Normally this is done through the art of divination, or clairvoyance. Putting themselves into trances with the aid of drugs, tobacco smoke, or monotonous drumming (see p. 225), shamans discover the name of the culprit. The people demand vengeance, and the culprit is ambushed and murdered.

The chances are that the murdered individual never attempted to carry out any witchcraft at all! In other words, the witches are probably wholly "innocent" of the crime with which they have been charged. Nonetheless, the shaman's witchcraft accusations usually conserve rather than destroy the group's feeling of unity because the person identified as the perpetrator is regarded as a troublemaker and lacks support from his kin (Box 11.2).

This system is not "fail-safe." Many cases are known of witchcraft systems that seem to have broken down, involving the community in a series of destructive retaliatory accusations and murders. These cases, however (especially in situations of intensive colonial contact, as in Africa and Melanesia), must be carefully related to the underlying conditions of communal life. In general, the incidence of witchcraft accusations varies with the amount of community dissension and frustration (Nadel 1952; Mair 1969). When a traditional culture is upset by exposure to new diseases, increased competition for land, and recruitment for wage labor, an epoch of increased dissension and frustration can be expected. This period will also be characterized by frenzied activity among those who are skilled in tracking down and exposing the malevolent effects of witches, as in the case of the breakup of feudal society in Europe and the great witch craze of the fifteenth to seventeenth centuries.

Box 11.1

INNUIT SONG

Something was whispered

Of a man and wife

Who could not agree

And what was it all about?

A wife who in rightful anger

Tore her husband's furs,

Took their boat

And rowed away with her son.

Ay-ay, all who listen,

What do you think of him

Who is great in his anger

But faint in strength,

Blubbering helplessly?

He got what he deserved

Though it was he who proudly

Started this quarrel with stupid words.

Adapted from Rasmussen 1929: 231–232.

Headmanship

To the extent that political leadership can be said to exist at all among small societies, it is exercised by headmen or, less commonly, headwomen. The *headman*, unlike such specialists as king, president, or dictator, is a relatively powerless figure incapable of compelling obedience. When he gives a command, he is never certain of being able to punish physically those who disobey. (Hence, if he wants to stay in "office," he gives few direct commands.) In contrast, the political power of genuine rulers depends on their ability to expel or exterminate any readily foreseeable combination of nonconforming individuals and groups. Genuine rulers control access to basic resources and to the tools and weapons for hurting or killing people.

Among the Innuit, leadership is especially diffuse, being closely related to success in hunting. A group will follow an outstanding hunter and defer to his opinion with respect to choice of hunting spots. But in all other matters, the "leader's" opinion carries no more weight than any other adult's opinion.

Similarly, among the !Kung San, each band has its recognized "leaders." Such leaders may speak out more than others and are listened to with a bit more deference than is usual, but they "have no formal authority" and "can only persuade, but never enforce their will on others" (Lee 1979: 333–334, 1982). When Richard Lee asked the !Kung San whether they had "headmen" in the sense of powerful chiefs, he was told: "Of course we have headmen! In fact we are all headmen. Each one of us is headman over himself" (Lee 1979: 348).

A similar pattern of leadership is reported for the Semai of Malaysia. Despite recent attempts by the Malaysian government to bolster the power of Semai leaders, the headman is merely the most prestigious figure among a group of peers. In the words of Robert Dentan, who carried out fieldwork among these egalitarian shifting horticulturalists, the headman

> keeps the peace by conciliation rather than coercion. He must be personally respected. Otherwise people will drift away from him or gradually stop paying attention to him. Moreover, the Semai recognize only two or three occasions on which he can assert his authority: dealing as a representative of his people with non-Semai; mediating a quarrel, if invited by the quarreling parties to do so but not otherwise; and selecting and apportioning land for fields. Furthermore, most of the time a good headman gauges the general feeling about an issue and bases his decision on that, so that he is more a spokesman for public opinion than a molder of it.

[1968: 681]

The impression given by descriptions of headmanship among Brazilian Indian groups, such as the Mehinacu of Brazil's Xingu National Park, is that it is a thankless and frustrating job (Box 11.3). The first one up in the morning, the headman tries to rouse his companions by standing in the middle of the village plaza and shouting. If a task needs to be done, it is the headman who starts doing it, and it is the headman who works at it harder than anyone else. Moreover, the headman must set an example not only for hard work but for generosity. After a fishing or hunting expedition, he is expected to give away more of the catch than anyone else; if trade goods are obtained, he must be careful not to keep the best pieces for himself (Fig. 11.4).

The Leopard Skin Chief

As we have seen, the ever-present danger confronting societies that lack genuine rulers is that their kinship groups tend to react as units to real or alleged aggression against one of their members. In this way, disputes involving individuals may escalate. The worst danger arises from disputes that lead

---

Box 11.2

How to Choose a Witch

Gertrude Dole (1966) reported the following events among the Kuikuru—an egalitarian Brazilian Indian society. Lightning had set fire to two houses (Fig. 11.3). The shaman went into a trance and discovered that the lightning had been sent by a man who had left the village some years previously and had never returned. This man had only one male relative, who was also no longer living in the village. Before the accused witch had departed, he had tried unsuccessfully to court a girl whom the shaman's brother wanted to marry. During his trance, the shaman carried out a dialogue with various members of the village. When he finally disclosed the identity of the culprit, he was readily believed. As the excitement grew, the shaman's brother and several companions left the village to kill the man suspected of witchcraft (1966: 761).

Among the Kuikuru, a change of residence from one village to another usually indicates that there is trouble brewing and that, in effect, the individual has been ostracized. Thus, the witch was not a randomly chosen figure but one who fulfilled several well-defined criteria: a history of disputes and quarrels within the village, a motivation for continuing to do harm (the unsuccessful courtship), and weak backing from kin.

Figure 11.3 Kuikuru Shaman
The shaman is leaving the village with his assistants on the way to a nearby lake to recover the lost soul of a patient lying ill in the house seen in the background. The shaman intends to dive to the bottom of the lake and wrest the soul away from the evil spirit who stole it from the patient, and then implant it back into the patient's body.

---

to homicide. The members of most simple band and village societies believe that the only proper reaction to a murder is to kill the murderer or any convenient member of the murderer's kin group. Yet, the absence of centralized political authority does not mean that blood feuds cannot be brought under control.

Mechanisms for preventing homicide from flaring into a protracted feud include the transfer of substantial amounts of prized possessions from the slayer's kin group to the victim's kin group. This practice is especially common and effective among pastoral peoples, whose animals are a concentrated form of material wealth and for whom bride-price is a regular aspect of kin-group exogamy.

For example, the Nuer, a pastoral and farming people who live amid the marshy grasslands of the Upper Nile in the Sudan, have no centralized political leadership (Box 11.4). The Nuer settle their feuds (or at least deescalate them) by transferring forty or more head of cattle to the victim's affines and kin. If a man has been killed, these animals will be used to "buy" a wife whose sons will fill the void left by his death. The dead man's closest kin are obliged to resist the offer of cattle, demanding instead a life for a life. However, more distant kin do their best to convince the others to accept the compensation. In this effort, they are aided by certain semisacred arbitration specialists. The latter, known as *leopard skin chiefs* (Fig. 11.5), are usually men whose kin groups are not

Box 11.3

THE RIGHT STUFF

The most significant qualifications for Mehinacu chieftainship [headman] are learned skills and personal attributes. The chief, for example, is expected to excel at public speaking. Each evening he should stand in the center of the plaza and exhort his fellow tribesmen to be good citizens. He must call upon them to work hard in their gardens, to take frequent baths, not to sleep during the day, not to be angry with each other, and not to have sexual relations too frequently. In addition to being a skilled orator, the chief is expected to be a generous man. This means that when he returns from a successful fishing trip, he will bring most of his catch out to the men's houses where it is cooked and shared by the men of the tribe. His wife must be generous, bringing manioc cakes and pepper to the men whenever they call for it. Further, the chief must be willing to part with possessions. When one of the men catches a harpy eagle, for example, the chief must buy it from him with a valuable shell belt in the name of the entire tribe. A chief should also be a man who never becomes angry in public. In his public speeches he should never criticize any of his fellow tribesmen, no matter how badly they may have affronted the chief or the tribe as a whole.

Gregor 1969: 88–89.

represented locally and who can hence act more readily as neutral intermediaries.

The leopard skin chief is the only one who can ritually cleanse a murderer. If a homicide takes place, the killer flees at once to the leopard skin chief's house, which is a sanctuary respected by all Nuer. Nonetheless, the leopard skin chief lacks even the rudiments of political power; the most he can do to the reluctant members of the slain man's relatives is to threaten them with various supernatural curses. Yet, the desire to prevent a feud is so great that the injured relatives eventually accept the cattle as compensation.

Nonkin Associations: Sodalities

Although relations of affinity and descent dominate the political life of headman-type societies, nonkin groups also occur to a limited extent. Such groups are called *sodalities*. A

common form of sodality is the exclusive men's or women's association, or club. These associations usually involve men and women drawn from different domestic groups who cooperate in secret ritual or craft performances. We will discuss these organizations in Chapter 15, which is devoted to gender hierarchies.

Age–grade associations are another common form of sodality, already mentioned with respect to the Masai warrior camps (p. 103). Among the Samburu, another group of East African pastoralists, all men initiated into manhood over a span of about 12 to 14 years composed an age set whose members had a special feeling of solidarity that cut across domestic and lineage kin groups. The age-set members advanced as a group from junior to senior status. As juniors, they were responsible for military combat, and as seniors, they were responsible for initiating and training the upcoming age sets (Spencer 1965; Kertzer 1978; Bernardi 1985).

A classic case of sodality is the native North American military associations that developed on the Great Plains after the introduction of the horse. Among the Crow and the Cheyenne, these associations tried to outdo one another in acts of daring during combat and in horse-stealing expeditions. Although the members of each club did not fight as a unit, they met in their tepees to reminisce and sing about their exploits, and they wore distinctive insignia and clothing.

Gretel and Pertti Pelto (1976: 324) have aptly compared them to organizations like the Veterans of Foreign Wars and the American Legion because their main function was to celebrate military exploits and to uphold the honor and prestige of the "tribe." However, on the occasion of a long march to a new territory or on large-scale collective hunts, the military clubs took turns supervising and policing the general population. For example, they prevented overeager hunters from stampeding the buffalo herds, and they suppressed rowdy behavior at ceremonials by fining or banishing disruptive individuals. But these were only seasonal functions since only during the spring and summer could large numbers of unrelated people congregate.

Warfare Among Hunters and Gatherers

We turn now to the subject of warfare as an aspect of the maintenance of law and order between nonstate societies. War is armed combat between groups of people who constitute separate territorial teams or political communities (Otterbein 1994). By this definition, feuds, "grudge fights," and "raiding" constitute warfare. Some anthropologists hold that warfare is universally practiced, and that it occurred as far back in time as the early Stone Age (Lizot 1979: 151). By excluding feuds and raids from their definitions of warfare, however, others hold that it was absent or uncommon until

Figure 11.4 Mehinacu Headmanship
In front of the men's house, the headman is redistributing presents given to him by the ethnographer.

The lack of governmental organs among the Nuer, the absence of legal institutions of developed leadership, and generally, of organized political life is remarkable. The ordered anarchy in which they live accords well with their character, for it is impossible to live among Nuer and conceive of rulers ruling over them. The Nuer is a product of hard and egalitarian upbringing, is deeply democratic, and is easily roused to violence. This turbulent spirit finds any restraint irksome and no man recognizes a superior. Wealth makes no difference. A man with many cattle is envied but not treated differently from a man with few cattle. Birth makes no difference. There is no master or servant in their society but only equals who regard themselves as God's noblest creation. Among themselves, even the suspicion of an order riles a man; he will not submit to any authority that clashes with his own interest, and he does not consider himself bound to anyone.

Adapted from Evans-Pritchard 1940: 181–182.

---

the advent of chiefdoms and states (Ferguson 1989a: 197; Reyna 1989). Several hunter–gatherer societies—the Andaman Islanders, the Shoshoni, the Yahgan, the Mission Indians of California (Lesser 1968; MacLeish 1972), and the Greenland Eskimo (Weyer 1932: 109–110)—have been offered as exceptions to the claim that warfare is a universal feature of human social life. But the peacefulness of these groups may result from their having suffered defeat when they practiced warfare in earlier times. William Divale (1972) lists thirty-seven hunting-and-gathering societies in which warfare (feuds and raids included) is known to have been practiced. But some anthropologists attribute these cases to the shocks of contact with state societies.

Archaeologists who have studied the pattern of dented, broken, and perforated bones suggest that warfare occurred among simple hunter-gatherers during periods of population increase and environmental stress. For example, in the Channel Islands off the coast of California, skull fractures attributable to clubs and projectiles increase in tandem with the growth of population during the prehistoric period. A similar increase on the mainland where populations could disperse was not observed (P. Walker 1988).

Tiwi Warfare

The slippery line between warfare and personal retribution among hunters and gatherers is well illustrated in the example of armed conflict among the Tiwi of Bathurst and Melville islands, northern Australia (Fig. 11.6). As recounted by C. W. Hart and Arnold Pilling (1960), a number of men from the Tiklauila and Rangwila bands developed personal grievances against a number of men who were residing with the Mandiimbula band. The aggrieved individuals,

Figure 11.5   Leopard Skin Chief

Figure 11.6   Tiwi Warrior
Tiwi man dressed in traditional body paint and feathers.

together with their relatives, put on the white paint of war, armed themselves, and set off, some thirty strong, to do battle with the Mandiimbula at a predetermined clearing. Both sides then exchanged a few insults and agreed to meet formally in the morning.

During the night, individuals from both groups visited each other, renewing acquaintances. In the morning, the two armies lined up at the opposite sides of the battlefield. Hostilities were begun by elders shouting insults and accusations at particular individuals in the enemy ranks. Although some of the old men urged that a general attack be launched, their grievances turned out to be directed not at the Mandiimbula band but at one or at most two or three individuals: "Hence when spears began to be thrown, they were thrown by individuals for reasons based on individual disputes (Hart and Pilling 1960: 84). Marksmanship was poor

because it was the old men who did most of the spear-throwing. Not infrequently the person hit was an old woman whose reflexes for dodging spears were not as fast as those of the men. As soon as somebody was wounded, fighting stopped immediately until the implications of this new incident could be assessed.

Although hunters and gatherers seldom try to annihilate each other and often retire from the field after one or two casualties have occurred, the cumulative effect may be quite considerable. Remember that the average !Kung San band has only about thirty people. If such a band engages in war only twice in a generation, each time with the loss of only one adult male, casualties due to warfare would account for more than 10 percent of all adult male deaths.

This is an extremely high figure when one realizes that less than 1 percent of all male deaths in Europe and the United States during the twentieth century have been battlefield casualties. In contrast, Lloyd Warner (1958) estimated that 28 percent of the adult male deaths among the Murngin, a hunter–gatherer society of northern Australia, resulted from battlefield casualties.

Warfare Among Sedentary Village Societies

Although village peoples (including complex hunter-gatherers and small agricultural societies) were not the first to practice warfare, they did expand the scale and ferocity of military engagements. Village peoples have more possessions to defend such as storehouses filled with food, garden lands with crops growing on them, or prime fishing spots. They cannot resolve disputes with other villages by simply moving off to a more remote territory. Thus, warfare among village societies is likely to be more costly in terms of battle casualties than among nonsedentary hunters and gatherers.

Among the Yanomami (Fig. 11.7) of Brazil and Venezuela, who are reputed to have one of the world's "fiercest" and most warlike cultures, sneak raids and ambushes account for about 33 percent of adult male deaths and about 7 percent of adult female deaths from all causes (Chagnon 1974: 160–161).

Among the more populous village-dwelling Dani of West Irian, New Guinea, warfare has an open-field, ritualistic phase (which resembles the encounters described for the Tiwi) in which casualties are light. But sneak "genocidal" attacks also occur, resulting in 100 fatalities at a time and in the destruction and expulsion of whole villages. Karl Heider (1972) estimates that the Dani lost about 0.5 percent of their population per year to warfare and that 29 percent of the men

and 3 percent of the women died as a result of battle injuries incurred primarily in raids and ambushes (Fig. 11.8).

Why War?

Anthropologists have offered a number of explanations for warfare in nonstate societies: (1) war as instinct, (2) war as sport and entertainment, (3) war as revenge, (4) war as a struggle for reproductive success, and (5) war as a struggle for material benefits.

1. War as instinct: This explanation proposes that we humans have innate aggressive tendencies that make us hate other people and want to kill them. Warfare is just one of the ways by which this tendency expresses itself (Lizot 1979: 151).

Comment: As a species, we are certainly capable of aggression on an unparalleled scale. But the capacity for collective violence does not explain the occurrence of war because even warlike societies fight only occasionally, and some societies have no war at all. This peacetime–wartime cycle cannot be explained by the constants of human nature. Rather the explanation must be sought in the variable conditions of society and culture (Ferguson 1984: 12). For example, aggressive tendencies could be suppressed, controlled, or expressed in ways other than by armed combat. War is a particular form

Figure 11.7 Yanomami Warriors
Preparations for battle include body painting and "line-ups."

Figure 11.8   Dani at War

of organized activity that has developed during cultural evolution just as have other structural features, such as trade, the division of labor, and domestic groups. Just as there is no instinct for trade, for domestic organization, or for the division of labor, so there is no instinct for war.

2. War as sport and entertainment: War is a big game. People enjoy the thrill of using martial arts and risking their lives in combat. (It's better than the movies.)

Comment: Combat is seldom entered into light-heartedly; the warriors need to "psych themselves up" with ritual dancing and singing, and often set out only after they have subdued their fears by taking psychotropic drugs.

3. War as revenge: This is the most common explanation for going to war given by nonstate combatants. It is frequently accompanied by the belief that the spirits of the ancestors who have been killed in previous battles will not rest unless a relative of the culprit is killed in turn. The desire for revenge keeps wars going generation after generation whether the combatants win or lose.

Comment: Vengeance is undoubtedly a powerful motivation. But it does not have an unlimited power to keep wars going. As Brian Ferguson (1992: 223) points out with respect to the Yanomami, combatants can declare that their ancestors have been avenged and stop fighting. Further, the avengers-to-be can simply forget the incident they are supposed to avenge or attribute it to a group that was not involved in past hostilities. Vengeance is thus a rationalization for continuing hostilities, but it does not explain why the hostilities got started, nor why old hostilities give way to new ones. "The decision to retaliate is a tactical one, a part of the process of war, rather than its cause." (Ferguson 1989: 564).

4. War as a struggle for reproductive success: Sociobiologists explain nonstate warfare as a means of obtaining higher rates of reproductive success. The fiercer the warrior, the more wives he will have, the greater the number of surviving children. Thus natural selection favors the practice of warfare. Napoleon Chagnon (1989, 1990) has attempted to show how this theory applies to warfare among the Yanomami where men who have killed, on the average, have more wives and children than men who have not killed.

Comment: Aside from more general criticisms of human sociobiology (see p. 278) that are applicable to this theory, the predicted relationship between fierceness in war and reproductive success is in doubt among the Yanomami (Ferguson 1989; cf. Chagnon 1989). One of the problems is that those who "live by the spear" are more likely to "die by the spear." In fact the man with the greatest number of kills among the Yanomami (twenty-two) died without leaving any descendants.

This theory has also been shown to be inapplicable to the Cheyenne, one of the most warlike of the Indian peoples who lived in the region of the Great Plains (see p. 132). The fiercest Cheyenne warriors were young men who were so indifferent to the risks of battle, that combat for them was in effect a form of suicide. Not only did they die young but many of them took vows of chastity in order to concentrate all of their energies on war, and died without heirs (Moore 1990).

5. War as a struggle for material benefits: Nonstate war is fought only to the extent that it is materially advantageous for some of the combatants. This is the point of view held by cultural materialists and the one that I favor (the theory, not the war!) (Balee 1984; Biolsi 1984; Ferguson 1984, 1989a and b; Shankman 1991; but see Knauft 1990 for contrary view).

Nonstate warfare almost always involves a response to population pressure. Population pressure manifests itself in hunger, malnutrition, poor health, high mortality rates, infanticide, diminishing returns, and environmental depletions. If a practice reduces the rate of growth or the density of a specific population and results in less hunger, better health, lower mortality, less infanticide, higher returns on labor, and less environmental depletion, it is a practice that reduces population pressure. (See p. 61 for distinction between population growth, population density, and population pressure.) In nonstate societies, warfare is such a practice, especially if you are on the winning side. It slows population growth through combat deaths, thins out population density by dispersing or routing the losers, and provides the winners with access to valuable resources such as game animals and garden lands. Of course, warfare has its costs, principally in the form of combat deaths. But the crucial question concerning these deaths is whether mortality rates would be higher or lower without them. If nonstate warfare does regulate population growth and if it does consequently prevent depletions, then the answer to this question is that it lowers rather than raises mortality rates, at least from the point of view of the winning side.

Much evidence suggest that nonstate warfare results in substantial immediate material gains related to the relief of population pressure. In his study of warfare among the Mae Enga of the western highlands of Papua, New Guinea, Mervyn Meggit estimates that aggressor groups succeeded in gaining significant amounts of enemy land in 75 percent of their wars. "Given that the initiation of warfare usually pays off for the aggressors, it is not surprising that the Mae count warfare as well worth the cost in human casualties" (1977: 14–15). More general confirmation of this point has been supplied by Melvin and Carol Ember (1992), who have found in a study of a sample of 186 societies that preindustrial people mostly go to war to cushion or moderate the impact of unpredictable (rather than chronic) food shortages and that the victorious side almost always takes some resources from the losers.

Game Animals and Warfare: The Yanomami

The Yanomami provide an important test of the theory that warfare has an infrastructural basis even among band and village groups that have very low population densities. The Yanomami, with a population density of less than one person per square mile, derive their main source of food calories, with little effort, from the plantains and banana trees that grow in their forest gardens. Like the Tsembaga Maring (p. 53), they burn the forest to get these gardens started, but bananas and plantains are perennials that provide high yields per unit of labor input for many consecutive years. Since the Yanomami live amid the world's greatest tropical forest, the little burning they do scarcely threatens to "eat up the trees." A typical Yanomami village has fewer than 100 people in it, a population that could easily grow enough bananas or plantains in nearby garden sites without ever having to move (Fig. 11.9). Yet the Yanomami villages constantly break up into factions that move off into new territories.

Despite the apparent abundance of resources, the high level of Yanomami warfare is probably caused by population pressure arising from resource depletion. The resource in question is meat. The Yanomami lack domesticated sources of meat and must obtain their animal foods from hunting and collecting. Moreover, unlike many other inhabitants of the Amazon Basin, the Yanomami traditionally did not have access to big-river fish and other aquatic animals that elsewhere in the Amazon region provided high-quality animal foods sufficient to supply villages inhabited by over 1,000 people.

Of course, human beings can remain healthy on diets that lack animal foods; however, meat, fish, and other animal products contain compact packages of proteins, fats, minerals, and vitamins that have made them extremely appealing and efficient sources of nutrients throughout most of history and prehistory (Eaton, Shostak, and Konner, 1988).

The theory relating meat to warfare among the Yanomami is this: As Yanomami villages grow, intensive hunting diminishes the availability of game nearby. Meat from large animals grows scarce, and people eat more small animals, insects, and larvae. The point of diminishing returns is reached. Increased tensions within and between villages lead to the breaking apart of villages before they permanently deplete the animal resources. Tensions also lead to the escalation of raiding, which disperses the Yanomami villages over a wide territory, and also protects vital resources by creating no-man's-lands, which function as game preserves (Harris 1984).

Some of the anthropologists who have extensive firsthand knowledge of the Yanomami have rejected this theory. They point to the fact that the Yanomami show no clinical signs of protein deficiency. Moreover, they have shown that in at least one village, whose population is thirty-five, daily per capita overall protein intake was 75 grams per day per adult, which is far higher than the minimum 35 grams recommended by the Food and Agricultural Organization. They have also shown that Yanomami villages with low levels of protein intake (36 grams) seem to engage in warfare just as frequently as those with high protein intake (75 grams) per adult. Finally, they point out that the other groups in the Amazon enjoy as much as 107 grams of animal protein per capita and still go to war frequently (Lizot 1977, 1979; Chagnon and Hames 1979).

Kenneth Good (1987, 1989), however, maintains that obtaining adequate supplies of meat is a constant preoccupation among the Yanomami and that meat is actually consumed only once or twice a week on the average. This accords with the observation made by Eric Ross (1979) that the average daily amount of animal food consumed is a misleading figure. Because of fluctuations in the number and size of animals captured, many days actually pass during which the village has little or no available meat. On days when a large animal such as a tapir is caught, the consumption rate may rise to 250 or more grams per adult, but for weeks at a time, the consumption rate may not rise above 30 grams per adult per day.

The absence of clinical signs of protein deficiency is not an argument against the theory that relates the quest for meat to warfare but rather supports the general point that band and village peoples can enjoy good health as long as they control population growth (see p. 52). The fact that villages with both high and low protein intake have the same level of warfare also does not test the theory because warfare necessarily pits villages at different stages of growth against each other. Hence, Yanomami groups with high levels of protein, and thus, little immediate material incentive to go to war, may have no choice but to engage in counterraids against large groups that are depleting their game reserves and raiding less populous neighbors in order to expand their hunting territory.

Figure 11.9   Yanomami Village
This scene is more representative of everyday life among the Yanomami, despite their warlike repu-
tation. Note the plantains, the staple food of the Yanomami, hanging from the rafters. (For more
photos of the everyday life of the Yanomami, see the photo essay following Chapter 11.)

The preponderance of evidence strongly supports the view that Amazonian fauna are a fragile resource, readily depleted with consequent decline in per capita meat consumption (Ferguson 1989a). Michael Baksh (1985), for example, has quantitatively documented the effect of the nucleation of dispersed Machiguenga homesteads (see p. 98) into a village of 250 people in eastern Peru. Baksh concludes that faunal resources in the vicinity of the village have been declining significantly in availability; that in the attempt to maintain previous levels of intake, men are working harder; that villagers must travel more often to distant hunting and fishing locations; and that faunal resources are limited in availability and encourage the existence of small, mobile groups. Men frequently arrive home empty-handed, or perhaps with a few grubs, some wild fruits, palm nuts, or manufacturing materials. A successful day-long or overnight trip might yield a small monkey or a few birds. Only one tapir and six peccary were obtained over a 17 month period (Baksh 1985: 150–151). Allyn Stearman (1994) also graphically describes the vulnerability of tropical forest game to depletions as experienced by the Yuquí of lowland Bolivia. Five years after an influx of coca farmers who began to compete with the Yuquí for game, large animals like peccary that had previously been abundant could no longer be found except in the most remote areas.

Trekking

The desire to maintain or increase their level of meat consumption explains an important feature of Yanomami life.

Three or four times a year, the Yanomami move out of their village as a group and go on a prolonged trek through the deep forest that lasts a month or more. Indeed, counting the time that the villagers also spend at distant campsites where they prepare new gardens, the Yanomami spend almost half the year away from their communal house. The desire for plant foods cannot provide the motive for going on a trek or planting new gardens since the Yanomami could easily increase the size of their existing gardens and have enough bananas and plantains to feed themselves by staying at home. Although they gather wild fruits while trekking, meat remains their main preoccupation. Good (1989) has shown that while on the trek, the efficiency of hunting improves considerably and the hunters find more meat. Were it not for these long sojourns away from the village, game near the village would soon be completely wiped out.

While on their treks (or shorter hunting trips), the villagers are constantly on the lookout for places to plant their new gardens. Once these gardens begin to bear bananas and plantains, the old communal house is abandoned and a new one is built near the new gardens. Good makes two crucial points regarding this move. First, plenty of forested land suitable for expanding the old gardens remains available near the old communal house. Second, the new communal house and gardens are not located near the old house and gardens but several kilometers away. Clearly then, the gardens are not moved in order to increase the efficiency of plant production; nor is the site of the house moved because it has become insect infested, decayed, or surrounded by human excrement (cf. Ferguson 1989b: 250). (Why not simply build the new house on the other side of the old gardens?) Rather, what moving accomplishes is that it improves the accessibility of game animals that have been hunted out or frightened away from the old sites. Warfare among the Yanomami and other tropical forest peoples therefore can be readily understood as a form of competition between autonomous villages for access to the best hunting territories. After all, since we have no difficulty in understanding why modern nations go to war to maintain access to oil, why, then, should we find it unlikely that the Yanomami go to war to maintain or increase access to game?

Warfare and Female Infanticide

Among patrilocal groups such as the Yanomami, female infanticide is an important component in demonstrating the relationship between population pressure and warfare.

It is generally accepted that slightly more boys than girls are born on a worldwide basis and that the average sex ratio at birth is about 105 males to 100 females. This imbalance, however, is much smaller than that found among the Yanomami whose sex ratios between boys and girls averages about 132:100. What accounts for this large imbalance? William Divale and I have shown that high junior-age sex ratios favoring males are characteristic of societies with high levels of warfare (Table 11.1) and that it probably reflects direct and indirect infanticide practiced against females more often than against males. (See Chapter 6 for a discussion of indirect infanticide.) There is a strong correlation between societies that admit to practicing infanticide and those that were actively engaged in warfare when they were first censused. In these societies, at least, female infanticide was more common than male infanticide.

A plausible reason for the killing and neglect of female children is that success in nonindustrial warfare depends on the size of the male combat teams. When weapons are muscle-powered clubs, spears, and bows and arrows, victory will belong to the group that has the largest number of aggressive males. Since infrastructure limits the number of people who

Table 11.1

Sex Ratios and Warfare

	Young males per 100 females
Warfare present	128
Stopped 5–25 years before census	113
Stopped over 25 years before census	109

Source: Divale and Harris 1976; Divale et al. 1978; cf. Hirschfeld et al. 1978.

can be reared by band and village societies, war-making band and village societies are compelled to rear more males than females. The favoring of male over female children reduces the rate of growth of regional populations and this effect, whether or not consciously intended, may help explain why warfare is so widely practiced by patrilocal prestate peoples who otherwise would find themselves with severely diminishing returns and irreversible depletions.

One consequence of female infanticide is a shortage of women, a shortage the Yanomami try to overcome by capturing women from enemy villages. It is not surprising, therefore, that when Chagnon (1992: 95) asked the Yanomami why they went to war, they replied it was to get women rather than to get meat. But if the Yanomami did not practice warfare, there would no shortage of women.

If female infanticide is so effective in reducing population pressure, you may wonder why the Yanomami do not simply practice female infanticide and forget about warfare. The answer is that the need to raise warriors provides the motive for female infanticide. Without that motive, the Yanomami would have as many daughters as they possibly could, leading to rapid population growth and the depletion of their fragile habitat (Fig. 11.10).

Warfare and Trade Goods

The Yanomami have long been presented as a people whose culture remained virtually free of Western influences and who had remained outside the orbit of the capitalist world system until the 1960s. For some interior groups, this isolation was said to have lasted even into the 1980s. Research carried out by R. Brian Ferguson has demonstrated that in fact the Yanomami have a long history of contact with gold miners, missionaries, travelers, and traders. Ferguson accepts the general principle that nonstate warfare is a means of competing for scarce resources, but in his view what the Yanomami are competing for is not game but Western trade goods.

> The Yanomami generally make great efforts to monopolize access to the Western provider, using pleas, threats, and deceptions to keep the distribution of goods within their local group. Beyond the source point, Western manufactures are passed along from village to village through networks of kinship.... An incomplete listing of goods distributed from the Catholic mission at Iyewei-teri for 1960 to 1972 includes 3,850 machetes, 620 axes, 2,850 pots, 759,000 fishhooks, and large quantities of other items. Most of these goods were traded to more remote villages.

> [Ferguson 1992: 209]

Although Ferguson does not deny that warfare occurred before trade goods intruded into the lives of the Yanomami, his point is that the level of warfare observed by Chagnon

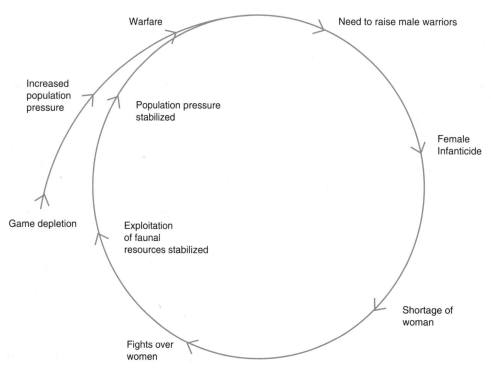

Figure 11.10   Model of Warfare Among Yanomami
Warfare prevents exploitation of game animals from passing point of irreversible depletions.

and others was not characteristic of former times. This interpretation of Yanomami warfare is compatible with the game depletion and population pressure models (Ferguson 1995).

Chapter Summary

Orderly relationships between the individuals and domestic groups in band and village societies are maintained without governments and law enforcement specialists. This is possible because of small size, predominance of kinship and reciprocity, and egalitarian access to vital resources. Public opinion is the chief source of law and order in these societies.

Individual or nuclear family ownership is absent among hunting-and-gathering bands and most village peoples. However, even in the most egalitarian societies, people privately own some items. The prevalence of the reciprocal mode of exchange and the absence of anonymous price markets render theft unnecessary and impractical.

The major threat to law and order among band and village societies stems from the tendency of domestic and kinship groups to escalate conflicts in support of real or imagined injuries to one of their members. Such support does not depend on abstract principles of right and wrong but on the probable outcome of a particular course of action in the face of public opinion. The Eskimo song duel is an illustration of how public opinion can be tested and used to end conflicts between individuals who belong to different domestic and kinship groups.

Witchcraft accusations also give public opinion an opportunity to identify and punish persistent violators of the rules of reciprocity and other troublemakers. Shamans act as the mouthpiece of the community. Under stressful conditions, witchcraft accusations may build to epidemic proportions and become a threat to the maintenance of law and order.

Headmanship reflects the egalitarian nature of the institutions of law and order in band and village societies. Headmen can do little more than harangue and plead with people for support. They lack physical or material means of enforcing their decisions. Their success rests on their ability to intuit public opinion. As exemplified by the Nuer, avoidance of blood feud can be facilitated by the payment of compensation and by appeal to ritual chiefs who have even less political power than headmen.

Other instances of nonkin political organization take the form of voluntary associations or sodalities such as men's and women's clubs, secret societies, and age–grade sets. However, all these nonkin modes of political organization remain rather rudimentary and are overshadowed by the pervasive networks of kinship alliances based on marriage and descent, which constitute the "glue" of band and village societies.

Warfare concerns the maintenance of law and order between separate societies and cultures. Although simple

YANOMAMO

Women dance and sing at night while their men are on a five-day hunt far from the village. They believe that singing about different animals and even imitating their behavior will give the men success on their hunt.

The hallucinogenic drug called epene is taken at all shamanistic rituals. The fine powder is derived from the seed of the spene tree and inhaled into the nostrils through a long tube.

A young man uses a set of poles lashed around the peach palm tree with thick vines so that he can shimmy up the tree without touching the branchless trunk, which is covered with extremely sharp, long needles.

The men of the village return from a five-day heniyomou *hunt to get meat for a village funeral-feast ceremony. On this occasion, thirty men hunting from morning to night for five days did not acquire enough game for the feast and had to go out again to a different locale. This is not uncommon.*

Aerial view of a Yanomamö shapono, or communal house. These are spaced throughout the forest, one or two days' walking distance apart. Although the house is communal, each family makes its section of the ring. If the leaves are woven tightly, the roof can last for five years. The village usually moves away before this time.

Grievances between villages can be resolved with a chest-pounding duel like this one. This event is more like a sporting contest and results in no further animosity unless someone is severely injured. Then emotions flare and more serious fights can ensue.

A visitor sits in his host's hammock, drinking plantain pap. He has walked for days through the forest to visit this community.

A young woman carries all the family possessions and her young child as she abandons her house and sets off on a trek in search of wild foods. This occurs when the gardens are exhausted and no foods are available near the communal house. The entire community participates in the trek. The man in the background is her husband and will carry only his bow and arrows so that he will be prepared to shoot animals encountered on the trail.

A man and his two young sons strip the peach palm fruit and store it in baskets to be boiled and distributed that day when a neighboring village arrives for a feast.

The headman of Hasupuweteri negotiates with his visitors in an early-morning trading session prior to their departure. Those villages with access to Western goods trade with more remote villages for Yanomamö goods such as hammocks, hunting dogs, and bows and arrows.

A mother paints her son with onoto *in the gardens of their hosts before entering and dancing in the central plaza.*

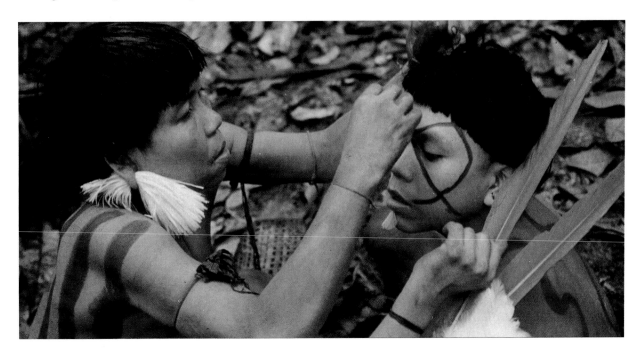

Women close in on the drugged fish in a nearby stream. Bark from a tree has been stripped and put in the water, causing the fish to become stupefied and float to the surface. This is done only once or twice during the dry season, when the streams are quite shallow. Large quantities of fish can be acquired, but this practice still does not change the relatively low importance of fish in the Yanomamö diet.

A boy learns from his father how to pluck feathers off a game bird.

The ethnographer's wife, Yarima, decorates herself with parrot feathers and buzzard down in preparation for an entrance and dance in the hosts' village.

hunter-gatherers engage in warfare, warfare is usually more intense among sedentary societies. Warfare cannot be explained as a consequence of innate aggression, an enjoyable sport, a thirst for revenge, or a struggle for reproductive success. Warfare is a particular form of organized activity and only one of the many ways in which cultures handle aggression. The causes of war in band and village societies are rooted in problems associated with production and reproduction, and almost always involve attempts to protect or improve standards of living.

Even where population densities are very low, as among the Yanomami, problems of depletion and declining efficiency may exist. Thus warfare in some nonstate contexts restrains population growth and thus protects resources from depletion. Among patrilocal band and village societies, warfare could have this effect through the encouragement of direct and indirect female infanticide. Evidence for population pressure as a cause of nonstate warfare consists of cross-cultural studies that correlate unbalanced sex ratios with active warfare.

Warfare among the Yanomami appears to be primarily a struggle for access to game and to hunting territories. The importance of game can be gauged by the fact that the Yanomami frequently split up their villages and move to new and distant garden sites even though they still have plenty of additional garden land nearby. The prominence of trekking by the Yanomami also indicates the importance of game in their lives. New data show that trade for Western manufactures may account for the special intensity and high frequency of Yanomami warfare, especially in recent decades.

Chapter 12

ORIGINS AND ANATOMY OF THE STATE

Liliuokalani. Queen of Hawaii (1891–93).

In this chapter, we contrast the forms of political life characteristic of band and village societies with those of chiefdoms and states. How did the relatively egalitarian societies that once prevailed throughout the world give way to class-structured societies that rank people high and low and divide them into rulers and ruled? In seeking the answer to the origin of states, we shall take account of both structural and infrastructural factors such as competitive feasting, territorial impaction, and warfare.

Bigmanship and Bigmandoms

As we have seen (p. 136), headmen often function as intensifiers of production and as redistributors. They get their relatives to work harder, and they collect and then give away the extra product. A village may have several headmen. Where technological and ecological conditions encourage intensification, headmen living in the same village may become rivals. They vie with one another to hold the most lavish feasts and to redistribute the greatest amount of valuables. Often, the most successful redistributors earn the reputation of being "big men" (Hayden 1993).

Anthropologist Douglas Oliver (1955) carried out a classic study of "bigmanship" during his fieldwork among the Siuai on Bougainville in the Solomon Islands. Among the Siuai, a "big man" is called a mumi, and to achieve mumi status is every youth's highest ambition (Fig. 12.1). A young man proves himself capable of becoming a mumi by working hard and by carefully restricting his consumption of meat and coconuts. Eventually, he impresses his wife, children, and near relatives with the seriousness of his intentions, and they vow to help him prepare for his first feast. If the feast is a success, his circle of supporters widens and he sets to work readying an even greater display of generosity.

He aims next at the construction of a men's clubhouse in which his male followers can lounge about and in which guests can be entertained and fed. Another feast is held at the consecration of the clubhouse, and if this is also a success, the circle of people willing to work for him grows still larger, and he will begin to be spoken of as a mumi. Larger and larger feasts mean that the mumi's demands on his supporters become more irksome. Although they grumble about how hard they have to work, they remain loyal as long as their mumi maintains or increases his renown as a "great provider."

Finally, the time comes for the new mumi to challenge the others who have risen before him. He does this at a muminai feast, where a tally is kept of all the pigs, coconut pies, and sago-almond puddings given away by the host mumi and his followers to the guest mumi and his followers. If the guest mumi cannot reciprocate in a year or so with a feast at least as lavish as that of his challengers, he suffers a great social humiliation, and his fall from mumihood is immediate. In deciding on whom to challenge, a mumi must be very careful. He tries to choose a guest whose downfall will increase his own reputation, but he must avoid one whose capacity to retaliate exceeds his own.

At the end of a successful feast, the greatest of mumis still faces a lifetime of personal toil and dependence on the moods and inclinations of his followers. Mumihood does not confer the power to coerce others into doing one's bidding, nor does it elevate one's standard of living above anyone else's. In fact, since giving things away is the essence of mumihood, great mumis may even consume less meat and other delicacies than an ordinary, undistinguished Siuai. The Kaoka, another Solomon Island group reported on by H. Ian Hogbin (1964: 66), have this saying: "The giver of the feast takes the bones and the stale cakes; the meat and the fat go to the others."

At one great feast attended by 1,100 people, the host mumi, whose name was Soni, gave away thirty-two pigs plus a large quantity of sago-almond puddings. Soni and his closest followers, however, went hungry. "We shall eat Soni's renown," his followers said.

Big Men and Warfare

Formerly, the mumis were as famous for their ability to get men to fight for them as they were for their ability to get men to work for them. Warfare had been suppressed by the colonial authorities long before Oliver carried out his study, but the memory of mumi war leaders was still vivid among the Siuai. As one old man put it:

> In the olden times there were greater mumi than there are today. Then they were fierce and relentless war leaders. They laid waste to the countryside and their clubhouses were lined with the skulls of people they had slain.

> [Oliver 1955: 411]

In singing praises of their mumis, the generation of pacified Siuai call them "warriors" and "killers of men and pigs."

Oliver's informants told him that mumis had more authority in the days when warfare was still practiced. Some mumi

Figure 12.1   Solomon Island Chiefs
They prefer to be called chiefs rather than mumis, as of old.

war leaders even kept one or two prisoners who were treated like slaves and forced to work in the mumi's family gardens, and people could not talk "loud and slanderously against their mumis without fear of punishment." This fits theoretical expectations since the ability to redistribute meat and other valuables goes hand in hand with the ability to attract a following of warriors, equip them for combat, and reward them with spoils of battle.

Rivalry among Bougainville's war-making mumis appeared to have been leading toward an islandwide political organization when the first European voyagers arrived. According to Oliver (1955: 420), "For certain periods of time many neighboring villages fought together so consistently that there emerged a pattern of war-making regions, each more or less internally peaceful and each containing one outstanding mumi whose war activities provided internal social cohesion." These mumis enjoyed regional fame, but their prerogatives remained rudimentary. For example, the mumis had to provide their warriors with prostitutes brought into the clubhouses and with gifts of pork and other delicacies. Said one old warrior:

> If the mumi didn't furnish us with women we were angry. All night long we would copulate and still want more. It was the same with eating. The clubhouse used to be filled with food, and we ate and ate and never had enough. Those were wonderful times.

[Oliver 1955: 415]

Furthermore, the mumi who wanted to lead a war party had to be prepared personally to pay an indemnity for any of his men who were killed in battle and to furnish a pig for each man's funeral feast.

Chiefs and Chiefdoms: Trobrianders and Cherokee

Headmen are the leaders of autonomous villages or bands. Chiefs are the leaders of more or less permanently allied groups of bands and villages called *chiefdoms*. The principal difference between autonomous bands and villages and chiefdoms is that chiefdoms consist of several communities or settlements. Chiefs have more power than headmen, but headmen who are successful redistributors are hard to distinguish from the leaders of small chiefdoms. Whereas headmen must achieve and constantly validate their status by recurrent feasts, chiefs inherit their offices and hold them even if they are temporarily unable to provide their followers with generous redistributions. Chiefs tend to live better than commoners; unlike headmen, they do not always keep only "the bones and the stale cakes" for themselves. Yet, in the long run, chiefs, too, must validate their titles by waging successful war, obtaining trade goods, and giving away food and other valuables to their followers (Earle 1991).

The Trobriand Chiefdoms

The difference between headmen and chiefs can be illustrated with the case of the Trobriand Islanders. Trobriander society was divided into several matrilineal clans and subclans of unequal rank and privilege through which access to garden lands was inherited. Bronislaw Malinowski (1920) reported that the Trobrianders were keen on fighting and that they conducted systematic and relentless wars, venturing across the open ocean in their canoes to trade—or, if need be, to fight—with the people of islands over 100 miles away. Unlike the Siuai mumis, the Trobriand chiefs occupied a hereditary office and could be deposed only through defeat in war. One of these, whom Malinowski considered to be the "paramount chief" of all the Trobrianders, held sway over more than a dozen villages, containing several thousand people. The Trobrianders attributed these inequalities to wars of conquest carried out long ago. Only the chiefs could wear certain shell ornaments as the insignia of high rank, and no commoner could stand or sit in a position that put a chief's head at a lower elevation than anyone else's. Malinowski (1920) tells of seeing all the people present in the village of Bwoytalu drop from their verandas as if blown down by a hurricane at the sound of a drawn-out cry announcing the arrival of an important chief.

The Trobriand chief's power rested ultimately on his ability to play the role of "great provider." Chiefs acquired up to a dozen or more wives, each of whom was entitled to an obligatory gift of yams from her brothers. These yams were delivered to the chief's village and displayed on special yam racks. Some of the yams were then distributed in elaborate feasts at which the chief validated his position as a "great provider"; the remainder were used to feed canoe-building specialists, artisans, magicians, and family servants who thereby became partially dependent on the chief's power. In former times, the yam stores also furnished the food for launching long-distance Kula trading expeditions among friendly groups and raids against enemies (Malinowski 1935; Brunton 1975; Geoffry 1983).

Even though the Trobrianders feared and respected their "great provider" war chiefs, they were still a long way from a state society. Living on islands, the Trobrianders were not free to spread out, and their population density had risen in Malinowski's time to sixty persons per square mile. Nonetheless, the chiefs could not control enough of the production system to acquire great power. Perhaps one reason for this is that Trobriand agriculture lacked cereal grains. Since yams rot after 4 or 5 months (unlike rice or maize), the Trobriand "great provider" could not manipulate people through dispensing food year-round, nor could he support a permanent police–military garrison out of his stores. Another important factor was the open resources of the lagoons and ocean from which the Trobrianders derived their protein supply. The Trobriand chief could not cut off access to these resources and hence could not exercise permanent coercive political control over subordinates.

The Cherokee Chiefdom

The political organization of the Cherokee of Tennessee (and of other southeastern woodland Native Americans) bears a striking resemblance to the Trobrianders' redistribution-warfare-trade-chief complex (Fig. 12.2). The Cherokee, like the Trobrianders, were matrilineal, and they waged external warfare over long distances. At the center of the principal settlements was a large, circular "council house" where the council of chiefs discussed issues involving several villages and where redistributive feasts were held. The council of chiefs had a supreme chief who was the central figure in the Cherokee redistributive network. At harvest time, a large crib, identified as the "chief's granary," was erected in each field. "To this each family carries and deposits a certain quantity according to his ability or inclination, or none at all if he so chooses." The chief's granaries functioned as "a public treasury to fly to for succor" in the case of crop failure, as a source of food "to accommodate strangers, or travellers," and as a military store "when they go forth on hostile expeditions." Although every citizen enjoyed "the right of free and public access," commoners had to acknowledge that the store really belonged to the supreme chief who had "an exclusive right and ability to distribute comfort and blessings to the necessitous" (Bartram 1958: 326).

Figure 12.2   Cherokee Chief Black Coat
Painted by George Catlin at Fort Gibson in 1834.

The Origins of States

Under certain conditions, large chiefdoms evolved into states. The *state* is a form of politically centralized society whose governing elites have the power to compel subordinates to pay taxes, render services, and obey the law (Carneiro 1981: 69). Three infrastructural conditions led to the transformation of chiefdoms into the first states:

1. Population pressure. After a period of population growth, the chiefdom's total production continued to rise, but the redistribution of the product became increasingly unequal.
2. Intensive agriculture. The staple was a grain such as rice, wheat, barley, millet, or maize, which provided a surplus above immediate needs at harvest and could be stored for long periods at low cost without becoming inedible.
3. Circumscription. The emigration of dissatisfied factions was blocked by similarly developed chiefdoms in adjacent territories or by features of the environment that required emigrants to adopt a new and less efficient

mode of production and to suffer a drastic decline in their standards of living. Most of the earliest states were circumscribed by their dependence on modes of production associated with fertile river valleys surrounded by arid or semiarid plains or mountains. But circumscription can also be caused by the transformation of low-yielding habitats into higher-yielding ones as a result of a long-term investment in the mounding, ditching, draining, and irrigating of a chiefdom's territory (Dickson 1987). The significance of circumscription, whatever its precise form, is that factions of discontented members of a chiefdom cannot escape from their elite overlords without suffering a sharp decline in their standard of living.

Given these infrastructural conditions, certain changes in a chiefdom's political and economic structure become likely. First, the larger and denser the population and the greater the harvest surplus, the greater the ability of the elites to support craft specialists, palace guards, and a standing professional army. Second, the more powerful the elite, the greater its ability to engage in long-distance warfare and trade, and to conquer, incorporate, and exploit new populations and territories. Third, the more powerful the elite, the more stratified its redistribution of trade wealth and harvest surplus. Fourth, the wider the territorial scope of political control and the larger the society's investment in the mode of production, the less opportunity there is to flee and the less there is to be gained by fleeing. Soon, contributions to the central store cease to be voluntary—they become taxes; access to the farmlands and natural resources cease to be rights—they become dispensations; food producers cease being the chief's followers—they become peasants who labor on their lands far from the ruler's palaces; redistributors cease being chiefs—they become kings; and chiefdoms cease being chiefdoms—they become states.

As the governing elites compel subordinates to pay taxes and tribute, provide military or labor services, and obey laws, the entire process of intensification, expansion, conquest, stratification, and centralization of control is continuously increased or "amplified" through a form of change known as *positive feedback* (Box 12.1) Where modes of production could sustain sufficient numbers of peasant farmers and warriors, this feedback process recurrently resulted in states conquering other states and in the emergence of preindustrial empires involving vast territories inhabited by millions of people (Fried 1978; Carneiro 1981; R. Cohen 1984a; Feinman and Neitzel 1984).

Once the first states came into existence, they themselves constituted barriers against the flight of people who sought to preserve egalitarian systems. Moreover, with states as neighbors, egalitarian peoples found themselves increasingly drawn into warfare and were compelled to increase production and to give their redistributor-war chiefs more and more power in order to prevail against the expansionist tendencies of their

Box 12.1

TWO KINDS OF FEEDBACK

Negative:
Changes are checked when certain limits are reached. Initial conditions tend to be restored. Example: Household temperature stays slightly above or slightly below the level set on a thermostat.
Positive:
Changes are not checked. Each successive change increases or amplifies the tendency to change. Example: A microphone picks up the sound of its own loudspeaker and sends the signal back through its amplifier, which sends a stronger signal to the loudspeaker, resulting in a louder and louder squeal.

neighbors. Thus, most states of the world were produced by a great diversity of specific historical and ecological conditions (Fried 1967); once states come into existence, they tend to spread, engulf, and overwhelm nonstate peoples (Carneiro 1970; Service 1975; Macneish 1981; Haas 1982; R. Cohen 1984a; Kirch 1984; Hommon 1986; Upman 1990).

Hawaii: On the Threshold of the State

When visited by Captain James Cook in A.D. 1778, the Hawaiian Islands were divided into four intensely hierarchical polities, each containing between 10,000 and 100,000 persons and each on the threshold (if not past it) of becoming a full-fledged state. Each was divided into named districts containing populations that ranged from about 4,000 to 25,000 people. The districts were in turn divided into many elongated territorial units called ahupua'a, which extended inland from the coast to the higher elevations of the island's interior, and were each inhabited by an average of 200 persons. These inhabitants were of the commoner class, the maka'ainana—fishermen, farmers, and craftsworkers.

Each ahupua'a was administered by officials of chiefly ranks, called konohiki, who were the local agents for the powerful district chiefs, called ali'i. These ali'i based their claims to high chiefly status on genealogies that extended upward for ten generations. (Such genealogies, however, were constantly adjusted and negotiated to accord with achieved political military status.) The chiefly class was topped off by a paramount figure called the ali'i nui, who was responsible for assigning privileges and administrative posts to the ali'i. In practice, the ali'i were in ceaseless turmoil over their relative rank, and the issue was decided by wars of conquest rather than genealogical reckoning. Until the time of contact, no ali'i nui had managed to gain firm control over all the districts on an island.

At the infrastructural level, the populous, incipient states of Hawaii were based on irrigation agriculture. Taro, sweet potatoes, and yams were the principal crops; both pigs and dogs were kept for meat. Hierarchical, taxlike forms of redistribution siphoned both food and craft items from the maka'ainana to the ali'i. It was the konohiki's main responsibility to see to it that the commoners in his charge produced enough to satisfy the demands of the ali'i. The ali'i in turn used these "gifts" to reward his warriors, priests, allies, and the konohiki.

Recent archaeological research demonstrates that the Hawaiian polities evolved out of more egalitarian chiefdoms as a result of the positive feedback between population increase, environmental depletions (deforestation and soil erosion), intensification of production (irrigation and pig husbandry), increased trade, escalating warfare, and competition for elite status. Three phases to this process have been identified (Kirch 1984; Hommon 1986; Earle 1989):

> Phase I: A.D. 500–1400. Initial colonization and population growth. Settlements are on best coastal sites. No irrigation is needed. Settlements are kinship-organized.
>
> Phase II: 1400–1600. Expansion into less desirable island sites. Use of flood-water irrigation, mulching, and reduction of fallow periods.
>
> Phase III: 1600–1778. Expansion of irrigation systems, use of marginal lands, deforestation, depletion of faunal resources, and soil erosion. Conquest, usurpation, and rebellion.

Would the Hawaiian polities have achieved a more stable and centralized state if their political history had not been interrupted by the landings of Europeans on their shores? (Actually, as a result of that contact, a unified Hawaiian kingdom was established in 1810.) According to the theory presented, the answer is no. All the conditions for state formation were present with one exception: The Hawaiian chiefs had no storageable grains. They did have storehouses that they used to sustain their followers. Indeed, David Malo, a nineteenth-century Hawaiian chief, noted that the storehouses of the Hawaiian kings were designed as a means of keeping people contented so that they would not desert him: "As the rat will not desert the pantry, so the people will not desert the king while they think there is food in his storehouse" (D'Altroy and Earle 1985: 192). Lacking staple grains that provided the nutritional and energetic basis for the emergence of states everywhere else, the Hawaiian chiefs were unable to sustain large numbers of followers, especially during times of drought and warfare-induced food shortage. Thus, no ali'i nui was able to achieve an enduring advantage over his rivals.

An African Kingdom: Bunyoro

The difference between a chiefdom and a state can be illustrated with the case of Bunyoro, a kingdom located in Uganda and studied by John Beattie (1960). At the time of Beattie's fieldwork, Bunyoro had a population of about 100,000 people and an area of 5,000 square miles. Supreme power over the Bunyoro territory and its inhabitants was vested in the Mukama, senior member of a royal lineage that reckoned its descent back to the beginning of time (Fig. 12.3). The use of all natural resources, especially of farming land, was a dispensation specifically granted by the Mukama to a dozen or more "chiefs" or to commoner peasants under their respective control. In return for these dispensations, quantities of food, handicrafts, and labor services were funneled up through the power hierarchy into the Mukama's headquarters. The Mukama in turn directed the use of these goods and services on behalf of state enterprises. Thus, the basic redistributive pattern was still plainly in evidence.

Although the Mukama had a reputation for generosity, he clearly did not give away as much as he received. He certainly did not follow the Solomon Island mumis and keep only

Figure 12.3 Mukama of Bunyoro
This is a king, not a chief.

the stale cakes and bones for himself. Moreover, much of what he gave away did not flow back down to the peasant producers; instead, it remained in the hands of his genealogically close kin, who constituted a clearly demarcated aristocratic class. Part of what the Mukama took away from the peasants was bestowed on nonkin who performed extraordinary services on behalf of the state, especially in connection with military exploits. Another part was used to support a permanent palace guard and resident staff who attended to the Mukama's personal needs and performed religious rites deemed essential for the welfare of the Mukama and the nation, including custodian of spears, custodian of royal graves, custodian of the royal drums, custodian of royal crowns, placers of royal crowns on the king's head, custodians of royal thrones (stools) and other regalia, cooks, bath attendants, herdsmen, potters, barkcloth makers, and musicians. Many of these officials had several assistants.

In addition, the king had a loosely defined category of advisers, diviners, and other retainers who hung around the court, attached to the Mukama's household as dependents, in the hope of being appointed to a chieftainship. And then there were the Mukama's extensive harem, his many children, and the polygynous households of his brothers and of other royal personages. To keep his power intact, the Mukama and portions of his court made frequent trips throughout Bunyoro land, staying at local palaces maintained at the expense of his chiefs and commoners.

A Native-American Empire: The Inca

Independently in both the Old and New Worlds, state systems arose in which scores of former small states were incorporated into highly centralized superstates or empires. In the New World, the largest and most powerful of these systems was the Inca Empire.

At its prime, the Inca Empire stretched 1,500 miles from northern Chile to southern Colombia and contained possibly as many as 6 million inhabitants. Because of government intervention in the basic mode of production, agriculture was organized in terms of villages, districts, and provinces. Each such unit was supervised by appointed government officials responsible for planning public works and for delivering government-established quotas of laborers, food, and other material (Morris 1976). Village lands were divided into three parts, the largest of which was probably the source of the workers' own subsistence; harvests from the second and third parts were turned over to religious and government agents, who stored them in granaries (D'Altroy and Earle 1985; D'Altroy 1992). The distribution of these supplies was entirely under the control of the central administration. Likewise, when labor power was needed to build roads, bridges, canals, fortresses, or other public works, government recruiters went directly into the villages.

Figure 12.4   Sacsahuaman
The principal fortress of the Inca Empire, near Cuzco, Peru.

Because of the size of the administrative network and the density of population, huge numbers of workers could be placed at the disposal of the Inca engineers. In the construction of Cuzco's fortress of Sacsahuaman (Fig. 12.4), probably the greatest masonry structure in the New World, 30,000 people were employed in cutting, quarrying, hauling, and erecting huge monoliths, some weighing as much as 200 tons. Labor contingents of this size were rare in medieval Europe but were common in ancient Egypt, the Middle East, and China.

Control over the entire empire was concentrated in the hands of the Inca. He was the firstborn of the firstborn, a descendant of the god of the sun and a celestial being of unparalleled holiness. This god-on-earth enjoyed power and luxury undreamed of by the poor Mehinacu chief in his plaintive daily quest for respect and obedience. Ordinary people could not approach the Inca face to face. His private audiences were conducted from behind a screen, and all who approached him did so with a burden of wood or stone on their backs. When traveling, he reclined on an ornate palanquin carried by special crews of bearers (Mason 1957: 184). A small army of sweepers, water carriers, woodcutters, cooks, wardrobe men, treasurers, gardeners, and hunters attended the domestic needs of the Inca in his palace in Cuzco, the capital of the empire.

The Inca ate his meals from gold and silver dishes in rooms whose walls were covered with precious metals. His clothing was made of the softest vicuña wool, and he gave away each change of clothing to members of the royal family, never wearing the same garment twice. The Inca enjoyed the services of a large number of concubines who were methodically culled from the empire's most beautiful young women. However, to conserve the holy line of descent from the god of the sun, his wife had to be his own full or half sister (see p.

113). When the Inca died, his wife, concubines, and many other retainers were strangled during a great drunken dance in order that he suffer no loss of comfort in the afterlife. Each Inca's body was eviscerated, wrapped in cloth, and mummified. Women with fans stood in constant attendance on these mummies, ready to drive away flies and to take care of the other things mummies need to stay happy.

The State and the Control of Thought

Large populations, anonymity, use of market money, and vast differences in wealth make the maintenance of law and order in state societies more difficult to achieve than in bands, villages, and chiefdoms. This accounts for the great elaboration of police and paramilitary forces and the other state-level institutions and specialists concerned with crime and punishment. Although every state ultimately stands prepared to crush criminals and political subversives by imprisoning, maiming, or killing them, most of the daily burdens of maintaining law and order against discontented individuals and groups is borne by institutions that seek to confuse, distract, and demoralize potential troublemakers before they have to be subdued by physical force. Therefore, every state, ancient and modern, has specialists who perform ideological services in support of the status quo. These services are often rendered in a manner and in contexts that seem unrelated to economic or political issues.

Thus the main thought-control apparatus of preindustrial states consists of magico-religious institutions (see p. 235). The elaborate religions of the Inca, Aztecs, ancient Egyptians, and other nonindustrial civilizations sanctified the privileges and powers of the ruling elite. They upheld the doctrine of the divine descent of the Inca and the pharaoh, and taught that the entire balance and continuity of the universe required the subordination of commoners to persons of noble and divine birth. Among the Aztecs, the priests were convinced and sought to convince others that the gods must be nourished with human blood, and they personally pulled out the beating hearts of the state's prisoners of war on top of Tenochtitlan's pyramids (see p. 233). In many states, religion has been used to condition large masses of people to accept relative deprivation as necessity, to look forward to material rewards in the afterlife rather than in the present one, and to be grateful for small favors from superiors lest ingratitude call down a fiery retribution in this life or in a hell to come. (Religion, of course, has other functions, as we shall see in Chapter 17.)

To deliver messages of this sort and demonstrate the truths they are based on, state societies invest a large portion of national wealth in monumental architecture. From the pyramids of Egypt or Teotihuac in Mexico to the Gothic cathedrals of medieval Europe, state-subsidized monumentality makes the individual feel powerless and insignificant. Great

Figure 12.5   The Great Pyramid of Khufu

public edifices—whether seeming to float, as in the case of the Gothic cathedral of Amiens, or to press down with the infinite heaviness of the pyramids of Khufu (Fig. 12.5)—teach the futility of discontent and the invincibility of those who rule, as well as the glory of heaven and the gods. (This is not to say that they teach nothing else.)

A considerable amount of conformity is achieved not by frightening or threatening people but by inviting them to identify with the governing elite and to enjoy vicariously the pomp of state occasions (Fig. 12.6). Public spectacles such as

Figure 12.6   Pomp and Ceremony
The crowning of Queen Elizabeth II in England.

religious processions, coronations, and victory parades work against the alienating effects of poverty and exploitation. During Roman times, the masses were kept under control by encouraging them to watch gladiators killing each other, chariot races, circuses, and other mass spectator events. Today, the movies, television, and radio provide states with far more powerful means of thought control. Through modern media, the consciousness of millions of listeners, readers, and watchers is often manipulated along rather precisely determined paths by censors and propaganda specialists. However, thought control via the mass media need not take the form of government-directed propaganda and censorship. More subtle forms of control arise from the voluntary filtering of news by reporters and commentators whose career advancements depend on avoiding objective coverage (Herman and Chomsky 1988; Chomsky 1989). "Entertainment" delivered through the air or by cable directly into the shantytown house or tenement apartment is another form of thought control—perhaps the most effective "Roman circus" yet devised (Parenti 1986; Kottak 1990).

Compulsory universal education is another powerful modern means of thought control. Teachers and schools serve the instrumental needs of complex industrial civilizations by training each generation to provide the skills and services necessary for survival and well-being. But schools also teach civics, history, citizenship, and social studies. These subjects are loaded with implicit or explicit assumptions about culture, people, and nature that favor the status quo.

All modern states use universal education to instill loyalty through mass rituals. These include saluting the flag; pronouncing oaths of allegiance; singing patriotic songs; and staging patriotic assemblies, plays, and pageants (Fig. 12.7) (Bowles and Gintis 1976; Ramirez and Meyer 1980).

In modern industrial states as in ancient ones, acceptance of extreme social and economic inequality depends on thought control more than on the exercise of naked repressive force. Children from economically deprived families are taught to believe that the main obstacle to achievement of wealth and power is their own intellectual merit, physical endurance, and will to compete. The poor are taught to blame themselves for being poor, and their resentment is directed primarily against themselves or against those with whom they must compete and who stand on the same rung of the ladder of upward mobility (Kleugel and Smith 1981; De Mott 1990).

The State and Physical Coercion

Although thought control can be an effective supplementary means of maintaining political control, there are limits to the lies and deceptions that governments can get away with. If people are experiencing stagnant or declining standards of living, no amount of propaganda and false promises can prevent them from becoming restless and dissatisfied. As discontent mounts, the ruling elites must either increase the use of direct force or make way for a restructuring of political economy. In China, popular dissatisfaction with the ruling class has been met in recent years by both more thought control and more direct physical repression (Fig. 12.8). The great upheavals in the Soviet Union and Eastern Europe during the 1980s and 1990s also illustrate dramatically what can happen when ruling classes fail to deliver on their promises of a better life (Fig. 12.9). No amount of thought control could hide the daily reality of long lines to buy food, the endless red tape, the shortages of housing and electricity, and the widespread industrial pollution characteristic of life behind the Iron Curtain.

Chapter Summary

Headmen, chiefs, and kings are found in three different forms of political organization: autonomous bands and villages, chiefdoms, and states, respectively. The "big man" is a rivalrous form of headmanship marked by competitive redistributions that expand and intensify production. As illustrated by the mumis of the Solomon Islands, bigmanship is a temporary status requiring constant validation through displays of generosity that leave the big man poor in possessions but rich in prestige and authority. Since they are highly respected, big men are well suited to act as leaders of war parties, long-distance trading expeditions, and other collective activities that require leadership among egalitarian peoples.

Chiefdoms consist of several more or less permanently allied communities. Like big men, chiefs also play the role of great provider, expand and intensify production, give feasts, and organize long-distance warfare and trading expeditions. However, as illustrated by the Trobriand and Cherokee chiefdoms, chiefs enjoy hereditary status, tend to live somewhat better than the average commoner, and can be deposed only through defeat in warfare. The power of chiefs is limited by their ability to support a permanent group of police–military specialists and to deprive significant numbers of their followers of access to the means of making a living. In the transition from band and village organizations through chiefdoms to states, a continuous series of cumulative changes occur in the balance of power between elites and commoners. The subtle gradations along this continuum make it difficult to say at exactly what point in the process we have chiefdoms rather than an alliance of villages, or states rather than a powerful chiefdom.

The polities of the Hawaiian Islands illustrate the incipient phases of state formation. Dense populations, intensifiable modes of production, trade, storageable grains, circumscription, and intense warfare underlay the emergence of pristine states. Secondary states, however, arose under a variety of conditions related to the spread of pristine states.

Figure 12.7   Thought Control in Japan
Children in native costume at Expo 85, Tsukuba, Japan.

The difference between chiefdoms and states is illustrated by the case of the Bunyoro. The Mukama was a great provider for himself and his closest supporters but not for the majority of the Bunyoro peasants. Unlike the Trobriand chief, the Mukama maintained a permanent court of personal retainers and a palace guard.

Figure 12.8   Free Speech Versus Tanks on Tiananmen Square,
Beijing, China.
The tanks won.

Figure 12.9   People Against Dictatorship in Bucharest, Romania
The people won.

The most developed and highly stratified form of statehood is that of empire. As illustrated by the Inca of Peru, the leaders of ancient empires possessed vast amounts of power and could not be approached by ordinary citizens. Production was supervised by a whole army of administrators and tax collectors. Though the Inca was concerned with the welfare of his people, he was viewed by them as a god to whom they owed everything rather than as a headman or chief who owed everything to them.

Since all state societies are based on marked inequalities between rich and poor, and rulers and ruled, maintenance of law and order presents a critical challenge. In the final analysis, it is the military with their control over the means of physical coercion that keep the poor and exploited in line. However, all states find it more expedient to maintain law and order by controlling people's thoughts. This is done in a variety of ways, ranging from state religions to public rites and spectacles and universal education.

AMERICA NOW UPDATE

Law and Disorder

The United States has one of the highest rates of violent crime found among industrial nations. In 1991, there were 24,700 murders, 106,000 rapes, 687,000 robberies, and 3 million burglaries. Someone is hit by gunfire in New York City every 88 minutes. In 1993, from January to November, 4,769 New Yorkers were hit by bullets. More people were murdered in New York in 1990 than died of colon cancer, or breast cancer, or from all accidents combined (Robert 1993).

Figure 12.10   Thought Control in the United States

One reason for the higher rate of violent crime in the United States is that U.S. citizens own far more pistols and rifles per capita than the Japanese or British. The right to "bear arms" is guaranteed by the U.S. Constitution. But the failure to pass stricter gun control laws itself reflects, in part at least, the pervasive, realistic fear of being robbed or attacked and the consequent desire to defend person and property. Hence, the cause of the high incidence of violent crimes must be sought at deeper levels of U.S. culture.

Much evidence links the unusually high rate of crime in the United States to the long-term, grinding poverty and economic hopelessness of America's inner-city minorities, especially of African-Americans and Hispanics. Although suburban crime is also on the rise, the principal locus of violent crime remains the inner cities. African-Americans constitute 12 percent of the population but account for 61 percent of arrests for robbery and 55 percent of arrests for murder and manslaughter (Hacker 1992: 181). One should note, however, that proportionately, African-Americans themselves suffer more from violent crimes than do whites. A poor black is twenty-five times more likely than a wealthy white to be a victim of a robbery resulting in injury and eight times more likely to be a homicide victim. In fact, homicide is the ranking killer of African-American males between 15 and 24 years of age. More black males die from homicide than from motor vehicle accidents, diabetes, emphysema, or pneumonia. (Two out of five black male children born in an American city in 1980 will not reach age 25.) Over half of all black teenagers are unemployed; further, in ghettos like Harlem in New York City, the unemployment rate among

Figure 12.11   The Breakdown of Law and Order
National Guard troops patrol the streets of Homestead, Florida, after Hurricane Andrew to prevent looting.

black youth may be as high as 86 percent (Brown 1978; National Urban League 1990.)

The dominant classes of Western democracies rely more on thought control (Fig. 12.10) than on physical coercion to maintain law and order, but in the final analysis they, too, depend on guns and jails to protect their privileges. Disasters such as Hurricane Andrew in 1992 (Fig. 12.11), and the Los Angeles riots in 1994 (Fig. 12.12) quickly led to extensive looting and widespread disorder, proving that thought control is not enough and that large numbers of ordinary citizens do not believe in the system and are held in check only by the threat of physical punishment (Curvin and Porter 1978; Weisman 1978).

Figure 12.12   Break Down of Law and Order Aftermath of rioting in Los Angeles.

Chapter 13

CLASS AND CASTE

❦

Down and out in São Pāulo, Brazil.

Now we examine the principal varieties of stratified groups found in state-level societies. We begin with groups known as classes. We will see that people who live in state-level societies think and behave in ways that are determined to a great extent by their membership in stratified groups and by their position in a stratification hierarchy. The values and behavior of such groups are in turn often related to a struggle for access to the structural and infrastructural sources of wealth and power. In this regard, to what extent can subordinated classes be seen as the authors of their own fates? Do the poor have cultural traditions that keep them down? Shall we blame the unemployed for being unemployed? Next, we move on to the hierarchical groups known as castes and compare them as they occur in Hindu India with other hierarchical groups.

Class and Power

All state societies are organized into a hierarchy of groups known as classes. A *class* is a group of people who have a similar relationship to the apparatus of control and who possess similar amounts of power (or lack of power) (Fig. 13.1). To be powerful in human affairs is to be able to get people to obey one's requests and demands. In practice, power depends on the ability to provide or take away essential goods and services, and this ability in turn ultimately depends on who controls access to energy, resources, technology, and the means of physical and psychological coercion.

The beginnings of class hierarchies can be traced to chiefdoms and bigman societies. Chiefdoms often kept war captives as slaves and drew further distinctions of rank between commoners and a ruling elite. Even bigman societies sometimes kept small numbers of slaves and recognized distinctions of rank for the members of the bigman's family and his closest allies. But the fullest elaboration of class systems occurs in state societies.

All state societies necessarily have at least two classes arranged hierarchically: rulers and ruled. But where more than two classes exist, they are not necessarily all arranged hierarchically with respect to each other. For example, fishermen and neighboring farmers are usefully regarded as two separate classes because they relate to the ruling class in distinctive ways; have different patterns of ownership, rent, and taxation; and exploit entirely different sectors of the environment. Yet neither has a clear-cut power advantage or disadvantage with respect to the other. Similarly, anthropologists often speak of an urban as opposed to a rural lower class although the quantitative power differentials between the two may be minimal.

One other feature of classes should be noted: They come in relatively closed or open systems. In open-class systems, people can move up or down the hierarchy as in modern Western democracies. In closed-class systems, there is little mobility up or down. In medieval Europe, for example, serfs remained serfs for life (see p. 164). At their extreme, closed-class systems strongly resemble castes and ethnic groups.

Emics, Etics, and Class Consciousness

Class is an aspect of culture in which emic and etic points of view differ sharply (Berreman 1981: 18). Many social scientists accept class distinction as real and important only when the members of the class are aware of their class identity and act in unison. For a group to be considered a class, its members must be conscious of having common interests and a common identity. Other social scientists believe that classes exist only when persons with similar forms and quantities of social power organize into interest groups such as political parties or labor unions. The position I favor is that classes exist if there are actual concentrations of power in certain groups regardless of any conscious awareness of these differences among the people concerned and regardless of the existence of special interest organizations.

From an etic and behavioral viewpoint, classes can exist even when the members of the class deny that they constitute a class, and even when, instead of collective organizations, they have organizations that compete, such as rival business corporations or rival unions (De Mott 1990). Subordinate classes lacking class consciousness are obviously not exempt from the domination of ruling classes. Similarly, ruling classes containing antagonistic and competitive elements nonetheless dominate those who lack social power. Members of ruling classes need not form permanent, hereditary, monolithic, conspiratorial organizations in order to protect and enhance their own interests. Nor does a struggle for power within the ruling class necessarily result in a fundamentally altered balance of power between the classes. For

(a)

(b)

Figure 13.1   Poverty and Power
These people are both impoverished and disempowered. (a) An inner-
city man; (b) this tragic figure haunts the streets of Washington, D.C.,
the capital of the richest country in the world.

example, competition among various corporations in the United States supports rather than subverts the class position of top management.

Of course, there is no disputing the importance of a people's belief about the shape and origin of their stratification system. Consciousness of a common plight among the members of a downtrodden and exploited class may very well lead to the outbreak of organized class warfare. Consciousness is thus an element in the struggle between classes, but it is not the cause of class differences.

Class and Lifestyle

Classes differ from one another not only in amount of power per capita but also in broad areas of culture and lifestyle. Peasants, urban industrial wage workers, middle-class suburbanites, and upper-class chief executive officers of industrial firms differ in their lifestyles (Figs. 13.2 and 13.3). The contrast between them is as great as the contrast

between life in an Innuit igloo and life in a Mbuti camp in the Ituri forest.

Classes have their own subcultures made up of distinctive work patterns, architecture, home furnishings, diet, dress, domestic routines, sex and mating practices, magico-religious rituals, art, and ideology. In many instances, different classes even have accents that make it difficult for them to talk to one another. Moreover, because of exposure of body parts to sun, wind, and callus-producing friction, working-class people tend to look different from their "superiors." Further distinctions result from dietary specialties—the fat and the rich were once synonymous. (Today, in advanced capitalist societies, fatness is a sign of a diet overloaded with fats and sugars, together with a lack of exercise, and is associated with poverty rather than with wealth.)

Throughout almost the entire evolutionary career of stratified societies, class identity has been at least as explicit as the distinction between male and female genders. The Chinese Han dynasty peasant, the Inca commoner, or the Russian serf could not expect to survive to maturity without knowing how

Figure 13.2   *Class and Lifestyle*
East Harlem

Figure 13.4   *Caracas Shantytown*
Squatters in Latin American cities often enjoy the best views since apartment houses were not built on hilltops because of lack of water. But this means that the squatters have to carry their water up the hill in cans.

to recognize members of the "superior" classes. Any lingering doubts were removed by state-enforced standards of dress: Only the Chinese nobility could wear silk clothing; only the European feudal overlords could carry daggers and swords; and only the Inca rulers could wear gold ornaments. Violators were put to death. In the presence of their "superiors," commoners still perform definite rituals of subordination, among which lowering the head, removing the hat, averting the eyes, kneeling, bowing, crawling, or maintaining silence unless spoken to occur almost universally.

Figure 13.3   *Class and Lifestyle*
Hampton Beach, New Hampshire.

Throughout much of the world, class identity continues to be sharp and unambiguous. Among most contemporary nations, differences in class-linked lifestyles show little prospect of diminishing or disappearing. Indeed, given the convergence in former communist countries toward market economies, extremes of poverty and wealth may be on the rise. The contrast between the lifestyles of the rich and powerful and those of people living in peasant villages or urban shantytowns (Fig. 13.4) may be greater than ever before.

During the recent epochs of industrial advance, governing classes throughout the world have gone from palanquins to Rolls Royces to private jets, whereas their subordinates find themselves without even a donkey or a pair of oxen. The elites now jet to the world's best medical centers to be treated with the most advanced medical technology, whereas vast numbers of less fortunate people have never even heard of the germ theory of disease and can't even afford the price of a bottle of aspirin. Elites attend the best universities, whereas over 1.4 billion of the world's adults remain illiterate (Brown et al. 1993: 122).

Peasant Classes

About 40 percent of the people in the world make a living from farming and are members of one kind of peasant class or another. *Peasants* are the subordinate food producers of state societies who use nonindustrial technologies of food production and who pay rent in the form of services, crops, cash, or taxes. Each major type of peasant is the subject of a vast research literature. Anthropologists have studied peasants more than they have studied village peoples or hunters and gatherers. Three major types of peasant classes can be distinguished:

1. Feudal peasants. These peasants are subject to the control of a decentralized hereditary ruling class whose members provide military assistance to one another but do not interfere in one another's territorial domains. Feudal peasants, or "serfs," inherit the opportunity to utilize a particular parcel of land; hence they are said to be "bound" to the land. For the privilege of raising their own food, feudal peasants render unto the lord rent in kind or in money. Rent may also take the form of labor service in the lord's kitchens, stables, or fields.

   Feudalism and feudal peasants are fast disappearing from the world, but a heritage of feudal class relations is an important component in the underdevelopment of many Third World countries. This heritage remains strong in several Central and South American countries, especially in Guatemala, El Salvador, Ecuador, and Peru. In these countries, land ownership continues to be concentrated in huge estates owned by small numbers of politically powerful families. The peasants who live on or near these estates depend on the big landowners for access to land, water, loans, and emergency assistance. The extreme disparity in land holdings and the semifeudal relationships between the estate owners and the peasants lie behind the guerilla movements that are found throughout this region (S. Stern 1988).

2. Agromanagerial state peasantries. Where the state is strongly centralized, as in ancient Peru, Egypt, Mesopotamia, and China, peasants may be directly subject to state control in addition to, or in the absence of, control by a local landlord class. Unlike the feudal peasants, agromanagerial peasants are subject to frequent conscription for labor brigades drawn from villages throughout the realm to build roads, dams, irrigation canals, palaces, temples, and monuments (Yates 1990). In return, the state makes an effort to feed its peasants in case of food shortages caused by droughts or other calamities. The pervasive bureaucratic control over production and lifestyles in the ancient agromanagerial states has often been compared to the treatment of peasants who until recently were under communist rule in China, Albania, and Cambodia. The state in these countries was all-powerful, setting production quotas, controlling prices, and extracting taxes in kind and in labor.

Figure 13.5   Peruvian Peasants
The man's wife is planting potatoes as he plows.

3. Capitalist peasants. In Africa, Latin America, India, and Southeast Asia, feudal and agromanagerial types of peasantries have been replaced by peasants who enjoy increased opportunities to buy and sell land, labor, and food in competitive price markets. Most of the existing peasantries of the world now belong to this category (Fig. 13.5). The varieties of structured inferiority within this group defy any simple taxonomy. Some capitalist peasants are subordinate to large landowners; others are subordinate to banks that hold mortgages and promissory notes. In more isolated or unproductive regions, holdings may be very small (Fig. 13.6), giving rise to the phenomenon known as "penny capitalism" (that is, frequent buying and selling of small quantities of food and handicrafts).

The Image of Limited Good

A recurrent question concerning the plight of contemporary peasant communities is the extent to which they are victims of their own values (Peletz 1983; Kahn 1985). It has often been noted, for example, that peasants distrust innovations and cling to their old ways of doing things. Based on his study of the village of Tzintzuntzan, in the state of Michoacan, Mexico, George Foster (1967) has developed a general theory of peasant life based on a concept called *the image of limited good*. According to Foster, the people of Tzintzuntzan, like many peasants throughout the world, believe that life is a dreary struggle, that very few people can achieve "success," and that they can improve themselves only at the expense of other people. If someone tries some-

Figure 13.6   Ecuadorian Peasants
Note the "postage-stamp" farms on the steep hillsides.

thing new and succeeds at it, the rest of the community resents it, becomes jealous, and snubs the "progressive" individual. Many peasants, therefore, are afraid to change their ways of life because they do not want to stir up the envy and hostility of friends and relatives.

Although an image of limited good exists in many peasant villages in Mexico and elsewhere, the role it plays in preventing economic development is not clear. Foster actually throws doubt on the importance of the image of limited good in Tzintzuntzan (Fig. 13.7). He tells the story of how a community development project sponsored by the United Nations achieved success initially, only to end in disasters that had more to do with inept aid policies than with the values held by the villagers. Further, most of the community's cash income came from jobs as migrant laborers in the United States. To get across the border, the migrants must bribe, scheme, and suffer great hardships. Yet 50 percent of them had succeeded in getting through, "many of them ten times or more" (Foster 1967: 277). As Foster suggests, the image of limited good is not a crippling illusion but rather a realistic appraisal of the facts of life in a society where economic success or failure is capricious and hinged to forces wholly beyond one's control or comprehension (Box 13.1).

James Acheson, who studied a community near Tzintzuntzan, has argued that without realistic economic opportunities, development would not occur. If opportunities present themselves, some individuals will always take advan-

tage of them, regardless of the image of limited good: "It is one thing to say that Tarascans [the people of the region of Tzintzuntzan] are suspicious, distrustful, and uncooperative; it is another to assume that this lack of cooperation precludes all possibility for positive economic change" (Acheson 1972: 1,165; Acheson 1974; Foster 1974).

A *"Culture of Poverty"?*

In studying the problems of people living in urban slums and shantytowns, Oscar Lewis thought he had found evidence for a distinct set of values and practices that he called the *"culture of poverty."* Although not exactly comparable point by point, the concepts of the culture of poverty and of the image of limited good resemble each other in many respects and represent similar attempts to explain the perpetuation of poverty by focusing on the traditions and values of subordinate classes. And they are both wrong for similar reasons.

Oscar Lewis (1966) pictured the poor in cities like Mexico City, New York, and Lima (Fig. 13.8) as tending to be fearful, suspicious, and apathetic toward the major institutions of the larger society; as hating the police and being mistrustful of government; and as "inclined to be cynical of the church." They also have "a strong present-time orientation with relatively little disposition to defer gratification and plan for the future." This statement implies that poor people are less willing to save money and are more interested in "getting mine now" in the form of stereos, color television, the latest-style clothing, and sporty automobiles. It also implies that the poor "blow" their earnings by getting drunk or going on buying sprees. Like George Foster, Lewis recognized that in some measure the culture of poverty was partly a rational response to the objective conditions of powerlessness and poverty: "an adaptation and a reaction of the poor to their marginal position in a class-stratified society" (1966: 21). But he also stated that once the culture of poverty comes into existence, it tends to perpetuate itself:

> By the time slum children are six or seven they have usually absorbed the basic attitudes and values of their subculture. Thereafter they are psychologically unready to take full advantage of changing conditions or improving opportunities that may develop in their lifetime.

[Lewis 1966]

Lewis proposed that only 20 percent of the urban poor actually have the culture of poverty, implying that 80 percent fall into the category of those whose poverty results from infrastructural and structural conditions rather than from the traditions and values of a culture of poverty. The concept of the culture of poverty has been criticized on the grounds that the poor have many values other than those stressed in the

Figure 13.7   Image of Limited Good
Peasant women of Tzintzuntzan with their homemade pottery.

culture of poverty—values they share with other classes. Furthermore, values said to be distinctive of the urban poor are actually shared equally by the middle class. For example, being suspicious of government, politicians, and organized religion is not an exclusive poverty-class trait; nor is the tendency to spend above one's means. There is little evidence that the middle class as a whole lives within its income more effectively than poor people do. But when the poor mismanage their incomes, the consequences are much more serious. If the male head of a poor family yields to the temptation to buy nonessential items, his children may go hungry or his wife may be deprived of medical attention. But these conse-

quences result from being poor, not from any demonstrable difference in the capacity to defer gratification.

Poverty in Naples

Thomas Belmonte lived for a year in a slum neighborhood of Naples, Italy, a city that is known as the "Calcutta of Europe." Belmonte describes the neighborhood, Fontana del Re (Fig. 13.9; Box 13.2), as being inhabited by a subproletariat, or underclass, who lacked steady employment and who produced so little that they could not even be said to be exploited because there was nothing to be taken away from them. Gabriele, for example, collected metal junk and broke it into pieces with the help of his four children but also ran a

---

Box 13.1

A WORLD OF LIMITED GOOD

For the underlying, fundamental truth is that in an economy like Tzintzuntzan's, hard work and thrift are moral qualities of only the slightest functional value. Because of the limitations on land and technology, additional hard work does not produce a significant increment in income. It is pointless to talk of thrift in a subsistence economy because usually there is no surplus with which to be thrifty. Foresight, with careful planning for the future, is also a virtue of dubious value in a world in which the best-laid plans must rest on a foundation of chance and capriciousness.

Foster 1967: 150–151.

Figure 13.8   Squatters in Lima
Life on a garbage heap.

Figure 13.9   Poverty in Naples
The infamous one-room hovels of the Bassi, usually without ventilation, running water, separate toilets, or heating, are home for tens of thousands of Neapolitan families.

little store during the day and drove a taxi for prostitutes at night. Others were part-time sailors, waiters, bartenders, dockworkers, and movers. Some groomed dogs, others were jacks-of-all-trades. Some were full-time smugglers, dope dealers, pickpockets, purse snatchers, and burglars. Still others were dressmakers, flower vendors, beggars, and old women who added to their small pensions "by selling contraband cig-

---

Box 13.2

THE BROKEN FOUNTAIN

At Fontana del Re in a corner strewn now with rubble, beneath the bruised, shattered visage of a lion, the eroded figure of a sculpted stone sea shell recedes into a wall. "This was our fountain," they told me. "Oh you should have seen it, Tommaso. The water played night and day. In summer, the children scampered about in it. At night, falling asleep, you heard it, and it was like music." The young men told me it was they who had destroyed it. As children, many years before, with iron rods, they had gone every day to hammer and smash it, until they were satisfied and there was nothing left to break.

Thereafter, whenever I passed that ruined corner, I tried to imagine what the fountain had once been like, and thought and wondered and sorrowed the more as I understood how it came to be broken.

Belmonte 1979: 144.

---

arettes and condoms, and greasy sandwiches and wine so bad it burned a hole through your gut." The children of Fontana del Re did odd jobs that earned them about 33 cents an hour. Pepe, the 11-year-old son of a cobbler, had a job in a TV repair shop; his face and chest were scarred from defective tubes that blew up when he tested them. Several neighborhood children made daily forays to pry open the trunks of parked cars. Other children carried trays of espresso to offices and shops.

The people of Fontana del Re have many of Oscar Lewis's culture of poverty traits. But Belmonte attributes most of these traits to being penniless and lacking steady employment.

Castes in India

Indian castes are closed, endogamous, and stratified descent groups. They bear many resemblances to closed classes, ethnic groups, and social races. No sharp line can be drawn between the castes of India and such groups as the Amish or blacks in the United States or the Inca elite. However, some features of the Indian caste hierarchy are unique and deserve special attention.

The unique features of Indian castes have to do with the fact that the caste hierarchy is an integral part of Hinduism, the religion of most people in India. (This does not mean that one must be a Hindu in order to belong to a caste. Muslim and Christian castes also exist in India.) It is a matter of religious conviction in India that all people are not spiritually equal and that the gods have established a hierarchy of groups. This hierarchy consists of the four major *varnas*, or grades of being. According to the earliest traditions (for example, the Hymns of Rigveda), the four varnas correspond to the physical parts of Manu, who gave rise to the human race through dismemberment. His head became the Brahmans (priests), his arms the Kshatriyas (warriors), his thighs the Vaishyas (merchants and craftsmen), and his feet the Shudras (menial workers). According to Hindu scripture, an individual's varna is determined by a descent rule; that is, it corresponds to the varna of one's parents and is unalterable during one's lifetime.

The basis of all Hindu morality is the idea that each varna has its appropriate rules of behavior, or "path of duty" (*dharma*). At the death of the body, the soul meets its fate in the form of a transmigration into a higher or lower being (*karma*). Those who follow their dharma will be rewarded with a higher point on Manu's body during their next life. Deviation from the dharma will result in reincarnation in the body of an outcaste or even an animal (Long 1987).

One of the most important aspects of the dharma is the practice of certain taboos regarding marriage, eating, and physical proximity. Marriage below one's varna is generally regarded as a defilement and pollution. Acceptance of food cooked or handled by persons below one's varna is also a defilement and pollution, and any bodily contact between Brahman and Shudra is forbidden. In parts of India, certain castes were not only untouchable but also unseeable, and therefore, these people could come out only at night. The worst of these restrictions became illegal after India gained its independence at mid-century.

Although the general outlines of this system are agreed on throughout Hindu India (Long 1987; Maloney 1987a, b), enormous regional and local differences occur in the finer details of the ideology and practice of caste relationships. The principal source of these differences is the fact that it is not the varna but thousands of internally stratified subdivisions known as *jatis* (or subcastes) that constitute the real functional endogamous units. Moreover, even jatis of the same name ("washermen," "shoemakers," "herders," and so on) further divide into local endogamous subgroups and exogamous lineages (Klass 1979).

Caste from the Top Down and Bottom Up

There are two very different views of the Hindu caste system. The view that predominates among Westerners conforms largely to the emics of the top-ranking Brahman caste. According to this view, each caste and subcaste has a hereditary occupation that guarantees its members basic subsistence and job security. The lower castes render vital services to the upper castes. Hence, the upper castes know they cannot get along without the lower castes and do not abuse them. In times of crisis, the upper castes will extend emergency assistance in the form of food or loans. Moreover, since the Hindu religion gives everyone a convincing explanation of why some are inferior and others superior, members of lower castes do not resent being regarded as a source of pollution and defilement and have no interest in changing the status of their caste in the local or regional hierarchy (Dumont 1970).

The other view—the view from the bottom up—makes the Indian caste system hard to distinguish from other kinds of hierarchical groups such as classes and ethnic groups with which Westerners are familiar. Critics of the top-down view point out that whites in the United States once insisted that the Bible justified slavery and that blacks were well treated, contented with their lot in life, and not interested in changing their status. According to Joan Mencher, who has worked and lived among the untouchable castes of southern India, the error in the top-down view is just as great in India as in the United States (Fig. 13.10).

Mencher reports that the lowest castes are not satisfied with their station in life and do not believe they are treated fairly by their caste superiors. As for the security allegedly provided by the monopoly over such professions as smiths, washermen, barbers, and potters, such occupations taken

Figure 13.10   Untouchables
Caste in India must be seen from the bottom up to be understood.

together never engaged more than 10 to 15 percent of the total Hindu population. Caste professions never provided basic subsistence for the majority of the members of most castes. Among the Chamars, for example, who are known as leatherworkers, only a small portion of the caste engages in leatherwork. In the countryside, almost all Chamars are a source of cheap agricultural labor. When questioned about their low station in life, many of Mencher's low-caste informants explained that they had to be dependent on the other castes since they had no land of their own. Did landowners in times of extreme need or crisis actually give free food and assistance to their low-caste dependents? "To my informants, both young and old, this sounds like a fairytale" (Mencher 1974b).

Anthropological studies of actual village life in India have yielded a picture of caste relationships drastically opposed to the ideals posited in Hindu theology (Carroll 1977). One of the most important discoveries is that local jatis recurrently try to raise their ritual status. Such attempts usually take place as part of a general process by which local ritual status is adjusted to actual local economic and political power. Some low-ranking subcastes may passively accept their lot in life as a result of their karma assignment; such groups, however, tend to be wholly lacking in the potential for economic and political mobility. "But let opportunities for political and economic advance appear barely possible and such resignation is likely to vanish more quickly than one might imagine" (Orans 1968: 878).

One symptom of this underlying propensity for jatis to redefine their spiritual level is a widespread lack of agreement over the shape of local ritual hierarchies as seen by inhabitants of the same village, town, or region. Even the lowest "untouchables" may (Khare 1984) reject the position others assign to them.

The study of caste "dissensus" has long been a central concern of village India researchers (Barber 1968). Kathleen Gough (1959) indicates that in villages of South India, the middle reaches of the caste hierarchy may have as many as fifteen castes whose positions are ambiguous or in dispute. Different individuals and families in the same caste give different versions of the rank order of these groups. Elsewhere, even the claims of Brahman subcastes to ritual superiority are openly contested (Srinivas 1955). The conflict among jatis concerning their ritual position may involve prolonged litigation in the local courts and if not resolved may lead to violence and bloodshed (see Cohn 1955; Berreman 1975).

The stratification system of India is noteworthy not merely for the presence of endogamous descent groups possessing real or imagined racial and cultural specialties. Every state-level society has such groups. It is, rather, the extraordinary profusion of such groups that merits our attention. Nonetheless, the caste system of India is fundamentally similar to the system of other countries that have closed classes and numerous ethnic and racial minorities. Like African-Americans in the United States or Catholics in Northern Ireland, low castes in India resist the status accorded them, with its concomitant disabilities and discrimination, and strive for higher accorded status and its attendant advantages. High castes attempt to prevent such striving and the implied threat to their positions. In this conflict of interests lies the explosive potential of all caste societies (Berreman 1966: 318).

Chapter Summary

Class differences involve both differential access to power and profound differences in lifestyles. The understanding of class and all other forms of social stratification is made difficult by the failure to separate emic and etic versions of stratification hierarchies. From an etic and behavioral point of view, classes can exist even if the members show no emic recognition of their existence and even if segments of the same class compete. Ruling classes need not form permanent, hereditary, monolithic, conspiratorial organizations. Ruling class membership can change rapidly, and they may actively deny that they constitute a ruling class. Similarly, subordinate classes need not be conscious of their identity and may exist only in an etic and behavioral sense.

About 40 percent of the people in the world today are members of peasant classes. Peasants are structured inferiors who farm with preindustrial technologies and pay rent or taxes. Three major varieties of peasants can be distinguished: feudal, agromanagerial, and capitalist. Their structured inferiority depends in the first case on the inability to acquire land; in the second, on the existence of a powerful managerial elite that sets production and labor quotas; and in the third, on the operation of a price market in land and labor controlled by big landlords, corporations, and banks.

Among peasant classes, an image of limited good is widespread. However, contradictory values and attitudes encourage innovations and risktaking under appropriate structural and infrastructural conditions. In Tzintzuntzan, despite the image of limited good, men struggled for a chance to work as migrant laborers, and both men and women participated in a series of ill-fated development experiments in the hope of bettering their lives.

The counterpart of the image of limited good for urban subordinate classes is the culture of poverty. This concept focuses on the values and traditions of the urban poor as an explanation for poverty. However, many of the values in the culture of poverty, such as distrust of authority, consumerism, and improvidence, are also found in more affluent classes. Much of the behavior of the underclass, as in the case of Naples, can be understood as a consequence of chronic unemployment.

Castes are closed endogamous groups that resemble classes and ethnic groups. They are epitomized by the varnas and jatis of India. Traditional views of Indian castes have been dominated by top-down idealizations in which the lower castes are represented as voluntarily accepting their subordinate status. Bottom-up studies show that Indian castes struggle for upward mobility and attempt to bring their caste's ranking in line with their economic status.

AMERICA NOW UPDATE

Is There a Ruling Class in the United States?

Most Americans do not think of themselves as being members of a class, and class has always been downplayed as a factor in American history. Thus, according to president George

Bush, "class is for European democracies or something else—it isn't for the United States of America. We are not going to be divided by class" (DeMott 1990: 11). But like all state-organized societies, the United States is a stratified society and has a complex system of classes, minorities, and other hierarchical groups.

There is no doubt that the United States is a highly stratified society. This can be seen from the data on the distribution of wealth among U.S. families. According to a Federal Reserve research survey, the richest 1 percent of U.S. families in 1989 owned 37 percent of the total net wealth; the next 9 percent owned 31 percent; and the remaining 90 percent owned 33 percent. That is, the top 10 percent owned more than twice the total of what the bottom 90 percent owned (Kinnickell and Woodburn 1992).

The most important question that can be asked about class in the United States is whether there is a ruling class. Paradoxically, this is a subject about which relatively little is known. The existence of a ruling class in the United States seems to be negated by the ability of the people as a whole to vote political officeholders in or out of office by secret ballot. Yet the fact that less than half of the voting-age population votes in presidential elections suggests that the majority of citizens distrust the candidates' promises or doubt that one candidate can do anything more than any other to make life significantly better (Hadley 1978; Ladd 1978). The actual selection of political candidates and the financing and conduct of election campaigns are controlled through special interest groups and political action committees. Small coalitions of powerful individuals working through lobbyists, law firms, legislatures, the courts, executive and administrative agencies, and the mass media can decisively influence the course of elections and of national affairs. The great bulk of the decision-making process consists of responses to pressures exerted by special interest groups (Drew 1983; Thomas 1986; Sabato 1989). In the campaigns for Congress, the candidate who spends the most money usually wins.

Those who claim that there is no ruling class in the United States argue that power is dispersed among many different contending blocs, lobbies, associations, clubs, industries, regions, income groups, ethnic groups, states, cities, age groups, legislatures, courts, and unions, and that no coalition powerful enough to dominate all the others can form (Dahl 1981). But the crucial question is this: Is there a category of people who share a set of underlying interests in the perpetuation of the status quo and who by virtue of their extreme wealth are able to set limits to the kinds of laws and executive policies that are enacted and followed out?

The evidence for the existence of such a category of people consists largely of studies of the extent of interlocking memberships on corporate boards of directors and the concentration of ownership and wealth in giant corporations and well-to-do families. This kind of data alone cannot prove the existence of a ruling class since the problem remains of how boards of directors and wealthy families actually influence decisions on crucial matters such as the rate of inflation, unemployment, national health service, energy policy, tax structure, resource depletion, pollution, military spending, and urban blight.

The concentration of wealth and economic power in the United States shows at least that there is a real potential for such influence to be exerted (Roberts and Brintnall 1982: 259). According to the Federal Reserve Board (Kennickell and Woodburn 1992), 1 percent of U.S. families owned:

45 percent of all nonresidential real estate

49 percent of all publicly held stock

78 percent of all trusts

62 percent of all business assets

About half of stocks and bonds are owned by institutional investors, who administer pension funds, trust funds, and insurance companies. It is the corporations, families, and people who control these institutional investors that have the greatest economic power. As a result of the wave of buyouts and mergers that took place in the United States during the 1980s, the concentration of economic power has continued to increase. A rough idea of the trend toward greater concentration of economic power can be derived from changes in family income. Between 1977 and 1989, the average pretax incomes of the top 1 percent of American families rose 77 percent while the pretax incomes of the bottom 40 percent of families fell by between 1 and 9 percent. The top 1 percent of families earned an average of $560,000 each in 1989, and their combined earnings were half a trillion dollars, an amount almost equivalent to the sum of all federal tax revenues in that year. Another revealing statistic is the change in the disparity between the incomes of employees and employers. In the 1970s, employers made 35 times what employees made; in 1990, they were making 120 times more (Noah 1992). It is entirely possible, therefore, that a small group of individuals and families exerts a decisive influence over the policies of a small but immensely powerful group of corporations. Some of the individuals and families involved are well known. Besides the Mellons, they include Rockefellers, Du Ponts, Fords, Hunts, Pews, and Gettys (Fig. 13.11). But it is a testament to the ability of the superrich to live in a world apart that the names of many other powerful families are unknown to the general public. Anthropologists have been remiss in not studying the patterns of thoughts and actions of the superrich (Nader 1972).

Figure 13.11   Members of the Ruling Class?
(a) H. Ross Perot. (b) William Gates (founder of Microsoft computer-software). (c) David Rockefeller.

Chapter 14

ETHNICITY, RACE, AND RACISM

German anti-racist protest march at Dachau.

Two other hierarchical groups associated with the rise of the state—ethnic groups and social races—are the subject of this chapter. How ethnic groups and social races differ from classes and castes is one of the questions to be considered. We shall also address the worldwide confusion concerning the relationship of biological race to social races and ethnic groups. Then we explore the dynamic processes that lead to more or less successful outcomes of the competition among social races and ethnic groups. We will pay special attention to the alternatives of assimilation and pluralism in the United States, where white racism against African-Americans and other "nonwhites" continues to flourish. This leads to a critique of the key evidence for white superiority. Not to be outdone, blacks have recently developed their own form of racism, and we end the chapter with a similar critique of the claims for black superiority. Ethnic and racial chauvinists of any ilk may have a hard time getting through this chapter. Keep your cool. We have to learn to live together.

Ethnicity

One of the most important consequences of the rise of the state was the appearance of *ethnic groups*. States achieved their prominence in political evolution precisely because of their ability to extend their boundaries to include near and distant polities such as chiefdoms and other states. Ethnic groups first formed when conquered populations retained distinctive linguistic and cultural features associated with their preconquest status. In modern times, ethnic groups have formed as much through migration as through conquest. Here is a rough definition of ethnic group: It is a group that has been incorporated into a state through conquest or migration and that maintains distinctive cultural and linguistic traditions, and a sense of having a separate identity.

The distinctiveness of ethnic groups—their ethnicity—stems from their distinctive cuisines, holidays, religious beliefs, dances, folklore, and dress (Fig. 14.1). But the most powerful source of ethnic identity is the possession of a common language or dialect. Use of a common language or dialect instills a sense of community that is powerful enough to override the absence of other kinds of cultural traditions.

The emergence in the United States of the ethnic category Hispanic illustrates this point. Hispanics include people who are recent immigrants from Spain, from the Spanish-speaking Caribbean islands, and from various parts of Mexico and Central and South America. The cultures of Hispanic-Americans, with the exception of their common language, differ at least as much among themselves as the cultures of Polish-Americans and Italian-Americans. Many prefer to be known as Puerto Ricans, Salvadorans, or Argentinians. Even Brazilian immigrants who speak Portuguese, not Spanish, often find themselves categorized as Hispanic (Margolis 1994).

Linguistic separateness is often accompanied by cultural differences that in fact or fancy represent long-standing traditions unique to the members of the ethnic group. A further criterion is group endogamy in combination with a rule of descent.

In practice, however, ethnic groups can maintain their identity and continuity by possessing many combinations of these traits. Ethnics do not necessarily speak the language of their ancestors. Moreover, their ancestral customs are not necessarily the heritage of remote ancestors. Some are actually the inventions of recent generations (Box 14.1). Some ethnic groups may neither speak the language of their ethnic ancestors nor preserve ancestral customs, old or new (Roosens 1989). Preservation of their ethnic identity may merely result from marrying endogamously and using family names indicative of ethnic descent. Even high rates of intermarriage do not necessarily impede the continuity of an ethnic group: Various rules of descent can be used to retain the children of mixed marriages within the ethnic group of one of the parents (Fig. 14.2).

Direct conquest continues to be an important source of ethnogenesis, but the founding of new Euro-American polities in North and South America and the rise of capitalism made migration an equally prominent source of new ethnic groups. The United States in particular, with its open labor markets and promise of cheap land (stolen from the Indians), attracted waves of non-English-speaking migrants who retained separate ethnic identities.

Biological Races Versus Social Races Versus Ethnic Groups

Biological races are etic populations in which several genes occur together with distinctive frequencies over many gener-

(a)

Figure 14.1   Ethnic Festivals
(a) An Irish Parade in New York. (b) Celebrating Chinese New Year.
(c) Jewish parade in New York. (d) Italian Festival in Boston.

(c)

(b)

(d)

Box 14.1

THE INVENTION OF TRADITION

A classic instance of traditions falsely attributed to remote ancestors is the wearing of kilts by the members of Scottish clans. Kilts were not used in Scotland until about 1746. They were introduced not by a Scotsman but by an Englishman who was interested in having his workers dress in a manner that gave them more freedom of movement than the traditional garb which consisted of a single piece of plaid cloth draped over the shoulders and belted around the waist to form a short petticoat. Initially there was no association between the plaid patterns and particular clans. Manufacturers of plaid cloth eagerly promoted such associations along with Celtic revivalists who produced dubious works of scholarship that were intended to settle the question of who could wear what. It was only in the 1850s that the association between plaids and clans was stabilized.

Trevor-Roper 1983.

ations. Scientists do not agree on which genes should be used to establish racial boundaries. The problem is that the more genes that are used to distinguish one race from another, the less likely it is that they occur together over many generations. This lack of genetic continuity results from the fact that human populations exchange genes through mating, creating ever-changing patterns of genetic variations (Armelagos 1993).

Social races consist of people who are believed to be (both by themselves and by others) physically and psychologically alike, regardless of scientifically established genetic relationships or even in direct contradiction to scientific knowledge about heredity. Social races differ from ethnic groups only as a matter of degree. Social races, like ethnic groups, gain their identity or claim to gain their identity from distinctive linguistic and other cultural patterns. They also claim common ancestry based on the practice of endogamy and rules of descent. They or others believe that they can be picked out in a crowd simply on the basis of their looks. The resemblance between social races and ethnic groups is so close that many people use the terms *ethnic* and *race* interchangeably. Others, however, claim that racial differences are more per-

manent and visible than the physical differences found among ethnics (see Wolf 1993).

Militant African-Americans, for example, claim that racial markers become the focus for discrimination by dominant ethnic and racial groups because they are indelible. As a result, racially different individuals have no chance to escape from the persecution and discrimination of the dominant group. The validity of this argument, however, depends on the culturally constructed principles such as descent and racial categorizations that are employed to give individuals a racial identity. As a matter of fact, social race identity is no more indelible than ethnic identity based on linguistic or cultural differences. For the continuity of social races depends on how much intermarriage takes place and on how the children of mixed marriages are classified.

The One Drop Rule

Various systems for identifying social races are in use throughout the world today. In the United States, African-Americans are not identified as a distinct social race solely on the basis of their skin color. Reliance on skin color alone would leave the identity of millions of people in doubt because skin color (and other "African" and "Caucasian" traits) varies across a broad spectrum of nuanced differences from very dark to brown to very light as a result of recent and remote interracial matings and marriages (Root 1992).

In the context of slavery and its aftermath, when it was official policy to discriminate against blacks, some rule or principle was needed to categorize people as either black or white so that the discriminatory measures could be applied to blacks who looked like whites, but not to whites who looked like blacks. To solve this quandary, a *one drop rule* was constructed: Blacks became anyone who had the slightest amount of black "blood" as attested to by their having even one ancestor who was known to have been identified as black (whether or not this ancestor himself or herself was also a child of a mixed marriage or mating). By the one drop rule still in force today, children of a mixed marriage between one biologically white and one biologically black parent are socially black (Spickard 1992: 16; Root 1992). But scientifically, we know that all of us inherit half of our genes from mother and half from father.

A very different construction of social race prevails in Latin America and the Caribbean Islands. In Brazil, for example, racial categorizations depend mainly on the perceptions that people have of each other's appearance, with equal emphasis on skin color and hair form. But a person's "racial" identity may also be influenced by his or her wealth and profession. A surprising number of terms are available for identifying any individual's particular combination of traits. (In

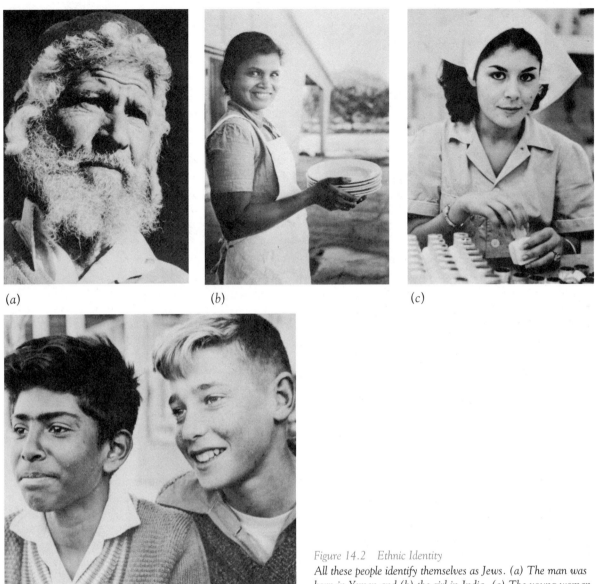

Figure 14.2   Ethnic Identity

All these people identify themselves as Jews. (a) The man was born in Yemen and (b) the girl in India. (c) The young woman was born in Morocco and (d) both boys in Israel.

one study, which I carried out, 492 different terms were encountered.) The one drop rule doesn't exist in Brazil; ancestry or descent is not important for racial identity. This means that children can have a racial identity that is different from that of their parents and further that one child can be identified as the equivalent of "white" while his or her full brother or sister can be identified as the equivalent of "black" (Harris et al. 1993; Fig. 14.3).

Biological Race and Culture

The relationship between biological race and culture is a source of much confusion the world over. One of the most

important tasks of anthropology is to clarify the difference between them. Etically, a race is a *population*—an interbreeding group of people defined by a set of distinctive gene frequencies. A culture is a way of life. A large-scale biological race does not have just one culture; it has hundreds of cultures. And these cultures cover the whole spectrum of cultural types, from bands and villages to states and empires. Thus people who belong to different biological races may possess very similar or even identical cultures. And people who possess very different cultures may belong to the same biological race.

In the United States, millions of racially diverse children and grandchildren of Asians and Africans have a way of life that is essentially similar to the way of life of the "Caucasian"

Figure 14.3   Brazilian Race–Color Variations
The great variety of facial features, skin color, and hair texture in modern Brazil suggests that it is futile to think about human beings in terms of a small number of fixed and sharply distinct races.

majority. These biological and anthropological facts, however, are often ignored in the construction of social races. It is widely believed that certain traditions are inseparable from and exclusive to each social race as implied, for example, in the concept "African culture." As we shall see momentarily, the sense of having a distinctive culture is important for the mobilization of resistance within disadvantaged social races and ethnic groups. However, a rigid linking of race and culture is a form of racism that runs counter to all that is scientifically known about the transmissibility of cultures across racial and ethnic boundaries. It bears repeating that at birth, every healthy human infant, regardless of race, has the capacity to acquire the traditions, practices, values, and languages found in any of the world's five thousand or so different cultures.

The Competitive Dynamics of Ethnic and Racial Groups

The most important point to bear in mind about ethnic groups and social races is that they are invariably locked into a more or less open and conscious form of political, social, and economic struggle to protect or raise their positions in the stratification system. To a surprising degree, the class struggle predicted by Karl Marx has been overshadowed by race and ethnic struggle. Although class differences have rarely led to class consciousness and class solidarity, racial and ethnic groups the world over have been at the forefront of conscious and often violent struggles aimed at changing the stratification hierarchy (Fig. 14.4).

Depending on their numbers, their special cultural strengths and weaknesses, and their initial advantages or dis-

Figure 14.4   Long Road to Freedom
Struggle between whites and backs in South Africa is not over. Sign says, "Kill Apartheid, Not Us."

advantages during the formation of the stratification system, ethnic and racial groups rise or fall in the hierarchy. Thus, although many ethnic groups and social races are subject to severe forms of discrimination, segregation, and exploitation, others may actually enjoy fairly high, though not dominant, positions.

Assimilation or Pluralism?

Pluralism denotes the continuity of social races and ethnic groups within the jurisdiction of a single state. The disappearance of an ethnic group or social race through absorption by dominant groups is called *assimilation*. The resurgence in recent times of an emphasis on ethnic and racial identity has made it clear that total assimilation is a rather rare outcome of the interaction of ethnic groups and social races with dominant groups. Some form of multiethnic and multiracial pluralism seems to be far more common. But the perpetuation of multiethnic and multiracial social groups differs in important ways from the preservation of their cultures.

Ethnic groups and social races may adopt the language of the majority, lose their old traditions, and become culturally similar to the dominant majority and yet remain unassimilated. (The change need not be one-sided—the dominant group may in turn adopt traditions such as ethnic foods and holidays, like pizza and St. Patrick's Day.) Even extensive intermarriage need not lead to assimilation. This appears to be true of the European immigrant groups in the United States such as Scots, Germans, Jews, English, French, and Italians, whose rates of exogamy range as high as 30 or 40 percent (Kivisto 1989; Alba 1990). These groups maintain their identity through a principal of ambilineal descent (see p. 121), whereby children of mixed marriages shift from one ethnic identity to another as they see fit. The children of an Irish and Italian intermarriage, for example, may invoke their Irish parent on Saint Patrick's Day and their Italian parent on the Feast of Saint Genaro.

Another important aspect of the dynamics of ethnic and racial groups is that these groups themselves consist of classes that do not necessarily have common interests. Ethnic and racial elites may stand to gain more than the average person from intensifying group solidarity in the name of resisting assimilation. Roger Sanjek (1972, 1977) studied the relationships among twenty-three different "tribal" groups who live in the city of Accra, Ghana, and found that in terms of language, behavior, dress, residence, and facial markings, one group hardly differed from another. Nonetheless, politicians relied heavily on their "tribal" identities in competing for political office. Similarly, the tragic history of Lebanon cannot be understood apart from the private fortunes that both Christian and Muslim elites were able to amass as a result of drawn-out communal strife (Joseph 1978).

New Yorker Cartoon, *Peace on Earth . . .*

"successful" adaptations that were followed by mass slaughter or forced migrations.

The Dynamics of Pluralism in the United States

Wars of conquest and migration have been the major sources of the racial and cultural diversity found in the United States. Captured and enslaved African peoples were transported against their will across the ocean while Native Americans, defeated in their attempt to safeguard their homelands, were forced to migrate to distant reservations. Conquest also lies at the root of the formation of the Hispanic ethnic group in the Southwest and California.

White ethnics, especially those from Ireland and Eastern and Southern Europe, migrated under various degrees of compulsion in search of relief from religious or political persecution, military impressment, economic insolvency, and the threat of outright starvation. A third wave of immigrants, legal and illegal, is currently pouring into the United States. Hispanics from Mexico, the Caribbean, and South America predominate, but substantial numbers of Haitians, Brazilians, English-speaking Caribbeans, Koreans, Indians, Vietnamese, Samoans, and Chinese are also part of this wave. Intent on achieving a better life, a bigger slice of the American dream, they are creating new conflicts over "turf" or intensifying old ones. As recent events have shown, the ethnic and racial frontiers of the inner cities, continue to be the breeding grounds of incivility and mindless violence.

Although each ethnic group has its distinctive history, they share many experiences and have evolved along similar lines in response to similar pressures. Most started out low in the social and economic hierarchy and have struggled to gain respect and to increase their access to local and national sources of wealth and power. Some groups were better prepared by their own cultural traditions to cope with the challenges of their new conditions of life. Those with strong literate traditions were preadapted for competing in the rapidly changing world of an urban industrial society. Knowledge of English was usually indispensable for success in this effort, leading to the gradual disuse and abandonment of ethnic native languages by the majority of white ethnics. Other influences such as the mass media and capitalist consumerism have led white ethnics to abandon a large part of their native cuisine and many of their other distinctive cultural traditions.

Does this mean that white ethnic groups are blending into a single white social race as in the theory of the melting pot? Yes and no. The evidence is equivocal. White ethnic groups continue to promote ethnic pride and to revitalize old ethnic traditions or to invent new ones. But the lifestyles of white Americans have become so homogeneous that young people

An emphasis on differences in language, religion, and other aspects of lifestyles increases a group's sense of solidarity, and this may help its members compete, especially in impersonalized, class-structured, capitalist societies. Jewish, Chinese, Japanese, Greek, Syrian, Hindu, or Muslim merchants and businesspeople, for example, frequently enjoy important commercial advantages as a result of sharing information and obtaining loans and credit from their ethnic associates. Moreover, racial and ethnic consciousness, like class consciousness, is a necessary condition for mobilizing the mental and physical resources of vulnerable or downtrodden groups on behalf of defending or improving their position in the hierarchy. Thus all ethnic and racial groups find themselves under pressure to cast their history and their achievements in the most favorable light. But unrestrained ethnic and racial chauvinism is a dangerous game.

The problem is that strong ethnic and racial solidarity carries with it the danger of backlash. In maintaining and increasing their own solidarity, social races and ethnic groups run the risk of increasing the dominant group's resentment and hence of becoming the scapegoats of discriminatory and even genocidal policies. The persecution of the Jews in Germany and Poland, the Hindu Indians in east and southern Africa, the Chinese in Indonesia, and the Muslims and Sikhs in India are some of the better-known examples of

from different ethnic groups are finding it increasingly acceptable to marry each other. In the absence of a rigid rule of descent (like the one drop rule), the ethnic identity of children and grandchildren of ethnically mixed marriages tends to grow weaker and to become more a matter of choice than of ascription.

Refuting White Racism

Despite the evidence that the vast majority of sociocultural differences and similarities cannot be explained by variant genotypes (see Appendix), racial explanations continue to find favor on a popular level and in certain scientific circles. Many people remain convinced that some racial groups are naturally smarter, more musical, more athletic, more spiritual, or sexier than others. These stereotypes arise from a common methodological problem: the failure to control for the effects of historical and cultural influences on the behavior of the groups in question.

In the nineteenth century, the failure of blacks and other "races" to compete successfully against "white nations" in manufacturing, commerce, and war was taken as incontrovertible evidence that whites were a superior race. Had not whites from Europe and their descendants in North America gained political and economic control over almost the entire human species? Eager to justify their imperial expansion, Europeans and North Americans failed to see the hollowness of this argument. They conveniently forgot that history is full of tales of empires brought to their knees by peoples who were at one time considered to be unalterably backward, such as the "barbarians" who conquered Rome and China (Boxes 14.2 and 14.3).

The Wages of Racism

Much humiliation suffered by U.S. industry and commerce at the hands of Japanese competitors stems from racial arrogance. In the 1930s, Americans knew the Japanese only as makers of cheap toys, paper fans, and watches with mainsprings that broke at the first winding. American engineers soberly declaimed that no matter how hard the Japanese might try, they could never catch up with the industrial superpowers, especially with the United States. They didn't have that special inborn quality that Americans called "Yankee ingenuity." How earnestly the Julius Caesars of American industry argued that Japan could only imitate! By no "sane stretch of fantasy" could they imagine that in 50 years Japanese auto imports would bring Detroit to its knees and that Japanese microscopes, cameras, digital watches, calculators, television sets, videorecorders, and dozens of other

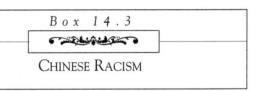

Box 1 4 . 2

ROMAN RACISM

Alfred Kroeber, founder of the Department of Anthropology at the University of California at Berkeley, succinctly conveyed the irony of Rome's collapse at the hands of despised barbarian races in these words:

> Had Julius Caesar or one of his contemporaries been asked whether by any sane stretch of fantasy he could imagine the Britons and the Germans as inherently the equals of Romans and Greeks, he would probably have replied that if these Northerners possessed the ability of the Mediterraneans they would long since have given vent to it, instead of continuing to live in disorganization, poverty, ignorance, rudeness, and without great men or products of the spirit.

(Kroeber 1948: 202)

Box 1 4 . 3

CHINESE RACISM

In 1792, Emperor Ch'ien-Lung rejected a "red-faced barbarian" delegation's request to open up trading relationships. England, the Emperor said, had nothing China wanted. "As your ambassador can see for himself, we possess all things." Ch'ien-Lung's empire stretched from the Arctic Circle to the Indian Ocean and 3,000 miles inland. It had a population of 300 million, all under the control of a single, centralized bureaucracy. It was the biggest and most powerful empire the world had ever seen. Yet in fewer than 50 years after Ch'ien-Lung's arrogant verdict, Chinese imperial power was destroyed, its armies humiliated by a handful of European troops, its seaports controlled by English, French, German, and American merchants, its peasant masses gripped by famine and pestilence.

made-in-Japan consumer products would dominate America's market.

Today, despite this record of supposedly inferior "races" gaining ascendancy over their erstwhile superiors, many people continue to think that black Africa is doomed by its genetic heritage to be a perpetual laggard in a world of high-tech industrialism. Are the genetic aptitudes for creating a United States or a Japan somehow in short supply in black Africa? In view of the frequency with which the roles of superior and inferior have been upended in the past, racial differences do not merit serious consideration as an explanation of black Africa's predicament, at least not until the historical reasons for black Africa's lagging pace of development have been thoroughly explored.

The IQ Controversy

In recent times, the question of the significance of racial differences has centered on the issue of whether some races are more intelligent than others. A vast amount of research has been devoted especially to the testing and comparison of the IQs of American whites and blacks. It has long been known that nationwide, whites score an average of 15 points higher than blacks. This gap allegedly persists even when samples of blacks and whites are matched for socioeconomic status—income, job type, and years of schooling (Shuey 1966; McGurk 1975).

The fact that a 15-point gap in IQ persists when whites and blacks are matched for socioeconomic status does not confirm the innateness of the difference between black and white IQs; rather, it points to the inadequacy of the socioeconomic factors being used to control for environmental and cultural differences. Chief among the factors that such studies fail to control for is the effect on test performance of being a member of a group that is demeaned, segregated, and discriminated against and that has never been able to develop a strong tradition of honoring scholastic and intellectual achievement. In order to control for these factors, we would have to place a sample of black infant twins for adoption, one from each pair in a white household and the other in a black household. Then we would do the same for a sample of white infant twins—half in white households and half in black households. And even then we would have to change the color of the white children to black and the black children to white to control for the possible effects of social rejection of transracial fostering. Needless to say, various ethical and practical considerations make it impossible to carry out this experiment. Small wonder that behavior geneticist Jerry Hirsch (1981: 36) reached the conclusion that the attempt to measure racial differences in intelligence is "impossible and therefore worthless."

Nonetheless, one study has approximated the conditions that are needed to control for the effects on IQ of being brought up in a white versus a black household. This study compared the IQ scores of black children who had been adopted by affluent white parents with the IQ scores of white children who had been adopted and brought up by the same parents as the black children (Scarr and Weinberg 1976). The main results of the study are these:

1. Both black and white adopted children had higher scores than the general population.
2. The IQs of the black and white adopted children were not statistically different.
3. Natural children of the white parents had higher test scores than their adopted siblings.

Even though the adopted children of both races achieved higher IQ scores than the general population, no measurable difference occurred between the scores of black adopted children and white adopted children. Biological children, however, scored higher than their adopted siblings, black and white (Silk and Boyd 1989; Fig. 14.5) The last point can be explained as an effect that some aspect(s) of the adoption process may have had on the ability of the adopted children to obtain the full benefit of being brought up in advantaged households. (Were the adopted children treated the same as the natural children?) One could alternatively argue that the adoptive parents had extra-high IQs, which gave their natural children a hereditary advantage over their adopted siblings—or some combination of these two.

There is evidence that poverty is the principal source of low IQs among children in the United States. Greg Duncan (1993) matched low-birth-weight black and white children who had experienced persistent poverty from birth to 5 years of age and found that both groups had IQs that were nine points lower than children who had low birth weights but no experience of persistent poverty. Poverty had more influence on the IQs of these children than family structure or the educational level of the mother.

Refuting African-American Racism

African-Americans have been confronted with some of the same pressures and alternatives as white ethnics, having lost most of their African cultural heritage and the knowledge of their ancestral languages. Like white ethnics, they have sought to increase their sense of unity and identity by revitalizing old and inventing new cultural traditions. Unlike white ethnics, however, they have never had the option of blending in with the rest of the population. Because of the one drop rule, intermarriage does not modify the socially and

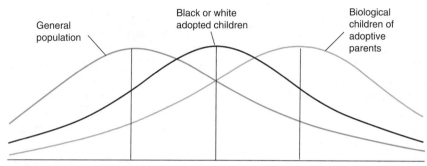

General population

Black or white adopted children

Biological children of adoptive parents

Figure 14.5   Distribution of IQ Scores in Transracial Adoptions
Although adopted children of both races achieved higher IQ scores than the general population,
no measurable difference occurred between the scores of black adopted children and white
adopted children. Biological children, however, scored higher than their adopted siblings, black
or white.

Source: Silk and Boyd, 1989.

legally allowable identities. Today intermarriage remains rare and subject to criticism from both whites and African-Americans. Under these circumstances, African-Americans have understandably turned their attention away from assimilation and have redoubled their efforts to instill pride in being black by emphasizing real or imagined cultural achievements. Increasingly, however, African-Americans have adopted a strategy of fighting the flames of white racism with the flames of black racism.

African-American scholars protest the domination of Eurocentric views regarding the history of civilization and seek to substitute their own Afrocentric views of the world. A major theme of Afrocentrism is that Africans preceded whites in all great technological, medical, political, and mathematical inventions. This follows from the belief that the ancient Egyptians were "black Africans." White scholars have allegedly suppressed this fact in order to create the impression that black Africans were incapable of great achievements (Adams 1990; Diop 1991; Brace 1993).

European scholars have certainly neglected the contribution of ancient Egypt to the development of Greece and other European cultures. It is also true that dark-skinned people from Nubia were incorporated into Egyptian society and that at least one Pharaoh was dark-skinned. Yet there is no basis to the claim that the Egyptian population was biologically closely related to Africans south of the Sahara (Brace et al. 1993). Today, as in dynastic times, Egyptian skin color ranges from dark to light. Only by imposing the criterion of social race used in the United States—the one drop rule—could the Egyptians be considered racially "black." Calling the ancient Egyptians black carelessly disposes of a genuine scientific puzzle. Africa does lag behind the rest of the world in terms of political and technological development. Why? See Box 14.4.

Melanin Theory

Afrocentric versions of the origins of civilization attribute the racial superiority of blacks to their greater supply of the pigment *melanin*. Not only does melanin protect against solar radiation, but the theory goes, it bestows special powers that are proportionate to the density of an individual's melanin supply. This supply is allegedly present both in the melanocyte cells of the skin and muscles and in the brain in the form of neuromelanin.

Melanin in the skin and muscles purportedly acts like a semiconductor. It traps free energy from the environment and thus accounts for the extra speed and agility of black athletes. Neuromelanin stimulates the immune system, expands memory and consciousness, and gives rise to higher forms of spirituality, which we call "soul." Jazz and similar musical styles, and religious forms of expression involving "shouting" and "speaking in tongues" supposedly derive from neuromelanin-induced spirituality. Neuromelanin can also pick up and decode cosmic rays and act as an infrared telescope. This accounts for the amazing knowledge that the people of the Dogon region of West Africa possessed concerning the existence of a companion star of Sirius, which is invisible to the naked eye and which European astronomers found out about only after they had telescopes. It is no exaggeration to say that according to melanin theory, the development of life depended on melanin, and the possession of melanin defines the very essence of being human.

Anthropologist Bernard Ortiz de Montellano (1993) has subjected melanin theory to careful scrutiny. He writes that melanin cannot be responsible for athletic prowess because it does not occur in muscle tissue (although it could conceivably have an effect on visual acuity). Melanin does occur in

---

Box 14.4

WHY AFRICA LAGS

In A.D. 500, West Africa had feudal king-doms—Ghana, Mali, Sanghay—which strong-ly resembled the feudal kingdoms of Europe except for the fact that the Africans were cut off by the Sahara from the heritage of tech-nology and engineering that Rome had be-queathed to Europe. Subsequently, the great desert also inhibited the southward flow of Arabic influences that did so much to revital-ize European science and commerce. The pres-ence of the Tse Tse fly in the forested regions of Africa south of the Sahara meant that cattle could not be used as a source of traction power and milk products. Without traction animals, hoes rather than plows became the main agri-cultural implements. Horses, which became the chief engines of war in medieval Europe, were scarce or absent in tropical Africa.

Although the people who lived in the Mediterranean basin carried out their trade and warfare on ships and became maritime powers, their dark-skinned counterparts south of the Sahara lacked the means of naval defense. So when the first Portuguese ships arrived off the Guinea coast in the fifteenth century, the Europeans were able to seize con-trol of the ports and seal the fate of Africa for the next 500 years.

After the Portuguese exhausted the gold mines, the Africans concentrated on hunting slaves to exchange for European cloth and firearms. The slave trade led to increased amounts of warfare, rebellion, and the breakup of the indigenous feudal states, cutting short the trajectory of Africa's political development and turning vast portions of the interior into a no-man's-land whose chief product was a human crop bred for export to the sugar, cot-ton, and tobacco plantations on the other side of the Atlantic.

When the slave trade ended, the Europeans tightened their control and forced the Africans to farm and mine for them. Meanwhile, colo-nial authorities tried to keep Africa subservient and backward by encouraging tribal wars, by limiting African education to the most rudi-mentary level possible, and above all, by pre-venting colonies from developing an industrial infrastructure that might have allowed them to compete on the world market after they achieved political independence.

---

the human brain as neuromelanin, but it forms as a byprod-uct in the biosynthesis of adrenaline and, as yet, has no known function. In any event, the amount of neuromelanin (which simply increases with age) has absolutely no correla-tion with the amount of skin melanin (whose abundance is regulated by the enzyme tyrosinase). Therefore, all the effects attributed to neuromelanin such as musical ability and "soul-ful" spirituality should be as common among whites as among blacks. As for the amazing discovery of the companion star of Sirius, restudies carried out by Walter van Beek (1991: 148) cast into doubt much that had been written about Dogon religion and world view: "That Sirius is a double star is unknown; astronomy is of very little importance in [Dogon] religion." Finally it is difficult to identify melanin as the pri-mordial source of life. As Ortiz de Montellano concludes, life began in the sea, the waters of which provided protection against solar radiation in the absence of melanin.

Although a critical appraisal of the racist claims of African-Americans may weaken their attempt to develop group consciousness and group pride, anthropologists who expose the errors of white racism have no choice but to expose and reject the errors of African-American racism as well (Box 14.5).

Racism on the Campus

One reason for the limited success of the black power movement in the United States is that it provoked a reactive increase in the solidarity sentiments and activities of the white ethnic groups. In response to real or imagined threats to their schools, neighborhoods, and jobs, "white ethnics"—people of Italian, Polish, Irish, and Jewish descent—fought back against black power. They mounted antibusing cam-

---

Box 14.5

HOW WE GOT THE COLOR OF OUR SKIN

The primary function of melanin is to protect the upper levels of the skin from being damaged by the sun's ultraviolet rays. This radiation poses a critical problem for our kind because we lack the dense coat of hair that acts as a sunscreen for most mammals. Hairlessness exposes us to two kinds of radiation hazards: ordinary sunburn, with its blisters, rashes, and risk of infection; and skin cancers, including malignant melanoma, one of the deadliest diseases known. Melanin is the body's first line of defense against these afflictions. The more melanin particles, the darker the skin, and the lower the risk of sunburn and all forms of skin cancer. This explains why the highest rates for skin cancer are found in sun-drenched lands such as Australia, where light-skinned people of European descent spend a good part of their lives outdoors wearing scanty attire. Very dark-skinned people such as heavily pigmented Africans of Zaire seldom get skin cancer, but when they do, they get it on depigmented parts of their bodies—palms and lips.

If exposure to solar radiation had nothing but harmful effects, natural selection would have favored inky black as the color for all human populations. But the sun's rays do not present an unmitigated threat. As it falls on the skin, sunshine converts a fatty substance in the epidermis into vitamin D. The blood carries vitamin D from the skin to the intestines (technically making it a hormone rather than a vitamin), where it plays a vital role in the absorption of calcium. In turn, calcium is vital for strong bones. Without it, people fall victim to the crippling diseases rickets and osteomalacia. In women, calcium deficiencies can result in a deformed birth canal, which makes childbirth lethal for both mother and fetus.

Vitamin D can be obtained from a few foods, primarily the oils and livers of marine fish. But inland populations must rely on the sun's rays and their own skins for the supply of this crucial substance. The particular color of a human population's skin, therefore, represents in large degree a trade-off between the hazards of too much versus too little solar radiation: acute sunburn and skin cancer on the one hand, and rickets and osteomalacia on the other. It is this trade-off that largely accounts for the preponderance of brown people in the world and for the general tendency for skin color to be darkest among equatorial populations and lightest among populations dwelling at higher latitudes.

At middle latitudes, the skin follows a strategy of changing colors with the seasons. Around the Mediterranean basin, for example, exposure to the summer sun brings high risk of cancer but low risk for rickets; the body produces more melanin and people grow darker (i.e., they get suntans).

---

paigns and created new private and public school systems based on segregated suburban residence patterns (Stein and Hill 1977; Katz and Taylor 1988; Glasser 1989). During the 1980s and 1990s, tensions between whites and blacks and other minorities increased in different regions and cities all across the United States. A wave of racially motivated verbal and physical abuse affected not only urban neighborhoods (such as New York's Howard Beach, Crown Heights, and Bensonhurst) but college campuses as well. This resurgence of overt racism results in part from the fact that successive conservative governments have devalued civil rights, encouraged resentment against affirmative action, and fostered racial polarization by cutting back on critical social programs (C. Murray 1984; Glasser 1989).

But there is a deeper level of sociocultural causation that needs to be considered. One must ask why such a political program became attractive during the 1980s. The answer may be that the electoral success of political leaders who were indifferent or even vindictive about the plight of the country's minorities was related to the marked deterioration in the economic prospects of the white majority. Polls reveal that many working- and middle-class whites have grown apprehensive about being able to improve or even maintain their level of socioeconomic well-being. For the first time in U.S. history, many young people are convinced that they will not be able to live as comfortably as their parents. These are not groundless fears. The wave of racial and ethnic unrest coincides with a period during which the average real weekly earnings of production and nonsupervisory employees declined by 18 percent (Morehouse and Dembo 1988: 7; Mishel and Frankel 1990). During the same period, U.S. hourly take-home wages for the first time slipped below those

---

Box 14.5

HOW WE GOT THE COLOR OF OUR SKIN (*CONTINUED*)

Winter reduces the risk of sunburn and cancer; the body produces less melanin, and the tan wears off.

The correlation between skin color and latitude is not perfect because other factors—such as the availability of foods containing vitamin D and calcium, regional cloud cover during the winter, amount of clothing worn, and cultural preferences—may work for or against the predicted relationship. Arctic-dwelling Eskimo, for example, are not as light-skinned as expected, but their habitat and economy afford them a diet that is exceptionally rich in both vitamin D and calcium.

Northern Europeans, obliged to wear heavy garments for protection against the long, cold, cloudy winters, were always at risk for rickets and osteomalacia from too little vitamin D and calcium. This risk increased sometime after 6000 B.C., when pioneer cattle herders who did not exploit marine resources began to appear in northern Europe. The risk would have been especially great for the brown-skinned Mediterranean peoples who migrated northward along with the crops and farm animals. Thus, in northern Europe, fair-skinned, nontanning individuals who could utilize the weakest and briefest doses of sunlight to synthesize vitamin D were strongly favored by natural selection. During the frigid winters, only a small circle of a child's face could be left to peek out at the sun through the heavy clothing, thereby favoring the survival of individuals with translucent patches of pink on their cheeks characteristic of many northern Europeans. But natural selection need not have acted alone. Cultural selection may also have played a role. It seems likely that whenever people consciously or unconsciously had to decide which infants to nourish and which to neglect, the advantage would go to those with lighter skin, experience having shown that such individuals tended to grow up to be taller, stronger, and healthier than their darker siblings. White was beautiful because white was healthy.

To account for the evolution of black skin in equatorial latitudes, one has merely to reverse the combined effects of natural and cultural selection. With the sun directly overhead most of the year, and clothing a hindrance to work and survival, vitamin D was never in short supply (and calcium was easily obtained from vegetables). Rickets and osteomalacia were rare. Skin cancer was the main problem, and what nature started, culture amplified. Darker infants were favored by parents because experience showed that they grew up to be freer of disfiguring and lethal malignancies. Black was beautiful because black was healthy.

Harris 1989.

---

of the other major industrial powers. It is understandable, therefore, why whites should increasingly regard any form of affirmative action as "reverse discrimination" and have lost interest in extending a helping hand to the poor, especially to poor blacks and Hispanics. Coming from segregated neighborhoods and segregated schools, blacks and whites seldom form friendships in their youth. They grow up as if they came from entirely different societies. It is no wonder, then, that when blacks and whites are thrown together in predominantly white high schools and colleges, the blacks feel insecure and huddle together for protection against insensitive or openly hateful treatment (Fleming 1984; Hacker 1989, 1992).

Chapter Summary

Ethnic groups are present in virtually all state societies. These groups differ from classes in having been formed through conquest or migration. They have internal class differences of their own and possess a high level of group consciousness.

Ethnic groups differ from social races only in the degree to which ethnic groups stress cultural differences (actual or invented) over physical appearance. Social race differs from biological race in its disregard for the scientific understanding of heredity—as illustrated in the one drop of blood rule and in the contrasting example of the Brazilian system for identifying the children of mixed matings.

Failure to understand the difference between biological race and culture is a common feature of the dynamics of social races and ethnic groups. Race denotes a population with a distinctive set of gene frequencies; culture denotes a way of life. A rigid linking of race and culture is a form of racism that runs counter to all that is scientifically known about the transmissibility of culture across racial and ethnic boundaries.

The most important point about the dynamics of racial and ethnic groups is that they almost always compete with other racial and ethnic groups, both dominant and subordinate, to defend and improve their standard of living. Although class struggle has been consistently difficult to identify and raise to conscious levels, race and ethnic struggle and race and ethnic consciousness are ubiquitous features of the contemporary world.

As part of their attempt to improve their position in the social and economic hierarchy, racial and ethnic groups attempt to mobilize their resources and instill a conscious pride in their identities. Thus all racial and ethnic groups that seek to survive and improve their condition tend to recast their historical achievements in the most favorable light and to emphasize their cultural separateness. As they do so, the threat of backlash is ever-present.

The United States provides a picture of how ethnic and racial dynamics operate in a complex multicultural society. Despite a high degree of homogenization of their cultures and much invention of tradition, white ethnic groups are maintaining their identities. By invoking ambilineal forms of descent, white European ethnics continue to identify with ancestral ethnic groups as a matter of choice.

The situation is less benign among African-Americans who are largely blocked by the one drop rule from choosing their social race. Racism remains a salient feature of the relations between whites of European origin and African-Americans (and other "nonwhite" groups).

In the nineteenth century, the dominant political position of the European powers was interpreted as proof of the superiority of the white race. But efforts to rank human races as inferior or superior based on technological, commercial, or military prowess are negated by the many historical examples of underdogs becoming topdogs, as in ancient Rome, China, and modern Japan. Racial explanations of black Africa's underdevelopment must be rejected in favor of explanations that take into account the effects of sub-Saharan ecology and colonialism and the slave trade.

The United States has paid a high price for its false stereotypes about the competitive disadvantages of nonwhites, not only at home but around the world as exemplified in the failure to take the challenge of Japanese inventiveness seriously.

Despite persistent efforts by racial determinists to prove that IQ test scores measure inherited differences in intelligence, no method exists for fully separating the influence on test score performance of culture and environment from the influence of heredity. However, very large changes in test scores can be achieved by altering the environment and culture. All correlations between race and IQ scores are spurious because it is impossible fully to control for the environmental and cultural differences to which different racial groups are exposed. The effects of subordinated status cannot be controlled for by any simple matching of socioeconomic indicators. We have no culture-free tests. Attempts to control for the minority factor by using transracial adoptions show no difference in the IQs of African-American black versus white children. Poverty is more powerfully correlated with low IQs in children than mother's education, family structure, or racial identity.

In view of the persistence of white racist views of African-Americans in the United States, it is not surprising that African-Americans have adopted their own brand of racism directed against whites. African-American racism seeks to invert the achievements of whites and blacks in world history by claiming that the Pharaohs and other inhabitants of ancient Egypt were black and that European civilization was therefore a derivative of black Africa. The weight of scientific evidence, however, indicates that Egyptians today and in the ancient past were a mixed population in which people who were biologically neither white nor black predominated.

Additional racist claims link the alleged innate superiority of blacks to their possession of extra amounts of melanin. Careful examination of these claims does not support melanin theory. From an anthropological point of view, racism must be rebutted whether espoused by the dominant or subordinate group.

A dangerous backlash by white ethnics in the United States has developed in relation to declining wage levels and a heightened sense of competition for scarce resources. This has resulted in the further withdrawal of African-Americans, including black-imposed segregation on college campuses.

AMERICA NOW UPDATE

Race, Poverty, Crime, Drugs, and Welfare

If one simply compares crime rates by state or city, those with low per capita incomes do not necessarily have high rates of criminal violence. Some scholars conclude, therefore, that African-American poverty and unemployment are not sufficient in themselves to account for the high rates of U.S. crime. But the poverty of the black inner-city ghetto is different from the poverty of rural whites or of an earlier gener-

(a)

Figure 14.6   Low-Cost Housing
(a) Pruitt-Igoe public housing complex in St.
Louis. (b) Scudder Homes housing project in
Newark. Despite the shortage of low-cost hous-
ing, these huge public housing projects were
dynamited into rubble. They had become drug
and crime infested and had been vandalized
beyond repair. Another futile approach to the
problem of inner-city housing is shown in (c).
All the windows in this building are fakes. The
shades and curtains are decals covering broken
and burned out rooms. The intent is to make
people believe that the neighborhood has a bright
future.

(b)

(c)

ation of urban ethnics. Unlike the rural poor, inner-city blacks have the opportunity as well as the motive to commit violent crimes. The city is an ideal setting for finding and surprising victims and successfully eluding the police. Most important, unlike the European immigrants of previous generations, blacks have with the passage of time become more, not less, concentrated inside their ghettos (Fig. 14.6). Under these conditions, the benefits of criminal behavior may seem to outweigh the risks of getting caught and being sent to jail. John Conyers, a member of the black congressional caucus, writes: "When survival is at stake, it should not be surprising that criminal activity begins to resemble an opportunity rather than a cost, work rather than deviance, and a possibly profitable undertaking that is superior to a coerced existence directed by welfare bureaucrats" (1978: 678).

The high odds against attaining economic success by going to school and acquiring the skills necessary to compete with whites for the better jobs lies behind the decision of many African-American, Hispanic, and other minority youth to traffic in illicit drugs. A week spent selling crack can bring more wealth than a year of working as a dishwasher or a fast-food server. Ironically, the most successful drug businesses are run by young men who refrain from taking drugs themselves and who display many of the characteristics associated with

Figure 14.7   Lower East Side
The vicinity of Jagna Sharff's study.

MALE HOMICIDES IN 24 AFDC FAMILIES,
1976–1979

VICTIM'S AGE	IMMEDIATE CAUSE OF DEATH
25	Shot in drug-related incident
19	Shot in dispute in grocery store
21	Shot in drug-related incident
28	Stabbed in drug-related incident
32	"Suicide" in a police precinct house
30	Stabbed in drug-related incident
28	Poisoned by adulterated heroin
30	Arson victim
24	Shot in drug-related incident
19	Tortured and stabbed in drug-related incident

Source: Sharff, 1980.

entrepreneurship in legitimate businesses. They break into the trade with a small investment, hire employees, keep careful accounts, strive to establish good relationships with their regular customers, encourage the consumption of their product, adjust prices to market conditions, and keep careful tabs on what their competitors are doing. Of course, the use of crack and other addictive substances has a devastating effect on the consumers who use drugs to escape from a squalid reality. The people of the United States pay an enormous price for the drug trade in the form of increased crime rates, overburdened courts and jails, and drug-related health problems such as AIDS (Massing 1989; T. Williams 1989).

A disproportionate share of violent urban crime in the United States is committed by black and Hispanic juveniles brought up in matrifocal families that receive AFDC allotments. This connection between juvenile delinquency and matrifocality reflects the fact that AFDC benefits are set below poverty-level incomes. Almost all inner-city AFDC women, therefore, count on supplementary incomes from husbands-in-hiding, coresident male consorts, or former consort fathers of their children. Anthropologist Jagna Sharff (1981) found that all the mothers in a group of twenty-four Hispanic AFDC families living in New York City's Lower East Side had some kind of male consort (Fig. 14.7). Few of the men in the house held regular full-time jobs, but even those who were unemployed chipped in something toward food and rent from selling stolen goods, dealing in marijuana or cocaine, and an occasional burglary or mugging. Some women had only one consort, whereas others picked up

money and gifts through more casual relationships. In their early teens, young inner-city boys make substantial contributions to their household's economic balance through their involvement in street crime and dope peddling. In addition, they confer an important benefit on their mothers in the form of protection against the risk of rape, mugging, and various kinds of ripoffs to which the ghetto families are perpetually exposed. Sharff found that AFDC mothers value sons for streetwise "macho" qualities, especially their ability to use knives or guns, which are needed to protect the family against unruly or predatory neighbors. Though the AFDC mothers did not actively encourage their sons to enter the drug trade, everyone recognized that a successful drug dealer could become a very rich man. To get ahead in the drug business, one needs the same macho qualities that are useful in defending one's family. When a young man brings home his first drug profits, mothers have mixed feelings of pride and apprehension. In her sample of AFDC families, Sharff compiled a record of ten male homicides in 3 years (see Table 14.1).

Since young ghetto males have a 40 percent chance of dying by age 25, a ghetto mother has to have more than one son if she hopes to enjoy the protection of a streetwise male. One must be careful not to conclude that every family on AFDC conforms to this pattern. For some mothers, AFDC represents a one-time emergency source of funds used in the aftermath of divorce or separation until they can find a job and arrange for child care. But several million inner-city women, mostly African-American and Hispanic, use AFDC not as a temporary crutch but as a regular or recurrent source of subsistence. It has been found that long-term welfare dependency is especially characteristic of unwed mothers who begin to receive AFDC when they have a first child. Almost 40 percent of these women will stay on welfare for 10 or more years (Besharov 1989: 151).

Chapter 15

GENDER HIERARCHIES

Kuwaiti woman driver.

Male and female and other genders are subject to the same kinds of hierarchical distinctions, advantages, and disabilities as classes, castes, ethnic groups, and social races. Here are some of the questions this chapter gets into: Do men and women interpret gender differences from the same perspective, or do they have different versions of who is up and who is down? Are males always dominant in public roles? Are matriarchies real or imagined? What is the effect of living in matrilineal societies on the position of women? Are men and women separate but equal in band-organized societies? Why are gender relations more equal in some agricultural societies than in others? Is there a relationship between warfare and male domination? Why is low female status so closely associated with the use of the plow? And finally, what kinds of changes in gender roles can we expect as the industrial nations continue to develop high-tech infrastructures and service and information economies? In answering these questions, we will see that gender relations in industrial societies have a long way to go before reaching equality, but not as long a way to go as class, caste, ethnic, and race relations.

Gender Ideologies

In many cultures, males believe that they are spiritually superior to females and that females are dangerous and polluting, weak and untrustworthy. For example, one of the most widespread of all gender ideologies has as its explicit aim the retention of a male monopoly on knowledge of the myths and rituals of human origins and of the nature of supernatural beings. The male knowledge monopoly embraces secret male initiation rites; male residence in a separate men's house (Fig. 15.1) from which women and children are excluded; masked male dancers who impersonate the gods and other spiritual beings; the bull roarer, which is said to be the voice of the gods and which is whirled about in the bush or under cover of darkness to frighten the women and uninitiated boys (see p. 192); storage of the masks, bull roarer, and other sacred paraphernalia in the men's house; threat of death or actual execution of any woman who admits to knowing the secrets of the cult; and threat of death or execution of any man who reveals the secrets to women or uninitiated boys (Gregor 1985: 94ff; Hays 1988).

Ecclesiastical types of religions (see p. 230) are also characterized by a pervasive functional interconnection between male-dominated rituals and myths on the one hand and male political–religious supremacy on the other. The established high priests of Rome, Greece, Mesopotamia, Egypt, ancient Israel, and the entire Muslim and Hindu world were or are men. High-ranking priestesses with autonomous control over their own temples, as in Minoan Crete, are the exception, even when the ecclesiastical cults include female deities. Males traditionally dominated the ecclesiastical organization of all the major world religions. All three chief religions of Western civilization—Christianity, Judaism, and Islam—stressed the priority of the male principle in the formation of the world. They identified the creator god as "He," and to the extent that they recognized female deities, as in Catholicism, traditionally assigned them a secondary role in myth and ritual. They all held that men were created first, and women second, out of a piece of a man (Fig. 15.2).

The Relativity of Gender Ideologies

How much of the male claim to spiritual superiority do women believe? To begin with, one must be skeptical that any subjugated group really accepts the reasons the subjugators give to justify their claims to superior status. In addition, much new evidence suggests that women have their own gender ideologies, which have not been properly recorded because earlier generations of ethnographers were primarily males and neglected or were unable to obtain the woman's point of view.

For example, the seclusion of menstruating women among the Yurok Indians of Northern California has consistently been interpreted by male ethnographers as a demonstration of the need to protect men from the pollution of menstrual blood. Only recently has it become clear that Yurok women had a completely different sense of what they were doing (Buckley 1982; Child and Child 1985). Rather than feeling that they were being confined for the benefit of Yurok men, they felt that they were enjoying a privileged opportunity to get away from the chores of everyday life, to meditate on their life goals, and to gather spiritual strength (Box 15.1).

Similarly, though men may have one idea about which gender is more valuable, women may have quite a different idea. Among the !Kung, who are generally regarded as having complementary and egalitarian gender roles, one woman

Figure 15.1 Interior of Men's House, New Guinea
The men use masks to terrify the women and children.

at least felt that men were dependent on women far more than women were dependent on men. Men would die without women, she said (Box 15.2). As for the exclusion of women from male-centered rituals, women do not necessarily resent being excluded because they do not attach much importance to what the men are doing with their bull roarers and masked dancing. Dorothy Counts tells how an old blind woman among the Kaliai of Papua New Guinea turned down the "honor" of being invited to remain in the village while the men performed their secret ceremonies. She left with the

other women as she had always done, to feast and make lewd fun of the men's "secrets" (1985: 61).

Male Bias: Trobriand Revisited

Women ethnographers (Kaberry 1970; Sacks 1971; Sanday 1981; Mathews 1985) have supplied much evidence that the power of women has often been substantially underestimated or misconstrued by male anthropologists, who until recently were the main sources of cross-cultural data on gender roles. Even one of the greatest ethnographers, Bronislaw Malinowski, fell short of providing a balanced view of gender roles in his classic study of the Trobriand Islanders. As discussed in Chapter 8, at harvest time in the Trobriands, brothers give their sisters' husbands gifts of yams. These yams provide much of the material basis for the political power of the Trobriand chiefs. Malinowski viewed the harvest gift as a kind of annual tribute from the wife's family to her husband, therefore as a means of enhancing and consolidating male power. Annette Weiner has shown, however, that the harvest yams are given in the name of the wife and are actually as much a means of bolstering the value of being a woman as a means of conferring power on men.

Malinowski did not record the fact that the gift of yams had to be reciprocated and that the husband had to give the counter gift not to his wife's brother but to his own wife. In return for the yams received in his wife's name, the Trobriand husband had to provide her with a distinct form of wealth consisting of women's skirts or bundles of pandanus and banana leaves, the materials used for making skirts. Moreover, much of a husband's economic activity is devoted to trading pigs and other valuables in order to supply his wife with large quantities of women's wealth. The skirts and bundles of leaves are publicly displayed and given away at huge funeral ceremonies known as *sagali* (which Malinowski knew about but did not describe in detail because he paid only lim-

(a)

(b)

Figure 15.2 Recreated Creation
(a) Michelangelo's Creation, *from the Sistine Chapel. God, depicted as a male, creates Adam first.*
(b) Redrawing.

Box 15.1

YUROK WOMAN'S VIEW OF MENSTRUAL SECLUSION

A menstruating woman should isolate herself because this is the time when she is at the height of her powers. Thus, the time should not be wasted in mundane tasks and social distractions, nor should one's concentration be broken by concerns with the opposite sex. Rather, all of one's energies should be applied in concentrated meditation on the nature of one's life, "to find out the purpose of your life," and toward the "accumulation" of spiritual energy. The menstrual shelter, or room, is "like the men's sweathouse," a place where you "go into yourself and make yourself stronger."

Buckley 1982: 48–49.

---

ited attention to female culture). Weiner (1976: 118) states that the sagali is one of the most important public events in Trobriand life (Fig. 15.3):

> Nothing is so dramatic as women standing at a sagali surrounded by thousands of bundles. Nor can anything be more impressive than watching the deportment of women as they attend to the distribution. When women walk to the center [of the plaza] to throw down their wealth, they carry them-

---

Box 15.2

!KUNG WOMAN'S POINT OF VIEW

Women are strong; women are important. Zhun/twa [!Kung San] men say that women are the chiefs, the rich ones, the wise ones. Because women possess something very important, something that enables men to live: their genitals. A woman can bring a man life even if he is almost dead. She can give him sex and make him alive again. If she were to refuse, he would die! If there were no women around, their semen would kill men. Did you know that? If there were only men, they would all die. Women make it possible for them to live.

The words of Nisa, a !Kung San woman, as recorded by Marjorie Shostak 1981: 288.

Figure 15.3   Trobriand Island Yam House
Woman on left is wearing traditional skirt.

selves with a pride as characteristic as that of any Melanesian bigman.

Failure of a husband to equip his wife with sufficient women's wealth to make a good showing at the sagali adversely affects his own prospects for becoming a bigman. His brothers-in-law may reduce or eliminate their yam harvest gift if their sister cannot display and give away large quantities of bundles and skirts to relatives of the deceased. In Weiner's account, not only are men more dependent on women for their power than in Malinowski's account, but women emerge as having far more influence in their own right. She concludes that all too often anthropologists "have allowed 'politics by men' to structure our thinking about other societies leading us to believe erroneously that if women are not dominant in the political sphere of interaction, their power, at best, remains peripheral" (1976: 228).

The distribution of power between the sexes is seldom simply a matter of women being completely at the mercy of men (or vice versa). As the Trobriand study shows, male anthropologists in the past may not have grasped the more subtle aspects of gender hierarchies. Yet, by emphasizing the ability of political subordinates to manipulate the system in their favor, we must not fall into the trap of minimizing the real power differences embodied in many gender hierarchies. It is well known that slaves can sometimes outwit masters, privates can frustrate generals, and children can get parents to wait on them like slaves. The ability to buffer the effects of institutionalized inequality is not the same as institutionalized equality.

Gender Hierarchy

Despite varying definitions of masculine and feminine, males tend in the majority of societies to be assigned more aggressive and violent roles than females (Schlegel 1972). From our previous discussions in Chapters 11 and 12 of the evolution of political organization, it is clear that males often preempt the major centers of public power and control. Headmen rather than headwomen dominate both egalitarian and stratified forms of trade and redistribution. The same male preeminence is evidenced by the Semai and Mehinacu headmen; the Solomon Island mumis and the New Guinea big men (but see Counts 1985); the Nuer leopard skin chief; the Kwakiutl and Trobriand chiefs; the Bunyoro mukama; the Inca, the Pharaohs, and the emperors of China and Japan. If queens reigned, they generally did so as temporary holders of power that belonged to the males of the lineage. Exceptions no doubt existed, especially in early states where matrilineal or ambilineal descent increased the importance of women as the link between generations of rulers. In the ancient Korean Kingdom of Silla, for example, male and female rulers were buried in tombs in adjacent burial mounds. It was the women's tombs that contained more gold ornaments and other precious objects, possibly showing that female royalty ranked higher than male royalty (Nelson 1993).

Today, nothing more dramatically exposes the political subordination of women than the fact that women comprise just over 10 percent of the members of the world's legislative bodies and 4 percent of national cabinets. In 1993, only six countries had women as heads of state (UNDP 1993: 25).

Early in this century, many anthropologists believed that political domination by women, or matriarchy (the opposite of patriarchy, or political domination by men), occurred as a regular stage in the evolution of social organization (see Appendix). Today, virtually all anthropologists doubt the existence of matriarchies at any phase of cultural evolution (Rosaldo and Lamphere 1974: 3). Claims for the existence of such societies often exaggerate the political significance of matrilineal descent and matrilocal residence. Ruby Rohrlich-Leavitt (1977: 57), for example, argues that in Minoan Crete, "Women participated at least equally with men in political decision making, while in religion and social life they were supreme." This contention, however, is based on inferences from archaeological data that can be given contradictory interpretations (Ehrenberg 1989: 109, 118). Most likely, Minoan Crete was matrilineal and women did enjoy a relatively high political status. However, the basis of Crete's economy was maritime trade and men, not women, dominated this activity. Rohrlich-Leavitt contends that the Cretan matriarchy was made possible by the absence of both warfare and a male military complex. However, it seems likely that military activities were focused on naval encounters that have left little archaeologically retrievable evidence (Reed 1984).

The Iroquois of New York State are another society that has been offered as an example of a matriarchy. According to Daniel McCall (1980), women dominated both domestic and political affairs in this matrilineal, matrilocal society prior to the coming of the Europeans and the intensification of warfare (but see Albers 1989: 140–142). However, McCall admits that after the arrival of the Europeans, male war chiefs dominated the tribal council. The question of Iroquois matriarchy, therefore, depends on the extent to which the Iroquois practiced warfare. In the absence of direct historical or archaeological evidence, one must turn to what we know about warfare in matrilineal societies in general: As we have seen, a high correlation exists between matrilineal–matrilocal chiefdoms and intense external warfare (see p. 127). Nonetheless, Iroquois women clearly wielded a great deal of power in political as well as in domestic affairs.

The absence of matriarchies is an important fact about gender hierarchies, but its significance should not be exaggerated. It does not mean that males universally dominate females, for many societies have gender roles that do not involve marked inequalities.

Gender and Exploitation

When males have power advantages over females based on access to strategic resources (Josephides 1985), ideas about female pollution, whether shared by women or not, will in all likelihood be associated with significant deprivations and disadvantages (Goodale 1971). The linking of negative stereotypes about females with various disadvantages has been stressed by Shirley Lindenbaum with respect to two strongly male-biased societies in which she has done fieldwork. In Bangladesh, Lindenbaum encountered an elaborate ideology of male supremacy expressed in symbols and rituals (see Box 15.3). She found similar beliefs and rituals among the Fore of highland New Guinea. In both instances, women were subject to important material deprivations. Among the Fore,

pregnant women were secluded in special huts, not, according to Lindenbaum, to celebrate and concentrate female powers but to limit them:

> Her (the Fore woman's) seclusion there is a sign of the half-wild condition brought on by the natural functions of her own body. Other women bring the food, for if she visited her gardens during this period of isolation she would blight all domesticated crops. Nor should she send food to her husband: ingesting food she had touched would make him feel weak, catch a cold, age prematurely.
>
> [Lindenbaum 1979: 129]

If a Fore woman gives birth to a deformed or stillborn child, the woman is held solely responsible. Her husband and the men of the hamlet denounce her, accuse her of trying to

---

B o x   1 5 . 3

SEXUAL SYMBOLISM IN BANGLADESH

Men are associated with the right, preferred side of things, women with the left. Village practitioners state that a basic physiological difference between the sexes makes it necessary to register a man's pulse in his right wrist, a woman's in her left, and they invariably examine patients in this way. Most villagers wear amulets to avert illness caused by evil spirits; men tie the amulet to the right upper arm, women to the left. Similarly, palmists and spiritualists read the right hands of men and the left hands of women. In village dramas, where both male and female parts are played by male actors, the audience may identify men gesturing with the right arm, women with the left. During religious celebrations there are separate entrances at such public places as the tombs of Muslim saints or Hindu images, the right avenue being reserved for men and the left for women. In popular belief, girls are said to commence walking by placing the left foot forward first, men the right.

In some instances, this right-left association indicates more than the social recognition of physiological difference, carrying additional connotations of prestige, honour and authority. Women who wish to behave respectfully to their husbands say they should, ideally, remain to the left side while eating, sitting and lying in bed. The same mark of respect should be shown also to all social superiors: to the rich, and in present times to those who are well-educated.

Thus, the right-left dichotomy denotes not only male-female but also authority-submission. It also has connotations of good-bad and purity-pollution. Muslims consider the right side to be the side of good augury, believing that angels dwell on the right shoulder to record good deeds in preparation for the Day of Judgment, while on the left side, devils record misdeeds. The left side is also associated with the concept of pollution. Islam decrees that the left hand be reserved for cleansing the anus after defecation. It must never, therefore, be used for conveying food to the mouth, or for rinsing the mouth with water before the proscribed daily prayers.

Lindenbaum 1977: 142.

obstruct male authority, and kill one of her pigs. Among the Fore as among many other New Guinea societies, men appropriate the best sources of meat for themselves. The men argue that women's animal foods—frogs, small game, and insects—would make men sick. These prejudices can have lethal effects. Throughout New Guinea, young girls die at much higher rates than young boys (Buchbinder 1977). The same lethal results are evident in Bangladesh:

> The male child receives preferential nutrition. With his father he eats first, and if there is a choice, luxury foods or scarce foods are given to him rather than to his female siblings. The result is a Bengalese population with a preponderance of males, and a demographic picture in which the mortality rate for females under 5 years of age is in some years 50% higher than that for males.

> [Lindenbaum 1975: 143]

Variations in Gender Hierarchies: Hunter-Gatherers

In the words of Eleanor Leacock (1978: 247), we cannot go from the proposition that "women are subordinate as regards political authority in most societies" to "women are subordinate in all respects in all societies." The very notions of "equality" and "inequality" may represent an ethnocentric misunderstanding of the kinds of gender roles that exist in many societies. Leacock (1978: 225) does not dispute the fact that when "unequal control over resources and subjugation by class and by sex developed," it was women who in general became subjugated to men (recognizing, of course, that the degree of subjugation varied depending on local ecological, economic, and political conditions). In the absence of classes and the state, Leacock argues that gender roles were merely different, not unequal. Much evidence indicates that power of any sort, whether of men over men or men over women, was trivial or nonexistent in many (but not all) band and village societies, for reasons discussed in Chapter 11. Writing of her fieldwork among the Montagnais-Naskapi foragers of Labrador, Leacock (1983: 116) recalls: "They gave me insight into a level of respect and consideration for the individuality of others, regardless of sex, that I had never before experienced."

In his study of the forest-dwelling Mbuti of Zaire, Colin Turnbull (1982) also found a high level of cooperation and mutual understanding between the males and females, with considerable authority and power vested in women. Despite his skills with bow and arrow, the Mbuti male does not see himself as superior to his wife. He "sees himself as the hunter, but then he could not hunt without a wife, and although hunting is more exciting than being a beater or a gatherer, he

knows that the bulk of his diet comes from the foods prepared by the women" (1982: 153).

Marjorie Shostak's (1981) biography of Nisa shows the !Kung to be another foraging society in which nearly egalitarian relationships between the sexes prevail. Shostak states that the !Kung do not show any preference for male children over female children. In matters relating to child rearing, both parents guide their offspring, and a mother's word carries about the same weight as a father's. Mothers play a major role in deciding whom their children will marry, and after marriage, !Kung couples live near the wife's family as often as the husband's. Women eat or distribute whatever food they have and bring back to camp whatever they choose.

All in all, !Kung women have a striking degree of autonomy over their own and their children's lives. Brought up to respect their own importance in community life, !Kung women become multifaceted adults and are likely to be competent and assertive as well as nurturant and cooperative (Shostak 1981: 246).

The fact is, however, that many hunter-gatherers do not have equal gender roles. This inequality seems to have been especially marked among the Aborigines of Australia (Burbank 1989; Goodale 1971). In northern Queensland, for example, polygyny was common, some men acquiring as many as four wives. Men discriminated against women in the distribution of food: A man "often keeps the animal food for himself, while the woman has to depend principally on vegetables for herself and her child." The sexual double standard prevailed: Men beat or killed their wives for adultery, but wives did not have similar recourse. Furthermore, the division of labor between the sexes was anything but equal, with women doing most of the drudge work (D. Harris 1987).

Gender Hierarchies In Matrilineal Societies

Although matrilineal, matrilocal societies should not be confused with matriarchies, women in matrilineal societies often dominated domestic life and exercised important prerogatives in political affairs. From their palisaded villages in upstate New York, the matrilocal and matrilineal Iroquois dispatched armies of up to 500 men to raid targets as far away as Quebec and Illinois. On returning to his native land, the Iroquois warrior joined his wife and children at their hearth in a village longhouse. The affairs of this communal dwelling were directed by a senior woman who was a close maternal relative of the man's wife. It was this matron who organized the work that the women of the longhouse performed at home and in the fields. She took charge of storing harvested crops and drawing on them as needed. When husbands were not off on some sort of expedition—absences of a year were common—they slept and ate in the female-headed longhouses but had virtually no control over how their wives lived and worked. If a husband was bossy or uncooperative, the matron might at any time order him to pick up his blanket and get out, leaving his children behind to be taken care of by his wife and the other women of the longhouse.

Turning to public life, the formal apex of political power among the Iroquois was the Council of Elders, consisting of elected male chiefs from different villages. The longhouse matrons nominated the members of this council and could prevent the seating of the men they opposed. But they did not serve on the council itself. Instead, they influenced the council's decisions by exercising control over the domestic economy. If a proposed action was not to their liking, the longhouse matrons could withhold the stored foods, wampum belts, feather work, moccasins, skins, and furs under their control. Warriors could not embark on foreign adventures unless the women filled their bearskin pouches with the mixture of dried corn and honey men ate while on the trail. Religious festivals could not take place, either, unless the women agreed to release the necessary stores. Even the Council of Elders did not convene if the women decided to withhold food for the occasion (J. Brown 1975; Gramby 1977).

Women in West Africa

Females had favorable gender relationships among chiefdoms and states in the forested areas of West Africa. Among the Yoruba, Ibo (also called Igbo), and Dahomey, for example, women had their own fields and grew their own crops. They dominated the local markets and could acquire considerable wealth from trade. To get married, West African men had to pay bride-price—iron hoes, goats, cloth, and in more recent times, cash. This transaction in itself indicated (see p. 112) that the groom and his family and the bride and her family agreed that the bride was a very valuable person and that her parents and relatives would not "give her away" without being compensated for her economic and reproductive capabilities (Bossen 1988; Schlegel and Eloul 1988). West African men and women believed that to have many daughters was to be rich.

Although men practiced polygyny, they could do so only if they consulted their senior wives and obtained their permission. Women, for their part, had considerable freedom of movement to travel to market towns, where they often had extramarital affairs. Furthermore, in many West African chiefdoms and states, women themselves could pay bride-price and "marry" other women. Among the Dahomey, as we have seen (p. 109), a female husband built a house for her "wife" and arranged for a male consort to get her pregnant. By paying bride-price for several such "wives," an ambitious

woman could establish control over a busy compound and become rich and powerful. West African women also achieved high status outside the domestic sphere. They belonged to female clubs and secret societies, participated in village councils, and mobilized en masse to seek redress against mistreatment by men.

Among the Ibo of Nigeria, women met in council to discuss matters that affected their interests as traders, farmers, or wives. A man who violated the woman's market rules, let his goats eat a woman's crops, or persistently mistreated his wife ran the risk of mass retaliation. The miscreant would be awakened in the middle of the night by a crowd of women banging on his hut. They danced lewd dances, sang songs mocking his manhood, and used his backyard as a latrine until he promised to mend his ways. They called it "sitting-on-a-man" (Van Allen 1972).

The supreme rulers of these West African chiefdoms and states were almost always males. However, their mothers, sisters, and other female relatives occupied offices that gave them considerable power over both men and women. In some Yoruba kingdoms, the king's female relatives directed the principal religious cults and managed the royal compounds. Anyone wanting to arrange rituals, hold festivals, or call up communal labor brigades had to deal with these powerful women first, before gaining access to the king. Among the Yoruba, women occupied an office known as "mother of all women," a kind of queen over females, who coordinated the voice of women in government, held court, settled quarrels, and decided what positions women should take on the opening and maintenance of markets, levying of taxes and tolls, declarations of war, and other important public issues. And in at least two Yoruba kingdoms, Ijesa and Ondo, the office of queen-over-women may have been as powerful as the office of king-over-men. Every grade of male chief under the king-over-men had a corresponding grade of female chief under the queen-over-women. The king-over-men and the queen-over-women met separately with their respective councils of chiefs to discuss matters of state. They then conferred with each other. No action was taken unless both councils were in agreement (Sudarkasa 1973; Aw 1977; Hart 1985).

Women in India

Parents in northern India express a strong preference for sons over daughters, unlike parents in West Africa. As Barbara Miller (1981, 1987a, b) has shown, the women of India are an "endangered sex" as a result of the high rate of female infant and child death caused by parental neglect. A north Indian man who had many daughters regarded them as an economic calamity rather than an economic bonanza. Instead of receiving bride-price, the north Indian father paid

Figure 15.4   Indian Dowry
Indian groom displays the gifts from his bride's parents at their wedding.

each daughter's husband a dowry (see p. 112) consisting of jewelry, cloth, or cash (Fig. 15.4).

In recent years, disgruntled or merely avaricious husbands have taken to demanding supplementary dowries. This has led to a spate of "bride-burnings" in which wives who fail to supply additional compensation are doused with kerosene and set on fire by husbands who pretend that the women killed themselves in cooking accidents (Sharma 1983; Crossette 1989; Rao 1993; Sakar 1993). Moreover, wife beating seems to be widespread in India, again, especially in the northern states (Miller 1992).

North Indian culture has always been extremely unfriendly to widows. In the past, a widow was given the opportunity of joining her dead husband on his funeral pyre. Facing a life of seclusion with no hope of remarrying, subject to food taboos that brought them close to starvation, and urged on by the family priest and their husbands' relatives, many women chose fiery death rather than widowhood.

Causes of Variation in Gender Hierarchies

Warfare is a major factor influencing the status of women in band and village societies. Since males in every human population on average have a physical advantage over females (Gray and Wolfe 1980: 442; Percival and Quinkert 1987: 136) with respect to the force they can exert with a club; the distance they can throw a spear, shoot an arrow, or hurl a stone; and the speed with which they can run short distances (see Table 15.1), males constitute the main fighting force in every known society (see Box 15.4 and Fig. 15.5). Males, therefore, are trained to be fierce and aggressive and to kill with a weapon far more often than women (Fig. 15.6).

The training, combat experience, and the monopoly that men possess over the weapons of war empower them to dominate women. Thus the gender-equal !Kung and Mbuti seldom if ever engage in warfare, whereas the Australian Aborigines and other hunter-gatherers with marked gender hierarchies do engage in frequent warfare.

Brian Hayden (Hayden et al. 1986) has tested the theory that wherever conditions favored the development of warfare among hunter-gatherers, the political and domestic subordination of women increased. Using a sample of thirty-three hunter–gatherer societies, he found that the correlation between low status for females and deaths due to armed combat was "unexpectedly high."

> The reasons for overwhelming male dominance in societies where warfare is pronounced seem relatively straightforward. The lives of group members depend to a greater degree on males and male assessment of social and political conditions. Male tasks during times of warfare are simply more critical to the survival of everyone than is female work. Moreover, male aggressiveness and the use of force engendered by warfare and fighting renders female opposition to male decisions not only futile but dangerous.
>
> [Hayden et al. 1986: 203]

A similar relationship holds between the intensity of warfare and male dominance among village peoples and simple patrilineal chiefdoms. Thus the Yanomami, with their high level of warfare, are well-known for strong male biases and their practice of female infanticide. Eastern highland New Guinea, noted for its male-centered communal cults and physical mistreatment of women, is also famous for its incessant warfare. As Daryl Feil (1987: 69) puts it, war was "general, pervasive, and perpetual." The treatment of women by men was proportionately brutal:

> Women were severely punished for adultery by having burning sticks thrust into their vaginas, or they were killed by their husbands; they were whipped with cane if they spoke out of turn or presumed to offer their opinions at public gatherings; and were physically abused in marital arguments. Men could never be seen to be weak or soft in dealings with women. Men do not require specific incidents or reasons to abuse or mistreat women; it is part of the normal course of events; indeed, in ritual and myth, it is portrayed as the essential order of things.
>
> [Feil 1987: 203]

Finally, as we have seen (p. 145), unbalanced gender ratios correlate with the practice of warfare (Divale and Harris 1976) among nonstate societies in general. We must remember, however, that the correlation between intense warfare and female subordination does not hold in the case of matrilocal and matrilineal societies where warfare is practiced against distant foes, and forestalls rather than encour-

Table 15.1

WORLD RECORDS

EVENT	MEN (MIN:SEC)	WOMEN (MIN:SEC)
100-meter dash	0:09.86	10.49
1 mile	3:46.32	4:15.61
400-meter hurdle	0:46.78	0:52.94*
	(ft) (in.)	(ft) (in.)
High jump	8 0	6 10¼

*Women's hurdles are set lower than men's.

Source: The World Almanac 1993.

Box 15.4

THE BODY AND CULTURE

Like everything else about human beings, the anatomical and physiological differences between men and women that are important for assigning combatant roles to males in preindustrial warfare are a product of the interaction of genetic and cultural influences. Feminist author Anne Oakley (1985: 28) has shown that the shape and strength of the human body can be greatly altered by the type of work each sex performs and the quality and quantity of food they consume. In some societies such as Bali, where men and women perform similar kinds of work, they are even difficult to tell apart. Indeed, theoretically, the strength and swiftness differences between the sexes could not only be effaced but completely reversed by sufficiently favoring the physical training and diet of women and by drastically curtailing male activities and food consumption (see Fig. 15.5). However, the point being made here is that any band or village society that chose to make its women physically better suited for hand-to-hand combat than its men would not survive combat with groups that invested primarily in conditioning its males for combat; genetic differences still guarantee that a maximum of investment in males will produce a brawnier and swifter combat team than a maximum investment in females.

Figure 15.5 Female Bodybuilding Champion
Gladys Portugese celebrates her victory at Madison Square Garden.

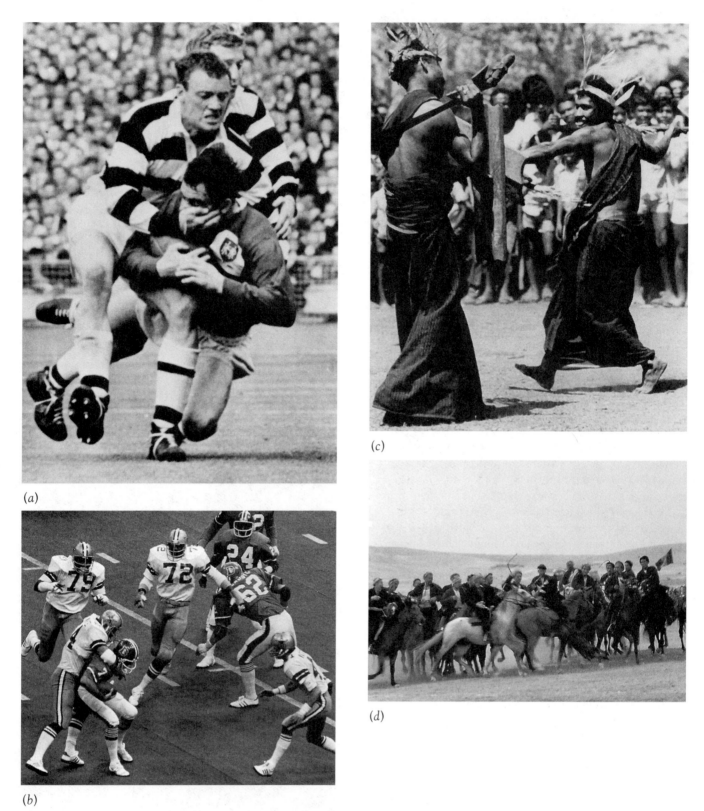

(a)

(b)

(c)

(d)

Figure 15.6   Aggressive Male Games
Aggressive male sports occur in warlike cultures. (a) The sporting life in England—rugby. (b) The gentle art of football in the United States. (c) Mock combat in Indonesia. (d) Afghan game (Buzkhashi) requires daring feats of horsemanship.

ages male control over production and domestic life (see p. 196).

The correlation between frequency and intensity of warfare and male dominance also does not hold for advanced chiefdoms and states. Although stratified societies have bigger armies and wage war on a much grander scale than classless societies, the effect of warfare on women is less direct and generally less severe than in bands and villages (but not as favorable as in matrilineal societies). What makes the difference is that in state societies, soldiering is a specialty reserved for professionals. Most males no longer train from infancy to be killers of men, or even killers of animals (since few large animals are left to hunt, except in royal preserves). Instead, they themselves become unarmed peasants and are no less terrified of professional warriors than their wives and children. Warfare does create a demand for suitably macho men to be trained as warriors, but in state societies, most women do not have to deal with husbands whose capacity for violence has been honed in battle. Nor does women's survival depend on training their sons to be cruel and aggressive. In advanced chiefdoms and states, therefore, female status depends less on the intensity, frequency, and scale of warfare than on whether the anatomical differences between men and women endow males or females with a decisive advantage in carrying out some crucial phase of production.

Hoes, Plows, and Gender Hierarchies

The contrasting gender hierarchies of West Africa and northern India are associated with two very different forms of agriculture. In West Africa, the main agricultural implement was not an ox-drawn plow, as in the plains of northern India, but a short-handled hoe (Goody 1976). The West Africans did not use plows because in their humid, shady habitat, the tsetse fly (see p. 183) made it difficult to rear plow animals. Besides, West African soils do not dry out and become hard-packed as in the arid plains of northern India so that West African women using nothing but hoes were as capable as men of preparing fields and had no need for men to grow, harvest, or market their crops.

In northern India, on the other hand, men maintained a monopoly over the use of ox-drawn plows. These implements were indispensable for breaking the long dry season's hard-packed soils. Men achieved this monopoly for essentially the same reasons that they achieved a monopoly over the weapons of hunting and warfare: Their greater bodily strength enabled them to be 15 to 20 percent more efficient than women. This advantage often means the difference between a family's survival and starvation, especially during prolonged dry spells when every fraction of an inch to which a plowshare penetrates beneath the surface and every minute

Figure 15.7 Man and Beast
An Indian farmer plowing with a pair of oxen.

less it takes a pair of oxen to complete a furrow are crucial for retaining moisture. As Morgan Maclachlan (1983) found in a study of the sexual division of labor in India, the question is not whether peasant women could be trained to manage a plow and a pair of oxen but whether, in most families, training men to do it leads to larger and more secure harvests (Fig. 15.7).

Further support for this theory can be found in the more female-favorable gender roles that characterize southern India and much of Southeast Asia and Indonesia (Peletz 1987). In these regions, noted for their strong matrifocal and complementary gender relationships, rice rather than wheat is the principal crop, and the principal function of traction animals in agriculture is puddling (softening and mixing the mud of rice paddies in preparation for planting) rather than plowing. Women and children can perform this operation as efficiently as men. Moreover, the operation of transplanting, which is as crucial as that of plowing or puddling, can also be carried out by women at least as efficiently as by men.

Is a factor as simple as male control over plowing sufficient to explain female infanticide, dowry, and widows throwing themselves onto their husbands' funeral pyres? Not if one thinks only of the direct effects of animal-drawn implements on agriculture itself. However, in evolutionary perspective, this male specialty was linked to a chain of additional specializations that together can plausibly explain many features of the depressed status of women in northern India as well as in other agrarian state societies with similar forms of agriculture in Europe, southwestern Asia, and northern China.

Wherever men gained control over the plow, they became the master of large traction animals. Wherever they yoked these animals to the plow, they also yoked them to all sorts of carts and vehicles. Therefore, with the invention of the wheel and its diffusion across Eurasia, men yoked animals to the principal means of land transport. This gave them control over the transportation of crops to market, and from there it was a short step to dominating long-distance trade and commerce. With the invention of money, men became the first merchants. As trade and commerce increased in importance, records had to be kept, and it was to men active in trade and commerce that the task fell of keeping these records. Therefore, with the invention of writing and arithmetic, men came to the fore as the first scribes and accountants. By extension, men became the literate sex; they did reading, writing, and arithmetic. Therefore, men, not women, were the first historically known philosophers, theologians, and mathematicians in the early agrarian states of Europe, southwestern Asia, India, and China.

All these indirect effects of male control over traction animals acted in concert with the continuing gender-role effects of warfare. By dominating the armed forces, men gained control over the highest administrative branches of government, including state religions. And the continuing need to recruit male warriors made the social construction of aggressive manhood a focus of national policy in every known state and empire. It is therefore no wonder that at the dawn of industrial times, men dominated politics, religion, art, science, law, industry, and commerce, as well as the armed forces, wherever animal-drawn plows had been the basic means of agricultural production.

Gender and Industrialism

During the smokestack phase of industrialism, women had little opportunity to overthrow the heritage of the classic Eurasian gender hierarchy. After an initial period of intense exploitation in factory employment, married women were excluded from industrial work and were confined to domestic tasks in order to assure the reproduction of the working class. Factory-employed male breadwinners collaborated in this effort in order to preserve their privileges while fending off the threat that women posed to the male wage rate. A decisive break came after World War II with the shift to the information and service infrastructure. This shift led to a call-up of literate women into low-paid, nonunionized information and service jobs, the feminization of the labor force, a fall in fertility rates to historic lows, and the destruction of the male breadwinner family (see p. 204).

Today's hyperindustrial mode of production is almost totally indifferent to the anatomical and physiological differences between men and women (except to the extent that women still may wish to have children). It is no accident that women's rights are rising as the strategic value of masculine brawn declines. Who needs extra muscle power when the decisive processes of production take place in automated fac-

tories or while people sit at desks in computerized offices? Men continue to fight for the retention of their old privileges, but they have been routed from one bastion after another as women fill the need for service and information workers by offering competent performance at lower wage rates than males. Even more than the market women of West Africa, women in today's advanced industrial societies have moved toward gender parity based on ability to earn a living without being dependent on husbands or other males (Fig. 15.8).

Chapter Summary

Gender groups are subject to the same kinds of hierarchical distinctions, advantages, and disabilities as classes, castes, ethnic groups, and social races. In many cultures, males believe that they are spiritually superior to females and that women are a source of pollution. These beliefs are present in the male-centered religions of Western civilization, which hold that women were created out of a piece of man. Women often do not accept these male versions of gender roles, as illustrated by the examples of the Yurok and Kaliai. Moreover, as demonstrated in the restudy of the Trobriand Islanders, male ethnographers have often underestimated the etic power of women. Nonetheless, men have more frequently dominated women politically, and the mirror image of patriarchy—matriarchy—is unknown. As illustrated by gender dominance in Bangladesh and the Fore, antifemale prejudices are often associated with high rates of illness and death among women.

Gender roles among hunter-gatherers are often egalitarian, as among the !Kung, Naskapi, and Mbuti, but in other hunter-gatherers—for example, the Queensland Aborigines—males are politically dominant. Female-favorable gender roles are found in many matrilineal societies such as the Iroquois, but perhaps the most powerful women in preindustrial societies lived in West Africa among the Yoruba, Ibo, and Dahomey. In contrast, the male-dominant gender roles of northern India, like those of Bangladesh, endanger the survival and well-being of females, especially when they are very young or very old.

Variations in gender hierarchies among hunter-gatherers and village societies are closely correlated with the frequency and intensity of warfare carried out against nearby groups. By contrast, long-distance warfare between village groups tends to promote matrilocality and a higher status for women. At the advanced chiefdom and state levels, only specialist warriors receive training for armed combat; consequently, variations in gender hierarchies depend less on the frequency and intensity of warfare than on the significance of the anatomical differences of men and women for carrying out certain crucial agricultural tasks. Underlying the contrast between

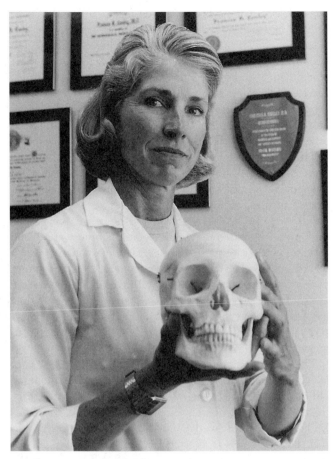

(a)

(b)

(d)

(c)

Figure 15.8   Breaking the Gender Barrier
(a) Neurosurgeon Frances Conley. (b) Cowgirl. (c) Construction engineer. (d) Firewoman.

West African gender relations and those of northern India are two different modes of agricultural production: hoe agriculture and plow agriculture, respectively. Women can use hoes as effectively as men, which leads to their controlling their own food supply, being involved in trade and markets, having an equal say in the management of household affairs, and wielding considerable political power. In northern India, men outperform women in the critical task of preparing hard-packed soils for planting by means of ox-drawn plows, leading to the preference for sons, female infanticide, dowry, and the mistreatment of widows, in contrast to the preferences for daughters and bride-price in West Africa.

Further consequences of the Eurasian animal-drawn plow complex include male control over trade, accounting, mathematics, literacy, and church and state bureaucracies, as well as continued control over the army. Southern India, Southeast Asia, and Indonesia, with their contrastive use of animals for puddling rather than plowing rice paddies and their more female-favorable gender roles, lend additional support to this theory.

In the smokestack phase of the industrial revolution, married women were excluded from factory work and confined to the home as dependents in male breadwinner families. After World War II, male muscular aptitudes were no longer significant in the emerging information and service economy; women entered the labor force in unprecedented numbers, leading to increased independence from men and radical changes in gender roles, gender hierarchy, and family life.

AMERICA NOW UPDATE

A Theory of Gender Hierarchy Change

All the recent trends toward parity in gender roles can be related to the hyperindustrial mode of production. The trend away from factory employment required and facilitated the call-up of female labor previously absorbed by child-and-home care; concurrently the premium placed on education for employment in nonmanufacturing jobs, together with the increase in the "opportunity costs" of pregnancy and parenting (that is, the amount of income forgone when women stop working to bear and raise children), inflated the costs of rearing children, weakened the marriage bond, depressed the fertility rate, and furthered the separation of the reproductive from the hedonistic components of sexuality.

The principal change that has occurred in the labor force is not merely an increase in the proportion of women who are employed but a growth in the proportion of employed women who are married and have children. Prior to World War II, only 15 percent of women living with husbands worked outside the home. By 1992, this proportion had risen to 67 percent (*Wall Street Journal* 1993: June 21, R4). What do these women do? Over 83 percent of them hold nonmanufacturing, service- and information-producing jobs—mostly low-level jobs that pay on the average only 70 percent of the wages earned by males (Serrin 1984: 1; *U.S. Bureau of the Census Statistical Abstract* 1990: 409).

The link between feminization and the information and service economy is reciprocal: Women, especially married women, had formerly been barred from unionized, male-dominated manufacturing jobs in which they were seen by husbands and unions as a threat to the wage scale. The nonunionized and traditionally feminine information and service occupations—secretaries, schoolteachers, health workers, saleswomen, and so on—offered less resistance. Seen from the perspective of capital investment, the reserve army of housewives constituted a source of cheap, docile labor that made the processing of information and people a profitable alternative to investment in factories devoted to goods production.

Thus the feminization of the labor force and the decline of goods manufacturing are closely related phenomena, although as we have seen (p. 202), this relationship has nothing to do with the inherent capacities of the sexes for physical labor and factory work. Why did U.S. women respond in such large numbers to the service and information call-up? Ironically, their primary motivation was to strengthen the traditional multichild, male breadwinner family in the face of rising costs of food, housing, and education. Despite their lower rate of remuneration, married women's wages became critical for maintaining or achieving middle-class status.

As we have seen in Chapters 9 and 10, family structure is closely correlated with infrastructural conditions. It is impossible in the present case to mistake the direction of causality. Though multiple and complex feedbacks have operated at all stages of the process, the main thrust emanated from changes occurring at the infrastructural level—the shift from goods production to service and information production. Alterations at the structural level—marriage and the organization of the family—did not show up until a substantial commitment to the new mode of production had taken place. For example, the number of women who had husbands present and who were participating in the work force had already risen from 15 to 30 percent by 1958. Yet it was not until 1970 that the feminist movement attained a level of national consciousness, when women shed their bras, held crockery-smashing parties, and marched down New York's Fifth Avenue shouting slogans like "Starve a rat tonight; don't feed your husband." These antics expressed the pent-up frustration of wives who were already in the labor force and experiencing the contradictions of the old and new gender

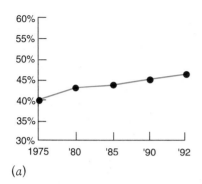

(a)

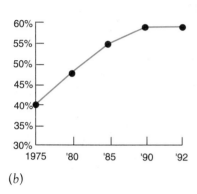

(b)

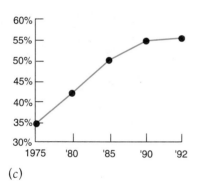

(c)

roles. As noted by Maxine Margolis in her book *Mothers and Such:* "While the media devoted much space to 'bra-burning' and other supposed atrocities of the women's movement, little attention was paid to the reality of women's work which had set the stage for the revival of feminism" (1984: 231). Writing from an economist's perspective, Valery Oppenheimer, in her book *Work and the Family,* makes the same point:

> There is no evidence that these substantial shifts in women's labor force participation were precipitated by prior changes in sex-role attitudes. On the contrary, they [changes in sex-role attitudes] lagged behind behavioral changes, indicating that changes in behavior have gradually brought about changes in sex role norms rather than the reverse. Moreover, the evidence clearly indicates that the start of the rapid changes in women's labor force behavior greatly preceded the rebirth of the feminist movement.

[1982: 30]

As Oppenheimer explains further, this is not to say that "more equalitarian sex-role attitudes and a feminist ideological perspective are not major motivating forces," but "that these attitudes reinforce or provide an ideological rationale (or normative justification)" (1982: 30).

To identify the infrastructural conditions of a social movement and to assign them a causal priority over values and ideas is not to diminish the role of values and ideas or of volition in the dynamism of history. Nonetheless, it is essential in this case, as well as in other controversial social movements, that both those who favor and those who oppose a particular change comprehend that some outcomes are more probable than others. In the present instance, for example, it seems highly improbable that women in the United States can be restored to their former situation as housewives. In order to resurrect the male breadwinner family and put women back behind the sink, the nation would have to revert to a more primitive phase of capitalism and industrialization, a course that even the most conservative antifeminists do not propose to take.

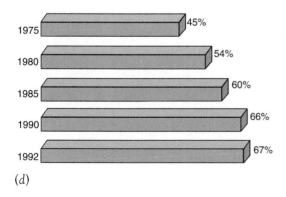

(d)

Figure 15.9

(a) Portion of the work force that is female (percent); (b) percentage of women in the labor force who have children under 6 years old; (c) percentage of women in the labor force who have children under 3 years old; (d) percentage of employed men who have employed wives.

Source: Bureau of Labor Statistics

Chapter 16

PSYCHOLOGICAL ANTHROPOLOGY

Father and son in Laos.

Earlier in this century psychologically oriented anthropologists began to study the relationship between culture and personality. Did cultures shape people's personalities, or did their personalities shape their cultures? According to the followers of Sigmund Freud, some personality complexes occur universally and affect cultures everywhere. We shall see if this is true. Others follow Freud in contending that culturally prescribed differences in childhood training greatly influence adult personality. But can it be said that all adults brought up in a particular culture have the same personality? Do the Japanese, for example, have a distinctive national character? And what of the relationship between culture and mental health? Do certain forms of mental illness occur in only one culture? And when people have dreams and visions, do they dream and hallucinate in culturally prescribed ways?

Culture and Personality

Culture refers to the patterned ways in which the members of a society think, feel, and behave. *Personality* also refers to patterned ways of thinking, feeling, and behaving, but the focus is on the individual. Personality, as defined by Victor Barnouw (1985: 8), "is a more or less enduring organization of forces within the individual associated with a complex of fairly consistent attitudes, values, and modes of perception which account, in part, for the individual's consistency of behavior." More simply, "personality is the tendency to behave in certain ways regardless of the specific setting" (Whiting and Whiting 1978: 57).

The concepts employed in describing the thinking, feeling, and behavior of personality types differ from those employed in describing infrastructure, structure, and superstructure. In describing personalities, psychologists use concepts such as aggressive, passive, anxious, obsessive, hysterical, manic, depressed, introverted, extroverted, paranoid, authoritarian, schizoid, masculine, feminine, infantile, repressed, and dependent. If you use such concepts to describe an entire group of people, the result will not add up to a description of modes of production and reproduction, domestic and political economy, systems of war and peace, or magico-religious rites and institutions. Rather, they will add up to a description of the kinds of personalities found in that group of people.

Freud's Influence

According to Sigmund Freud, the founder of psychoanalysis, adult personality is largely shaped by an individual's experiences in resolving certain recurrent conflicts during infancy and childhood. The most important conflict is known as the Oedipus complex. (Oedipus, according to ancient Greek legend, killed his father and committed incest with his mother.)

The conflict is allegedly caused by biologically determined sexual strivings and jealousies within the nuclear family.

Freud held that a young boy's first sexual feelings are directed toward his mother. But the boy soon discovers that mother is the sexual object of his father and that he is in competition with his father for sexual "mastery" of the same woman. The father, while providing protection, also provides stern discipline (Fig. 16.1). He suppresses his son's attempt to express sexual love for mother. The son is frustrated and fantasizes that he is strong enough to kill his father. This fantasy arouses fear and guilt in the young boy: fear because the father in fact or in the boy's fantasy threatens to cut off the child's penis, and guilt because the child loves the father as well as fears him. To resolve this conflict successfully, the young boy must learn to control his hostility and to redirect his sexuality toward females other than his mother.

For the young girl, Freud envisioned a parallel but fundamentally different trauma. A girl's sexuality is also initially directed toward her mother, but she soon makes a fateful discovery: She lacks a penis. She blames her mother for this and redirects her sexual desires away from her mother and toward her father. However, her love for the father and for other men is mixed with a feeling of envy for they possess something she lacks. Freud believed that women suffer from penis envy all of their lives. In this fashion, Freud sought to ground the subordination of women to the unalterable facts of anatomy—hence the aphorism "anatomy is destiny." Thus, women were relegated to a passive and secondary role, the role of the "second sex." The best hope of overcoming her penis envy is for a woman to be passive and attractive, get married, and have babies: "Her happiness is great if later on this wish for a baby finds fulfillment in reality, and quite especially so if the baby is a little boy who brings the longed-for penis with him" (Freud, in Millett 1970: 185). Clearly, Freud's notions about gender roles were projections of his own experiences as a male in highly male-centered late nineteenth-century Vienna where he lived and formulated his ideas. Sexual pol-

Figure 16.1 Freud's Milieu
A turn-of-the-century middle-class father with his two sons. He is stern but protective.

itics aimed at perpetuating the gender hierarchy, not science, provided the basis for his idea that women necessarily envied men and were destined always to be the second sex.

Is the Oedipus Complex Universal?

Starting with Bronislaw Malinowski's (1927) research on the avunculocal Trobriand family (see Chapter 10), anthropologists have criticized Freud on the grounds that the Oedipus complex imposes on the rest of the world a view of personality development appropriate to monogamous, patriarchical, nineteenth-century middle-class Vienna. Malinowski pointed out that Trobriand males couldn't develop the same kind of complex because their mother's brother and not their father exercised authority over them. Thus, Trobriand males grew up without the hate–love feelings toward their father that Freud postulated as being universal.

Melford Spiro (1982) has attempted to rescue the Freudian position by separating the hate-love engendered by sexual jealousy from the hate-love engendered by authority. For example, the Trobriand male lives with his father and mother until he is an adolescent. Although his father is an easygoing and nonauthoritarian figure, father and son still have plenty of opportunity to develop feelings of sexual rivalry over the mother and wife. Spiro concludes, therefore, that Malinowski did not prove that the Trobrianders were without any basis for developing the Oedipus complex. Malinowski was on the right track, however, since the severity of the Oedipus complex must vary in relation to the amount and quality of the control that parents exercise over their children, and such control varies with the structure of the domestic group.

Most anthropologists interested in culture and personality studies today reject the idea that the Oedipus complex is universal. Freud's continuing influence, however, can be seen in the idea that personality is largely determined as a result of the individual's experiences during infancy and childhood. What anthropologists have added is the qualification that these experiences vary widely in conformity with the specific forms of family life and gender roles characteristic of particular sociocultural systems.

Childhood Training and Personality

Parents in a particular culture tend to follow similar childhood training practices involving the feeding, cleaning, and handling of infants and children. These childhood training practices vary widely from one society to another and are probably responsible for some cross-cultural differences in adult personalities (Box 16.1). In many cultures, for example, infants are constrained by swaddling bandages or cradle boards that immobilize their limbs. Elsewhere, freedom of movement is encouraged. Similarly, nursing may be either on demand at the first cry of hunger or at regular intervals at the convenience of the mother. Nursing at the mother's breast may last for a few months or several years or may not take place at all. Supplementary foods may be taken in the first few weeks; they may be stuffed into the baby's mouth, prechewed by the mother, played with by the baby, or omitted entirely.

Weaning may take place abruptly, as when the mother's nipples are painted with bitter substances, and it may or may not be associated with the birth of another child. In some cultures, infants are kept next to their mother's skin and carried wherever the mother goes (Fig. 16.2); elsewhere, they may be left behind with relatives or other caretakers. In some cultures, infants are fondled, hugged, kissed, and fussed over by large groups of adoring children and adults; in others, they are kept relatively isolated and touched infrequently.

Toilet training may begin as early as 6 weeks or as late as 36 months. The mode of training may involve many different techniques, some based on intense forms of punishment, shame, and ridicule, and others involving suggestion, emulation, and no punishment (Fig. 16.3).

Treatment of infant sexuality also varies widely. In many cultures, mothers or fathers stroke their babies' genitals to soothe them and stop them from crying. Tibetan mothers go one step further, as reported by anthropologist Hildegard Diemberger (1993: 89):

Caili, an energetic and sensual woman, is playing with her youngest son, Migmar. I enter the house. Caili offers me a cup of barley beer and then continues to play with Migmar who really does not want to be disturbed. He drinks some milk from the breast and plays with his erect little penis. He

---

Box 16.1

TAKING CARE OF BABY AMONG HUNTER-GATHERERS

AMONG THE AGTA

The infant is eagerly passed from person to person until all in attendance have had an opportunity to snuggle, nuzzle, sniff, and admire the newborn. A child's first experience, then, involves a community of relatives and friends. Thereafter, he enjoys constant cuddling, carrying, loving, sniffing, and affectionate genital stimulation.

[Peterson 1978: 16]

AMONG THE MBUTI

The mother emerges and presents the child to the camp and she hands the boy to a few of her closest friends and family, not just for them to look at him but for them to hold him close to their bodies. In this way an initial model of predictability and security becomes multiplied, and so it is throughout the educational process: vital lessons, such as non-

aggressivity, are learned through a plurality of models.

[Turnbull 1978: 172]

AMONG THE EFE PYGMY

A recent study of Efe Pygmy infant caring practices (Tronick et al. 1987) found that the mother often was not the first one to nurse her infant and that other women frequently nursed the child during infancy. Four-month old infants spent only 40 percent of their time with their mother and were transferred among caretakers frequently—8.3 times per hour on average. Many individuals contributed to an infant's care: an average of 14.2 different people cared for an infant during eight hours of observation.

[Hewlett 1991: 15]

---

offers it to his mother who sucks it tenderly and then continues to chat with me. Migmar is five years old."

Elsewhere, even the baby is prevented from touching its own genitals, and masturbation is severely punished. In the United States, Caili's behavior would be considered child sexual abuse and she would be hauled off to jail!

Another series of variables relevant to personality formation consists of later childhood and adolescent experiences: numbers of siblings, their relationships and mutual responsibilities (Fig. 16.4), patterns of play, opportunities to observe adult intercourse, opportunities to engage in homosexual or heterosexual experimentation, incest restrictions, and type of threat and punishment used against culturally prohibited sexual practices (Weisner and Gilmore 1977).

Male Initiation and Childhood Training

John Whiting (1969) and his associates proposed an interesting theory that relates childhood experiences to the formation of adult personality. They showed that statistical correlations exist between (1) protein scarcities, (2) nursing of children for 1 year or more, (3) prohibition of sexual relations

between husband and wife for 1 year or more after the birth of their child, (4) polygyny, (5) domestic sleeping arrangements in which mother and child sleep together and father sleeps elsewhere, (6) child training by women, (7) patrilocality, and (8) severe male initiation rites.

> Following our model, the following chain develops: Low protein availability and the risk of Kwashiorkor [a protein-deficiency disease] were correlated with an extended postpartum sex taboo to allow the mother time to nurse the infant through the critical stage before becoming pregnant again. The postpartum sex taboo was significantly correlated with the institution of polygyny, providing alternate sexual outlets for the male. Polygyny, in turn, is associated with mother–child households, child training by women, resultant cross-sex identity, and where patrilocality is also present, with initiation rites to resolve the conflict and properly inculcate male identity.

[Harrington and Whiting 1972: 491]

"Cross-sex identity" refers to the psycho-dynamic process by which boys who are reared exclusively by their mothers and older women identify themselves with their mothers and other women. Where patrilocality is present, reasons Whiting, functional consistency demands that adult males

(a)

(b)

Figure 16.2   Care of Children
Cultures vary greatly in the amount of body contact between mother and infant. (a) Swazi mother and child. (b) Arunta mother and child; mother has all-purpose carrying dish on her head and a digging stick in her hand.

must make a strong identification with their fathers and other males. Hence, what the male must do and think as an adult conflicts with what he is trained to do and think as an infant. Severe male initiation ceremonies involving circumcision or other forms of mutilation, prolonged seclusion, beatings, and trials of courage and stamina are thus required to resolve this conflict by breaking the prepubescent identity (Fig. 16.5).

Patterns and Themes

Many other proposals have been made concerning how to treat the relationship between personality and culture. One popular option acknowledges that culture and personality represent two different ways of looking at the propensity to think, feel, and behave that characterize a given population and uses psychological terms to characterize both personality and the cultural system. For example, Ruth Benedict, in her famous book *Patterns of Culture* (1934), characterized the institution of the Kwakiutl potlatch (see p. 92) as a "megalomaniacal" performance—behavior dominated by fantasies of wealth and power. She saw potlatch as part of a "Dionysian" pattern that was characteristic of all the institutions of Kwakiutl culture. By Dionysian she meant the desire to achieve emotional excess, as in drunkenness or frenzy. Other cultures, such as that of the Pueblo Indians, she saw as Apollonian—given to moderation and the "middle of the

Figure 16.3   Toilet Training, Russian Style
Soviet children were toilet trained in their nursery schools by their
teachers. How might this have influenced their personalities in compari-
son with American children, who are usually toilet trained by their par-
ents before they go to nursery school?

Figure 16.4   Javanese Girl and Brother
One way to free mother for work in the fields is to turn over the care of
infants to a 7-year-old sister.

road" in all things. Benedict's patterns were psychological elements reputedly found throughout a culture, "comparable to the chromosomes found in most of the cells of a body" (Wallace 1970: 149). Most anthropologists have rejected such attempts to use one or two psychological terms to describe whole cultures. Even the most simple hunter–gatherer cultures have too many personalities to be summed up in such a manner.

Rather than attempt to sum up whole cultures under one or two psychological concepts, some anthropologists point to dominant themes or values that express the essential or main thought and feeling of a particular culture. The "image of limited good" is one such theme (see p. 164). Themes and values are readily translatable into personality traits.

For example, the image of limited good reputedly produces personalities that are jealous, suspicious, secretive, and fearful. The culture of poverty (see p. 165) also has its psychological components—improvidence, lack of future time orientation, and sexual promiscuity. An important theme in Hindu India is the "sacredness of life," and an important theme in the United States is "keeping up with the Joneses."

The problem with attempts to portray cultures in terms of a few dominant values and attitudes is that contradictory values and attitudes can usually be identified within the same cultures and even within the same individuals. Thus, although Hindu farmers believe in the sacredness of life (Opler 1968), they also believe in the necessity of having more bullocks than cows (see p. 240); and although many people in the United States believe in trying to keep up with the Joneses, others believe that conspicuous consumption is foolish and wasteful.

Schemas and Cognition

Psychological anthropologists have long been interested in the question of the relationship between culture and cognitive processes (how people think). Recently they have found that the concept of *schema*, borrowed from cognitive psychology, promises to reveal how thoughts about culture are organized within the minds of individuals. Schemas provide people with simplified models of what the world is like and how one ought to act and feel and think (D'Andrade 1992).

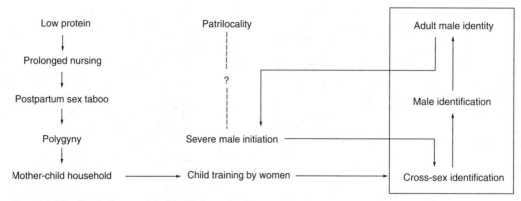

Figure 16.5   Psychodynamic Model of Relationship Between Low-Protein Diet and Severe Male Initiation

A classic instance of a schema is our knowledge of what one should do in a restaurant:

> sit at a table
>
> order from a menu
>
> tell a waiter or waitress what we want
>
> eat
>
> wait for a check
>
> pay it
>
> go out

Adapted from Strauss 1992: 198.

Cultures differ in their repertoire of schemas. One that is found in Samoa, for example, is organized around the concept of an encounter with an old person, carrying a heavy burden, walking along the road, on a hot day. Just as a New Yorker knows the "script" for a restaurant, so a Samoan knows what to do if such an encounter takes place:

> offer to carry the burden
>
> bring the old person into the shade
>
> serve a cooling drink

Adapted from Strauss 1992: 198.

According to Roy D'Andrade (1992: 55), cultural schemas are organized into levels of generality and motivational force. Top-level schemas give the most general view of what is going on and contain a general set of powerful goals. They constitute a person's "master set" of schemas, such as, for Americans, love, success, security, and fun. At a lower level and subservient to the master set are schemas for marriage, jobs, and surfing. At a still lower level lie the schemas for dirt, memos, and birthdays. These lower schemas generate

goals only when they are activated by the higher-level schemas. "The goal of cleaning up dirt, for example, generally is triggered only when schemas having to do with ownership, health, beauty, etc., are also invoked" (D'Andrade 1992).

This picture of a well-ordered set of scripts, motivations, and goals may not be adequate for capturing the complexity of the cognitive structures in the human "mind." First of all, as Dorothy Holland (1992) points out, the actual behavior associated with a given schema may be completely novel and unpredictable. She cites the example of "The Woman Who Climbed Up the House." In a village in Nepal, Holland and a colleague were interviewing villagers on the second-story balcony of a house that belonged to a high-caste family. When a low-caste woman who was to be interviewed next appeared below, Holland's colleague hastened downstairs to welcome her and escort her to the balcony, knowing that the schemas governing caste relations barred anyone of low caste from entering the house. Before she could be intercepted and escorted up the stairway, the woman, using fingers and toes, clawed her way up the outside of the house and clambered over the balcony rail. This action cannot be explained by any neat interaction of schemas.

Schemas may also contradict each other as often as they support each other. For example, Janet Keller interviewed twenty people in a study of how Americans conceptualize the family. She found the following contradictory positions:

> Family members should strive for the good of the whole.
>
> Family as a group is secondary to each individual.
>
> Family is permanent.
>
> Family is always in transition.
>
> Family is a refuge.
>
> Family is a place to prepare and rehearse public roles.

Family is nurturant.

Family is smothering.

Family is divisive, a cauldron of tension and domination.

Family is an opportunity for mutual support, unity, and warmth.

Adapted from Keller 1992: 61–62.

Evidently, schema theory has a long way to go before it can supply a valid model of how cultural knowledge is organized and activated.

Basic Personality and National Character

One approach to culture and personality postulates that every culture produces a deep or *basic personality* structure that can be found in virtually every individual member of the culture. When the populations involved are organized into a state, the basic personality is often called *national character.*

The notion of basic personality structure has always enjoyed considerable popularity among travelers to foreign lands as well as among scholars (Fig. 16.6). One often hears it said that the English are "reserved," the Brazilians "carefree," the French "romantic," the Italians "uninhibited," the Japanese "orderly," the Americans "outgoing," and so forth. Gerardus Mercator, the father of mapmaking, wrote the following descriptions of European basic personalities in the sixteenth century (see if you can guess Mercator's nationality):

Franks: Simple, blockish, furious.

Bavarians: Sumptuous, gluttons, brazenfaced.

Swedes: Light, babblers, boasters.

Saxons: Dissemblers, double-hearted, opinionative.

Spaniards: Disdainful, cautious, greedy.

Belgians: Good horsemen, tender, docile, delicate.

The concept of basic personality type is hard to reconcile with the fact that every society includes a great range of personalities and that the more populous, complex, and stratified the society, the greater the variability. In every society, many individuals have personalities that deviate widely from the statistical mode (most frequent type), and the range of individual personalities produces wide overlaps between different cultures. For example, it would certainly be correct to characterize the basic type of Plains Native-American male personality as aggressive, independent, fearless. Yet, as we

Figure 16.6   National Character Stereotypes
Allen Funt's popular TV show "Candid Camera" frequently explored national character differences by means of informal cross-cultural experiments. The three scenes represented here show the same young woman in three different countries, standing at a curb with a suitcase filled with 100 pounds of bricks. In each scene, she solicits a male passerby to help her get her suitcase across the street. In Country A, the man tugs and pulls at the suitcase with all of his might, finally managing to get it across the street. In Country B, the man tries to move the suitcase, but when he finds it unexpectedly heavy, he gives up and goes on his way. In Country C, on finding the bag too heavy for one person to pick up, the man enlists the aid of another male passerby, and the two of them carry it across with no difficulty. Can you guess which country each scene depicts? In view of the recent changes in gender roles, what other scenarios might be likely to occur today?
Answers: (A) England; (B) France; (C) United States.

have seen (p. 81), some young men always found themselves temperamentally unsuited to the male role. Very little is actually known about the amount of personality variance in different societies. However, complex state-level populations consisting of millions of people must contain an enormous variety of personality types.

Japanese National Character

Despite the varieties of personalities found in a given society, many psychological traits and their associated behaviors may be rare, "strange," or utterly alien to certain societies and not to others. This variation follows logically from the fact that a society's personality is culture described in psychological terms (see p. 207). Valid interpretations of personality configurations in alien cultures, however, require great familiarity with the language and deep immersion in the context of everyday life. The experience of being a member of another society often cannot be adequately represented by simple contrasts and conventional categories.

For example, the Japanese are stereotyped by Westerners as a people who are deferential, shy, self-effacing, conformist, and dependent on group approval. "Few Japanese," writes one anthropologist, "achieve a sense of self that is independent of the attitude of others" (cited in Kumagai and Kumagai 1986: 314; cf. Plath 1983). Examples of exaggerated deference are found in the frequent bowing and elaborate courtesy of Japanese business conferences and the readiness with which Japanese identify themselves as a work team or a corporation rather than as individuals. Indeed, self-effacement has been linked by many observers to the secret of Japan's industrial success. Japanese management style plays down the difference between executives and workers. Everyone eats in the same company cafeteria, and groups of workers regularly join with management to solve problems of mutual interest in a cooperative rather than adversarial manner.

However, another side of the Japanese personality is reserved for private and intimate occasions. If you are not a member of a Japanese family group and do not interact with family members when there are no guests or outside observers present, you would not see the strength of individual ego-assertion that is also part of Japanese daily life (Box 16.2).

Most Japanese are brought up to be adept at changing back and forth between the private assertive self and the deferential public self. The significance of these different modes of presenting one's self has little if anything to do with the inner psychological strength of the Japanese ego. Since Westerners have no real equivalent of a public-formal mode of self-effacement, they have often incorrectly and unfavorably perceived Japanese personality. Lacking a Western equivalent, Westerners interpret the posture of self-effacement as indica-

---

Box 16.2

THE JAPANESE AT HOME

People are relaxed and do not worry about formalities. They can talk and joke about their innermost concerns. Even the most formal of women may be informal with close friends. They even tease each other about the formalities which they notice on other occasions. With close friends, one can argue, criticize, and be stubborn without endangering the relationship. There is inevitably a great deal of laughter mixed with mutual support and respect. It is partly the sharp contrast between seeing a close friend and a mere acquaintance that makes contacts with outsiders seem so stiff. The visitor to Japan who does not appreciate the difference in behavior toward friends and acquaintances is likely to consider the Japanese as more formal than they actually are.

Quoted in Sugimoto and Mouer 1983.

---

tive of hypocrisy and deviousness. On the other side, the Japanese are equally befuddled by the failure of Westerners to make a distinction between expressions of one's ego in public-formal versus intimate-private situations. As recounted by a Japanese social scientist, being a dinner guest in an American home can be especially perplexing:

Another thing that made me nervous was the custom whereby an American host will ask a guest, before the meal, whether he would prefer a strong or a soft drink [and after dinner] whether [he takes] coffee or tea, and—in even greater detail—whether one wants it with sugar, and milk, and so on.

Kumagai 1986: 12

Although the visitor soon realized that the hosts were trying to be polite, he felt extremely uncomfortable with having to say what he would like since in the self-effacing and deferential posture appropriate to being a guest in a Japanese home, one avoids expressions of personal preference with respect to what is being served. Guests are dependent on hosts and surrender all vestiges of personal preference. The hosts in turn must avoid embarrassing their guests by asking them to choose their own food. Unlike Americans, Japanese hosts do not discuss how they prepared the main dish. They say, "This may not suit your taste, but it is the best we could do." The guests are not supposed to be interested in knowing any of the details of this effort.

Compliant Japanese?

Japan's managerial and governing elites have long advocated and extolled the virtues of team spirit, loyalty to firm and state, and peaceful family-style acquiescence to authority. But social conflict is also part of Japan's traditions.

In 1897, Oka Minoru, later the chief architect of Japan's first factory law, predicted that Japanese labor relations would resemble the "beautiful customs" of "master and retainer" that had prevailed during feudalism. He envisioned the factory as "one big family" and predicted that "strikes will become unthinkable" (quoted in Garon 1987: 30). But early in its career as an industrial nation, Japan was troubled by labor unrest. Bitter labor management confrontations occurred in 1906, and during World War I, the 1920s, and again in the 1940s. During the American occupation, the Japanese were at first encouraged to develop national trade unions as a step toward democratization. "From an insignificant base of five thousand in October 1945, union membership soared to nearly five million by December 1946" (Garon 1987: 40–41; Gordon 1987: 238). Strikes occurred at a rate similar to U.S. rates but with a far more radical and disharmonious objective: The unions planned a general strike for February 1, 1947. Frightened by the specter of a communist-inspired class war, the Americans stepped in and reversed course on unionization.

In addition to labor unrest and strikes, much additional evidence indicates that Japan, like the rest of the industrial world, is not exclusively under the sway of harmony-promoting values. Peasant revolts were commonplace during the past century. For the decade 1868–1877, there are accounts of 499 peasant uprisings and 24 urban mass disturbances (Mouer and Sugimoto 1986: 101). In 1918, a sharp increase in the price of rice led to widespread rioting and looting that lasted 53 days, spread to 42 prefectures, and required the attention of 92,000 troops before order was restored (Garon 1987: 40–41; Lewis 1990: 97).

After World War II, Japanese teachers engaged in massive boycotts and demonstrations against political censorship, complete with fistfights in the Japanese Diet between socialist and conservative members. In more recent years, dissent, often accompanied by violence, has been registered by various antipollution and environmental movements, the student movement, the consumer movement, the movement against nuclear weapons, the movement against noise pollution, and the decade-long farmers movement to prevent the expansion of Tokyo's Narita Airport (Fig. 16.7).

Little credence should be given to the view that because these movements and demonstrations are themselves structured by groupist values, they therefore merely confirm the pervasiveness of such values and correspondingly fail to demonstrate the existence of alternative confrontational ideologies. Nothing in the notion of protest requires activists to

Figure 16.7 Japanese Riot
Police and demonstrators clash during a protest against expansion of Tokyo airport.

act like a mob, especially in an age when performance for the media is the key to winning public support (Ben-Ari et al. 1990).

Culture and Mental Illness

Anthropologists do not agree on the role that cultural differences play in the incidence and nature of mental illness. Recent medical research has shown that such classic mental disorders as schizophrenia and manic-depressive psychosis probably have important viral genetic and chemical-neurological bases (Torrey 1980). This accords with the evidence that the rates of those diseases among groups as diverse as Swedes, Innuits, the Yoruba of West Africa, and modern Canadians do not show marked differences (Murphy 1976; Warner 1985). However, there is no doubt that, though broad symptoms of the same mental diseases can be found cross-culturally, specific symptoms found in different cultures vary considerably.

For example, American patients have delusions about putting Cadillac engines into people's heads or of talking with angels in spacesuits, themes that one does not expect to hear from people who do not own cars or watch rocket lift-offs. Westerners began to have delusions about being controlled by rays of electricity only around the beginning of the century. Similarly, a common delusion of modern schizophrenics is that they have become robots. This delusion did not exist before the word and concept of *robot* was introduced in 1921 in a play by Karel Capek (Barnouw 1985: 361).

Moreover, as psychiatrist Richard Warner (1985) has shown, the severity of schizophrenia and the prospects of spontaneously recovering from it vary from culture to culture. In nonindustrial societies with extended families, small face-to-face communities, and religions that stress the existence of a multitude of ever-present spirit beings (see p. 222), the schizophrenic individual is not regarded as a shameful or threatening presence or even as a person who has gone crazy. Relatives continue to render emotional and physical support, while the community blames the schizophrenic's bizarre behavior on some pesky spirit. In contrast, schizophrenics in industrial societies are often expelled from both family and community, deprived of emotional and physical support, isolated, and made to feel worthless and guilty. These culturally constructed conditions make the prospect for recovery much poorer in industrial societies despite the availability of modern medical therapies.

Culture-Specific Psychoses

Evidence for more powerful effects of culture on mental illness can be found in culture-specific psychoses—disorders that have a distinctive set of symptoms limited to only one or a few cultures (Simmons and Hughes 1985).

A well-known example of these culture-specific psychoses occurs among the Innuits and is called Arctic hysteria, or pibloktoq (Fig. 16.8). Unlike classic psychoses, pibloktoq strikes suddenly. Its victims leap up, tear off their clothes, move their limbs convulsively, and roll about naked in the snow and ice. One explanation for this behavior likens it to a severe case of "cabin fever." Cooped up in their small, crowded dwellings for long periods during which they are

unable to vent their feelings of hostility, pibloktoq victims may become hysterical as a means of dealing with their pent-up frustrations. It seems more likely, however, that the underlying cause also lies in the highly carnivorous diet of the Innuits. Lacking plant foods and solar radiation, the Innuits are forced to rely on the consumption of sea mammal and polar bear livers for their supply of vitamin A and vitamin D. Eating too much of these livers produces a poisonous excess of vitamin A, but eating too little can result in a deficit of vitamin D, which in turn leads to a deficit of calcium in the bloodstream (see p. 184). Both conditions—too much vitamin A and too little calcium in the blood—are known to be associated with convulsions and psychotic episodes (Landy 1985; Wallace 1972). Thus, pibloktoq is probably a consequence of the interaction between culturally determined living conditions and the chemistry of nutrition.

Windigo Psychosis?

Among the hunter–gatherer northern Ojibwa and Cree of the Canadian subarctic forest, there is a widespread belief that humans can become possessed by the spirit of Windigo, a cannibal monster whose heart is made out of ice. This belief has given rise to the hypothesis that the Cree and Ojibwa are subject to a culture-specific malady called Windigo psychosis. Those who are possessed by Windigo are said to experience an overwhelming desire to kill and eat their campmates. Living in a harsh environment, the Cree and Ojibwa often find themselves snowbound and close to starvation in their isolated winter camps. The likelihood of someone becoming

(a)

(b)

Figure 16.8   Arctic Hysteria
The victim is an Innuit woman from Greenland.

a Windigo is said to have been greatest under such conditions. Various reports verify the fact that famished campmates did sometimes eat the bodies of their deceased companions in order to keep themselves alive. (Similar accounts of "crisis cannibalism" have been reported from many parts of the world, most recently from a soccer team whose plane crashed in the Andes mountains.) Once having experienced human flesh, human Windigos are said to crave more. They lose their taste for ordinary food, their hearts feel like a lump of ice, and the people around them no longer look like people but like deer, moose, or other game animals. Unless they are killed first, they will kill and devour their companions.

As Louis Marano (1982) has shown, there are many authenticated cases of the killing of people said to be Windigos by their alarmed campmates. Recurrently, Windigo killers cite evidence that justifies their homicides: The victims looked at them strangely, tossed about and mumbled in their sleep, had saliva dripping from their mouths, or tried to attack and bite their companions. In one instance, the alleged Windigo even seemed to hover off the ground and had to be pulled down by his attackers. The alleged Windigos themselves are said to have asked that they be killed lest they eat their campmates one by one. What is lacking in all these accounts, however, is any hard data showing that the alleged Windigos thought and acted in the manner described by their executioners. Without such data, the existence of a genuine Windigo psychosis remains in doubt, and a much simpler explanation can be offered for the belief in Windigo possession (Box 16.3). Under conditions of extreme hunger and stress, the northern Ojibwa and Cree accused certain troublesome campmates of being Windigos as a justification for getting rid of them, thereby increasing the chances of survival for the rest of the camp. Thus, the typical executed Windigo was a sickly individual delirious with a high fever, someone who was too ill to walk, a senile old man or woman, or a stranger from another ethnic group. In Marano's words, the Windigo beliefs were not evidence of a psychosis but of a system of "triage homicide" (letting some die in order that others might live) in which the fear of being eaten was used to overcome the fear of breaking the taboo on killing a campmate.

Dreams and Hallucinations

The cultural patterning of mental life affects the content of dreams, visions, and drug-induced hallucinations. For example, a form of individualistic religion (see p. 224) common in North and South America involves the acquisition of a personal guardian spirit or supernatural protector. Typically, this spirit protector is acquired by means of a visionary experience induced by fasting, self-inflicted torture, or hallucinogenic drugs (see p. 227). Although each vision is slightly different

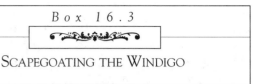

Box 16.3

SCAPEGOATING THE WINDIGO

Upon close scrutiny the Windigo psychosis discloses itself not as a culturally isolated anthropophagic (i.e., cannibal) obsession, but instead as a rather predictable—though culturally conditioned—variant of triage homicide and witch hunting typical of societies under stress. In this process, as in all witch hunts, the victims of the aggression are socially redefined as the aggressors. Here the specific form of the redefinition was determined by the constant threat of starvation, a situation in which cannibalism has proved to be a tempting recourse for persons of all cultures throughout history. By attributing society's most salient fear to the scapegoat, the group was able to project its modal anxiety onto the individual, thus generating a rationale for homicide with which everyone could identify.

Marano 1982: 385.

from the next, they all follow a similar culturally constructed pattern.

For many native North Americans, a hallucinatory vision was the central experience of life (Fig. 16.9). Young men needed this hallucinatory experience to succeed in love, warfare, horse stealing, trading, and all other important endeavors. In keeping with their code of personal bravery and endurance, they sought these visions primarily through self-inflicted torture. Among the Crow, for example, a youth who craved a visionary experience went alone into the mountains, stripped off his clothes, and abstained from food and drink. If the vision still did not come, he chopped off part of the fourth finger of his left hand.

Coached from childhood to expect that a vision would come, most Crow vision-seekers were successful. A buffalo, snake, chicken hawk, thunderbird, dwarf, or mysterious stranger would appear; miraculous events would unfold; and then these strange beings would "adopt" the vision-seeker and disappear. Scratches-face, who was one of Robert Lowie's informants, prayed to the morning star: "Old woman's grandson, I give you this [finger joint]. Give me something good in exchange . . . a good horse a good-natured woman a tent of my own to live in" (Lowie 1948: 6). Lowie reports that after cutting off his finger, Scratches-face had a successful vision. "As a consequence of his blessing Scratches-face struck and killed an enemy without ever getting wounded. He also

(a)

(b)

Figure 16.9 Sioux Vision

Section of pictographic biography done by Rain in the Face. (a) In a dream, the lightning tells him that unless he gives a buffalo feast, the lightning will kill him. He gives the feast, one part of which consists of filling a kettle with red-hot buffalo tongues, which he eats in order to save his life. (b) He dreams of buffalo again. While dancing, he is shot by an arrow that enters the feathers. In removing it, he soon vomits and, grabbing a handful of earth, rubs it into the wound, healing it rapidly.

obtained horses and married a good-tempered and industrious woman."

Although each Crow's vision had some unique elements, they were usually similar in the following regards: (1) Some revelation of future success in warfare, horse raiding, or other act of bravery was involved; (2) the visions usually occurred at the end of the fourth day—four being the sacred number of the native North Americans; (3) practically every vision was accompanied by the acquisition of a sacred song; (4) the friendly spirits in the vision adopted the youth; and (5) trees or rocks often turned into enemies who vainly shot at the invulnerable spirit being. Lowie concludes:

> He sees and hears not merely what any faster, say in British Columbia or South Africa, would see and hear under like conditions of physiological exhaustion and under the urge of generally human desires, but what the social tradition of the Crow tribe imperatively suggests.

[1948: 14]

Chapter Summary

Culture and personality are closely related concepts concerned with the patterning of thoughts, feelings, and behavior. Personality is primarily a characteristic of individuals; culture is primarily a characteristic of groups. Yet it is possible to speak of the personality of a group—of a basic, modal,

or typical personality. However, the technical vocabulary used to describe culture differs from the vocabulary used to describe personality.

Anthropologists who study personality generally accept the Freudian premise that personality is molded by childhood experiences. This premise has led to an interest in how adults interact with and relate to infants and young children, especially in such matters as toilet training, nursing, weaning, and sexual discipline.

Other approaches to culture and personality attempt to characterize whole cultures in terms of central themes or patterns. More recently, the concept of schemas has been used to identify the cognitive organization of cultures. Care is necessary in order to avoid overgeneralizing the applicability of such concepts. Contradictory themes and schema are common. Moreover, a wide range of personality types is found in any large population.

This is not to deny that profound differences exist between personality patterns in different cultures. The Japanese, for example, have a distinctive disposition to separate ego-effacing from ego-asserting situations. This disposition, however, cannot be reduced to the stereotype that Japanese are hypocritical or devious. Similarly, the notion that the Japanese are compliant and respectful of authority fails to take into account a history of civil and industrial conflict.

The relationship between culture and mental disease remains problematical. Classic disorders such as schizophrenia and manic-depressive psychosis are somewhat modified by cultural influences, yet they occur in many societies and probably result from interactions between cultural, biochemical, and genetic variables. Culture-specific psychoses such as pibloktoq indicate that cultural factors may powerfully influence the state of mental health, but as the case of Windigo psychosis shows, caution is needed in evaluating allegations concerning the existence of such psychoses.

The pervasive effect of culture on mental life is further revealed by the patterning of dreams and hallucinations. As in the vision quests of native North and South Americans, the content of what is seen when under the influence of trance-inducing substances and procedures is specific to each culture's traditions.

Chapter 17

RELIGION

Buddhist Monk, Rangoon, Myanmar.

Now we are entering the inner sanctum of superstructure, the domain of religion, myth, magic, ritual, and all the other aspects of cultures that are intended to mediate between ordinary beings and forces, on the one hand, and extraordinary beings and forces on the other. First, some basic definitions will be needed. Then we shall try to classify the basic types of religious organizations and rituals. Finally, we shall range over the vast variety of religious behaviors, from puberty rites to messianic cults, from prayer to cannibal feasts, and from abominable pigs to sacred cows. Can aspects of religion be explained in terms of structure and infrastructure? To a considerable degree. Yet religion can frequently become a powerful force in its own right. Although infrastructural and structural conditions provide a means for understanding the origin of many specific beliefs and rituals, religion frequently plays a crucial role in strengthening the impulses leading toward major transformations in social life.

Animism

What is religion? The earliest anthropological attempt to define religion was that of E. B. Tylor (1871). In his book *Primitive Culture,* he demonstrated that members of every society believe that inside the ordinary, visible, tangible body there is a normally invisible, normally intangible being: the soul. He gave the name *animism* to this belief. Throughout the world, people believe that souls can be seen in dreams, trances, visions, shadows, and reflections, and that souls are implicated in fainting, loss of consciousness, and birth and death. Tylor reasoned that the basic idea of soul must have been invented in order to explain all these puzzling phenomena. The basic soul idea then led to belief in a variety of soul-like beings, including the souls of animals, plants, and material objects, as well as gods, demons, spirits, devils, ghosts, saints, fairies, gnomes, elves, angels, and so forth.

Tylor has been criticized by twentieth-century anthropologists for his suggestion that animism arose merely as a result of the attempt to understand puzzling human and natural phenomena. Today, we know that religion is much more than an attempt to explain puzzling phenomena. Like other aspects of superstructure, religion serves a multitude of economic, political, and psychological functions.

Another important criticism of Tylor's stress on the puzzle-solving function of religion concerns the role of hallucinations in shaping religious beliefs. During drug-induced trances and other forms of hallucinatory experience, people "see" and "hear" extraordinary things that seem even more "real" than ordinary people and animals. One can argue, therefore, that animistic theories are not intellectual attempts to explain trances and dreams but direct expressions of extraordinary psychological experiences. Nonetheless, it cannot be denied that religion and the doctrine of souls also provides people with answers to fundamental questions about

the meaning of life and death and the causes of events (Pandian 1991: 88).

Although certain animistic beliefs are universal, each culture has its own distinctive animistic beings and its own specific elaboration of the soul concept. Even the number of a person's souls varies cross-culturally. The ancient Egyptians had two and so do many West African cultures: one from mother's ancestors and one from father's. The Jivaro of Ecuador (Harner 1984) have three souls. The first soul—the mekas—gives life to the body. The second soul—the arutam—has to be captured through a drug-induced visionary experience at a sacred waterfall. It confers bravery in battle to the possessor. The third soul—the musiak—forms inside the head of a dying warrior and attempts to avenge his death. It is to gain control over the musiak soul that the Jivaro cut off the fallen warrior's head, "shrink" it, and bring it back to their village where it is the focus of rituals designed to transfer its powers to its captor (Fig. 17.1).

The Dahomey say that women have three souls and that men have four. Both sexes have an ancestor soul, a personal soul, and a mawn soul. The ancestor soul gives protection during life, the personal soul is accountable for what people do with their lives, and the mawn soul is a bit of the creator god, Mawn, who supplies divine guidance. The exclusively male fourth soul guides men to positions of leadership in their households and lineages.

The record for plural souls may be held by the Fang of Gabon. They have seven: a soul inside the brain, a heart soul, a name soul, a life force soul, a body soul, a shadow soul, and a ghost soul (Riviere 1987).

Animatism and Mana

Robert Marett (1914) complained that Tylor's definition of religion as animism was too narrow. When people attribute

Figure 17.1   Jivaro Shrunken Head

"unlucky," which can be interpreted as a belief that they control varying quantities of mana.

Natural and Supernatural

Marett's idea that religion includes a belief in mana is problematical. If a belief in a powerful force constitutes religion, then what prevents belief in the force of gravity, electricity, or other concepts of physics from being regarded as religion? This problem cannot be solved by saying that mana is a supernatural force while electricity is a natural force. Most cultures do not distinguish between natural and supernatural realms. In a society where people believe ghosts are always present, it is not necessarily either natural or supernatural to provide dead ancestors with food and drink. The culture may simply lack emic categories for "natural" and "supernatural." Similarly, when a shaman blows smoke over a patient and triumphantly removes a sliver of bone allegedly inserted by the patient's enemy, the question of whether the performance is natural or supernatural may have no emic meaning.

Writing of the Gururumba (Fig. 17.2) of the highlands of western New Guinea, Philip Newman notes that they "have

lifelike properties to rocks, pots, storms, and volcanoes, they do not necessarily believe that souls cause the lifelike behavior of these objects. Hence, he wanted to distinguish a concept of a supernatural force that does not derive its effect from souls. Marett therefore introduced the term *animatism* to designate the belief in such nonsoul forces. Possession of concentrated animatistic force can give certain objects, animals, and people extraordinary powers independent of power derived from souls and gods. To label this concentrated form of animatistic force, Marett used the Melanesian word *mana*. An adze that makes intricate carvings, a fishhook that catches large fish, a club that kills many enemies, or a horseshoe that brings "good luck" have large amounts of mana. People, too, may be spoken of as having more or less mana. A woodcarver whose work is especially intricate and beautiful possesses mana, whereas a warrior captured by the enemy has obviously lost his mana.

In its broadest range of meaning, mana simply indicates belief in a powerful force. Many vernacular relationships not normally recognized as religious beliefs in Western cultures can be regarded as mana. For example, vitamin pills are consumed by many millions of people in expectation that they will exert a powerful effect on health and well-being. Soaps and detergents are said to clean because of "cleaning power"; gasolines provide engines with "starting power" or "go-power"; salespeople are prized for their "selling power"; and politicians are said to have charisma or "vote-getting power." Many people fervently believe that they are "lucky" or

Figure 17.2   Gururumba Medicine
This man is inducing vomiting by swallowing a 3-foot length of cane. After he pushes it all the way into his stomach, he works it up and down until he vomits. Gururumba men do this to rid the individual of contaminating influences gotten through contact with women.

a series of beliefs postulating the existence of entities and forces we would call supernatural." Yet the contrast between natural and supernatural is not emically relevant to the Gururumba themselves:

> It should be mentioned that our use of the notion "supernatural" does not correspond to any Gururumba concept: they do not divide the world into natural and supernatural parts. Certain entities, forces, and processes must be controlled partially through lusu, a term denoting rituals relating to growth, curing, or the stimulation of strength, while others need only rarely be controlled in this way. However, lusu does not contrast with any term denoting a realm of control where the nature of controls differ from lusu. Consequently lusu is simply part of all control techniques and what it controls is simply part of all things requiring human control.
>
> [Newman 1965: 83]

Magic and Religion

Sir James Frazer attempted to define religion in his famous book, *The Golden Bough*. For Frazer, the question of whether a belief was religious or not centered on the extent to which the participants felt they could make an entity or force do their bidding. If the participants felt insecure and humble and were inclined to supplicate and request favors and dispensations, their beliefs and actions were essentially religious. If they thought they were in control of the entities and forces governing events, felt no uncertainty about the outcome, and experienced no need for humble supplication, their beliefs and practices were examples of magic rather than of religion.

Frazer regarded prayer as the essence of religious ritual. But prayers are not always rendered in a mood of supplication. For example, prayers among the Navajo must be letter-perfect to be effective. Yet the Navajo do not expect that letter-perfect prayers will always get results. Thus, the line between prayers and "magical spells" is actually hard to draw.

Not all cultures approach their gods as supplicants. In many cultures, people try to intimidate, bribe, and lie to their gods. The Tsimshian of the Canadian Pacific Coast stamp their feet and shake their fists at the heavens and call their gods "slaves" as a term of reproach. The Manus of the Bismarck Archipelago keep the skulls of their ancestors in a corner of the house and try their best to please "Sir Ghost." However, if someone gets sick, the Manus may angrily threaten to throw Sir Ghost out of the house. This is what they tell Sir Ghost: "This man dies and you rest in no house. You will but wander about the edges of the island [used for excretory functions]" (Fortune 1965: 216). Thus, Frazer's definition of religion has not withstood the test of fieldwork. Religious thought and behavior is a complex mixture of awe and wonder, boredom and excitement, power and weakness.

The Organization of Religious Beliefs and Practices

Anthropologist Anthony Wallace (1966) distinguished four principal varieties of religious "cults"—that is, forms of organization of religious doctrines and activities—that have broad evolutionary implications. The passage of time has not brought forth a better classification. Wallace's four principal forms are (1) individualistic cults, (2) shamanistic cults, (3) communal cults, and (4) ecclesiastical cults, defined as follows:

1. *Individualistic cults*: The most basic form of religious life involves individualistic (but culturally patterned) beliefs and rituals. Each person is a specialist; each one enters into a relationship with animistic and animatistic beings and forces as each personally experiences the need for control and protection. One might call this "do-it-yourself" religion.

2. *Shamanistic cults*: No culture known to anthropology has a religion that is completely individualistic, although the Innuit and other hunters and gatherers lean heavily in this direction. Every known society also exhibits at least the shamanistic level of religious specialization (Fig. 17.3). The term *shaman* derives from the word used by the Tungus-speaking peoples of Siberia to designate the part-time religious specialist consulted in times of stress and anxiety. In cross-cultural applications, however, shaman may refer to individuals who act as diviners, curers, spirit mediums, and magicians for other people in return for gifts, fees, prestige, and power.

3. *Communal cults*: At a more complex level of political economy, communal forms of beliefs and practices become more elaborate. Groups of nonspecialists organized in terms of age grades, men's societies, clans, or lineages assume responsibility for regular or occasional performance of rituals deemed essential for their own welfare or for the survival of the society. Although communal rituals may employ specialists such as shamans, orators, and highly skilled dancers and musicians, once the ritual performance is concluded, the participants revert to a common daily routine. There are no full-time religious specialists.

4. *Ecclesiastical cults*: The ecclesiastical level of religious organization involves a full-time professional clergy or priesthood. These professionals form a bureaucracy that monopolizes the performance of certain rites on behalf of individuals, groups, and the whole society. Ecclesiastical bureaucracies are usually closely associated with state-level political systems. In many instances, the leaders of the ecclesiastical hierarchy are members of the ruling class, and in some cases, a state's political and ecclesiastical hierarchies are indistinguishable.

the dangers of travel over the ice and the threats of storms and month-long nights. The Innuit hunter was equipped with an ingenious array of technological devices that made life possible in the Arctic, but the outcome of the daily struggle remained in doubt. From the Innuit's point of view, it was not enough to be well equipped with snow goggles, fur parkas, spring-bone traps, detachable barbed harpoon points, and powerful compound bows. One also had to be equipped to handle unseen spirits and forces that lurked in all parts of nature and that, if offended or not properly warded off, could reduce the greatest hunter to a starving wretch.

Vigilant individual effort was needed to deal with wandering human and animal souls, place spirits, Sedna (the Keeper of the Sea Animals), the Sun, the Moon, and the Spirit of the Air. Part of each hunter's equipment was his hunting song, a combination of chant, prayer, and magic formula that he inherited from his father or father's brothers or purchased from some famous hunter or shaman. This he would sing under his breath as he prepared himself for the day's activities. Around his neck, he wore a little bag filled with tiny ani-

Figure 17.3 San Curing
Shaman in a trance.

Wallace noted that the individualistic, shamanistic, communal, and ecclesiastical forms of beliefs and rituals constitute a scale. That is, the more complex levels contain the beliefs and practices of all the less complex levels. Thus, societies with ecclesiastical cults also have communal cults, shamanistic cults, and strictly individualistic beliefs and rituals (Fig. 17.4). In the following sections, examples of each of these forms of religious organization will be given.

Individualistic Beliefs and Rituals: The Innuit

The individualism of much of Innuit belief and ritual parallels the individualism of the Innuit mode of production. Hunters alone or in small groups constantly match their wits against the cunning and strength of animal prey and confront

Figure 17.5 Female Shaman
Piegan "medicine woman." Female shamans are as common as male shamans.

(a)

(b)

Figure 17.4   Levels of Religious Organization
(a) A Guatemalan shaman obtaining personal power at a mixed Maya and Catholic shrine. This does not prevent him from participating in ecclesiastical rites such as (b) the celebration of Good Friday in Chichicastenango.

mal carvings, bits of claws and fur, pebbles, insects, and other items, each corresponding to some Spirit Helper with whom he maintained a special relationship. In return for protection and hunting success given by his Spirit Helpers, the hunter had to observe certain taboos, refrain from hunting or eating certain species, or avoid trespassing in a particular locale. Moreover, a hunter should never sleep out on the ice edge. Every evening he had to return to land or to the old firm ice that lies some distance back from the open sea because the Sea Spirit does not like her creatures to smell human beings while they are not hunting (Rasmussen 1929: 76). Care also must be taken not to cook land and sea mammals in the same pot; fresh water must be placed in the mouth of recently killed sea mammals, and fat must be placed in the mouth of slain land mammals (Wallace 1966). Note that some of these "superstitions" may have alleviated psychological stress or have had a practical value for hunting or some other aspect of Eskimo life. Not sleeping out on the ice, for example, is a safety precaution.

Shamanistic Cults

Shamans are women or men who are socially recognized as having special abilities for entering into contact with spirit beings and for controlling supernatural forces. The full shamanistic complex includes some form of trance experience during which the shaman's powers are increased. Possession, the invasion of the human body by a god or spirit, is the most common form of shamanistic trance. The shaman goes into a trance by smoking tobacco, taking drugs, beating on a drum, dancing monotonously, or simply by closing his or her eyes and concentrating. The trance begins with rigidity of the body, sweating, and heavy breathing. While in the trance, the shaman may act as a medium, transmitting messages from the ancestors. With the help of friendly spirits, shamans predict future events, locate lost objects, identify the cause of illness, prescribe cures, and give advice on how clients can protect themselves against the evil intentions of enemies.

There is a close relationship between shamanistic cults and individualistic vision quests. Shamans are usually personalities who are psychologically predisposed toward hallucinatory experiences. In cultures that use hallucinogenic substances freely in order to penetrate the mysteries of the other world, many people may claim shamanistic status (Fig. 17.5). Among the Jivaro, one out of every four men is a shaman since the use of hallucinogenic vines makes it possible for almost everyone to achieve the trance states essential for the practice of shamanism (Harner 1972: 154). Elsewhere, becoming a shaman may be restricted to people who are prone to having auditory and visual hallucinations.

An important part of shamanistic performance in many regions of the world consists of simple tricks of ventriloquism, sleight of hand, and illusion. The Siberian shamans, for example, signaled the arrival of the possessing spirit by secretly shaking the walls of a darkened tent. Throughout South America, the standard shamanistic curing ceremony involves the sleight-of-hand removal of slivers of bone, pebbles, bugs, and other foreign objects from the patient's body. The practice of these tricks should not be regarded as evidence that the shaman has a cynical or disbelieving attitude toward the rest of the performance. Michael Harner (1982), a modern proponent of shamanic rituals, insists there is nothing fraudulent about the sucking cure (see Box 17.1). It is not the object itself that is in the patient's body and causing the trouble; rather, it is the object's spiritual counterpart. Shamans put the material object in their mouth during the sucking cure because this helps withdraw its spiritual counterpart.

Although trance is part of the shamanistic repertory in hundreds of cultures, it is not universal. Many cultures have part-time specialists who do not make use of trance but who diagnose and cure disease, find lost objects, foretell the future, and confer immunity in war and success in love. Such persons may be referred to variously as magicians, seers, sorcerers, witch doctors, medicine men or medicine women, and curers. The full shamanistic complex embodies all these roles (Atkinson 1992; but see Winhelman 1990).

Among the Tapirapé, a village people of central Brazil (Wagley 1977), shamans (Fig. 17.6) derive their powers from dreams in which they encounter spirits who become the shaman's helpers. Dreams are caused by souls leaving the body and going on journeys. Frequent dreaming is a sign of shamanistic talent. Mature shamans, with the help of the spirit familiars, can turn into birds or launch themselves through the air in gourd "canoes," visit with ghosts and demons, or travel to distant villages forward and backward through time.

Tapirapé shamans are frequently called on to cure illness. This they do with sleight of hand and the help of their spirit familiars while in a semitrance condition induced by gulping huge quantities of tobacco, which makes them vomit. It is interesting to note in conjunction with the widespread use of

---

Box 17.1

THE TAPIRAPÉ SUCKING CURE

Unless the illness is serious enough to warrant immediate treatment, shamans always cure in the late evening. A shaman comes to his patient, and squats near the patient's hammock; his first act is always to light his pipe. When the patient has a fever or has fallen unconscious from the sight of a ghost, the principal method of treatment is by massage. The shaman blows smoke over the entire body of the patient; then he blows smoke over his own hands, spits into them, and massages the patient slowly and firmly, always toward the extremities of the body. He shows that he is removing a foreign substance by quick movement of his hands as he reaches the end of an arm or leg.

The more frequent method of curing, however, is by the extraction of a malignant object by sucking. The shaman squats alongside the hammock of his patient and begins to "eat smoke"—swallow large gulps of tobacco smoke from his pipe. He forces the smoke with great intakes of breath deep down into his stomach; soon he becomes intoxicated and nauseated; he vomits violently and smoke spews from his stomach. He groans and clears his throat in the manner of a person gagging with nausea but unable to vomit. By sucking back what he vomits he accumulates saliva in his mouth.

In the midst of this process he stops several times to suck on the body of his patient and finally, with one awful heave, he spews all the accumulated material on the ground. He then searches in this mess for the intrusive object that has been causing the illness. Never once did I see a shaman show the intrusive object to observers. At one treatment a Tapirapé [shaman] usually repeats this process of "eating smoke," sucking, and vomiting several times. Sometimes, when a man of prestige is ill, two or even three shamans will cure side by side in this manner and the noise of violent vomiting resounds throughout the village.

Wagley 1943: 73–74.

Figure 17.6 Tapirape Shaman
The shaman has fallen into a tobacco-induced trance and cannot walk unaided.

tobacco in Native American rituals that tobacco contains hallucinogenic alkaloids and may have induced visions when consumed in large quantities.

Communal Cults

No society is completely without communally organized religious beliefs and practices. Even the Innuit have group rites. Frightened and sick, Innuit individuals under the cross-examinations of shamans publicly confess violations of taboos that have made them ill and that have endangered the rest of the community.

Native Americans of the Western Plains held annual public rites of self-torture and vision quest known as the Sun Dance (Fig. 17.7). Under the direction of shaman leaders, the sun dancers tied themselves to a pole by means of a cord passed through a slit in their skin. Watched by the assembled group, they walked or danced around the pole and tugged at the cord until they fainted or the skin ripped apart. These public displays of endurance and bravery were part of the intense marauding and warfare complex that developed after the coming of the Europeans.

Communal rites fall into two major categories: (1) rites of solidarity and (2) rites of passage. In the *rites of solidarity*, participation in dramatic public rituals enhances the sense of group identity, coordinates the actions of the individual members of the group, and prepares the group for immediate or future cooperative action. *Rites of passage* celebrate the social movement of individuals into and out of groups or into or out of statuses of critical importance to the individual and to the community. Reproduction, the achievement of manhood and womanhood, marriage, and death are the principal worldwide occasions for rites of passage.

COMMUNAL RITES OF SOLIDARITY: TOTEMISM

Rites of solidarity are common among clans and other descent groups. Such groups usually have names and emblems that identify group members and set one group off from another. Animal names and emblems predominate, but insects, plants, and natural phenomena such as rain and clouds also occur. These group-identifying objects are known as *totems*. Many totems such as bear, breadfruit, or kangaroo are useful or edible species, and often a descent relationship is stipulated between the members of the group and their totemic ancestor. Sometimes the members of the group must refrain from harming or eating their totem. The specific form of totemic belief, however, varies greatly, and no single totemic complex can be said to exist.

The Aranda of Australia provide one of the classic cases of totemic ritual. Here an individual identifies with the totem of the sacred place near which one's mother passed shortly before becoming pregnant (see p. 121). These places contain the stone objects known as *churinga*, which are the visible manifestations of each person's spirit (Fig. 17.8). The churinga are believed to have been left behind by the totemic ancestors as they traveled about the countryside at the beginning of the world. The ancestors later turned into animals, objects, and other phenomena constituting the inventory of totems. The sacred places of each totem are visited annually.

These rituals have many meanings and functions. The participants are earnestly concerned with protecting their totems and ensuring their reproduction. But the exclusive membership of the ritual group also indicates that they are acting out the mythological dogma of their common ancestry. The totem ceremonies reaffirm and intensify the sense of common identity of the members of a regional community. The handling of the churinga confirms the fact that the totemic group has "stones" or, in a more familiar metaphor, "roots" in a particular land.

Figure 17.7   Dakota Sun Dance
*Painted by Short-Bull, chief of the Oglala Dakota (Sioux), this painting represents the Sun Dance of
more than 90 years ago. The circle in the center represents a windbreak formed of fresh cottonwood
boughs. In the center is the Sun Dance pole, and hanging from it are the figures of a man and buffalo.
Outside the Sun Dance enclosure, devotees perform. One of them is dragging four buffalo skulls by cords
run through openings in the skin on his back. He will continue to drag these until they tear loose.*

Figure 17.8   Bull Roarer Churinga
*A string is tied through the hole and used to whirl
the bull roarer around one's head. This specimen is
from Australia. It is made out of stone and is
known as a churinga. It represents a human spirit-
soul.*

COMMUNAL RITUALS: RITES OF PASSAGE

Because they involve a web of interrelated status changes for the entire community, birth, puberty, marriage, and death are the most common occasions for rites of passage (Fig. 17.9). The individual who is born, who reaches adulthood, who takes a spouse, or who dies is not the only one implicated in these events. Many other people must adjust to these momentous changes. Being born not only defines a new life but brings into existence or modifies the position of parent, grandparent, sibling, heir, agemate, and many other domestic and political relationships. The main function of rites of passage is to give communal recognition to the entire complex of new or altered relationships and not merely to the changes experienced by the individuals who get born, marry, or die. Rites of passage conform to a remarkably similar pattern among widely dispersed cultures (Eliade 1958; Schlegel and Barry 1979). First, the principal performers are separated from the routines associated with their earlier life. Second, decisive physical and symbolic steps are taken to extinguish the old status. Often these steps include the notion of killing the old personality. To promote "death and transfiguration," old clothing and ornaments are exchanged for new, and the body is painted or mutilated. Finally, the participants are ceremoniously returned to normal life.

The pattern of rites of passage can be seen in the male initiation ceremonies of the Ndembu of northern Zambia (Fig.

(a)

Figure 17.9   Religion and Life Crisis
(a) Dogon funeral dancers. The Crow scaffold burial (b) shows a common means of disposing of the dead in sparsely inhabited regions. (c) The Peruvian mummies show another method, which is common in arid climates.

(b)

(c)

(a)

(b)

Figure 17.10 Ndembu Rites
(a) Although the women are supposed to be terrified of the "monster,"
they are actually amused and skeptical. (b) The circumcision camp—
the "place of dying."

17.10). Here, as among many African and Middle Eastern peoples, the transition from boyhood to manhood involves the rite of circumcision. Young boys are taken from their separate villages and placed in a special bush "school." They are circumcised by their own kinsmen or neighbors, and after their wounds heal, they are returned to normal life (see Box 17.2).

In many cultures, girls are subject to similar rites of separation, seclusion, and return in relationship to their first menses and their eligibility for marriage (Fig. 17.11). Genital mutilation is also common among girls, and an operation known as clitoridectomy is widely practiced in parts of Africa. In this operation, the external tip of the clitoris is cut off. Among many Australian groups, both circumcision and clitoridectomy were practiced. In addition, the Australians knocked out the pubescent child's front tooth. Males were subject to the further operation of subincision, in which the

underside of the penis was slit open to the depth of the urethra. In several parts of Africa, clitoridectomy was followed by a procedure in which the two sides of the vulva are attached to each other by stitching with silk or catgut sutures or by thorns, thus preventing vaginal intercourse until their removal at the time of marriage (Dualeh 1982; Gruenbaum 1988; Lightfoot-Klein 1989; Hicks 1993).

Ecclesiastical Cults

As stated earlier, ecclesiastical cults have a professional clergy or priesthood organized into a bureaucracy. This bureaucracy is usually associated with and under the control of a central temple. At secondary or provincial temple centers, the clergy may exercise a considerable amount of independence. In general, the more highly centralized the politi-

---

Box 17.2

No Rites Hurt Too

Westerners are likely to be shocked and dismayed by examples of painful puberty rituals, but the system that has been substituted for such rituals may not have any clear advantage as far as eliminating pain and suffering. The passage from child to adult in advanced industrial societies is not marked by any rituals at all. No one is quite sure when adulthood begins. As a result, the young girl or boy must pass through a prolonged period of stress, known as adolescence, which is marked by high rates of accidents, suicides, and antisocial behavior. (The Jewish bar mitzvah and bat mitzvah held at age 13 for boys and girls, respectively, creates boy-men and girl-women for whom adult status lies many years ahead.) Which system is more cruel?

Figure 17.11   Apache Girl's Puberty Ceremony
The old life of the child is washed away.

---

cal system, the more highly centralized the ecclesiastical bureaucracy.

The ecclesiastic specialists are different from both the Tapirape shamans and the Ndembu circumcisers and guardians. They are formally designated persons who devote themselves to the rituals of their office (Fig. 17.12). These rituals usually include a wide variety of techniques for influencing and controlling animistic beings and animatistic forces. The material support for these full-time specialists is usually closely related to power and privileges of taxation. As among the Inca (see p. 154), the state and the priesthood may divide up the rent and tribute exacted from the peasants. Under feudalism (see p. 164), the ecclesiastical hierar-

chy derives its earnings from its own estates and from the gifts of powerful princes and kings. High officials in feudal ecclesiastical hierarchies are almost always kin or appointees of members of the ruling class.

The presence of ecclesiastical organizations produces a profound split among those who participate in ritual performances. On the one hand, there is an active segment, the priesthood; on the other, the passive "congregation," who are virtual spectators. The members of the priesthood must acquire intricate ritual, historical, calendrical, and astronomical knowledge. Often they are scribes and learned persons. It must be stressed, however, that the "congregation" does not altogether abandon individualistic shamanistic and

Figure 17.12   Ecclesiastical Cult
Celebration of Roman Catholic high mass.

communal beliefs and rituals. These practices are all continued, sometimes secretly, in neighborhoods, villages, or households, side by side with the "higher" rituals, despite more or
less energetic efforts by the ecclesiastical hierarchy to stamp
out what it often calls idolatrous, superstitious, pagan, hea-
then, or heretical beliefs and performances.

The Religion of the Aztecs

Many characteristics of belief and ritual in stratified contexts can be seen in the ecclesiastical organization of the
Aztecs of Mexico. The Aztecs held their priests responsible
for the maintenance and renewal of the entire universe. By
performing annual rituals, priests could obtain the blessing of
the Aztec gods, ensure the well-being of the Aztec people,
and guard the world against collapse into chaos and darkness.
According to Aztec theology, the world had already passed
through four ages, each of which ended in cataclysmic
destruction. The first age ended when the reigning god transformed himself into the sun, and all the people of the earth
were devoured by jaguars. The second age, ruled over by the
feathered serpent (Fig. 17.13), was destroyed by hurricanes
that changed people into monkeys. The third age, ruled over
by the god of rain, was brought to a close when the heavens
rained fire. Then came the rule of the goddess of water, whose
time ended with a universal flood, during which people

Figure 17.13   Temple of Quetzalcoatl
Temple of the plumed serpent, Teotihuacan.

turned into fish. The fifth age is in progress, ruled over by the
sun god and doomed to destruction sooner or later by earthquakes.

The principal function of the 5,000 priests living in the
Aztec capital was to make sure that the end of the world
came later rather than sooner. They could assure this only by
pleasing the legions of gods reputed to govern the world. The
best way to please the gods was to give them gifts, the most
precious being fresh human hearts. The hearts of war captives
were the most esteemed gifts since they were won only at
great expense and risk.

Aztec ceremonial centers were dominated by large pyrami-
dal platforms topped by temples (Fig. 17.14). These structures were vast stages on which the drama of human sacrifice
was enacted at least once a day throughout the year. On especially critical days, multiple sacrifices took place. The set pattern for these performances involved first the victim's ascent
of the huge staircase to the top of the pyramid; then, at the
summit, the victim was seized by four priests, one for each
limb, and bent face up, spread-eagled over the sacrificial
stone. A fifth priest cut the victim's chest open with an obsidian knife and wrenched out the beating heart. The heart was
smeared over the statue of the god and later burned. Finally,
the lifeless body was flung over the edge of the pyramid where

Figure 17.14   Tenochtitlan
A reconstructed view of the Aztec capital, with its numerous temple-topped pyramids. The large struc-
ture at right center is the main skull rack constructed out of tall wooden poles with rows of skulls visible
as white dots strung on cross beams.

it was rolled back down the steps. During a 4-day dedication ceremony of the main Aztec temple in Tenochtitlan, 20,000 prisoners of war may have been or were sacrificed in this manner. A yearly toll estimated that nearly 15,000 people were sent to death to placate the bloodthirsty gods. Most of these victims were prisoners of war, although local youths, maidens, and children were also sacrificed from time to time (Vaillant 1966; Soustelle 1970; Coe 1977; Berdan 1982). After being killed, the bodies of most of those who were sacrificed were rolled down the pyramid steps, dismembered, and probably cooked and eaten (Harner 1977; see Box 17.3 for evidence of Aztec cannibalism).

Aztec Cannibalism

Prior to the emergence of the state, many societies practiced human sacrifice and ritually consumed all or part of the bodies of prisoners of war (Harris 1985, 1989). Lacking the political–military means to tax and conscript large populations, chiefdoms had little interest in preserving the lives of their defeated enemies. With the advent of the state, however, cannibalism and human sacrifice tended to disappear. As we have seen (see p. 152), conquered territories were incorporated into the state, and the labor power of defeated populations was tapped through taxation, conscription, and tribute. Thus, the preservation of the lives of defeated peoples became an essential part of the process of state expansion.

The Aztec, however, were an exception to this general trend. Instead of tabooing human sacrifice and cannibalism and encouraging charity and kindness toward defeated enemy peoples, the Aztec state made human sacrifice and cannibalism the main focus of ecclesiastical beliefs and rituals (Fig. 17.15). As the Aztec became more powerful, they sacrificed increasing numbers of prisoners of war and became more rather than less cannibalistic (Fig. 17.16).

Although it is considered controversial, Michael Harner's (1977) explanation of the Aztec state's unique ecclesiastical cannibalism remains the best theory available. Harner starts from the fact that as a result of millennia of intensification and population growth, the central Mexican highlands had lost their best domesticable animal species. Unlike the Inca, who obtained animal foods from llama, alpaca, and guinea pigs—or the Old World states that had sheep, goats, pigs, and cattle—the Aztec had only semidomesticated ducks and turkeys, and hairless dogs. Wild fauna, such as deer and migrating waterfowl, were not abundant enough to provide the Aztecs with more than 1 or 2 grams of animal protein per capita per day (compared with over 60 grams in the United States). The depleted condition of the natural fauna is shown by the prominence in the Aztec diet of bugs, worms, and "scum cakes," which were made out of algae skimmed off the surface of Lake Texcoco (see Sahlins 1978; Harris 1979b).

According to Harner, the severe depletion of animal resources made it uniquely difficult for the Aztec state to prohibit the consumption of human flesh in order to facilitate its expansionist aims. Because of the severe depletion of animal resources, human flesh rather than animal flesh was redistributed as a means of rewarding loyalty to the throne and bravery in combat. Moreover, to have made serfs or slaves out of captives would only have worsened the animal food shortage. The Aztec state had much to lose by prohibiting cannibalism and little to gain.

It would have been far more puzzling if the Aztecs did not consume the flesh of their prisoners of war after expending so

---

Box 17.3

THE EVIDENCE FOR AZTEC CANNIBALISM

Bernadino de Sahagun, who started collecting data on the Aztecs in the 1540s, is generally considered to be the most honest and reliable historian and ethnographer of Aztec culture. In his *General History of the Things of New Spain*, he repeatedly describes the fate of the Aztec's sacrificial victims as follows:

> After they had slain them and torn out their hearts, they took them away gently, rolling them down the steps. When they had reached the bottom, they cut off their heads and inserted a rod through them, and they carried the bodies to the houses which they called calpulli, where they divided them up in order to eat them.

Sahagun 1951: 24.

Many other passages written by Sahagun and other historians of the conquest of Mexico tell the same story.

---

much effort in capturing and killing them. In etic perspective, it cannot be said that the Aztecs went to war primarily to obtain prisoners and meat. Like all states, the Aztec went to war primarily for reasons that are associated with the inherently expansionist nature of the state (see p. 152; Hassig 1988). From an emic perspective, as reported to the Spanish by the Aztecs, however, one could say that the desire to capture prisoners for sacrifice and consumption was an important objective of the participants.

This theory cannot be disproved by showing that the Aztecs could have obtained all of their essential nutrients from worms, insects, algae, corn, beans, and other plant foods (Ortiz de Montellano 1978, 1983). The issue is whether a diet that includes meat is a more efficient source of proteins, fats, and energy than one that does not. America went to war in the Middle East to protect the supply of oil even though all its energy requirements can be met by using domestic supplies of coal. Coal, however, is not as desirable as oil because it is environmentally more hazardous and it costs more. Similarly, compared to meat, insects and plant foods are very inefficient packages of essential nutrients. Hence, the high value that the Aztecs placed on the consumption of human flesh was not a purely arbitrary consequence of their religious beliefs.

Rather than eat scum cakes and leave the bodies of their enemies to rot on the battlefield, they marched their prisoners home to Tenochtitlan and ate human flesh. Nothing compelled the Aztec to let this source of nourishment go to waste. In the history of humankind, it is not cannibalism that needs to be explained but the taboo against cannibalism. Thus

Figure 17.15   Aztec Sacrificial Knife

Figure 17.16 Skull Rack
One of the smaller racks in the Aztec capital. The skulls in the photo-
graph are sculpted in stone; during Aztec times, real skulls were exhib-
ited on wooden structures raised on the sculpted base (see Fig. 17.14).
Part of the ongoing excavation in Mexico City.

Aztec religious beliefs (the cravings of their gods for human blood) reflected the importance of animal foods in relation to human dietary needs and the depleted supply of nonhuman animals in their habitat. Note that most of the cultures of the world attach special value to the consumption of meat or other animal products rich in fat and protein. So-called "vegetarian cultures" like India are in reality lacto-vegetarians or ovo-vegetarians—that is, they spurn meat but eat dairy products and eggs. Also bear in mind the role that perennial shortages of meat have played in recent world politics. Such shortages were an important source of discontent that contributed to the collapse of Soviet communism (Box 17.4).

Box 17.4

MEAT AND POLITICS IN THE SOVIET UNION

If we could put 80 kilograms [176 pounds] of meat a year on the consumer's table, all other problems that we have would not be as acute as they are now. It is no exaggeration to say that the shortage of meat products is a problem that is worrying the whole nation.

Mikhail Gorbachev addressing the Soviet Central Committee. Quoted in Gumbel 1988.

Religion and Political Economy: High Gods

Full-time specialists, monumental temples, dramatic processions, and elaborate rites performed for spectator congregations are incompatible with the infrastructure and political economy of hunters and gatherers. Similarly, the complex astronomical and mathematical basis of ecclesiastical beliefs and rituals is never found among band and village peoples.

The level of political economy also influences the way in which gods are thought to relate to each other and to human beings. For example, the idea of a single high god who creates the universe is found among cultures at all levels of economic and political development. These high gods, however, play different kinds of roles in running the universe after they have brought it into existence. Among hunter-gatherers and other nonstate peoples, the high gods tend to become inactive after their creation task is done (Sullivan 1987). It is to a host of lesser gods, demons, and ancestor souls that one must turn in order to obtain assistance (cf. Hayden 1987). On the other hand, in stratified societies the high god bosses the lesser gods and tends to be a more active figure to whom priests and commoners address their prayers (Swanson 1960), although the lesser gods may still be revered more actively by ordinary people.

A plausible explanation for this difference is that nonstate cultures have no need for the idea of a central or supreme authority. Just as centralized control over people and strategic resources is absent in life, so in religious belief, the inhabitants of the spirit world lack decisive control over each other. They form a more or less egalitarian group. On the other hand, the belief that superordination and subordination characterize relationships among the gods helps obtain the cooperation of the commoner classes in stratified societies (Fig. 17.17; see p. 155).

One way to achieve conformity in stratified societies is to convince commoners that the gods demand obedience to the state. Disobedience and nonconformity result not only in retribution administered through the state's police–military apparatus but also in punishments in present or future life administered by the high gods themselves. In nonstate societies, for reasons discussed in Chapter 11, law and order are rooted in common interest. Consequently, there is little need for high gods to administer punishments to those who have been "bad" and rewards to those who have been "good." But as Table 17.1 shows, where class differences exist, the gods are believed to take a lively interest in the degree to which each individual's thoughts and behavior are immoral or ethically subversive.

Revitalization

The relationship of religion to structure and infrastructure can also be seen in the process known as *revitalization*. Under

Figure 17.17 Religion and Stratification
Bishops and other high prelates of the Corpus Christi
Cathedral in Cuzco, Peru, are an awe-inspiring sight to an Indian
peasant.

the severe stresses associated with colonial conquest and intense class or minority exploitation, religions tend to become movements concerned with achieving a drastic improvement in the immediate conditions of life or in the prospects for an afterlife. These movements are sometimes referred to as nativistic, revivalistic, millenarian, or messianic. The concept of revitalization is intended to embrace all the specific cognitive and ritual variants implied by these terms (Wallace 1966).

Revitalization is a process of political and religious interaction between a depressed caste, class, minority, or other subordinate social group and a superordinate group. Some revitalization movements emphasize passive attitudes, the adoption of old rather than new cultural practices, or salvation through rewards after death; others advocate more or less open resistance or aggressive political or military action. These differences largely reflect the extent to which the subordinate groups are prepared to cope with the challenge to their power and authority. Revitalizations that take place under conditions of massive suffering and exploitation sooner or later result in political and even military probes or confrontations, even though both sides may overtly desire to avoid conflict (Worsley 1968).

Native-American Revitalizations

Widespread revitalizations were provoked by the European invasion of the New World, the conquest and expulsion of the Native-American peoples, and the destruction of their natural resources. The most famous of the nineteenth-century revitalization movements was the Ghost Dance, also known (by whites) as the Messiah craze. The main phase of the Ghost Dance began in 1889 under the inspiration of a Paviotso prophet, named Wovoka (Fig. 17.18). Wovoka and his followers envisioned a day when all of their ancestors would return to life. Songs and dances revealed to Wovoka would make this happen. Ostensibly, Wovoka's teachings lacked political content, and as the Ghost Dance spread eastward across the Rockies, its political implications remained ambiguous. Yet for the Native Americans of the Plains, the return of the dead meant that they would outnumber the whites and hence be more powerful.

The Sioux initiated a version that included the return of all the bison and the extermination of the whites under a huge landslide. The Sioux warriors put on Ghost Dance shirts, which they believed would make them invulnerable to bullets. Clashes between the U.S. Army and the Sioux became more frequent, and the Sioux leader Sitting Bull was arrested and killed. The second Ghost Dance movement came to an end with the massacre of 200 Sioux at Wounded Knee, South Dakota (Fig. 17.19), on December 29, 1890 (Mooney 1965).

After all chance of military resistance was crushed, the Native-American revitalization movement became more

T a b l e   1 7 . 1

RELIGION, CLASS, AND MORALITY

GOD INTERESTED IN MORALITY	SOCIETIES WITH SOCIAL CLASSES	SOCIETIES WITHOUT SOCIAL CLASSES
Present	25	2
Absent	8	12

Source: Adapted from Swanson, 1960: 166.

Figure 17.18 Wovoka
Leader of the Ghost Dance.

introverted and passive. Visions in which all the whites were wiped out ceased to be experienced, confirming once again the responsiveness of religion to political reality. The development and spread of beliefs and rituals centering on peyote, mescal, and other hallucinogenic drugs are characteristic of many twentieth-century Native-American revitalizations. Peyote ritual, as practiced in the Native-American Church, involves a night of praying, singing, peyote eating, and ecstatic contemplation followed by a communal breakfast (Fig. 17.20). The peyote eaters are not interested in bringing back the buffalo or making themselves invulnerable to bullets; they seek self-knowledge, personal moral strength, and physical health (Stewart 1987).

Peyotism and allied cult movements do not, of course, signal the end of political action by the Native Americans. With the emergence of the "Red Power" movement, the Native Americans' attempt to hold on to and regain their stolen lands is now being carried out through the work of lawyers, politicians, novelists, Washington lobbyists, sit-ins, and land-ins (Fig. 17.21) (DeLoria 1969; Walker 1972; Josephy 1982).

Cargo Cults

In New Guinea and Melanesia, revitalization is associated with the concept of cargo. The typical vision of the leaders of Melanesian revitalization movements is that of a ship bringing back the ancestors and a cargo of European goods. In recent times, airplanes and spaceships have become the favorite means of delivering the cargo.

As a result of the abundance of goods displayed by U.S. military forces during the Pacific island campaigns of World War II, some revitalizations stressed the return of the Americans. In Espiritu Santo in 1944, Tsek urged his people to destroy all trade goods and throw away their clothes in preparation for the return of the mysteriously departed Americans. Some of the American-oriented revitalizations have placed specific American soldiers in the role of cargo deliverers. On the island of Tana in the New Hebrides, the John Frumm cult cherishes an old GI jacket as the relic of one John Frumm, whose identity is not otherwise known (Fig. 17.22). The followers of John Frumm build landing strips, bamboo control towers, and grass-thatched cargo sheds. In some cases, beacons are kept ablaze at night and radio operators stand ready with tin-can microphones and earphones to guide the cargo planes to a safe landing.

An important theme is that the cargo planes and ships have been successfully loaded by the ancestors at U.S. ports and are on their way, but the local authorities have refused to permit the cargo to be landed. In other versions, the cargo planes are tricked into landing at the wrong airport. In a metaphorical sense, these sentiments apply to the actual conditions under colonialism. The peoples of the South Seas were indeed often tricked out of their lands and resources.

The confusion of the Melanesian revitalization prophets stems from lack of knowledge of the workings of cultural systems. They do not understand how modern industrial wage–labor societies are organized, nor comprehend how law and order are maintained among state-level peoples. To them, the material abundance of the industrial nations and the penury of others constitute an irrational flaw, a massive contradiction in the structure of the world. The belief system of the cargo cults vividly demonstrates why the assumption that all people distinguish between natural and supernatural categories is incorrect (see p. 222). Cargo leaders who have been taken to see modern Australian stores and factories in the hope that they would give up their beliefs, return home more convinced than ever that they are following the best prescription for obtaining cargo. With their own eyes, they have observed the fantastic abundance the authorities refuse to let them have (Lawrence 1964).

(a)

Figure 17.19   Wounded Knee
(a) In the first battle, in 1890, 200 Sioux Indians were killed by the U.S. Army. (b) In the second battle, in 1973, militant Indians occupied the village of Wounded Knee, South Dakota, and exchanged gunfire with U.S. marshals.

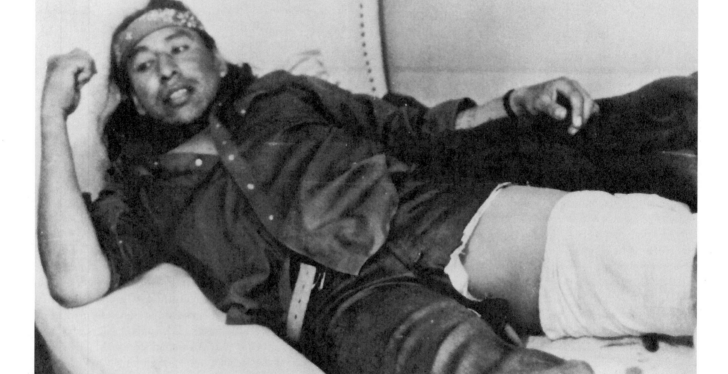

(b)

Figure 17.20   Peyote Ceremony
Delaware Indians of Oklahoma spend the night in prayer and meditation. At right, they emerge to greet
the dawn.

Taboo, Religion, and Ecology

Anthropologists have long debated the issue of whether strongly held religious beliefs result in lowered productivity and the mismanagement of a society's resources. Do various religiously sanctioned taboos on the consumption of certain foods, for example, have negative nutritional consequences? Or is the reverse true? Do such taboos sometimes actually contribute to a more efficient use of a society's infrastructural potential? In answering these questions, both the costs and benefits of not eating a particular food and the availability of more efficient alternatives must be considered.

Consider, for example, the ancient Israelite prohibition on the consumption of pork. Pigs require shade and moisture to regulate their body temperature. Moreover, unlike the domesticated ruminants such as cattle, sheep, and goats, pigs don't give milk. They also can't pull carts or plows, nor can they subsist on grass. With the progressive deforestation and desertification of the Middle East caused by the spread and intensification of agriculture and stock raising and by population growth, habitat zones suitable for pig rearing became scarce. Hence, an animal that was at one time reared and consumed as a relatively inexpensive source of fat and protein could no longer be reared and consumed by large numbers of people without reducing the efficiency of the main system of food production (Harris 1985). The temptation to continue the practice of pig raising persisted, however— hence, the invocation of sacred commandments in the ancient Hebrew religion. Note that the explanation of the ancient origins of this taboo does not account for its perpetuation into the present. Once in existence, the taboo against pork (and other foods) acquired the function of demarcating or bounding Jewish ethnic minorities from other groups and of increasing their sense of identity and solidarity (see p. 178). Outside the Middle East, the taboo no longer served an ecological function, but it continued to be useful on the level of structural relationships.

Figure 17.21   Native-American Militants
With Molotov cocktails and machine guns, armed Mohawks near
Montreal attempt to prevent the takeover of their lands for the building
of a golf course.

Figure 17.22   John Frumm
This cult is active on the Island of Tana in the New Hebrides.

The Sacred Cow

The case of the sacred cow of India conforms to the general theory that the flesh of certain animals is made taboo when it becomes very expensive as a result of ecological changes. Like pigs in the Middle East, cattle were sacrificed and eaten quite freely in India during the Neolithic. With the rise of the state and of dense rural and urban populations, however, cattle could no longer be raised in sufficient numbers to be used both as a source of meat and as the principal source of traction power for pulling plows. But as the taboo on cattle use developed, it took a form quite different from the Israelite taboo on the pig. Whereas the pig was valued almost exclusively for its flesh, cattle were also valued for their milk and especially for their traction power. When pigs became too costly to be raised for meat, the whole animal became taboo and an abomination. But as cattle in India became too costly to be raised for meat, their value as a source of traction power increased. (The land had to be plowed more intensively as population grew.) Therefore, they had to be protected rather than abominated, and so the Hindu religion came to emphasize everyone's sacred duty to refrain from killing cattle or eating beef.

Interestingly enough, the Brahmans (see p. 167), who at one time were the caste responsible for ritually slaughtering cattle, later became the caste most concerned with their protection and most opposed to the development of a beef-slaughtering industry in India (Harris 1977, 1979a, 1985; cf. Simoons 1979).

What about the sacred cow today? Is the religious ban on the slaughter of cattle and the consumption of beef a functionally useful feature of modern Hinduism? Everyone agrees that the human population of India needs more calories and proteins, yet the Hindu religion bans the slaughter of cattle and taboos the eating of beef. These taboos are often held responsible for the creation of large numbers of aged, decrepit, barren, and useless cattle. Such animals are depicted as roaming aimlessly across the Indian countryside, clogging the roads, stopping the trains, stealing food from the marketplace, and blocking city streets (Fig. 17.23). A closer look at some of the details of the ecology and economy of the Indian subcontinent, however, suggests that the taboo in question does not decrease the capacity of the present Indian system of food production to support human life (see Box 17.5).

The basis of traditional Indian agriculture is the ox-drawn plow (see p. 201). Each peasant farmer needs at least two oxen to plow the fields at the proper time of the year. Despite the impression of surplus cattle, the central fact of Indian rural life is that there is a shortage of oxen since one-third of the peasant households own less than the minimum pair. It is true that many cows are too old, decrepit, and sick to do a

Figure 17.23 Sacred Cows
(a) These residents of Calcutta are not wandering aimlessly; their owner knows where they are. (b) These cows are "parked," not blocking traffic.

(a)

(b)

Box 17.5

Other Favorable Consequences of the Taboo on the Consumption of Beef

A number of additional reasons support the theory that the Hindu taboos against slaughtering cattle and consuming beef have a positive rather than a negative effect on agricultural productivity in India. First, the ban on slaughter discourages the development of a meat-packing industry. Such an industry would be ecologically disastrous in a land as densely populated as India. Second, in this connection, it should be pointed out that the animal fat and protein output of the existing system is substantial. Although the Indian cows are very poor milkers by Western standards, they nonetheless contribute critical if small quantities of fat and protein to the diets of millions of people. Moreover, a considerable amount of beef does get eaten during the year since animals that die a natural death are consumed by carrion-eating outcastes. Finally, the critical function of the ban on slaughter during famines should be noted. When hunger stalks the Indian countryside, the slaughter taboo helps the peasants resist the temptation to eat their cattle. If this temptation were to win out over their religious scruples, they would be unable to plant new crops when the rains begin again. Thus the intense resistance among Hindu saints to the slaughter and consumption of beef takes on a new meaning in the context of the Indian infrastructure. In the words of Mahatma Gandhi:

> Why the cow was selected for apotheosis is obvious to me. The cow was in India the best companion. She was the giver of plenty. Not only did she give milk but she also made agriculture possible.

[1954: 3]

proper job of reproducing. At this point, the ban on slaughter and beef consumption is thought to exert its harmful effect. For rather than kill dry, barren, and aged cows, the Hindu farmer is depicted as ritually obsessed with preserving the life of each sacred beast, no matter how useless it may become. From the point of view of the poor farmer, however, these relatively undesirable creatures may be quite essential and useful. The farmer would prefer to have more vigorous cows, but is prevented from achieving this goal not by the taboos against slaughter but by the shortage of land and pasture (Chakravarti 1985a, b).

Even barren cows, however, are by no means a total loss. Their dung makes an essential contribution to the energy system as fertilizer and as cooking fuel. Millions of tons of artificial fertilizer at prices beyond the reach of the small farmer would be required to make up for the loss of dung if substantial numbers of cattle were sent to slaughter. Since cattle dung is also a major source of cooking fuel, the slaughter of substantial numbers of animals would require the purchase of expensive dung substitutes, such as wood, coal, or kerosene. Cattle dung is relatively cheap because the cattle do not eat foods that can be eaten by people. Instead, they eat the stubble left in the fields and the marginal patches of grass on steep hillsides, roadside ditches, railroad embankments, and other nonarable lands. This constant scavenging gives the impression that cows are roaming around aimlessly, devouring everything in sight. But most cows have an owner, and in the cities, after poking about in the market refuse and nibbling on neighbors' lawns, each cow returns to its stall at the end of the day.

In a study of the bioenergetic balances involved in the cattle complex of villages in West Bengal, Stuart Odend'hal (1972) found that "basically, the cattle convert items of little direct human value into products of immediate human utility." Their gross energetic efficiency in supplying useful products was several times greater than that characteristic of agroindustrial beef production. He concludes that "judging the productive value of Indian cattle based on Western standards is inappropriate."

Although it might be possible to maintain or exceed the present level of production of oxen (castrated male cattle) with substantially fewer cows (female cattle) of larger and better breeds, the question arises of how these cows would be distributed among the poor farmers. Are the farmers who have only one or two decrepit animals to be driven from the land?

Aside from the problem of whether present levels of population and productivity could be maintained with fewer cows, there is the theoretically more crucial question of whether it is the taboo on slaughter that accounts for the ratio of cows to oxen. Despite the ban on slaughter, Hindu farmers cull their herds and adjust sex ratios to crops, weather, and regional conditions. The cattle are killed by various indirect means equivalent to the forms of neglect discussed in

Chapter 6 with respect to human population controls. And as discussed in Chapter 2, culling of unwanted female calves results in having over 200 oxen for every 100 cows in the Gangetic plain, one of the most religiously orthodox regions of India (Vaidyanathan et al. 1982).

Chapter Summary

E. B. Tylor defined religion as animism or the doctrine of souls. According to Tylor, from the idea of the soul the idea of all godlike beings arose, and the idea of the soul itself arose as an attempt to explain phenomena such as trances, dreams, shadows, and reflections. Tylor's definition has been criticized for failing to consider the multifunctional nature of religion and for overlooking the compelling reality of direct hallucinatory contact with extraordinary beings. And as the Jivaro belief in three souls demonstrates, each culture uses the basic concepts of animism in its own distinctive fashion.

Marett sought to supplement Tylor's definition of religion with the concepts of animatism and mana. Animatism refers to the belief in an impersonal life force in people, animals, and objects. The concentration of this force gives people, animals, and objects mana, or the capacity to be extraordinarily powerful and successful. This concept does not readily separate mana from such forces as electricity or gravity. Moreover, the Western distinction between natural and supernatural is of limited utility for defining religion. As the case of the Gururumba indicates, in many cultures there are no supernatural versus natural controls, only controls.

Next, Frazer tried to cope with the enormous variety of religious experience by separating religion from magic. Humility, supplication, and doubt characterize religion; routine cause and effect characterize magic. This distinction is difficult to maintain in view of the routine and coercive fashion in which animistic beings are often manipulated.

The principal varieties of beliefs and rituals show broad correlations with levels of political economic organization. Four levels of religious organizations or cults can be distinguished: individualistic, shamanistic, communal, and ecclesiastical.

Innuit religion illustrates the individualistic or do-it-yourself level. Each individual carries out a series of rituals and observes a series of taboos that are deemed essential for survival and well-being, without the help of any part-time or full-time specialist.

No culture is devoid of shamanistic cults, the next level, defined by the presence of part-time magico-religious experts, or shamans, who have special talents and knowledge, usually involving sleight of hand, trances, and possession. As the case of Tapirape shamanism indicates, shamans are frequently employed to cure sick people, as well as to identify and destroy evildoers.

Communal cults, involving public rituals deemed essential for the welfare or survival of the entire social group, also occur to some extent at all political–economic levels. Two principal types of communal ritual can be distinguished: rites of solidarity and rites of passage. As illustrated by the Arunta totemic rituals, rites of solidarity reaffirm and intensify a group's sense of common identity and express in symbolic form the group's claims to territory and resources. As illustrated in the Ndembu circumcision rituals, rites of passage symbolically and publicly denote the extinction or "death" of an individual's or group's socially significant status and the acquisition or "birth" of a new socially significant status.

Finally, ecclesiastical cults are those that are dominated by a hierarchy of full-time specialists or "priests" whose knowledge and skills are usually commanded by a state-level ruling class. To preserve and enhance the well-being of the state and of the universe, historical, astronomical, and ritual information must be acquired by the ecclesiastical specialists. Ecclesiastical cults are also characterized by huge investments in buildings, monuments, and personnel and by a thoroughgoing split between the specialist performers of ritual and the great mass of more or less passive spectators who constitute the "congregation."

With the development of the state, the objective of warfare shifted from that of routing enemy populations to incorporating them within imperial systems. This brought an end to the practice of sacrificing and eating prisoners of war. However, it was difficult for the Aztec state to refrain from rewarding its armies with the flesh of enemy soldiers in its effort to justify, expand, and consolidate ruling-class power. The Aztecs' consumption of human flesh was an expression of an adaptive strategy; it could not be suppressed because of the depletion of alternative sources of animal foods.

Revitalization movements, such as those of Native Americans and Melanesians, is another category of religious phenomena that cannot be understood apart from political–economic conditions. Under political–economic stress, subordinate castes, classes, minorities, and ethnic groups develop beliefs and rituals concerned with achieving a drastic improvement in their immediate well-being or their well-being in a life after death. These movements have the latent capacity to attack the dominant group directly or indirectly through political or military action; on the other hand, they may turn inward and accommodate by means of passive doctrines and rituals involving individual guilt, drugs, and contemplation.

Religious beliefs and rituals also exhibit adaptive relationships in the form of taboos. The ancient Israelite pig taboo, for example, can be understood as an adaptation to the changing costs and benefits of pig rearing brought about by population increase, deforestation, and desertification. The sacred cow of India serves as a final example of the way in which taboos and whole religions adapt to changing political, economic, and ecological contexts.

AMERICA NOW UPDATE

The Electronic Church

Protestant fundamentalism and the various born-again Christian revitalization movements have been able to use television to expand membership and raise funds. These so-called electronic churches recruit their membership through a personal "gospel of wealth"—they promise material success and physical well-being to the true believer. Their message appeals especially to people who are sick, old, or isolated; impoverished by unemployment or underemployment; bewildered by the changes in sex mores and the family; and frightened by crime in the streets. According to TV preacher Jim Bakker: "The scripture says, 'Delight yourself in the Lord and he'll give you the desire of your heart.' Give and it shall be given unto you." Bakker tells how one man prayed for a Winnebago mobile home, color brown, and got just that. Says Bakker: "Diamonds and gold aren't just for Satan—they're for Christians, too" (Bakker 1976). (Unfortunately, Bakker's appetite for diamonds and gold led him to sell lifetime vacations in nonexistent condos and he was sentenced to jail for fraud and embezzlement.)

On his "Old Time Gospel Hour," Moral Majority leader Jerry Falwell (Fig. 17.24) asks the faithful to turn over one-tenth of their income: "Christ has not captured a man's heart until He has your pocketbook." Two million potential contributors whose names and addresses are kept in a computer databank receive frequent requests for money, one of which reads: "Maybe your financial situation seems impossible. Put Jesus first in your stewardship and allow him to bless you financially" (*Time*, 1 October 1979: 68).

Finding himself $50 million short of the funds needed to complete his City of Faith hospital complex near Tulsa, Oklahoma, video evangelist Oral Roberts raised money with the aid of swatches from a "miracle cloth." "My hands feel as if there is a supernatural heat in them," he declared. "My right hand is especially hot right now." Following God's instructions, Roberts began to turn out millions of swatches imprinted with his right hand. In return, those who acquire the cloth are promised "special miracles" (*Newsweek*, 10 September 1979).

Another TV evangelist, Pat Robertson, recruits followers and raises funds through what he calls the Kingdom Principles: The Bible says the more you give to Jesus the more you will get back in return. And the harder it is to give, the greater will be the increase. Thus, as described in Rifkind and Howard (1979: 108), "a woman in California who was on a limited income and in poor health decided to trust God and

Figure 17.24   The Electronic Church
*Jerry Falwell's "Old Time Gospel Hour" being televised live from Lynchburg, Virginia, to a network of
391 television stations. Cameras can be seen on the balcony and in the center of the audience.*

to step out in faith on the Kingdom Principles. She was already giving half her disability money to the 700 Club to spread the gospel of Jesus Christ. But just last week, she decided to go all the way and give God the money she spends for cancer medicine—$120 a month. And three days later— get this!—from an entirely unexpected source, she got a check for $3,000!"

Since all the other aspects of U.S. culture are in flux, it is not surprising that religious beliefs and practices are going through a period of change and ferment. The experience of other cultures and historical epochs demonstrates that stresses brought on by rapid cultural change usually find expression in spiritual yearning, questing, and experimenting that lead to an expansion and intensification of religious activity, broadly defined.

All the major world religions were born during times of rapid cultural transformations. Buddhism and Hinduism arose in the Ganges Valley of northern India during an epoch of deforestation, population increase, and state formation. Judaism arose during the prolonged migrations of the ancient Israelites. Christianity arose in conjunction with attempts to break the yoke of Roman imperialism. Islam arose during the transition from a life of pastoral nomadism to that of trade and empires in Arabia and North Africa. Protestants split from Catholicism as feudalism gave way to capitalism. As we have seen (p. 236), messianic and millenarian cults swept across the Great Plains as the American Indians lost their lands and hunting grounds, while in the wake of the European colonization of New Guinea and Melanesia, hundreds of cargo cults, devoted to acquiring worldly wealth with the assistance of ancestors returned from the dead, spread from island to island. There is reason to believe, therefore, that the rising intensity of nontraditional religious activity in the United States constitutes an attempt to solve or to escape from the problems of malfunctioning consumerism, unemployment, the upending of gender roles, the breakup of the breadwinner family, alienation from work, oppressive government and corporate bureaucracies, feelings of isolation and loneliness, fear of crime, and bewilderment about the root cause of why so many changes are happening at once.

Chapter 18

ART

❦

Masked dancers, Dogon, Mali.

This chapter is concerned with additional aspects of superstructure—namely, the thought and behavior associated with painting, music, poetry, sculpture, dance, and other media of art. What is art? Is art as defined by Western art critics a valid definition of art in other cultures? How and why do the specific forms and styles of artistic expression vary from one culture to another? Is art ever created only for art's sake? We shall see that art is not an isolated sector of human experience. It is intimately connected with and embedded in religion, politics, technology, and many other components of human social life.

What Is Art?

Alexander Alland (1977: 39) defines *art* as "play with form producing some aesthetically successful transformation-representation." The key ingredients in this definition are play, form, aesthetic, and transformation:

Play is an enjoyable, self-rewarding aspect of activity that cannot be accounted for simply by the utilitarian or survival functions of that activity.

Form designates a set of restrictions on how the art play is to be organized in time and space—the rules of the game of art.

Aesthetic designates the existence of a universal human capacity for an emotionally charged response of appreciation and pleasure when art is successful.

Transformation-representation refers to the communicative aspect of art. Art always represents something—communicates information—but this something is never represented in its literal shape, sound, color, movement, or feeling. To be art, as distinct from other forms of communication, the representation must be transformed into some metaphoric or symbolic statement, movement, image, or object that stands for whatever is being represented. A portrait, for example, no matter how "realistic," can only be a transformation-representation of the individual it depicts.

As Alland points out, play, adherence to form, and an aesthetic sense are found in many nonhuman animals. Chimpanzees, for example, like to play with paints (Fig. 18.1). Their adherence to form can be demonstrated by their placement of designs in the center of blank spaces or by their balancing of designs on different parts of a page. (They don't simply paint right off the page.) An aesthetic sense can be inferred by their repeated attempts to copy simple designs such as circles and triangles accurately. Moreover, as we have seen in Chapter 3, the capacity to use symbols and to learn rules of symbolic transformation is not entirely confined to human beings. The 3-year-old chimp Moja drew a bird and gave the sign for it. The trainer tried to make sure that it was a bird rather than a berry, so he asked her to draw a berry, which she promptly did (Hill 1978: 98).

Nonetheless, just as grammatical language remains rudimentary among apes in nature, so too does their artistry. Although the rudiments of art can be found in our primate heritage, only *Homo sapiens* can justly be called the "artistic animal."

Art as a Cultural Category

Although it is possible to identify art as an etic category of thought and behavior in all human cultures, an emic distinction between art and nonart is not universal (just as the distinction between natural and supernatural is not universal). What most Westerners mean by art is a particular emic category of modern Euro-American civilization. Euro-American schoolchildren are enculturated to the idea that art is a category of activities and products that stands opposed to the category of nonart. They learn to believe, in other words, that some paintings, carvings, songs, dances, and stories are not art. In Western civilization, a particular performance is deemed artistic or not by a distinct group of authorities—an art establishment—who make or judge art and who control the museums, conservatories, critical journals, and other organizations and institutions devoted to art as a livelihood and style of life. Most cultures lack any semblance of an art establishment. This does not mean they lack art or artistic standards (Anderson 1992). A painted design on a pot or a rock, a carved mask or club, or a song or chant in a puberty ordeal is subject to critical evaluation by both performers and spectators. All cultures distinguish between less satisfactory and more satisfactory aesthetic experiences in decorative, pictorial, and expressive matters.

Basic to the modern Western idea of art and nonart is the exclusion of designs, stories, and artifacts that have a definite

(a)

(b)

(c)

Figure 18.1   Chimpanzee Artists
(a), (b) A 2-year-old chimpanzee finger painting at the Baltimore Zoo.
Note attempt to center painting. (c) A chimpanzee named Candy
exhibits her artwork at the San Francisco Zoo.

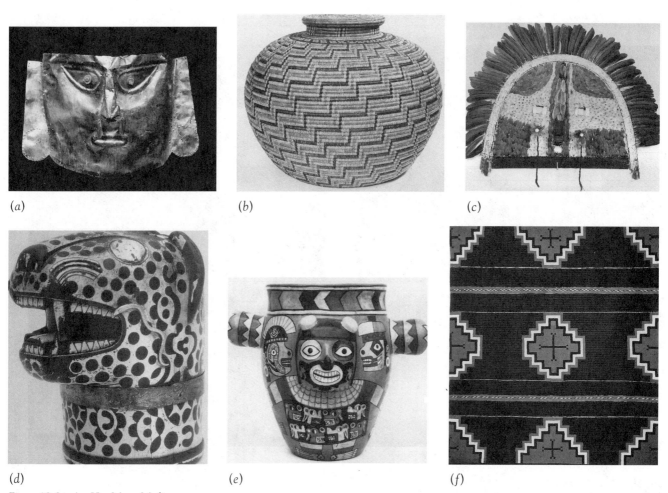

(a)   (b)   (c)

(d)   (e)   (f)

Figure 18.2   Art Has Many Media
Native-American cultures produced these objects. (a) Gold mummy mask with green stone eyes: Chimu,
Peru. (b) Globular basket with coiled weave: Chumash, California. (c) Feathers of blue and yellow
form the design of a Tapirapé mask: Brazil. (d) Painted wooden kero, or beaker, representing ocelot
head: Inca, Peru. (e) Ceramic jar: Nazca, Peru. (f) Blanket, in blue, black, and white, with stripes and
frets: Navajo.

use in day-to-day subsistence activities and that are produced primarily for practical purposes or for commercial sale. Carpenters are distinguished from people who make wooden sculptures, bricklayers from architects, house painters from those who apply paint to canvas, and so forth. A similar opposition between art and practicality is seldom found in other cultures. Many works of art are produced and performed in complete harmony with utilitarian objectives. People everywhere, whether specialists or nonspecialists, derive pleasure from playfully embellishing and transforming the contours and surfaces of pots, fabrics, wood, and metal products (Fig. 18.2). All cultures, however, recognize that certain individuals are more skilled than others in making

utilitarian objects and in embellishing them with pleasurable designs. Most anthropologists regard the skilled wood carver, basketmaker, potter, weaver, or sandalmaker as an artist.

Art and Invention

Play is a form of exploratory behavior that permits human beings to try out new and possibly useful responses in a controlled and protected context. The playful creative urge that lies behind art, therefore, is probably closely related to the creative urge that lies behind the development of science, technology, and new institutions.

Figure 18.3   !Kung San Plays the Bow
Thumb plucks the string; mouth opens and closes, moving along string to control tone and resonance. Which came first: bow for hunting or bow for making music?

Art and technology often interact, and it is difficult to say where technology ends and art begins, or where art ends and technology begins. The beautiful symmetry of nets, baskets, and woven fabrics is essential for their proper functioning. Even the development of musical expression may have technological benefits. For example, there was probably some kind of feedback between the invention of the bow as a hunting weapon and the twanging of taut strings for musical effect (Fig. 18.3). No one can say which came first, but cultures with bows and arrows usually have musical strings. Wind instruments, blowguns, pistons, and bellows are all related. Similarly, metallurgy and chemistry relate to experimentation with the ornamental shape, texture, and color of ceramic and textile products. The first fired ceramics were figurines rather than utilitarian pots (Vandiver et al. 1989). Thus, it is practical to encourage craftworkers to experiment with new techniques and materials. Small wonder that many cultures regard technical virtuosity as mana (see p. 221). Others regard it as the gift of the gods, as in the classical Greek idea of the Muses—goddesses of oratory, dance, and music—whose assistance was needed if worthy artistic performances were to occur.

Art and Cultural Patterning

Most artwork is deliberately fashioned in the image of preexisting forms. It is the task of the artist to replicate these forms by original combinations of culturally standardized elements—familiar and pleasing sounds, colors, lines, shapes, movements, and so on. Of course, the artist must always add some playful and creative ingredient, or it will not be art. On the other hand, if the transformation-representation is to communicate something—and it must communicate something if it is to be a successful work of art—the rules of the game cannot be the artist's own private invention. Complete originality, therefore, is not what most cultures strive after in their art.

Each culture tends to repeat traditional and familiar elements, thus generating a characteristic sound, look, or feel. For example, Northwest Coast Native-American sculpture is well known for its consistent attention to animal and human motifs rendered in such a way as to indicate internal as well as external organs. These organs are symmetrically arranged within bounded geometrical forms (Fig. 18.4). Maori sculpture, on the other hand, requires that wooden surfaces be broken into bold but intricate filigrees and whorls (Fig. 18.5). Among the Mochica of ancient Peru, the sculptural medium was pottery, and Mochica pots are famous for their representational realism in portraiture and in depictions of domestic and sexual behavior (Fig. 18.6). Hundreds of other easily recognizable and distinctive art styles of different cultures can be identified. The continuity and integrity of these styles provide the basic context for a people's understanding and liking of art.

Establishment art in modern Western culture is again unique in its emphasis on formal originality. Westerners take it as normal that art must be interpreted and explained by experts in order to be understood and appreciated. Since the end of the nineteenth century, the greatest artists of the Western art establishment are those who break with tradition, introduce new formal rules, and at least for a time render their work incomprehensible to a large number of people. Joined to this deemphasis of tradition is the peculiar and recent Western notion of artists as lonely people struggling in poverty against limitations set by the preexisting capability of their audience to appreciate and understand true genius.

Thus, the creative, playful, and transformational aspects of modern art have gotten the upper hand over the formal and representational aspects (Fig. 18.7). Contemporary Euro-American artists consciously strive to be the originators of entirely new formal rules. They compete to invent new transformations to replace the traditional ones. Modern aesthetic standards hold that originality is more important than intelligibility. Indeed, a work of art that is too easily understood may be condemned. Many artists take it for granted that novelty must result in a certain amount of obscurity. What accounts for this obsession with being original?

One important influence is the reaction to mass production. Mass production leads to a downgrading of technical

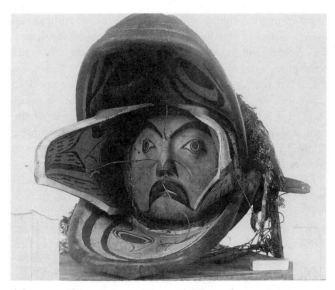

(a)   (b)

Figure 18.4   Kwakiutl Masks
(a) Mask within a mask within a mask. Whale conceals bird, which conceals human face, which conceals face of wearer; another Kwakiutl masterpiece. (b) Mask within a mask. Wearer of the Kwakiutl
mask uses strings to pull eagle apart, revealing human face.

virtuosity. It also leads to a downgrading of all artwork that closely resembles the objects or performances others have produced. Another factor to be considered is the involvement of the modern artist in a commercial market in which supply perennially exceeds demand. Artists in band and village societies are not obsessed with being original except to the extent that it enhances the aesthetic enjoyment of their work. Their livelihood does not depend on obtaining an artistic identity and a personal following.

Another factor to be considered is the high rate of cultural change in modern societies. To some extent, the emphasis on artistic originality merely reflects this rate of change.

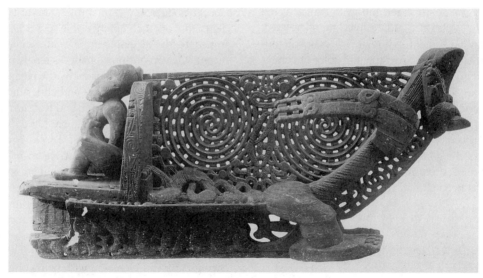

Figure 18.5   Maori Canoe Prow
The Maori of New Zealand are among the world's great wood carvers.

Finally, the alienating and isolating tendencies of modern mass society may also play a role. Much modern art reflects the loneliness, puzzlement, and anxiety of the creative individual in a depersonalized and hostile urban, industrial milieu.

Art and Religion

The history and ethnography of art are inseparable from the history and ethnography of religion. The earliest paintings found on the walls of caves are generally assumed to have been painted as part of ancient religious rituals. Art is intimately associated with all four organizational levels of religion. For example, at the individualistic level, magical songs are often included among the revelations granted the vision seekers of the Great Plains. Even the preparation of trophy heads among the Jivaro must meet aesthetic standards, and singing and chanting are widely used during shamanistic performances. On the communal level, puberty rituals, as among the Ndembu (p. 228), provide occasions for dancing and myth and storytelling. Body painting is also widely practiced in communal ceremonies, as among the Arunta. Singing, dancing, and the wearing of masks are common at both puberty and funeral rituals. Furthermore, much artistic effort is expended in the preparation of religiously significant funeral equipment such as coffins and graveposts

Figure 18.6   Mochica Pot
A pre-Columbian portrait made by the Mochica of northern Peru.

(a)

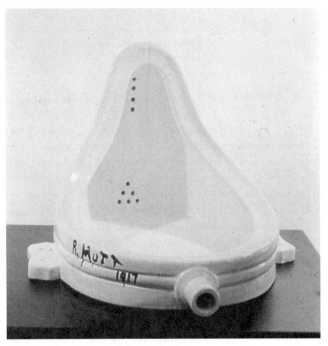

(b)

Figure 18.7   What Does It Mean?
(a) Fur-covered cup, saucer, and spoon by Meret Oppenheim. (b).
Marcel Duchamp, Fountain.

Figure 18.8   Ba Kota Funerary Figures
The Ba Kota of the Gabon Republic place the skeletal remains of dead chiefs in bark boxes or baskets surmounted by Mbulu-ngulu guardian figures of wood, faced with brass or copper sheets or strips. Although the figures each express the creative individuality of the artist, they conform to the same stylistic pattern.

(Figs. 18.8 and 18.9). Many cultures include among a deceased person's grave goods ceremonial artifacts such as pottery and clubs, points, and other weapons. Ancestors and gods are often depicted in statues and masks that are kept in men's houses or in shrines (Fig. 18.10). Churingas (p. 228), the Aranda's most sacred objects, are artfully incised with whorls and loops depicting the route followed by the ancestors during the dream time.

Finally, on the ecclesiastical level, art and religion are fused in pyramids, monumental avenues, stone statuary, monolithic calendar carvings, temples, altars, priestly garments, and a nearly infinite variety of ritual ornaments and sacred paraphernalia.

Clearly, art, religion, and magic satisfy many overlapping psychological needs in human beings. They are media for expressing sentiments and emotions not easily expressed in ordinary life. They impart a sense of mastery over or communion with unpredictable events and mysterious, unseen pow-

ers. They impose human meanings and values on an indifferent world—a world that has no humanly intelligible meanings and values of its own. They seek to penetrate behind the facade of ordinary appearance into the true, cosmic significance of things. And they use illusions, dramatic tricks, and sleight of hand to get people to believe in them.

Art and Politics

Art is also intimately related to politics. The relationship is especially clear in the context of state-sponsored art. As we have seen, in stratified societies, religion is a means of social control. To strengthen this control, the skills of the artist are harnessed by the ruling class to implant religious notions of obedience and to sanctify the status quo (Fig. 18.11). Contrary to the popular modern image of the artist as a free spirit disdainful of authority, most state-level art is politically

Figure 18.9 Asmat Gravepost
Around the world, much talent has been lavished on commemorating the dead, but styles and media vary enormously.

Figure 18.10 Art and Architecture
Brightly painted faces on a men's house in Sepik River basin, New Guinea.

conservative (Paztory 1984: 20). Ecclesiastical art generally interprets the world in conformity with prevailing myths and ideologies justifying inequities and exploitation. Art makes the gods visible as idols. Gazing on massive stone blocks carved as if by superhuman hands, commoners comprehend the necessity for subservience. They are awed by the immense size of pyramids and by the processions, prayers, pomp, and sacrifices carried out by priests in dramatic settings—golden altars, colonnaded temples, great vaulted roofs, huge ramps and stairways, windows through which only the light from heaven passes (Fig. 18.12).

The church and state have been the greatest patrons of the arts in all but the last few hundred years of history. With the rise of capitalism, ecclesiastical and civil institutions in the West became more decentralized, and wealthy individuals largely replaced church and state as patrons of the arts. Individualized sponsorship promoted greater flexibility and freedom of expression. Politically neutral, secular, and even revolutionary and sacrilegious themes became common. The arts became established as individualistic, secular forms of expression and entertainment. To protect and preserve its newfound autonomy, the art establishment adopted the doctrine of "art for art's sake." But once they were free to express themselves as they saw fit, artists were no longer sure what they wanted to express. They devoted themselves more and more to idiosyncratic and obscure symbols organized into novel and unintelligible patterns, as noted earlier in this chapter. And the patrons of art, concerned less and less with communication, increasingly looked toward the acquisition and sponsorship of art as a prestigious commercial venture that yielded substantial profits, tax deductions, and a hedge against inflation.

The Evolution of Music and Dance

Some anthropologists hold that the influence on art of structural and infrastructural components extends directly

Figure 18.11   Gold Death Mask of Tut
Another example of the interrelationship of art, religion, and politics.

Figure 18.12   Art and Religion
Notre Dame Cathedral, Paris. No one ever had to ask what it means,
but how it was built remains a mystery.

into the formal characteristics and aesthetic standards of different cultural styles. According to Allan Lomax and his associates (Lomax 1968; Lomax and Arensberg 1977), for example, certain broad characteristics of song, music, and dance are closely correlated with a culture's level of subsistence. Band and village peoples in general tend to have a different complex of music, song, and dance than do chiefdoms and states. Dividing cultures into those that are low and those that are high on the scale of subsistence technology leads to the following correlations:

Musical intervals: The less advanced subsistence systems employ musical scales in which notes are widely separated—that is, have intervals of a third or more. Advanced subsistence systems employ scales that are marked by more and smaller intervals.

Repetition in song text: The less advanced subsistence cultures employ more repetition in their lyrics—fewer words, over and over again.

Complexity and type of orchestra: Less advanced subsistence systems use only one or two kinds of instruments and small numbers of each. Advanced subsistence is correlated with musical performances involving more performers and a greater variety of instruments.

Dance styles: The advanced subsistence systems are correlated with dance styles in which many body parts—fingers, wrists, arms, torso, legs, feet, toes—have distinctive movements to make or "parts to play." Further, the more advanced the subsistence system, the more the dance style tends to emphasize complex curving motions, as opposed to simple up-and-down or side-to-side steps like hopping or shuffling.

Lomax sees these correlations as resulting from direct and indirect influence of subsistence. Large, complex orchestration, for example, reflects the structural ability of a society to form large, coordinated groups. Dance styles, on the other hand, may simply express the characteristic movements employed in using such implements of production as digging sticks versus plows or complex machines. Some dances can be regarded as training for work, warfare, or self-defense, but obviously dance has many other functions (Box 18.1). Modern rock, for example, has a strong erotic component, expressed through pelvic gyrations and thrusts.

Lomax's correlations have been criticized on technical grounds relating to sampling and coding procedures (see Kaeppler 1978). Nonetheless, Lomax's attempt to measure and compare music and dance styles, and to relate them to

---

Box 18.1

SOME SOCIAL FUNCTIONS OF MUSIC, SONG, AND DANCE

1. Emotes: Lets people "blow off steam," makes them feel good.
2. Socializes: Teaches traditions.
3. Educates: Develops poise and confidence in performance.
4. Bonds: Creates a sense of togetherness among performers.
5. Rallies: Prepares for dangerous situations (for example, warfare and journeys).
6. Aggresses: Lets people "show their stuff" harmlessly.
7. Worships: Brings people closer to the gods.
8. Seduces: Arouses sexual passions, displays charms.
9. Coordinates: Gets people to work or move together, as in sea chanties or military marches.
10. Entertains: Prevents boredom.

---

social structure and subsistence, constitutes an important avenue of approach.

The Complexity of Primitive Art: Campa Rhetoric

A common misconception about the arts of band and village societies is that they are necessarily more simple or naive than art in modern industrial societies (Titon et al. 1984). Although, as we have just seen, many stylistic aspects of art have undergone an evolution from simple to more complex forms, other aspects may have been as complex among Stone Age hunter-gatherers as they are today. The case of Campa rhetoric illustrates this point.

Rhetoric is the art of persuasive public discourse and is closely related to the theatrical arts. As Gerald Weiss (1977b) has discovered, the preliterate Campa, who live in eastern Peru near the headwaters of the Amazon river, use most of the important rhetorical devices cultivated by the great philosophers and orators of ancient Greece and Rome. Their object in public discourse is not merely to inform, but to persuade and convince. "Campa narration is 'a separate time,' where a spellbinding relationship between narrator and audience is developed, with powerful rhetorical devices employed to create and enhance the quality of that relationship" (1977b: 173).

Here are a few examples of these devices, as translated by Weiss from the Campa language, which belongs to the native American family of languages known as Arawak:

Rhetorical questions: The speaker makes the point that the Campa are deficient in their worship of the sky god, the sun, by asking a question that he himself will then answer: "Do we supplicate him, he here, he who lives in the sky, the sun? We do not know how to supplicate him."

Iterations (effect by repetition): The speaker imparts an emphatic, graphic, cinematic quality to the point by repeating some key words: "The enemy comes out of the lake: And so they emerged in great numbers—he saw them emerge, emerge, emerge, emerge, emerge, emerge, emerge, emerge, emerge, all, all."

Imagery and metaphor: Death is alluded to in the phrase "the earth will eat him." The body is described as "the clothing of the soul."

Appeal to evidence: To prove that the oilbird was formerly human in shape: "Yes, he was formerly human—doesn't he have whiskers?"

Appeal to authority: "They told me long ago, the elders, they who heard these words, long ago, so it was."

Antithesis (effect by contrast): A hummingbird is about to raise the sky rope, which the other larger creatures have failed to do: "They are all big whereas I am small and chubby."

In addition, the Campa orator uses a wide variety of gestures, exclamations, sudden calls for attention ("watch out, here it comes"), asides ("imagine it, then"; "careful that you don't believe, now"). Altogether, Weiss lists nineteen formal rhetorical devices used by the Campa.

Myth and Binary Contrasts

Anthropologists have found considerable evidence suggesting that certain formal structures recur in widely different traditions of oral and written literature, including myths and folktales. These structures are characterized by binary contrasts—that is, by two elements or themes that can be viewed as standing in diametric opposition to each other. Many examples of recurrent binary contrasts can be found in Western religion, literature, and mythology: good versus bad, up versus down, male versus female, cultural versus natural, young versus old, and so forth. According to the French anthropologist Levi-Strauss, the founder of the research strategy known as *structuralism* (see Appendix), the reason these binary contrasts recur so often is that the human brain is "wired" in such a way as to make binary contrasts especially appealing, or "good to think." From the structuralist point of view, the main task of the anthropological study of literature, mythology, and folklore is to identify the common, unconscious binary contrasts that lie beneath the surface of human thought and to show how these binary contrasts undergo unconscious transformation-representations.

Consider the familiar tale of Cinderella: A mother has two daughters and one stepdaughter. The two daughters are older, the stepdaughter is younger; the older ones are ugly and mean, whereas Cinderella is beautiful and kind. The older sisters are aggressive; Cinderella is passive. Through a kind fairy godmother, as opposed to her mean stepmother, Cinderella goes to the ball, dances with the prince, and loses her magical shoe. Her sisters have big feet, she has little feet. Cinderella wins the prince. The unconscious deep structure of this story might include the following binary oppositions:

passive	aggressive
younger	older
smaller	larger
good	evil
beautiful	ugly
culture	nature
fairy godmother	stepmother

Structuralists contend that the enjoyment people derive from such tales and their durability across space and time derive mainly from the unconscious oppositions and their familiar yet surprising representations.

Structural analyses of literature, art, myths, rituals, and religion abound in anthropology. However, they are surrounded by considerable controversy, primarily because it is not clear whether the binary matrices discerned by the anthropologists really exist as unconscious realities in the minds of the people being studied. It is always possible to reduce complex and subtle symbols to less complex and gross symbols and then finally to emerge with such flat oppositions as culture versus nature or male versus female.

Chapter Summary

Creative play, formal structure, aesthetic feelings, and symbolic transformations are the essential ingredients in art. Although the capacity for art is foreshadowed in the behavior of nonhuman primates, only humans are capable of art involving "transformation-representations." The distinctive human capacity for art is thus closely related to the distinctive human capacity for the symbolic transformations that underlie the semantic universality of human language.

Western emic definitions of art depend on the existence of art authorities and critics who place many examples of play, structured aesthetic, and symbolic transformation into the category of nonart. The distinction between crafts and art is part of this tradition. In contrast, anthropologists regard skilled craftspersons as artists.

Art has adaptive functions related to creative changes in other sectors of social life. Art and technology influence each other, as in the case of instruments of music and the hunt, or in the search for new shapes, colors, textures, and materials in ceramics and textiles.

Despite the emphasis on creative innovation, most cultures have art traditions or styles that maintain formal continuity through time. This makes it possible to identify the styles of cultures such as the Northwest Coast, Maori, or Mochica. The continuity and integrity of such styles provide the basic context for a people's understanding of and liking for the artist's creative transformations. Establishment art in modern Western culture is unique in emphasizing structural or formal creativity as well as creative transformations. This results in the isolation of the artist. Lack of communication between the Western artist and the rest of society may be caused by a reaction to mass production, commercialization of art markets, rapid rate of cultural change, and the depersonalized milieu of urban industrial life.

Art and religion are closely related. This relationship can be seen in the songs of the vision quest; preparation of shrunken heads; singing and chanting in shamanistic performances; Tapirape shamanistic myths; storytelling; singing and dancing; Arunta churingas; and many other aspects of individual, shamanistic, communal, and ecclesiastical cults.

Art and religion satisfy many similar psychological needs, and it is often difficult to tell them apart.

Art and politics are also closely related. This relationship is clear in state-sponsored ecclesiastical art, much of which functions to keep people in awe of their rulers. It is only in recent times, with the rise of decentralized capitalist states, that art has enjoyed any significant degree of freedom from direct political control.

To the extent that bands, villages, chiefdoms, and states represent evolutionary levels, and to the extent that art is functionally related to technology, economy, politics, religion, and other aspects of the universal cultural pattern, the content of art has clearly evolved. A more controversial finding is that styles of song, music, and dance—including musical intervals, repetition in song texts, complexity and type of orchestra, body part involvement, and amount of curvilinear motion—have also undergone evolutionary changes. But as the example of Campa rhetoric shows, the art styles of band and village peoples can be highly sophisticated.

The structuralist approach to art attempts to interpret myths, rituals, and other expressive performances in terms of a series of unconscious universal binary oppositions. Common binary oppositions can be found in the Cinderella myth, but these may not be emically valid categories.

Chapter 19

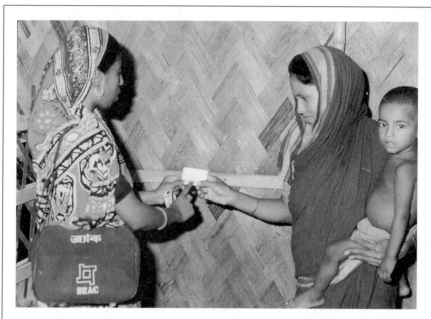

APPLIED ANTHROPOLOGY

Family planning worker, Bangladesh.

Up to now, you have probably been thinking that at least some of this is pretty interesting stuff (I hope). But what good is it?

Does it have any practical use? Well, it so happens that a lot of people (and not only anthropologists) think it does. Herein we explore some of the relationships between anthropological research and the attempt to achieve practical goals by organizations that sponsor or use such research. The sample of cases presented in this brief survey does not fairly represent the great variety of applied projects being carried out by anthropologists. This is a rapidly growing field that is hard to keep up with.

What is Applied Anthropology?

Since World War II, an increasing number of cultural anthropologists have become involved in research that has immediate practical applications. Such anthropologists are said to practice *applied anthropology*.

The core of applied anthropology consists of research commissioned by public or private organizations in the hope of achieving practical goals of interest to those organizations. Such organizations include federal, state, local, and international government bureaus and agencies, such as the U.S. Department of Agriculture, the Department of Defense, the National Park Service, the Agency for International Development, the Bureau of Indian Affairs, the World Bank, the World Health Organization, the Food and Agricultural Organization, various drug abuse agencies, education and urban planning departments of major cities, and municipal hospitals, to mention only a few. In addition, private organizations that have hired or contracted with anthropologists to carry out practical, goal-oriented research include major industrial corporations, research foundations such as Planned Parenthood and the Population Council, and various branches of the Rockefeller and Ford Foundations' International Crops Research Institutes (Chambers 1985; Willigen 1986).

It should be emphasized that cultural anthropologists do not have a monopoly on applied anthropology: Physical anthropology, archaeology, and linguistics also have their applied aspects. But here we shall deal mainly with the applied aspects of cultural anthropology.

Research, Theory, and Action

Although the hallmark of applied anthropology is involvement in research aimed at achieving a special practical result, the extent to which the applied anthropologist actually participates in bringing about the desired result varies from one assignment to another. At one extreme, the applied anthro-
pologist may merely be charged with developing information the sponsoring organization needs in order to make decisions. In other instances, the applied anthropologist may be asked to evaluate the feasibility of a planned program or even to draw up a set of plans for achieving a desired goal (Husain 1976). More rarely, the anthropologist, alone or as a member of a team, may be responsible for planning, implementing, and evaluating a whole program from beginning to end. When anthropologists help implement a program, they are said to be practicing action anthropology.

It is often difficult to draw a line between applied and nonapplied research. Abstract theorizing about the causes of sociocultural differences and similarities can itself be construed as applied anthropology if it provides a general set of principles to which any action program must conform if it is to achieve success. For example, general theories about the causes of underdevelopment or of urban poverty (see pp. 164 and 165) can have considerable practical consequences even though the research behind these theories may not have been sponsored by organizations with the expressed goal of eliminating underdevelopment and urban poverty. Similarly, a better understanding of the processes that are responsible for the evolution of advanced industrial societies may be of immediate relevance to organizations that advise firms and governments on investment policies. Applied anthropology premised on blatantly incorrect theory is misapplied anthropology (Cohen 1984b).

What Do Applied Anthropologists Have to Offer?

The effectiveness of applied anthropology is enhanced by three distinctive attributes of general anthropology (see p. 2): (1) relative freedom from ethnocentrism and Western biases, (2) concern with holistic sociocultural systems, and (3) concern with both ordinary etic behavioral events and the emics of mental life.

DETECTING AND CONTROLLING ETHNOCENTRISM

The applied anthropologist can be of assistance to sponsoring organizations by exposing the ethnocentric, culture-bound assumptions that often characterize cross-cultural contacts and that prevent change-oriented programs from achieving their goals. For example, Western-trained agricultural scientists tend to dismiss peasant forms of agriculture as backward and inefficient, thereby overlooking the cumulative wisdom embodied in age-old practices handed down from generation to generation (Netting 1993). The attitude of Western experts toward the use of cattle in India is a case in point (see p. 240). Anthropologists are more likely to reserve judgment about a traditional practice such as using cattle to plow fields, whereas a narrowly trained specialist might automatically wish to replace the animals with tractors.

Again, applied anthropologists could add a valuable perspective to the attempt to set up a health care delivery system. Simply modeling it after those with which Western-trained doctors are familiar may represent nothing more than an attempt to replace the culturally unfamiliar with the culturally familiar. Expensive staffs, costly hospitals, and the latest electronic gadgetry, for example, are not necessarily the way to improve the quality of health services (Cattle 1977: 38). Furthermore, the American notion that milk is the "perfect food" has led to much grief and dismay throughout the world since many populations in less developed countries to which tons of surplus milk in powdered form were sent as nutritional supplements lacked the enzyme needed to digest lactose, the predominant form of sugar in milk (Harris 1985). Finally, Western notions of hygiene automatically suggest that mothers must be persuaded not to chew food and then put it in their babies' mouths. Yet it was found that in the case of the Pijoan Indians of the U.S. Southwest, premastication of infant foods effectively combatted the iron-deficiency anemia that afflicts infants who are fed exclusively on mother's milk (Freedman 1977: 8).

A HOLISTIC VIEW

As industrial society becomes increasingly specialized and technocratic (that is, dominated by narrowly trained experts who have mastered techniques and the use of machines others do not understand), the need for anthropology's holistic view of social life becomes more urgent. In diverse fields (for example, education, health, economic development), narrow sets of easily quantified variables are increasingly being used to verify objectively the accomplishment or lack of accomplishment of an organization's goals. All too often, however, the gain in verifiability is accomplished at the expense of a loss in "validity" (or "meaningfulness"). Easily quantified variables may represent only a small part of a much bigger system whose larger set of difficult-to-measure variables has the capacity to cancel out the observed effects of the small set of variables (Bernard 1981: 5).

For example, after World War II, the U.S. auto industry found it could earn more money by building heavier and more powerful cars without paying too much attention to the question of how long the cars would function without need of repairs. Other sets of variables—namely, the ecological consequences of auto emission pollution, the political and military conditions that made it possible for the United States to enjoy low oil prices, and the perception by foreign auto pro-

---

KAZANGA

The Universal Bank, having decided to launch a big development program in a remote region, sent a team of development experts to visit the country and talk to the chiefs. The team arrived at a settlement of mud huts and cattle corrals. The team leader asked the chief to assemble the villagers so that he could explain all the good things that the Universal Bank was going to do for them. When the villagers were seated the development expert stood up and said:

"You are very lucky that the Universal Bank has decided to bring progress to your land".

"Kazanga!" The people shouted.

"You are going to get roads, schools and hospitals."

"Kazanga!" They shouted again.

"You are going to have electic lights and running water."

"Kazanga!" They roared back.

"TVs, VCRs, Big Macs, and a landing strip for jumbo jets."

"Kazanga!"

With everybody in a jovial mood, smiling and laughing, the chief asked the development experts if they would like to see the rest of the village. They agreed and he led them down the path that went to the cattle corrals, with the whole village following. As they neared the first corral, the chief pointed downward and said,

"Oh, by the way, be careful. Don't step in the Kazanga."

ducers that there was a market for small, fuel-efficient, reliable, and long-lasting vehicles—were considered irrelevant to the task of maximizing the U.S. auto industry's profits. Hence, what appeared in a narrow context to be a highly objective measure of success (large profits and domination of the U.S. auto market) turned out in a longer time frame to be devoid of validity.

Thus, in commonsense language, anthropological holism boils down to being aware of the long term as well as the short term, the distant as well as the near, parts other than the one being studied, and the whole as well as the parts. Without these perspectives, even a seemingly straightforward and simple project can end up as a disaster (Box 19.1).

ETIC AND EMIC VIEWS OF ORGANIZATIONS

Technification and specialization are usually accompanied by the growth of bureaucracy. An essential component of bureaucracy is an emic plan by which the units within an organization are related to each other and according to which individuals are expected to perform their tasks. As in most sociocultural systems, the etic behavioral substance of organizations and situations differs substantially from the mental emics of the bureaucratic plan. Anthropologists who are trained to approach social life from the ground up, and who are concerned with everyday events as they actually unfold, often can provide a view of organizations and situations that the bureaucracy lacks. Thus, anthropologists have studied schools, factories, corporations, and hospitals in a manner that provides both emic and etic viewpoints (Box 19.2).

Agricultural Development

One of the most important subfields of applied anthropology focuses on the problem of agricultural development in peasant and small farmer communities. As mentioned previously (p. 164), anthropologists have studied peasants more often than they have studied other kinds of groups. Their knowledge of the conditions and aspirations of peasant life makes anthropologists useful as consultants to or members of interdisciplinary projects aimed at raising Third World standards of living (Barlett and Brown 1985).

The Vicos Project

A classic example of an anthropological development effort took place in the 1950s under the auspices of the Cornell–Peru Vicos project. Vicos was a hacienda (a large farm on which a variety of crops is grown, worked by resident peasants) in the Peruvian highlands inhabited by 373 economically serflike, depressed, and exploited families of Indian peasants (Fig. 19.1). Cornell University leased the hacienda

---

Box 19.1

WITHOUT HOLISM: AN ANDEAN FIASCO

International experts tried without success to get the peasant Indians of Chimborazo Province in Ecuador to substitute high-yield Australian merino sheep for the scrawny sheep the Indians owned. If the Indians would use them to breed new flocks, they could have them free of charge. Finally, one "progressive" Indian accepted the offer and raised a flock of cross-bred merinos that were far woollier and heavier than the traditional Indian sheep. Unfortunately, the Indians of Chimborazo compete with other ethnic and racial groups for scarce resources. Non-Indian, Spanish-speaking farmers who live in the lower valleys resented the attention being paid to the Indians; they began to fear that the Indians would be emboldened to press for additional economic and social gains, which would undermine their own positions. The merinos attracted someone's attention, and the whole flock was herded into a truck and stolen. The rustlers were well protected by public opinion, which regarded the animals as "too good for the Indians anyway." The "progressive" innovator was left as the only one in the village without sheep. Variables such as ethnic and class antagonisms, opportunities for theft, and the political subservience of peasants are not part of the expertise of sheep breeders, but awareness of these factors nonetheless proved essential to the achievement of their goals.

Box 19.2

EMICS AND ETICS IN A HOSPITAL BUREAUCRACY

During the 1970s, a series of community health centers was established by the department of health and hospitals of a large northeastern city. These centers were located in poor neighborhoods and designed to provide health care for the local people. All but one of the centers was used to capacity. Anthropologist Delmos Jones (1976) was charged with the task of discovering why this particular facility was underused.

Jones proceeded on the assumption that the main reasons for the underutilization of the health center would be found not in the characteristics of the population it was designed to serve but in certain traits of the center itself. Initial investigation showed that many people in the neighborhood did not know about the center's existence. Unlike the other centers, this one was located inside a hospital and could not be seen from the street. Moreover, among those who had heard about the center, few were aware of where it was or what it did.

Probing further, Jones discovered that the neighborhood people had a negative image of the hospital in which the clinic was located. It had the reputation of being very "fancy" and not for poor people. Thus, they could not believe that somewhere inside the hospital there was a free clinic. Rumor had it that poor people were even turned away from the hospital's emergency room. People who had persisted in trying to use the clinic reported that they couldn't find it. When they got to the hospital, they couldn't find any signs telling them where to go. Even some of the hospital's receptionists didn't know where it was, or refused to say. Jones suspected the latter was the case because key members of the staff expressed displeasure at having a free clinic in their fancy hospital. As at the other centers, this one had several neighborhood representatives. But these representatives had developed a defeatist attitude toward the client population and made little effort to contact people in the neighborhood.

Figure 19.1   Vicos
A community work party begins its potato harvest.

and turned it over to anthropologist Allen Holmberg with the objective of raising the Indians' standard of living and making them economically independent. At the time of intervention, the people of Vicos were unable to grow enough food to feed themselves, their farming lands were broken up into thousands of tiny scattered plots, their potato crop was subject to frequent failure, and they lacked motivation for producing a surplus since they were constantly in debt or at the beck and call of the landlords.

Under the feudal rules of the hacienda system, the peasants were required to labor on the owner's fields for three days per week. Holmberg decided to take advantage of this obligation by using it to familiarize the peasants with improved varieties of potatoes, fertilizers, fungicides, and insecticides. After seeing how well the new seeds and methods succeeded during their obligatory labor on the new boss's plot, the peasants were more willing to do the same on their own plots. Their willingness was further facilitated by advancing the seeds and other materials on a sharecrop basis. Anthropologists and technicians carefully supervised the use of the new methods to ensure their success.

Meanwhile, other activities were underway: a full-scale educational program; a school hot-lunch program that introduced fruits and eggs, previously not part of the diet; a demonstration garden for growing leafy vegetables; and sewing machine lessons that enabled the women to make their own clothes. In addition, through frequent communal meetings and discussions, the peasants gradually came to place more trust in one another and to seek cooperative, communal solutions to their problems.

The culmination of all these changes was the purchase of the hacienda by the families living on it. Along with higher incomes, better health, and literacy, this event was considered dramatic evidence of the success of the project (Dobyns 1972: 201). Most important, the people of Vicos continued to improve their standard of living long after all the applied anthropologists had left the community. Studies show that other communities in the same region have had much lower rates of improvement in per capita income, literacy, health conditions, and political representation (Doughty 1987: 152).

As a model for developing the entire peasant sector of the Peruvian Andes, however, the plan has attracted certain criticisms. The per capita cash outlays were quite modest in comparison with those of other international development efforts, yet there were hidden investment costs that are not likely to be duplicated on a scale large enough to affect a significant portion of the Peruvian peasantry. Vicos benefited from highly trained, honest, and relatively unselfish experts (including Holmberg) who worked diligently to improve the lot of the peasants. They were paid by universities and foundations, and many of them worked for next to nothing as graduate students hoping to be compensated by getting their Ph.D.s and making their careers in anthropology. Thus, although extremely interesting as a demonstration of what can be done by action anthropologists who had considerable power to manage the people in their charge, the Vicos project fell short of providing a more general solution to the problem of underdevelopment in the Peruvian Andes. But such criticisms fail to take into account the limited goals of the project. The organizers wanted to demonstrate that it was possible for a low-budget, face-to-face collaborative effort by anthropologists, preexisting government agencies, and the people themselves to overcome centuries of poverty, isolation, ignorance, and prejudice. Judged on this limited basis, the project was a success.

The Haitian Agroforestry Project

If agricultural development is to be meaningful, it cannot be confined to one or two peasant communities. It must use scientific knowledge to ensure that beneficial innovations will be spread rapidly throughout a region or a country by local participants rather than by foreign experts. Thus, the Haitian Agroforestry Project shows more promise in this regard than the Vicos project.

Planned and directed in its initial phase by anthropologist Gerald Murray, the Agroforestry Project has successfully induced Haitian peasants to plant millions of fast-growing trees in steep hillside farmlands threatened by erosion. Depletion of soil as a result of rapid run-off from treeless hillsides has long been recognized as one of Haiti's greatest problems. In addition, trees are needed as a source of charcoal—the principal cooking fuel in poor households—and as a source of building materials. Many other reforestation programs have been tried in Haiti, but they have met with little or no success either because the funds for planting were squandered or diverted by government bureaucrats or because peasants refused to cooperate and protect the seedlings from hungry goats.

The Haitian Agroforestry Project was designed to avoid both pitfalls. In accepting a $4 million grant from the United States Agency for International Development (USAID), Murray insisted on an unusual stipulation: No funds were to be transferred to the Haitian government or through the Haitian government. Instead, the funds were to be given to local community groups—private voluntary organizations—interested in peasant welfare. In practice, the majority of these groups were grass-roots religious associations formed by Catholic or Protestant priests, pastors, or missionaries. The project provided these groups with seedlings of fast-growing species matched to local ecological conditions and with expert advisors. The private voluntary organizations, in turn, undertook to assemble and instruct the local farmers and to distribute the seedlings to them free of charge, provided each farmer agreed to plant a minimum of 500 (G. Murray 1984).

Clearly, unless the peasants themselves were motivated to plant the seedlings and to protect them, the project could not succeed. Murray's analysis of why previous projects had been unable to obtain the peasants' cooperation was based on his firsthand knowledge of Haitian peasant life and on certain principles of anthropological theory. Haitian peasants are market oriented—they produce crops for cash sale. Yet previous attempts to get them to plant trees stipulated that the trees should not be sold. Instead the peasants were told that they were an unmarketable national treasure. Thus, trees were presented as exactly the opposite of the cash crops that the peasants planted on their own behalf. Putting himself in the peasants' shoes, Murray realized that previous reforestation projects had created an adverse balance of costs over benefits for the peasants. It was perfectly rational for the peasants to let their goats eat the seedlings instead of donating their labor and land to trees that they would be forbidden to harvest (or could only harvest 30 or 40 years in the future). Accordingly, Murray decided to distribute the trees as a cash crop over which the peasants would have complete control. The project merely informed the peasants how to plant the trees and take care of them. They were also shown how to set the seedlings in rows between which other crops could be planted until the trees matured. They were told, too, how fast the trees would grow and how much lumber or charcoal they could expect to get at various stages of growth. Then the peasants were left on their own to decide when it would be in their best interest to cut some or all of them.

The project's goal was to assist 5,000 peasant families to plant 3 million trees in 4 years. After 4 years (1981–1985), it had in fact assisted 40,000 families to plant 20 million trees (Fig. 19.2). Considerable numbers of trees have already been used for charcoal and for building purposes. Though it remains to be seen how much extra income will eventually be generated and how much erosion has been curtailed, Murray's basic analysis appears to have been correct.

The Theory Behind the Haitian Reforestation Project

Murray predicts that cash-oriented agroforestry (see Box 19.3) will become a major feature of peasant agriculture throughout the Third World. He interprets cash-oriented agroforestry as a response to a set of infrastructural conditions that are similar to the conditions associated with the rise of agricultural modes of production out of hunting and gathering: widespread depletion of a natural resource and population pressure (see p. 61). Peasants, having depleted the trees on which they depend for soil regeneration, fuel, and building material, will now find it to their advantage to plant trees

Figure 19.2   Haitian Agroforestry Project
These trees are of the species Leucaena leucophala *and are about two-and-one-half years old. Several other species are also being planted.*

as one of their basic crops. In Murray's words (personal communication):

> The anthropologically most important element of the model is the diachronic (evolutionary) component in which I am positing a scarcity-and-stress-generated readiness for a repeat in the domain of fuel and wood of the transition from foraging to planting which began some 15 millennia ago in the domain of food.

The Not-So-Green Revolution

A more typical role for the applied anthropologist is that of critic-observer of the change process. An important example of this role can be found in the anthropological critique of the "Green Revolution." This critique again illustrates the importance of a holistic perspective for development projects.

The Green Revolution had its origin in the late 1950s in the dwarf varieties of "wonder wheat" developed by Nobel Prize winner and plant geneticist Norman Borlaug at the Rockefeller Foundation's research center in northwest Mexico. Designed to double and triple yields per acre, wonder wheat was soon followed by dwarf varieties of "miracle rice" engineered at a joint Rockefeller and Ford Foundation

---

B o x   1 9 . 3

CO-OPTING THE "DEMON" BEHIND DEFORESTATION

I propose that we look carefully at the "demon" which is currently blamed for putting the final touches on the environment of Haiti—the market which currently exists for charcoal and construction materials. It is this market, many would argue, which sabotages forever any hopes of preserving the few remaining trees in Haiti.

I would like to argue that it is precisely this market which can restore tree growth to the hills of Haiti. The demon can be "baptized" and joined in wedlock to the ecological imperatives whose major adversary he has been up till now. With creative programming we can turn the tables on history and utilize the awe-inspiring cash-generating energy present throughout Haitian society in a manner which plants trees in the ground faster than they are being cut down. If this is to be done, it must be the peasant who does it. But he will not do it voluntarily or spontaneously unless tree planting contributes to the flow of desperately needed cash into his home. I propose that the mechanism for achieving this is the introduction of cash-oriented agroforestry.

G. Murray 1984: 147.

---

research center in the Philippines. (The significance of the dwarfed forms is that short, thick stems can bear heavy loads of ripe grain without bending over.) On the basis of initial successes in Mexico and the Philippines, the new seeds were hailed as the solution to the problem of feeding the expanding population of the underdeveloped world and were soon planted in vast areas of Pakistan, India, and Indonesia. The new seeds did result in a rapid increase of grain production per capita for a brief period. However, the pace of agricultural development has been adversely affected by a number of side effects associated with intensification: a growing scarcity of suitable land, lack of water for irrigation, and floods caused by deforestation. In addition, the point of diminishing returns for the application of chemical fertilizer to the new seeds has been reached. Thus between 1984 and 1990, growth in rice yields per acre virtually ceased. And the overall rate of increase in per capita production of all grains fell to 1 percent per year while the rate of population growth remained at 2 percent. As a result, grain production per person is declining throughout much of the world, despite the Green Revolution (Brown et al. 1991: 12–13; Brown 1994: 186; see Table 19.1).

The main problem with the miracle seeds is that they were engineered to outperform native varieties of rice and wheat only if grown in fields heavily irrigated and treated with large inputs of chemical fertilizers, pesticides, insecticides, and fungicides. Without such inputs, the high-yield varieties perform little better than the native varieties, especially under adverse soil and weather conditions.

How farmers are to obtain these inputs and how and to whom they are to be distributed are difficult questions. Most peasants in the underdeveloped world not only lack access to irrigation water but are unable to pay for expensive chemical fertilizers and other chemical inputs. This means that unless extraordinary efforts are made by the governments of countries switching to miracle seeds, the chief beneficiaries of the Green Revolution are the wealthy farmers who already occupy the irrigated lands and who are best able to pay for the chemical inputs (Walsh, 1991; Sharma and Poleman 1993).

The Green Revolution in Java

Anthropologist Richard Franke (1974) studied the Green Revolution in central Java. Even though yield increases of up to 70 percent were being obtained, in the village studied by Franke only 20 percent of the farming households had joined the program. The chief beneficiaries were the farmers who were already better off than average, owned the most land,

T a b l e   1 9 . 1

REGIONAL AND WORLD GRAIN PRODUCTION PER PERSON,

PEAK YEAR AND 1990

REGION	PEAK PRODUCTION		1990 PRODUCTION	CHANGE SINCE PEAK YEAR
	(year)	(kilograms)	(kilograms)	(percent)
Africa	1967	169	121	−28
E. Europe and Soviet Union	1978	826	763	− 8
Latin America	1981	250	210	−16
North America	1981	1,509	1,324	−12
Western Europe	1984	538	496	− 8
Asia	1984	227	217	− 4
World	1984	343	329	− 4

Source: Brown et al. 1991:13.

and had adequate supplies of water. The poorest families did not adopt the new seeds. They made ends meet by working part time for well-to-do farmers who lent them money to buy food or who paid them in kind (Fig. 19.3). Moreover, the richer farmers prevented their part-time workers from adopting the new seeds. The wealthier farmers feared they would lose their supply of cheap labor, and the poor farmers feared that if they cut themselves off from their patrons, they would have no one to turn to in case of sickness or drought. Franke concludes that the theories behind the Green Revolution are primarily rationalizations for ruling elites trying to find a way to achieve economic development without the social and political transformation their societies need.

Purely technological solutions often fail to achieve their intended purpose because of the failure to take into account other and equally important parts of sociocultural systems.

Medical Anthropology

Another central focus of applied anthropology is the interaction between culture, disease, and health care (Johnson and Sargent 1990). Anthropologists have, for example, studied the ethnography of everyday life in hospitals, organizations that offer a rich source of jarring discrepancies between the emics of various staff specialists and the etics of patient care. From the perspective of the hospital bureaucracy, its various rules and regulations are designed to promote the health and well-being of patients. In fact, numerous studies have shown that the main effect of many rules and regulations is to shock and depersonalize the patients and to create in them a level of apprehension comparable to that which

can be observed in an Ndembu boy awaiting the rite of circumcision in the "place of death" (see p. 230).

On entering the hospital, patients are stripped of their clothing and their money. They become a case in a numbered room wearing a numbered bracelet for identification (the same way newborn babies are numbered). Groups of costumed personnel (some even wearing masks) speak to them in a strange new dialect: "Did you void this morning?" "When was your last B.M.?" (bowel movement). "You're going to have an EEG" (electroencephalogram). Patients are awakened, fed, and put to sleep according to a rigid schedule, and they are often kept uninformed about their condition and what is happening to them (Fig. 19.4). One might conclude that many hospital rules exist primarily for the convenience of the staff and have an adverse effect on the health and well-being of the patients (Foster and Anderson 1978: 170–171).

Unfortunately, discovering what is wrong with hospitals and health care delivery is easier than discovering how to change them for the better. As Melvin Konner, who is an M.D. and an anthropologist, has pointed out, medical anthropologists may be lessening their effectiveness as agents of change by adopting an adversarial and negative tone. "Modern medicine," writes Konner (1991: 81), is "not a conspiracy against humanitarianism, cost efficiency, comprehensible language, patient compliance, patient autonomy, cultural differences, folk beliefs about health, or any of the other nonmedical dimensions it handles less than perfectly." Konner does not deny that physicians tend to ignore cultural factors in disease, practice "defensive medicine" aimed more at protecting themselves against lawsuits than at curing their patients, and rely excessively on technology. But these defects arise from systemic forces rather than the venality of physicians as a group:

Figure 19.3   Rice Harvest, Java
Threshing harvested bundles of rice stalks.

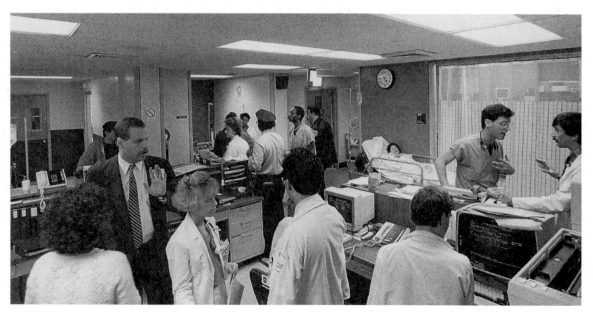

Figure 19.4   Emergency Room of a Metropolitan Hospital
Bewildered patients?

If third party payers [insurance companies] prefer to pay for expensive hospital care of the dying rather than dignified hospices or home care, that is not the fault of physicians. If society lacks compassion for the ill poor, making the doctor–patient encounter intolerably brief, stressful and inadequate for both, it is neither fair or analytically satisfying to blame the doctor or to rail against 'bourgeois' medicine.

[Konner 1991: 81]

KURU

Medical anthropology has an important role to play in helping physical anthropologists and medical researchers understand the interaction between cultural and natural factors that cause people to become ill. The solution of the mystery of Kuru is a classic instance of how medical knowledge can be advanced by examining the interaction between cultural and natural causes of a deadly disease.

During the late 1950s, reports that a previously unknown disease was rampant among the Fore peoples of highland New Guinea made headlines around the world. Victims of the disease, called Kuru, were said to be laughing themselves to death. As reliable accounts began to replace rumor, Kuru turned out to be no laughing matter. Its victims progressively lost control over their central nervous systems, including the nerves controlling their facial muscles, so that their faces were often contorted by ghastly grimaces and smiles. The disease was always fatal within a year or two of its first symptoms (Fig. 19.5).

Researchers led by Carleton Gajdusek found a puzzling epidemiological pattern (distribution and incidence of the disease in the population). Most of the victims were women and girls. Although a few young men came down with it, adult men never did. None of the neighboring tribespeople ever got Kuru, nor was it ever passed on to the Europeans who were in close contact with the Fore.

The first hypothesis was that the disease was genetic and was passed on in family lines from generation to generation. But genetics could not explain the preponderance of female victims plus the occasional young man. Rejecting the genetic explanation, Gajdusek, who was trained as a physical anthropologist and as a virologist (one who studies viruses), began to explore the possibility that Kuru was caused by a type of virus known as a slow virus, whose existence in human beings had never been demonstrated but had been long suspected. Beginning in 1963, Gajdusek inoculated chimpanzees with brain extracts of Kuru victims. After long incubation periods, the chimpanzees began to show the Kuru symptoms. The demonstration that humans could harbor slow viruses has important implications for the study of many puzzling diseases, such as multiple sclerosis, acquired immune deficiency syndrome (AIDS), and certain forms of cancer.

Figure 19.5   Young Girl with Advanced Kuru Disease

For his work, Gajdusek received the Nobel Prize for medicine in 1976.

It was left to two cultural anthropologists, Robert Glasse and Shirley Lindenbaum, however, to complete the explanations for the puzzling epidemiological pattern. Glasse and Lindenbaum drew attention to the fact that in years prior to the outbreak of Kuru, the Fore had begun to practice a form of cannibalism as part of their funeral rituals. Female relatives of the deceased consumed the dead person's brain. Since it was women who were always charged with the task of disposing of the dead, and never men, the Kuru virus never infected adult males. But what about the young men who also occasionally got Kuru? As in many cultures, the Fore's distinction between male and female roles was held less rigidly before puberty than after. Occasionally, therefore, a boy would be permitted to partake of what otherwise was defined as strictly female food. And some years later, this occasional youth would succumb to Kuru along with the much greater number of girls and women (Lindenbaum 1979).

Since neither Gajdusek nor Lindenbaum actually witnessed the eating of human flesh by the Fore, the suggestion has been made that the virus was spread merely by contact with the corpse rather than by consumption of infected morsels. Yet Fore women themselves freely told several researchers that they had previously engaged in cannibalism as part of mortuary rituals (Gajdusek 1977; Steadman and Merbs 1982; Harris 1985). Today, since the Fore have given up their cannibalism, Kuru has virtually ceased to exist among them.

AIDS (ACQUIRED IMMUNE DEFICIENCY SYNDROME)

As of 1993, over 13 million people worldwide have been infected with HIV (human immunodeficiency virus), which is the cause of AIDS. AIDS is a sexually transmitted disease that like Kuru has a complex epidemiology. The risk for getting AIDs seems to be related to patterns of sexual and related behaviors as exhibited by different populations. One way to stop or slow the spread of the virus and the disease it causes is to identify and modify risk-increasing and risk-decreasing patterns of behavior. Anthropologists are making a contribution to this effort by providing detailed ethnographic studies of the behavior of high- and low-risk populations (Merson 1993).

The case of AIDS among the Baganda of Uganda illustrates the need for detailed ethnographic knowledge. Uganda has one of the highest HIV infection rates in the world. And the rate is highest, not among men, but among women aged 20–30. AIDS prevention programs advise women to protect themselves by sticking to one partner. In theory, this advice corresponds to traditional mating patterns and should be readily accepted. Why then are the infection rates so high? One problem is that the Baganda have rules for breaking the rule of monogamy. Thus Baganda women recognize the need to seek an additional partner if they find themselves under severe economic distress. Women who affirm this rule were actually found to have significantly higher rates of infection. Clearly, therefore, a woman can follow the advice to stick with one man only if she has alternative means of supplementing her income. Moreover, though women may practice monogamy, the men traditionally expect to have more than one wife plus additional sexual partners. Finally, most men and women know that condoms reduce the risk of contracting AIDS, but men are adamant in their refusal to use them, and Baganda women cannot refuse to have sex with their husbands (adapted from McGrath et al. 1992).

A particularly tragic aspect of the AIDS epidemic is that mothers can transmit the virus to newborns during birth. This outcome is not automatic, however; not all children of infected mothers become infected. But if they do, they have a short life expectancy. Of all HIV-positive women, intravenous drug users are the least likely to opt for terminating their pregnancies. The reason for this seems obvious: As intravenous drug users, these women have lost their sense of responsibility and are unable to think of the consequences of their behavior for their children. The full extent of their depravity is revealed by the fact that many of these women already have children whom they are unable to take care of and who are being raised by relatives or adoptive parents. But this reasoning can be stood on its head. An anthropological study carried out in the Bronx, New York, suggests a wholly different interpretation: Women who find themselves isolated by disease, poverty, and drug addiction desperately want to have children of their own to reaffirm their status as women and as human beings. It is the very fact that their children have been taken away from them that motivates them to get pregnant and have another child despite the terrible risk that they may not be able to see the child grow to adulthood (adapted from Pivnik et al. 1991).

Advocacy Anthropology

The fact that the implementation phase of a project is often controlled by administrators or politicians who will not accept the anthropologist's analysis or suggestions has led a number of applied anthropologists to adopt the role of advocate. Advocacy anthropologists have fought to improve conditions in women's jails, lobbied in state legislatures for raising welfare allotments, submitted testimony before congressional committees in support of child health care programs, lobbied against the construction of dams and highways that would have an adverse effect on local communities, and engaged in many other consciousness-raising and political activities.

Witnessing for the Hungry and Homeless

The distinction between acting on behalf of a group's interests and serving as an expert witness concerning the violation of a group's rights is an important one. Anthropologist Anna Lou Dehavenon (1989–1990) has studied the causes of urban hunger and homelessness in New York City and has served as an expert witness in court cases designed to help the poor. Her work has focused on two problems: the plight of individuals and families who need food and shelter on an emergency basis and the plight of individuals and families whose welfare entitlements have lapsed as a result of bureaucratic apathy and ineptitude.

By doing fieldwork in the city's emergency assistance units, Dehavenon was able to document the failure of these units to find temporary shelter for homeless families until the early hours of the morning. A lawsuit brought against the city used her data to compel the city's human resource administration to find suitable shelter during regular working hours if possible but in no case later than midnight.

Dehavenon discovered that the appearance of families seeking emergency food help was also closely connected with the administrative phenomenon known as "churning." Churning results when people on welfare lose their entitlements as a result of a real or inaccurately recorded failure on their part to comply with bureaucratic requirements. The requirements most often at issue have to do with failure to keep appointments with a caseworker as indicated in a mailed notification or failure to supply requested information or fill out a questionnaire. The most common reasons for not complying with these administrative rules stem from problems of communication. Mailboxes are frequently broken into; postal employees give up trying to find the persons being contacted and write "whereabouts unknown." And, of course, a considerable amount of correspondence sent by people in compliance to welfare offices is not routed to the proper desk. Moreover, many welfare recipients are ill and cannot keep their appointments. Regardless of the reason, the welfare recipients lose their entitlement until the case can be reopened pending completion of proper forms and other procedures that may take as long as 2 or 3 months. While this administrative churning is going on, an estimated 18,000 people a month who are legally entitled to assistance find themselves in a food emergency, which often means that an individual or family has been without solid food for two days or incurred considerable weight loss over the previous month. Others find themselves without money for rent—hence, the connection between churning and the people showing up at the emergency assistance units (see Box 19.4).

By documenting and measuring these problems, by bringing them to the attention of high-ranking administrators in the city government, by proposing administrative reforms, and by releasing information to the news media, Dehavenon's research has helped bring about a substantial reduction in the amount of churning. For example, welfare recipients are now alerted to look for mail setting up appointments. The human resources administration has also made a start toward abandoning the policy of dropping people whose mail comes back "whereabouts unknown" or who fail to return questionnaires. But much remains to be done. Some of Dehavenon's additional targets and goals:

> People who have medical problems or lack a fixed address should receive important notices by messenger.
>
> All missed appointments should be automatically rescheduled once.
>
> Recipients should have 60 days to comply with an administrative requirement. Their cases should not be

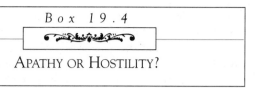

Box 19.4

APATHY OR HOSTILITY?

A profound indifference to the plight of the poor may explain their ever-worsening condition of the past several years. Churning, however, is difficult to explain as a product of indifference alone. Rather, it is the direct and logical consequence of a government policy that places a high premium on preventing the erroneous issuance of benefits, but often seems to care much less if eligible recipients are denied the assistance they desperately need to survive. Unless our society is one consumed by hostility to the poor, it must put a stop to this perverse policy and secure for poor people the benefits to which they are entitled.

Dehavenon, 1990: 254.

closed but suspended so that as soon as they are in compliance, their payments can resume retroactively.

To Advocate or Not to Advocate: Is That the Question?

Despite her involvement with poverty problems, Dehavenon regards herself as an expert witness rather than as an advocate for the poor. Many other applied anthropologists prefer not to be categorized as professional advocates. They hold the view that the only legitimate professional function of the applied anthropologist is to provide administrators, politicians, or lawyers with an objective analysis of a situation or organization and that, at most, action should be limited to suggesting but not implementing a plan. In this way, applied anthropologists hope to preserve the scientific standing of anthropology since an all-out attempt to achieve a practical goal frequently involves rhetorical skills and cajolery, and may increase the risk of biased presentations.

Against this view, advocacy anthropologists insist that the objectivity of anthropology and the other social sciences is illusory and that failure to push for the implementation of a goal represents a form of advocacy in itself. The objectivity is illusory, they argue, because political and personal biases control the commitment to study one situation rather than another (to study the poor rather than the wealthy, for example; see p. 170). And refraining from action is itself a form of action and therefore a form of advocacy because one's inaction assures that someone else's actions will weigh more heavily in the final outcome. Anthropologists who do not actively use their skills and knowledge to bring about what they believe to be a solution simply make it easier for others with opposite beliefs to prevail. Such anthropologists are themselves part of the problem (Cohen 1984b).

No consensus exists among anthropologists about how to resolve these views of the proper relationship between knowledge and the achievement of controversial practical goals. Perhaps the only resolution of this dilemma is the one that now exists: We must search our individual consciences and act accordingly.

In conclusion, it should be emphasized that we have looked at only a few of the many faces of applied anthropology. As Box 19.5 suggests, many other equally important and interesting cases could have been presented.

Chapter Summary

Applied anthropology is concerned with research that has practical applications. Its core consists of research sponsored by public and private organizations with an interest in achieving practical goals. The role of the applied cultural anthropologist may consist merely in researching the possible means of attaining such goals; sometimes it includes drawing up plans and helping implement them, as well as evaluating the results of implementation. Applied anthropologists involved in implementation are known as practitioners of action anthropology. Beyond that core, other forms of research may also be considered part of applied anthropology. For example, abstract theorizing often has important practical implications, as in the case of alternative theories about the causes of underdevelopment or urban poverty.

Box 19.5

PUTTING ANTHROPOLOGY TO PRACTICAL USE

TYPE OF ACTION	ANTHROPOLOGIST
Designed and spread inexpensive storage facilities for potatoes in highland Peru and the Philippines.	Werge 1979; Rhoades 1984
Prevented construction of dam that threatened a preexisting irrigation system in the Southwest.	Jacobs 1978
Helped mothers feed babies a life-saving remedy for dehydration resulting from diarrhea in Third World countries.	
Helped get fraud charges against Bannock-Shoshoni women dismissed, on grounds of cultural misunderstanding by English-speaking social workers.	Joans 1984
Evaluated community health projects in Tumaco, Colombia.	Buzzard 1982; Kendall 1984
Helped prepare litigation for a $47 million award to the Pembina Chippewa Indians for the loss of their tribal lands.	Feraca 1984
Developed quality-control procedures for the hotel industry.	Glover et al. 1984
Designed, implemented, and evaluated a community health program in Miami to take account of ethnically diverse medical needs.	Weidman 1983

Applied anthropology has three major and distinctive contributions to make to the analysis and solution of urgent practical problems: (1) exposure of ethnocentric biases; (2) a holistic viewpoint stressing the long as well as the short term, the interconnectedness of the parts of a sociocultural system, and the whole of the system as well as its parts; and (3) a commitment to distinguishing etic behavioral events from emic plans and ideologies. All too often, the intended effects of an organization's plans and policies differ sharply from their actual everyday etic consequences.

One important focus of applied anthropology is the problem of underdevelopment. This problem was the focus of the Cornell–Peru Vicos project, in which applied anthropologists covered the entire range of research, planning, implementation, and evaluation.

The Haitian Agroforestry Project is another example of anthropological research, planning, implementation, and evaluation—in this case, applied to the goal of getting peasants to plant and protect trees.

Finally, the case of the Not-So-Green Revolution illustrates the importance both of a holistic perspective for development projects and of the role of the applied anthropologist as critic rather than change agent. It is futile to seek a purely technical solution to poverty and underdevelopment since the effects on every technological innovation are modified by the total sociocultural context into which it is introduced.

Another focus of applied anthropology is medical anthropology. Studies of health care delivery systems and of everyday life in hospitals have attracted considerable interest among anthropologists. The case of Kuru illustrates the importance of knowing the cultural context in which diseases occur. Understanding the role of cannibalism in funerary rituals and the development of distinct dietary patterns among men and women provided the key to solving the disease's mysterious epidemiology.

Many anthropologists have recently become involved in the attempt to slow the spread of HIV. As in the case of Kuru, the epidemiology of AIDS presents puzzles that can be solved only by a detailed ethnographic knowledge of the sexual behavior of people who have and have not contracted the disease.

As brought out in the case of the "churning" of welfare recipients in a merciless bureaucratic machine, there is a legitimate role for anthropologists who hope to see their research used to help people who cannot help themselves.

Appendix

A HISTORY OF THEORIES OF CULTURE

The Enlightenment

Nineteenth-Century Evolutionism

Social Darwinism

Marxist Evolutionism

The Reaction to Nineteenth-Century
Evolutionism

Diffusionism

British Functionalism and Structural
Functionalism

Culture and Personality

The New Evolutionism

Dialectical Materialism

Cultural Materialism

Sociobiology

Structuralism

Particularizing Approaches

This appendix serves as a brief outline of the history of the development of anthropological theories. It also presents the main research strategies employed by contemporary anthropologists.

The impulse lying behind the development of cultural anthropology is probably as old as our species. Members of different human groups have always been curious about the customs and traditions of strangers. The fact that people who live in different societies build different kinds of shelters, wear different kinds of clothing, practice different kinds of marriages, worship different spirits and gods, and speak different languages has always been a source of puzzlement. The most ancient and still most common approach to these differences is to assume that one's own beliefs and practices are normal expressions of the true or right way of life, as justified by the teachings of one's ancestors and the commandments or instructions of supernatural beings. Most cultures have origin myths that set forth the sequence of events leading to the beginning of the world and of humanity, and to the adoption of the group's way of life. The failure of other groups to share the same way of life can then be attributed to their failure to be true, real, or normal human beings.

The Enlightenment

As Europe entered the age of exploration and mercantile expansion, interest in describing and explaining cultural diversity increased. The discovery and exploration of a whole "New World"—the Americas—opened the eyes of philosophers, political leaders, theologians, and scientists to astonishing contrasts in the human condition.

Toward the middle of the eighteenth century, during the period known as the Enlightenment, the first systematic attempts to offer scientific theories of cultural differences began to emerge. The common theme of these theories was the idea of progress. It was held by scholars such as Adam Smith, Adam Ferguson, Jean Turgot, and Denis Diderot that cultures differed not because they expressed innate differences in human capacities or preferences, but because they manifested different levels of rational knowledge and achievement. It was believed that humankind, including Europe's ancestors, had at one time lived in an "uncivilized" condition, lacking a knowledge of farming and animal husbandry, laws, and governments. Gradually, however, guided by the ever-expanding role of reason in human affairs, humankind progressed from a "state of nature" to a state of

enlightened civilization. Cultural differences thus largely resulted from the different degrees of intellectual and moral progress achieved by different peoples.

Nineteenth-Century Evolutionism

The idea of cultural progress was the forerunner of the concept of cultural evolution that dominated theories of culture during the nineteenth century. Cultures were usually seen as moving through various stages of development, ending up with something resembling Euro-American lifestyles. Auguste Comte postulated a progression from theological to metaphysical to positivistic (scientific) modes of thought. Georg Wilhelm Friedrich Hegel saw a movement from a time when only one man was free (the Asiatic tyrant) to a time when some were free (Greek city-states) to a time when all would be free (European constitutional monarchies). Others wrote of an evolution from status (such as slave, noble, or commoner) to contract (employee and employer, buyer and seller); from small communities of people who knew each other's faces to large, impersonal societies; from slave to military to industrial societies; from animism to polytheism to monotheism; from magic to science; from female-dominated horticultural societies to male-dominated agricultural societies; and from many other hypothetical earlier and simpler stages to later and more complex ones.

One of the most influential schemes was that proposed by the American anthropologist Lewis Henry Morgan in his book *Ancient Society*. Morgan divided the evolution of culture into three main stages: savagery, barbarism, and civilization. These stages had figured in evolutionary schemes as early as the sixteenth century, but Morgan subdivided them and filled them out in greater detail and with greater reference to ethnographic evidence than had anyone else. (Morgan himself carried out a lifelong study of the Iroquois, who lived near his hometown of Rochester, New York.) Morgan held that "lower savagery" subsistence had been gained exclusively by gathering wild foods, that people mated promiscuously, and that the basic unit of society was the small nomadic "horde" that owned its resources communally. By the period of "upper savagery," the bow and arrow had been invented, brother–sister marriage was prohibited, and descent was reckoned primarily through women. With the invention of pottery and the beginning of farming came the transition to barbarism. Incest prohibitions were extended to include all descendants in the female line, and clan and village became the basic structural units.

The development of metallurgy marked the upper phase of barbarism; descent shifted from the female to the male line, men married several women at one time (polygyny), and private property appeared. Finally, the invention of writing, the development of civil government, and the emergence of the monogamous family marked the beginning of "civilization."

Social Darwinism

In addition to the greater complexity and detail of the nineteenth-century evolutionary schemes, they differed in one fundamental way from eighteenth-century notions of universal progress. Almost all the nineteenth-century schemes (with the conspicuous exception of Marxism) postulated that cultures evolved in conjunction with the evolution of human biological types and races. Not only were the cultures of modern-day Europe and America seen as the pinnacle of cultural progress, but the white race (especially its male half) was seen as the epitome of biological progress.

This fusion of biological evolutionism with cultural evolutionism is often but incorrectly attributed to the influence of Charles Darwin. In fact, the development of biological interpretations of cultural evolution preceded the appearance of Darwin's *Origin of Species,* and Darwin was himself greatly influenced by social philosophers such as Thomas Malthus and Herbert Spencer. Malthus's notion that population growth led to an inevitable "struggle for existence" had been elaborated by Spencer into the idea of the "survival of the fittest" in social life before Darwin published his theories of biological evolution.

The success of Darwin's biological theory of the survival of the fittest (he called it "natural selection") greatly enhanced the popularity of the view that social and cultural evolution also depended on biological evolution. After the publication of Darwin's *Origin of Species,* a movement known as Social Darwinism appeared based on the belief that cultural and biological progress depended on the free play of competitive forces in the struggle of individual against individual, nation against nation, and race against race. The most influential Social Darwinist was Herbert Spencer, who went so far as to advocate the end of all attempts to provide charity and relief for the unemployed and impoverished classes and the so-called backward races on the grounds that such assistance interfered with the operation of the "law of the survival of the fittest" and merely prolonged the agony and deepened the misery of those who were "unfit." Spencer used Social Darwinism to justify the capitalist free enterprise system, and his influence continues to be felt among advocates of unrestrained capitalism as well as among advocates of white supremacy.

Marxist Evolutionism

Although the writings and thoughts of Karl Marx were diametrically opposed to Social Darwinism, Marxism was also heavily influenced by the prevailing nineteenth-century notions of cultural evolution and progress. Marx saw cultures passing through the stages of primitive communism, slave society, feudalism, capitalism, and communism. Moreover, like many of his contemporaries, Marx stressed the importance of the role of struggle in achieving cultural evolution and progress. All history, according to Marx, was the outcome of the struggle between social classes for control over the means of production. The proletarian class, brought into existence by capitalism, was destined to abolish private property and bring about the final stage of history: communism. On reading Morgan's *Ancient Society,* Marx and his associate Friedrich Engels thought they had found a confirmation of their idea that during the first stage of cultural evolution there was no private property and that the successive stages of cultural progress had been brought about by changes in the "mode of production"—as, for example, in the co-occurrence of the development of agriculture and the transition between savagery and barbarism in Morgan's scheme. Morgan's *Ancient Society* provided the basis for Engels's *The Origin of the Family, Private Property and the State,* which until the middle of the twentieth century served as a cornerstone of Marxist anthropology.

The Reaction to Nineteenth-Century Evolutionism

Early in the twentieth century, anthropologists took the lead in challenging the evolutionary schemes and doctrines of both the Social Darwinists and the Marxist Communists. In the United States, the dominant theoretical position was developed by Franz Boas and his students and was known as historical particularism. According to Boas, nineteenth-century attempts to discover the laws of cultural evolution and to schematize the stages of cultural progress were founded on insufficient empirical evidence. Boas argued that each culture has its own long and unique history. To understand or explain a particular culture, the best one can do is to reconstruct the unique path it had followed. The emphasis on the uniqueness of each culture amounted to a denial of the prospects for a generalizing science of culture. Another important feature of historical particularism is the notion of cultural relativism, which holds that there are no higher or lower forms of culture. Such terms as savagery, barbarism, and civilization merely express the ethnocentrism of people who think that their way of life is more normal than those of other peoples.

To counter the speculative "armchair" theories and ethnocentrism of the evolutionists, Boas and his students also stressed the importance of carrying out ethnographic fieldwork among non-Western peoples. As the ethnographic reports and monographs produced by the historical particularists multiplied, it became clear that the evolutionists had indeed misrepresented or overlooked the complexities of so-called primitive cultures and that they had grossly underestimated the intelligence and ingenuity of the non-Caucasoid, non-European peoples of the world.

Boas' most important achievement was his demonstration that race, language, and culture were independent aspects of the human condition. Since both similar and dissimilar cultures and languages are found among people of the same race, the Social Darwinist notion that biological and cultural evolution were part of a single process had no merit.

Diffusionism

Another early twentieth-century reaction to nineteenth-century evolutionism is known as diffusionism. According to its advocates, the principal source of cultural differences and similarities is not the inventiveness of the human mind but the tendency of humans to imitate one another. Diffusionists see cultures as a patchwork of elements derived from a haphazard series of borrowings from near and distant peoples. In the critical case of the origin of Native-American civilizations, for example, diffusionists argued that the technology and architecture of the Inca of Peru and the Aztecs of Mexico were diffused from Egypt or from Southeast Asia rather than invented independently (see p. 11 for a critique of diffusionism).

British Functionalism and Structural Functionalism

In Great Britain, the dominant early twentieth-century research strategies are known as functionalism and structural functionalism. According to the functionalists, the main task of cultural anthropology is to describe the recurrent functions of customs and institutions rather than to explain the origins of cultural differences and similarities. According to one of the leading functionalists, Bronislaw Malinowski, the attempt to discover the origins of cultural elements was doomed to be speculative and unscientific because of the absence of written records. Once we have understood the function of an institution, argued Malinowski, then we have understood all we will ever understand about its origins.

A. R. Radcliffe-Brown was the principal advocate of structural functionalism. According to Radcliffe-Brown, the main task of cultural anthropology was even narrower than that proposed by Malinowski. Whereas Malinowski emphasized the contribution of cultural elements to the biological and psychological welfare of individuals, Radcliffe-Brown and the structural functionalists stressed the contribution of the biological and psychological welfare of individuals to the maintenance of the social system. For the structural functionalists, the function of maintaining the system took precedence over all others. But like Malinowski, the structural functionalists labeled all attempts to find origins as speculative history.

Thus, the functionalists and structural functionalists evaded the question of the general, recurrent causes of cultural differences, while emphasizing the general, recurrent functional reasons for similarities. This set the functionalists and structural functionalists apart from the diffusionists as much as from the nineteenth-century evolutionists. Nor were the functionalists and structural functionalists sympathetic to Boas' historical particularism. But like Boas and his students, the British functionalists and structural functionalists stressed the importance of carrying out fieldwork, insisting that only after 2 or more years of immersion in the language, thoughts, and events of another culture could anthropologists provide valid and reliable ethnographic descriptions.

Culture and Personality

In turning away from the nineteenth-century notions of causality and evolution, many anthropologists, influenced by the writings of Sigmund Freud, attempted to interpret cultures in psychological terms. The writings of Freud and the antievolutionism of Boas set the stage for the development of the approach known as culture and personality. Two of Boas' most famous students, Ruth Benedict and Margaret Mead, pioneered in the development of culture and personality theories. Such theories in general may be described as psychological forms of functionalism that relate cultural beliefs and practices to individual personality, and individual personality to cultural beliefs and practices. As we saw in Chapter 16, many advocates of the culture and personality approach stress the importance of early childhood experiences such as toilet training, breast feeding, and sex training in the formation of a basic or modal type of adult personality or national character. Some culture and personality theories attempt to explain cultural differences and similarities as a consequence of basic or modal personality. In general, however, culture and personality advocates do not deal with the problem of why the beliefs and practices that mold particular personality types or national characters occur in some cultures but not in others.

The New Evolutionism

After World War II, increasing numbers of anthropologists became dissatisfied with the antievolutionism and lack of broad generalizations and causal explanations characteristic of the first half of the century. Under the influence of Leslie White, an effort was launched to reexamine the works of the nineteenth-century evolutionists such as Lewis Henry Morgan, to correct their ethnographic errors, and to identify their positive contribution to the development of a science of culture. White pioneered in postulating that the overall direction of cultural evolution was largely determined by the quantities of energy that could be captured and put to work per capita per year (see p. 15).

At the same time (about 1940 to 1950), Julian Steward laid the basis for the development of the approach known as cultural ecology, which stressed the interaction between natural conditions such as soils, rainfall, and temperature with cultural factors such as technology and economy as the cause of both cultural differences and similarities.

The return to broad evolutionary points of view in the second half of the twentieth century among American cultural anthropologists was stimulated by archaeological evidence that diffusion could not account for the remarkable similarities between the development of states and empires in the New and Old Worlds (see p. 56). The step-by-step process by which Native-American peoples in the Andean and Mesoamerican regions independently developed their own elaborate civilizations is now fairly well known, thanks to modern archaeological research.

Julian Steward was especially impressed with the parallels in the evolution of the ancient civilizations of Peru, Mexico, Egypt, Mesopotamia, and China, and called for a renewed effort by anthropologists to examine and explain these remarkable uniformities. Yet Steward was careful to distinguish his scheme of cultural evolution from the more extreme versions of nineteenth-century evolutionism. According to Steward, the problem with these earlier evolutionists was that they postulated a single or unilinear set of stages for all cultures, whereas he postulated many, or multilinear, paths of development depending on initial environmental, technological, and other conditions.

Dialectical Materialism

Both White and Steward were influenced by Marx and Engels' emphasis on changes in the material aspects of modes of reproduction as the mainspring of cultural evolution. However, neither accepted the full set of Marxist propositions embodied in the point of view known as dialectical materialism, which gained considerable popularity among Western anthropologists for the first time in the 1960s and 1970s. Dialectical materialists hold that history has a determined direction—namely, that of the emergence of communism and of classless society. The sources of this movement are the class conflicts caused by the internal contradictions of sociocultural systems. To understand the causes of sociocultural differences and similarities, social scientists must not only study these contradictions but must take part in the "dialectical" struggles that lead to progress toward communism. The most important contradiction in all societies is that between the means of production (roughly, the technology) and the relations of production (who owns the means of production). In the words of Karl Marx: "The mode of production in material life determines the general character of the social, political, and spiritual process of life. It is not the consciousness of men that determines their existence, but on the contrary, their social existence determines their consciousness" (1970 [1859]: 21).

Cultural Materialism

Further elaboration of the theoretical perspectives of Marx, White, and Steward has led to the appearance of the point of view known as cultural materialism. This research strategy holds that the primary task of anthropology is to give causal explanations for the differences and similarities in thought and behavior found among human groups. Like dialectical materialists, cultural materialists hold that this task can best be carried out by studying the material constraints to which human existence is subjected. These constraints arise from the need to produce food, shelter, tools, and machines, and to reproduce human populations within limits set by biology and the environment. These are called material constraints or conditions in order to distinguish them from constraints or conditions imposed by ideas and other mental or spiritual aspects of human life such as values, religion, and art. For cultural materialists, the most likely causes of variation in the mental or spiritual aspects of human life are the differences in the material costs and benefits of satisfying basic needs in a particular habitat.

Cultural materialists differ from dialectical materialists mainly in rejecting the notion that anthropology must become part of a political movement aimed at destroying capitalism and at furthering the interests of the proletariat. Cultural materialists allow for a diversity of political motivation among anthropologists united by a common commitment to the development of a science of culture. In addition, cultural materialists reject the notion that all important cultural changes result from the playing out of dialectical contradictions, holding that much of cultural evolution has resulted from the gradual accumulation of useful traits through a process of trial and error.

Sociobiology

Sociobiology is a research strategy that attempts to explain some sociocultural differences and similarities in terms of natural selection. It is based on a refinement of natural selection known as the principle of inclusive fitness. This principle states that natural selection favors traits that spread an individual's genes by increasing not only the number of an individual's offspring, but the number of offspring of close relatives, such as brothers and sisters, who carry many of the same genes. What controls biological evolution, therefore, is whether a trait increases the inclusive total of an individual's genes in succeeding generations and not merely the number of one's own progeny.

Applied to cultural evolution, human sociobiology states that cultural traits are selected if they maximize an individual's reproductive success reckoned in terms of inclusive fitness. Selection does not necessarily bring about a one-to-one correlation between genes and behavior but between genes and tendencies to behave in certain ways rather than others. For example, sociobiologists hold that the tendency for humans to forage in a manner that optimizes energy produced per unit of time is selected because it maximizes reproductive success (Wilson 1975, 1978; Lewontin et al. 1984).

From a cultural materialist perspective, it is not necessary to posit that useful traits are always selected because they maximize reproductive success. In the case of optimal foraging theory, for example (see p. 52), the favorable balance of energetic benefits over costs in satisfying an individual's nutritional needs is sufficient to understand why certain animals are captured and others are not, without reference to its effects on reproductive success. Moreover, it is clear, contrary to sociobiological principle, that humans do not always seek to maximize reproductive success. The most glaring discrepancy is the low rate of reproductive success characteristic of the affluent classes in industrial society. The behavior of one-child American families scarcely seems to be dominated by the urge to have as many children as possible.

Structuralism

Not all post–World War II approaches to cultural theory are aimed at explaining the origin of cultural differences and similarities. In France, under the leadership of Claude Levi-Strauss, the point of view known as structuralism has been widely accepted. Structuralism is concerned only with the psychological uniformities that underlie apparent differences in thought and behavior. According to Levi-Strauss, these uniformities arise from the structure of the human brain and of unconscious thought processes. The most important structural feature of the human mind is the tendency to dichotomize, or to think in terms of binary oppositions, and then to attempt to mediate this opposition by a third concept, which may serve as the basis for yet another opposition. A recurrent opposition present in many myths, for example, is culture versus nature. From the structuralist point of view, the more cultures change, the more they remain the same, since they are all merely variations on the theme of recurrent oppositions and their resolutions. Structuralism, therefore, is concerned with explaining the similarities among cultures, but not with explaining the differences. See the section "Myth and Binary Contrasts" in Chapter 18 for an example of a structuralist analysis.

Particularizing Approaches

Mention must also be made of the fact that many anthropologists continue to reject all general causal viewpoints, holding that the chief aim of ethnography ought to be the study and interpretation of the emics of different cultures—their world views, symbols, values, religions, philosophies, and systems of meanings. During the 1980s, these approaches grew in popularity and were characterized by rejection of the distinction between observer and observed, etics and emics, and science and nonscience. Extreme relativism (see p. 8) and antievolutionism reminiscent of Franz Boas' historical particularism also characterize recent approaches. For many contemporary cultural anthropologists, the main task of ethnography is to become familiar with a culture in the way one becomes familiar with a book or a poem, and then to "read" or interpret it as if one were a literary critic. The goal of these anthropologists is not to discover the scientific truth about a culture but to compose interpretations about the "other"—the other culture—that are elegant and convincing.

One recent manifestation of this line of development is called deconstruction. It focuses on the hidden intentions and unexpressed biases of the author of an ethnography rather than on the question of what the culture being described is really like.

Although deconstructionists make valid points about the need to expose biases and prejudices in scientific descriptions (remember Malinoswski), their flat rejection of scientific truth as a goal of ethnography results in fragmented, contradictory, and essentially nihilistic notions about the human condition.

GLOSSARY

Adaptation The process by which organisms, or cultural elements, undergo change in form or function in response to threats to their existence and replication.

Adaptive Capacity Previously established ability of a minority to compete for upward mobility in a given sociocultural context.

Affinal A relationship based on marriage.

Affixes Bound MORPHEMES that occur at the initial position in a word.

Age Grades In some societies, formally institutionalized segmentation of the population, by sex and chronological age, with RITES OF PASSAGE announcing the transition from one status to the next.

Agriculture The cultivation of domesticated crops.

Alleles Variants of GENES that occupy the same location on corresponding CHROMOSOMES.

Allophone A variant of a PHONEME; all the contrastive sounds with the class of sounds designated by a particular phoneme.

Ambilineal Descent The reckoning of descent through a combination of male and female ancestors establishing a descent relationship with a particular ancestor; resembles BILATERAL DESCENT but maintains a narrow rather than a broadening span of kin on each ascending generation.

Ambilocality Residence of a couple after marriage alternatively with either the husband's or wife's kin.

Animatism The attribution of humanlike consciousness and powers to inanimate objects, natural phenomena, plants, and animals.

Animism Belief in personalized yet disembodied beings such as souls, ghosts, spirits, and gods. Compare ANIMATISM.

Anthropological Linguistics The study of the great variety of languages spoken by human beings.

Archaeology The scientific study of the remains of cultures of past ages.

Artifacts Material objects made by human hands, and having specifiable uses and functions.

Ascribed Status The attributes of an individual's position in SOCIETY that are involuntary and often inevitable, based on sex or descent.

Ascription See ASCRIBED STATUS.

Assimilation Disappearance of a group—usually a MINORITY—through the loss of biological and/or cultural distinctiveness.

Avunculocality Residence of a couple after marriage with or near the groom's mother's brother.

Band, Local A small, loosely organized group of hunter-gatherer families, occupying a specifiable territory and tending toward self-sufficiency.

Basic Personality Certain culturally defined psychological traits exhibited by members of a social group.

Berdache A male transvestite who assumes a sanctioned female role among Native American peoples.

Bilateral Descent Rule by which ego traces descent equally through both parents and through both sexes in all ascending and descending generations and collateral lines.

Blood Feud Vengeful confrontation between opposing groups of kin, set off by real or alleged homicide or other crimes, and involving continuing alternative retaliation in kind.

Bride-Price Goods or valuables transferred by the groom's kin to recompense the bride's relatives for her absence.

Cargo Cult A revitalization movement native to Melanesia based on the expectation of the imminent return of ancestors in ships, planes, and trains bringing treasures of European-manufactured goods.

Carrying Capacity The population of a species that a particular area or ECOSYSTEM can support without suffering irreversible deterioration.

Caste Widely applied as a term to a self-enclosed CLASS or Ethnic group; a stratified, endogamous descent group.

Chromosomes Threadlike structures within the cell nucleus, containing DNA, that transmit information that determines heredity.

Circulating Connubia A system of marriages in which several groups exchange spouses in one direction in a circle or in directions that alternate in each generation.

Circumcision The ritual removal of the foreskin of a male's penis or of the tip of a woman's clitoris.

Clans Kin groups whose members assume—but need not demonstrate—descent from a common ancestor.

Class, Social One of the stratified groupings within a society, characterized by specific attitudes and behavior and by differential access to power and to basic resources. Less endogamous and more open than castes or minorities.

Clines The gradual changes in traits and gene frequencies displayed by the populations of a species as the distance between them increases.

Clitoridectomy The ritual removal of a portion of a female's clitoris.

Cognatic Lineage A group whose members trace their descent genealogically from a common ancestor through the application of ambilineal descent.

Collaterals Persons who are CONSANGUINEAL kin, possessing a common ancestor, but in different lines of descent, such as cousins.

Communal Rites Ceremonies, largely religious, carried out by the social group—usually by nonprofessional specialists and celebrants.

Complementary Opposition The process by which groups unite into more and more inclusive units as they are confronted with more and more inclusive coalitions of antagonistic groups.

Consanguineal A relationship between persons based on descent, in contrast to the AFFINAL relationship of marriage.

Corvée A forced labor draft imposed by a government for public road and building construction, often in lieu of monetary taxes.

Couvade Customary restrictions on the activities of a man often associated with his wife's lying-in and birth of their child.

Cross Cousins Persons of either sex whose parents are siblings of the opposite sex; offspring of a father's sister and mother's brother. Compare PARALLEL COUSINS.

Cultural Anthropology The description and analysis of cultures of past and present ages.

Cultural Materialism The research strategy that attempts to explain the differences and similarities in thought and behavior found among human groups by studying the material constraints to which humans are subjected. These material constraints include the need to produce food, shelter, tools, and machines, and to reproduce human populations within limits set by biology and the environment.

Cultural Relativism The principle that all cultural systems are inherently equal in value and that the traits characteristic of each system need to be assessed and explained within the context in which they occur.

Culture The learned patterns of behavior and thought characteristic of a societal group.

Deep Structure The form of an utterance that is not directly observable but that accounts for the intelligibility of its SURFACE STRUCTURE.

Descent The rule for ascertaining an individual's kinship affiliation from among the range of actual or presumed connections provided by birth to a particular culturally defined father and/or mother.

Diffusion The process by which cultural traits, ways, complexes, and institutions are transferred from one cultural group to another.

Displacement The ability to communicate about items or events with which the communicators are not in direct contact.

Divination Arrival at an expectation or judgment of future events through the interpretation of omens construed as evidence.

DNA (Deoxyribonucleic Acid) The long-stranded molecules that are the principal component of CHROMOSOMES. Varied arrangements of DNA determine the GENETIC CODE and the GENOTYPE.

Dowry Compensation given at marriage to a husband or his group by his wife's group; in some instances, it is the wife who controls the compensation, in which case the transfer of wealth resembles a predeath form of inheritance for the bride.

Ecology The study of the total system of relationships among all the organisms and environmental conditions characteristic of a given area or region.

Economy The management of the production, distribution, and consumption of the natural resources, labor, and other forms of wealth available to a cultural system.

Egalitarian A type of societal group that lacks formalized differentiation in access to, and power over, basic resources among its members.

Ego The person of reference at the center of kin terminological systems.

Emics Descriptions or judgments concerning behavior, customs, beliefs, values, and so on, held by members of a societal group as culturally appropriate and valid. See also ETICS.

Enculturation The process by which individuals—usually as children—acquire behavioral patterns and other aspects of their culture from others, through observation, instruction, and reinforcement.

Endogamy The principle that requires ego to take a spouse from a group or status of which ego is a member.

Ethnocentrism The tendency to view the traits, ways, ideas, and values observed in other cultural groups as invariably inferior and less natural or logical than those of one's own group.

Ethnography The systematic description of contemporary cultures.

Etics The techniques and results of making generalizations about cultural events, behavior patterns, artifacts, thought, and ideology that are independent of the distinctions and beliefs that are significant and appropriate from the native actors' point of view. See also EMICS.

Exogamy The rule that forbids an individual from taking a spouse from within a prescribed local, kin, status, or other group in which they are both members.

Extended Family A domestic group consisting of two or more NUCLEAR FAMILIES, comprising siblings and their spouses and children, and often including their parents and married children.

Family A domiciliary and or kin grouping, variously constituted of married and related persons and their offspring, residing together for economic and reproductive purposes. See also NUCLEAR FAMILY; EXTENDED FAMILY.

Feudal System A type of historical socioeconomic organization involving a network of obligations, in which the PEASANTS are structured inferiors to their lord and are bound to provide certain payments and services in exchange for apparent privileges.

Fossils Remains or traces of plants or animals preserved—usually by mineralization—from the geological past.

Functions The systemic needs served by artifacts, patterns of behavior, and ideas; the ways in which cultural traits contribute toward maintenance, efficiency, and adaptation of the cultural system.

Gene Flow The movement of genetic material from one GENE POOL to another as a consequence of interbreeding.

Gene Pool The sum and range of variety of genes present within a given breeding population.

Genes The basic chemical units of heredity, found at particular loci on the CHROMOSOMES.

Genitor The etic male source of the sperm responsible for the birth of a particular child.

Genotype The total gene complement received by an individual organism from its parents; as distinguished from the external appearance manifest in the phenotype.

Geographic Race A breeding population, usually of considerable spatial extent, that can be described in terms of the frequencies of specifiable, characterizing genetic traits.

Ghost Dance A REVITALIZATION MOVEMENT that appeared on the North American Plains during the nineteenth century, awaiting the departure of the whites and the restoration of Indian traditional ways.

Groom Price Compensation given to a man's MATRILINEAL GROUP when he resides with his wife's matrilineal group. Very rare.

Headman In an egalitarian group, the titular head who may lead those who will follow, but is usually unable to impose sanctions to enforce his decisions or requests or deprive others of equal access to basic resources.

Hominids (Hominidae) The taxonomic family, including all living and extinct types and races of humans and proto-humans.

Ideology Cognitive and emotional aspects of the emic superstructure.

Incest Socially prohibited mating and or marriage, as within certain specified limits of real or putative KINSHIP.

Industrialization An advanced stage of techno-economic development observed particularly in modern states and colonizing powers, characterized by advanced technologies, mass production, and consumerism.

Irrigation Civilization An advanced type of preindustrial society associated with the control of extensive facilities for crop irrigation and land drainage. Usually characterized by highly centralized political institutions.

Kindred A bilateral kin group in which ego traces relationships in ever-widening collateral and lineal descent and ascent through both ego's maternal and paternal kin and ego's sons and daughters.

Kin Group A social aggregate of individuals related by either CONSANGUINEAL ties of descent or AFFINAL ties of marriage.

Kinship The network of culturally recognized interpersonal relations through which individuals are related to one another by ties of descent or marriage.

Kinship Terminology The system of terms by which members of a KIN GROUP customarily address or refer to one another, denoting their relationship.

Language Family A group of related languages historically derived from a common antecedent language.

Levirate Custom favoring the remarriage of a widow to her deceased husband's brother.

Linneage A KIN GROUP whose members can actually trace their relationship through specific, known genealogical links along the recognized line of descent, as either MATRILINEAL or PATRILINEAL.

Magic The practice of certain rituals that are presumed to coerce desired practical outcomes.

Majority The superordinate group in a hierarchy of racial, cultural, or religious minorities. The majority is usually, but not necessarily, not only politically and economically dominant but more numerous as well.

Mana A term for the impersonal pervasive power expected in certain objects and roles. See also ANIMATISM.

Marriage A socially sanctioned form of heterosexual mating and coresidence establishing duties and obligations with respect to sex and reproduction; variant forms are homosexual matings and childless marriages.

Matriarchy The political and economic dominance of men by women; no cases have been confirmed.

Matrifocal Family A domestic group comprising one or more adult women, and their offspring, within which husbands-fathers are not permanent residents.

Matrilineality Descent reckoning is through females exclusively.

Matrilocality Residence of a couple after marriage in or near the wife's mother's domicile.

Messianic Movement A movement offering REVITALIZATION or salvation through following the spiritual or activist leadership of a prophetic individual or messiah; often against vested authority.

Minority Subordinate endogamous descent groups based on racial, cultural, or religious criteria found in all state societies.

Modal Personality The type of BASIC PERSONALITY that is most common in a given society.

Monogamy Marriage between one man and one woman for their lifetimes.

Morphemes The smallest sequence of sounds to which a definite meaning is attached.

Natural Selection The process by which differential reproductive success changes the frequency of genes in populations. One of the major forces of evolution.

Neolocal Residence Residence of a couple after marriage apart from the parental domicile of either spouse.

Nuclear Family A basic social grouping comprising married male and female parents and their offspring.

Oedipus Complex Sexually charged hostility, usually repressed, between parents and children of the same sex.

Parallel Cousins Persons whose parents are siblings of the same sex; the sons and daughters of two sisters or of two brothers.

Parallel Cultural Evolution Evolution represented by instances in which significant aspects, patternings, or institutions in two or more cultural systems undergo similar adaptations and transformations; presumably in response to the operations of similar causal and dynamic factors.

Pastoral Nomads Peoples who raise domesticated animals and do not depend on hunting, gathering, or the planting of their own crops for a significant portion of their diets.

Patrilineality Descent reckoning is through males exclusively.

Patrilocality Residence of a couple after marriage in or near the husband's father's domicile.

Peasants Food-producing farm workers who form the lower economic stratum in preindustrial and underdeveloped societies, subject to exploitative obligations in the form of rent, taxes, tribute, and forced labor service.

Personality The structuring of the inherent constitutional, emotional, and intellectual factors that determine how a person feels, thinks, and behaves in relation to the patterning of a particular cultural context.

Phenotype The characteristics of an individual organism that are the external, apparent manifestations of its hereditary genetic composition, resulting from the interaction of its genotype with its environment. See also GENOTYPE.

Phonemes A sound (PHONE), or the several variants of such a sound (ALLOPHONES), that native speakers perceive as contrastive with each other and as significant for the meaning of an utterance.

Physical Anthropology The study of the animal origins and biologically determined nature of humankind and of physical variations among human populations.

Pluralism Where a national or regional population is composed of several social, cultural, ethnic, or religious minorities concerned with maintaining their separate identities.

Political Economy The role of political authority and power in production, distribution, and consumption of goods and services.

Polyandry Marriage of one woman with two or more males simultaneously.

Polygamy Marriage involving more than one spouse of either sex.

Polygyny Marriage of one male with two or more women simultaneously.

Race Large populations characterized by a bundle of distinctive gene frequencies and associated with continents or extensive regions.

Raciology The scientific study of the relationship between race and culture.

Racism The attitude that the genetic composition of various RACES determines the principal cultural differences manifested by different groups of people.

Reciprocity A mode of exchanging goods and/or valuables without overt reckoning of economic worth or overt reckoning that a balance need be reached, to establish or reinforce ties between persons.

Redistribution A mode of exchange in which the labor products of several different individuals are brought to a central place, sorted by type, counted, and then given away to producers and nonproducers alike.

Rent A payment in kind or in money for the opportunity to live or work on the owner's land.

Revitalization Movement Reaction by a minority group to coercion and disruption, often under MESSIANIC leadership, aiming to reclaim lost status, identity, and well-being.

Rites of Passage Communally celebrated rituals that mark the transition of an individual from one institutionalized STATUS to another.

Rites of Solidarity Rites that confirm the unity of a group.

Roles Patterns of behavior associated with specific statuses.

Semantic Universality Potential of all human languages for generating utterances capable of conveying information relevant to all aspects of experience and thought, without limits as to time or place.

Shaman A part-time practitioner of magico-religious rites of DIVINATION and curing, skilled in sleight of hand and the techniques of trance and possession.

Sister Exchange A form of marriage in which two males marry each other's sister (or sisters).

Society A group within which all aspects of the UNIVERSAL PATTERN occur with a high density of interaction among its members and having a geographical locus.

Sodality A group based on nonkinship principles such as a club or a professional association.

Sororate Custom by which a deceased wife is replaced by a sister.

Status Position or standing, socially recognized, ascribed to or achieved by an individual or group. Compare ROLE.

Subculture A culture associated with a MINORITY, MAJORITY, CLASS, CASTE, or other group within a larger sociocultural system.

Suitor Service BRIDE-PRICE rendered in the form of labor.

Surface Structure The directly observed form of an utterance.

Taboo A culturally determined prohibition on an activity, plant, animal, person, or place.

Tool An object, not part of the user's body, that the user holds or carries during or just prior to use and that is used to alter the form or location of a second object with which it was previously unconnected.

Totems Plants, animals, phenomena, or objects symbolically associated with particular descent groups as identifying insignia.

Unilineal Descent The reckoning of descent either exclusively through males or exclusively through females.

Universal Pattern A set of categories comprehensive enough to afford logical and classificatory organization for the range of artifacts, traits, ways, and institutions to be observed in all cultural systems.

Uxorilocal Residence When the husband lives in the wife's home.

Virilocal Residence When the wife lives in the husband's home.

Warfare Formalized armed combat by teams of people who represent rival territories or political communities.

BIBLIOGRAPHY

In the citation system used in this text, the names in parentheses are the authors of the publication mentioned or of publications that support the description or interpretations of matters being discussed. The year following the name is the year of the publication and should be used to identify specific sources when more than one publication of an author is included. Letters following a date (e.g., 1990a) distinguish different publications of the same author for the year. Specific page numbers following the date are provided only for direct quotes or for controversial points. All items in the bibliography have been cited in the text.

Acheson, James M. 1972. "Limited Good or Limited Goods: Response to Economic Opportunity in a Tarascan Pueblo." *American Anthropologist,* 74:1152–1169.

———. 1974. "Reply to George Foster." *American Anthropologist,* 76:57–62.

Adair, Linda and Barry Popkin. 1992. "Prolonged Lactation Contributes to Depletion of Maternal Energy Reserves in Filipino Women." *Journal of Nutrition,* 122:1643–1655.

Adams, H. 1990. African and African American Contributions In Science. Base Line Essay. Portland: Multnomah School District.

Agar, Michael. 1994. *Language Shock: Understanding the Culture of Conversation.* New York: William Morrow.

Akmajian, Adrian, et al. 1992. *Linguistics: An Introduction to Language and Communication.* 3rd edition. Cambridge: MIT Press.

Alba, Richard. 1990. *Ethnic Identity: The Transformation of White America.* New Haven: Yale University Press.

Albers, Patricia. 1989. "From Illusion to Illumination: Anthropological Studies of American Indian Women." In *Gender and Anthropology,* Sandra Morgan, ed., pp. 132–170. Washington D.C.: American Anthropological Association.

Alexander, Richard. 1977. "Natural Selection and the Analysis of Human Sociality." In *The Changing Scenes in the Natural Sciences, 1776–1976,* C. E. Goulden, ed., pp. 283–337. Philadelphia: Academy of Natural Science, Special Publication 12.

Algaze, Guillermo. 1993. "Expansionary Dynamics of Some Early Pristine States." *American Anthropologist,* 95:304–333.

Alland, Alexander, Jr. 1977. *The Artistic Animal: An Inquiry into the Biological Roots of Art.* Garden City, New York: Doubleday/Anchor Books.

American Anthropological Association. 1994. *AAA Guide.* Washington, D.C.

Ames, Kenneth. 1994. "The Northwest Coast: Complex Hunter-Gatherers, Ecology and Social Evolution." *Annual Review of Anthropology,* 23: 209-229.

Anderson, Richard. 1992. "Do Other Cultures Have Art?" *American Anthropologist,* 94:926–929.

Armelagos, George. 1990. "Health and Disease in Prehistoric Populations in Transition." In *Disease in Populations in Transition: Anthropological and Epidemiological Perspectives,* A. Swedlund and G. Armelagos, eds., pp. 127–144. New York: Bergin and Garvey.

Armelagos, George and Allan Goodman. 1994. "The Case Against Race." Paper read at the Southern Anthropological Society Meeting, Atlanta, April 28.

Armelagos, George, A. Goodman and K. Jacobs. 1994. "The Origins of Agriculture: Population Growth During a Period of Declining Health." *Population and Environment,* in press.

Atkinson, Jane. 1992. "Shaminisms Today." *Annual Review of Anthropology,* 21:307–330.

Awe, Bolanlie. 1977. "The Iyalod in Traditional Yoruba Political

Systems." In *Sexual Stratification: A Cross Cultural View*, Alice Schlegel, ed., pp. 270–291. New York: Columbia University Press.

Bailey, Robert. 1989. "Hunting and Gathering in Tropical Rain Forest: Is It Possible?" *American Anthropologist*, 91:59–82.

Bailey, Robert and Thomas Headland. 1991. "The Tropical Rain Forest: Is It a Productive Environment for Human Foragers?" *Human Ecology*, 19:261–285.

Bakker, Jim. 1976. *Move That Mountain*. Plainfield, New Jersey: Logos International.

Baksh, Michael. 1985. "Faunal Food as a 'Limiting Factor' on Amazonian Cultural Behavior: A Machiguenga Example." *Research in Economic Anthropology*, 7:145–175.

Balee, William. 1984. "The Ecology of Ancient Tupi Warfare." In *Warfare, Culture and Environment*, Brian Ferguson, ed., pp. 241–265. Orlando, Florida: Academic Press.

Barber, Bernard. 1968. "Social Mobility in Hindu India." In *Social Mobility in the Caste System*, J. Silverberg, ed., pp. 18–35. The Hague: Mouton.

Barlett, Peggy. 1989. "Industrial Agriculture." In *Economic Anthropology*, Stuart Plattner, ed. Stanford: Stanford University Press.

Barlett, Peggy and Peter Brown. 1985. "Agricultural Development and the Quality of Life: An Anthropological View." *Agriculture and Human Values*, 2:28–35.

Barnes, J. A. 1960. "Marriage and Residential Continuity." *American Anthropologist*, 62:850–866.

Barnouw, Victor. 1985. *Culture and Personality*, 4th edition. Homewood, Illinois: Dorsey Press.

Barth, Frederick. 1961. *Nomads of South Persia*. Boston: Little, Brown.

Bartram, William. 1958. *The Travels of William Bartram*, Francis Harper, ed. New Haven: Yale University Press.

Bar-Yosef, Ofer and B. Vandermeersch. 1993. "Modern Humans in the Levant." *Scientific American*, April: 94–100.

Bayliss-Smith, Timothy. 1977. "Human Ecology and Island Populations: The Problems of Change." In *Subsistence and Survival: Rural Ecology in the Pacific*, T. Bayliss-Smith and R. Feachem, eds., pp. 11–20. New York: Academic Press.

Beattie, John. 1960. *Bunyoro: An African Kingdom*. New York: Holt, Rinehart and Winston.

Bell, Daniel. 1973. *The Coming of Post-Industrial Society: A Venture in Social Forecasting*. New York: Basic Books.

Belmonte, Thomas. 1979. *The Broken Fountain*. New York: Columbia University Press.

Ben-Ari, E., B. Moeran and J. Valentine 1990. *Unwrapping Japan: Society and Culture in Anthropological Perspective*. Manchester: University of Manchester.

Bender, Donald. 1967. "A Refinement of the Concept of Household: Families, Co-Residence, Domestic Functions." *American Anthropologist*, 69:493–503.

Benedict, Ruth. 1934. *Patterns of Culture*. Boston: Houghton Mifflin.

———. 1960. *Patterns of Culture*. New York: Mentor.

Berdan, Frances. 1982. *Aztecs of Central Mexico*. New York: Holt, Rinehart and Winston.

Berlin, Brent and Paul Kay. 1991. *Basic Color Terms: Their Universality and Evolution*. Berkeley: University of California Press.

Bermejo, M., G. Illera, and J. Sabater-PI. 1989. "New Observations on the Tool-behavior of Chimpanzees from Mt. Assirik (Senegal, West Africa)." *Primates*, 30(1):65–73.

Bernard, H. Russell. 1981. "Issues in Training in Applied Anthropology." *Practicing Anthropology*, 3:(Winter).

———. 1994. *Research Methods in Anthropology*, 2nd edition. Thousand Oaks, California: Sage.

Bernardi, Bernado. 1985. *Age Class Systems: Social Institutions and Politics Based on Age*. New York: Cambridge University Press.

Berra, Tim M. 1990. *Evolutionism and the Myth of Creationism: A Basic Guide to the Facts in the Evolution Debate*. Stanford, California: Stanford University Press.

Berreman, Gerald. 1966. "Caste in Cross-cultural Perspective." In *Japan's Invisible Race: Caste in Culture and Personality*, G. de Vos and H. Wagatsuma, eds., pp. 275–324. Berkeley: University of California Press.

———. 1975. "Bazaar Behavior: Social Identity and Social Interaction in Urban India." In *Ethnic Identity: Cultural Continuity and Change*, L. Romanucci-Ross and G. de Vos, eds., pp. 71–105. Palo Alto, California: Mayfield.

———. 1981. *Social Inequality*. New York: Academic Press.

Besharov, Douglas J. 1989. "Targeting Long-Term Welfare Recipients." In *Welfare Policy for the 1990's*, Phoebe H. Cottingham and David T. Ellwood, eds., pp. 146–164. Cambridge: Harvard University Press.

Bickerton, Derek. 1990. *Language and Species*. Chicago: University of Chicago Press.

Biolsi, Thomas. 1984. "Ecological and Cultural Factors in Plains Indians Warfare." In *Warfare, Culture and Environment*, Brian Ferguson, ed., pp. 141–168. Orlando, Florida: Academic Press.

Bittles, Alan, et al. 1991. "Reproductive Behavior and Health in Consanguineous Marriages." *Science*, 2(52):789–794.

Bixler, Ray. 1982. "Comment on the Incidence and Purpose of Royal Sibling Incest." *American Ethnologist*, 9:580–582.

Blackwood, Evelyn. 1984. "Sexuality and Gender in Certain North American Indian Tribes: The Case of Cross-Gender Females." *Signs*, 10:27–42.

———. 1986. "Breaking the Mirror: The Construction of Lesbianism and the Anthropological Discourse on Homosexuality." In *Anthropology and Homosexual Behavior*, Evelyn Blackwood, ed., pp. 1–18. New York: Haworth Press.

Boesch, Christope and Hedwige Boesch. 1984. "Mental Map in Wild Chimpanzees: An Analysis of Hammer Transports for Nut Cracking." *Primates*, 25(2):169–170.

———. 1991. "Dim Forest, Bright Chimps." *Natural History*, (September):50–56.

Bongaarts, John. 1980. "Does Malnutrition Affect Fertility? A Summary of the Evidence." *Science*, 208:564–569.

———. 1994a. "Can the Growing Human Population Feed Itself?" *Scientific American*, (March):36–42.

———. 1994b. "Population Policy Options in the Developing World." *Science*, 263:771–776.

Bongaarts, John and F. Odile. 1984. "The Proximate Determinants of Fertility in Sub-Saharan Africa." *Population and Development Review*, 10:511–537.

Boserup, Ester. 1965. *The Condition of Agricultural Growth: The Economics of Agrarian Change Under Population Pressure*. Chicago: Aldine.

Bossen, Laurel. 1988. "Toward a Theory of Marriage: The Economic Anthropology of Marriage Transactions." *Ethnology*, 27:127–144.

Bowles, S. and H. Gintis. 1976. *Schooling in Capitalist America*. New York: Basic Books.

Brace, Loring, et al. 1993. "Clines and Clusters Versus 'Race': A Test in Ancient Egypt and the Case of Death on the Nile." *American Journal of Physical Anthropology*, 36:1–31.

Brown, Judith K. 1975. "Iroquois Women: An Ethnohistoric Note." In *Toward an Anthropology of Women*, Rayna Reiter, ed., pp. 235–251. New York: Monthly Review Press.

Brown, Lester, H. Kane, and E. Ayres. 1993. *Vital Signs*. New York: W.W. Norton.

Brown, Lester, et al. 1991. *State of the World 1991: A Worldwatch Institute Report on Progress Toward a Sustainable Society*. New York/London: Norton.

———. 1994. "Facing Food Insecurity." In *State of the World 1994*, Lester Brown, ed., pp. 177–197. New York: W.W. Norton.

Brozan, Nadine. 1985. "U.S. Leads Industrialized Nations in Teen Age Births and Abortions." *The New York Times*, March 13, pp. 1, 22.

Brunton, Ron. 1975. "Why Do the Trobriands Have Chiefs?" *Man*, 10(4):545–550.

Buchbinder, Geogeda. 1977. "Nutritional Stress and Population Decline Among the Maring of New Guinea." In *Malnutrition, Behavior and Social Organization*, Lawrence S. Greene, ed., pp. 109–142. New York: Academic Press.

Buckley, Thomas. 1982. "Menstruation and the Power of Yurok Women." *American Ethnologist*, 9:47–90.

Burbank, Victoria. 1989. "Gender and the Anthropology Curriculum: Aboriginal Australia." In *Gender and Anthropology*, Sandra Morgan, ed., pp. 116–131. Washington, D.C.: American Anthropological Association.

Bureau of the Census. 1994. Statistical Abstract.

Burton, Michael and D. White. 1987. "Sexual Division of Labor in Agriculture." In *Household Economies*, M. Maclachlan, ed. Lanham, Maryland: University Press of America.

Buzzard, Shirley. 1982. *The PLAN Primary Health Care Project, Tumaco, Colombia: A Case Study*. Warwick, Rhode Island: Foster Parents Plan International.

Cain, Meade. 1977. "The Economic Activities of Children in a Village in Bangladesh." *Population and Development*, Review 3:201–227.

Caldwell, John. 1982. *Theory of Fertility Decline*. New York: Academic Press.

Caldwell, J., et al. 1983. "The Causes of Demographic Change in Rural South India: A Micro Approach." *Population and Demographic Review*, 8:689–727.

Callender, Charles and Lee Kochems. 1983. "The North American Berdache." *Current Anthropology*, 24:443–470.

Campbell, Shirley. 1983. "Kula in Vakuta: The Mechanics of Keda." In *The Kula: New Perspectives on Massim Exchange*, J. Leach and E. Leach, eds., pp. 201–227. Cambridge: Cambridge University Press.

Carneiro, Robert. 1970. "A theory of the Origin of the State." *Science*, 169:733–738.

———. 1981. "Chiefdom: Precursor of the State." In *The Transition to Statehood in the New World*, Grant Jones and Robert Kautz, eds., pp. 37–75. New York: Cambridge University Press.

Carroll, Lucy. 1977."'Sanskritization,' 'Westernization,' and 'Social Mobility': A Reappraisal of the Relevence of Anthropological Concepts to the Social Historian of Modern India." *Journal of Anthropological Research*, 33(4):355–371.

Carstairs, G. M. 1967. *The Twice Born*. Bloomington: Indiana University Press.

Cashdan, Elizabeth. 1989. "Hunters and Gatherers: Economic Behavior in Bands." In *Economic Anthropology*, Stuart Plattner, ed., pp. 21–48. Stanford: Stanford University Press.

Cattle, Dorothy. 1977. "An Alternative to Nutritional Particularism." In *Nutrition and Anthropology in Action*, Thomas Fitzgerald, ed., pp. 35–45. Amsterdam: Van Gorcum.

Chagnon, Napoleon. 1974. *Studying the Yanomam*. New York: Holt, Rinehart and Winston.

———. 1989. "Response to Ferguson." *American Ethnologist* 1989:565–569.

———. 1992. *Yanomamo*, 4th edition. New York: Harcourt Brace Javanovich.

Chagnon, Napoleon and Raymond Hames. 1979. "Protein Deficiency and Tribal Warfare in Amazonia: New Data." *Science*, 203:910–913.

Chakravarti, A.K. 1985a. "Cattle Development Problems and Programs In India: A Regional Analysis." *Geo Journal*, 10:21–45.

———. 1985b. "The Question of Surplus Cattle In India: A Spatial View. *Geografska Annala*, 67B:121–130.

Chambers, Erve. 1985. *Applied Anthropology: A Professional Guide*. Englewood Cliffs, New Jersey: Prentice-Hall.

Child, Alice and J. Child. 1985. "Biology, Ethnocentrism, and Sex Differences." *American Anthropologist*, 87:125–128.

Chomsky, Noam. 1973. "The General Properties of Language." In *Explorations in Anthropology: Readings in Culture, Man, and Nature*, Morton Fried, ed., pp. 115–123. New York: Crowell.

———. 1989. *Necessary Illusions: Thought Control in Democratic Societies*. Boston: South End Press.

Cicchetti, Dante and Vicki Carlson, eds. 1989. *Child Maltreatment: Theory and Research on the Causes and Consequences of Child Abuse and Neglect*. New York: Cambridge University Press.

Ciochon, Russel. 1985. "Hominoid Cladistics and the Ancestry of Modern Apes and Humans." In *Primate Evolution and Human Origins*, R. L. Ciochon and J. G. Fleagle, eds., pp. 345–362. Menlo Park, California: Benjamin/Cummings.

Coe, Michael. 1977. *Mexico*, 2nd edition. New York: Praeger.

Cohen, Mark N. 1977. *The Food Crisis in Prehistory*. New Haven: Yale University Press.

———. 1987. "The Significance of Long-Term Changes in Human Diet and Food Economy." In *Food and Evolution: Toward a Theory of Human Food Habits*, M. Harris and E. Ross, eds., pp. 261–283. Philadelphia: Temple University Press.

Cohen, Mark and G. Armelagos, eds. 1984. *Paleopathology and the Origin of Agriculture*. New York: Academic Press.

Cohen, Myron. 1976. *House United, House Divided*. New York: Columbia University Press.

Cohen, Ronald. 1984a. "Wafare and State Foundation: Wars Make States and States Make Wars." In *Warfare, Culture and Environment*, Brian Ferguson, ed., pp. 329–355. Orlando, Florida: Academic Press.

———. 1984b. "Approaches to Applied Anthropology." *Communication and Cognition*, 17:135–162.

Cohen, Yehudi. 1978. "The Disappearance of the Incest Taboo." *Human Nature,* 1(7):72–78.

Cohn, Bernard. 1955. "Changing Status of a Depressed Caste." In *Village India: Studies in the Little Community,* M. Marriott, ed. American Anthropological Association Memoirs, 83:55–77.

Collins, Glenn. 1985. "Remarriage: Bigger Ready-Made Families." *The New York Times,* May 13, p. 15.

Collins, Randall. 1989. "Sociology: Proscience or Antiscience?" *American Sociological Review,* 54:124–139.

Collinvaux, Paul and Mark Bush. 1991. "The Rain-Forest Ecosystem As a Resource for Hunting and Gathering." *American Anthropologist,* 93:153–162.

Condominas, George. 1977. *We Have Eaten the Forest.* New York: Hill and Wang.

Conyers, John. 1978. "Unemployment Is Cruel and Unusual Punishment." Hearings before the House Subcommittee on Crime, House of Representatives. Ninety-fifth Congress, Serial No. 47, pp. 647–679. Washington, D.C.: U.S. Government Printing Office.

Constanza, R. 1991. *The Science and Management of Sustainability.* New York: Columbia University Press.

Counts, Dorothy. 1985. "Tamparonga: The Big Women of Kaliai (Papua New Guinea)." In *In Her Prime: A New View of Middle-Aged Women,* J. Brown and V. Kerns, eds., pp. 49–64. South Hadley, Massachusetts: Bergin and Garvey.

Craig, Daniel. 1979. "Immortality Through Kinship: The Vertical Transmission of Substance and Symbolic Estate." *American Anthropologist,* 81:94–96.

Crossette, Barbara. 1989. "India Studying the 'Accidental' Deaths of Hindu Wives." *The New York Times,* January 15, p. 4.

Curvin, Robert and Bruce Porter. 1978. "The Myth of Blackout Looters." *The New York Times,* July 13, p. 21.

Dahl, Robert. 1981. *Democracy in the United States* 4th edition. Boston: Houghton Mifflin.

Dalton, George. 1969. "Theoretical Issues in Economic Anthropology." *Current Anthropology,* 10:63–102.

D'Altroy, T. and T. K. Earle. 1985. "Staple Finance, Wealth Finance, and Storage in the Inca Political Economy." *Current Anthropology,* 26:187–206.

D'Altroy, Terrence. 1992. *Provincial Power in the Inca Empire.* Washington, D.C.: Smithsonian Institution Press.

D'Andrade, Roy. 1992. "Cognitive Anthropology". In *New Directions in Psychological Anthropology,* T. Schwartz, G. White, and C. Lutz, eds., pp. 47–67. New York: Cambridge University Press.

Darwin, Charles and Alfred Wallace. 1895. "On the Tendency of Species etc." *Journal of Proceedings of the Linean Society—Zoology,* 3:45–46.

Das Gupta, Monica. 1978. "Production Relations and Population: Rampur." *Journal of Development Studies,* 14(4):177–185.

Dehavenon, Anna Lou. 1989–1990. "Charles Dickens Meets Franz Kafka: The Maladministration of New York City's Public Assistance Programs." *New York University Review of Law and Social Change,* 17:231–254.

———. 1993. "An Etic Model for the Scientific Study of the Causes of Matrifocality." In *Where Did All the Men Go?,* Joan Mencher and Anne Okongwu, eds., pp. 53–69. Boulder: Westview.

Deloria, Vine. 1969. *Custer Died for Your Sins.* London: Collier-Macmillan.

De Mott, Benjamin. 1980. "The Pro-Incest Lobby." *Psychology Today,* (March):11–16.

———. 1990 *The Imperial Middle: Why Americans Can't Think Straight About Class.* New York: Morrow.

Dentan, Robert. 1968. *The Semai: A Non-Violent People of Malaya.* New York: Holt, Rinehart and Winston.

Devereaux, George. 1967. "A Typological Study of Abortion in 350 Primitive, Ancient, and Pre-Industrial Societies." In *Abortion in America,* H. Rosen, ed., pp. 95–152. Boston: Beacon Press.

Dickson, D. Bruce. 1987. "Circumscription by Anthropogenic Environmental Destruction: An Expansion of Carneiro's (1970) Theory of the Origin of the State." *American Antiquity,* 52(4):709–716.

Diemberger, Hildegard 1993. "Blood, Sperm, Soul and the Mountain." In *Gendered Anthropology,* Teresa del Valle, ed., pp. 88–127. New York: Routledge.

Dillingham, Beth and B. Isaac. 1975. "Defining Marriage Cross-culturally." In *Being Female: Reproduction, Power and Change,* D. Raphael, ed., pp. 55–63. The Hague: Mouton.

Diop, Cheik Anta. 1991. *Civilization or Barbarism: An Authentic Anthropology.* Brooklyn, New York: Lawrence Hill Books.

Divale, William. 1972. "Systematic Population Control in the Middle and Upper Paleolithic: Inferences Based on Contemporary Hunters and Gatherers." *World Archaeology,* 4:221–243.

———. 1974. "Migration, External Warfare, and Matrilocal Residence." *Behavior Science Research,* 9:75–133.

Divale, William and Marvin Harris. 1976. "Population, Warfare and the Male Supremacist Complex." *American Anthropologist,* 78:521–538.

Divale, William, M. Harris, and D. Williams. 1978. "On the Misuse of Statistics: A Reply to Hirschfeld et al." *American Anthropologist,* 80:379–386.

Dobyns, Henry. 1972. "The Cornell-Peru Project: Experimental Intervention in Vicos." In *Contemporary Societies and Cultures of Latin America,* Dwight Heath, ed., pp. 201–210. New York: Random House.

Dole, Gertrude. 1966. "Anarchy Without Chaos: Alternatives to Political Authority Among the Kui-Kuru." In *Political Authority,* M. J. Swartz, V. W. Turner, and A. Tuden, eds., pp. 73–88. Chicago: Aldine.

Doughty, Paul. 1987. "Against the Odds: Collaboration and Development at Vicos." In *Collaborative Research and Social Change: Applied Anthropology in Action,* Donald Stull and J. Schensul, eds., pp. 129–157. Boulder, Colorado: Westview.

Drachman, A.G. 1963. *The Mechanical Technology of Greek and Roman Antiquity.* Copenhagen: Monksgaard.

Drew, Elizabeth. 1983. *Politics and Money: The New Road to Corruption.* New York: Macmillan.

Dualeh, Raqiya. 1982. *Sisters in Affliction: Circumcision and Infibulation of Women in Africa.* London: Zed Press.

Dumond, Don. 1975. "The Limitation of Human Population: A Natural History." *Science,* 1987:713–721.

Dumont, Louis. 1970. *Homo Hierarchicus: The Caste System and Its Implications,* Mark Sainsbury, trans. Chicago: University of Chicago Press.

Duncan, Greg, Jeanne Brooks-Gunn, and Pamela Klebanov. 1993. "Economic Deprivation and Early Childhood Development". Ann Arbor: University of Michigan (Xerox).

Earle, Timothy. 1989 "The Evolution of Chiefdoms." *Current Anthropology*, 30:84–88.

Earle, Timothy, ed. 1991 *Chiefdoms: Power, Economy, and Ideology.* Cambridge: Cambridge University Press.

Eaton, S. Boyd, Marjorie Shostak, and Melvin Konner. 1988. *The Paleolithic Prescription: A Program for Diet and Exercise and a Design for Living.* New York: Harper and Row.

Ehrenberg, Margaret. 1989. *Women in Prehistory.* Norman: University of Oklahoma Press.

Eliade, M. 1958. *Birth and Rebirth: The Religious Meaning of Initiation in Human Culture.* New York: Harper & Row.

Ember, Carol and Melvin Ember. 1992 "Resource Unpredictability, Mistrust, and War." *Journal of Conflict Resolution*, 36:242–262.

Ember, Carol, Melvin Ember, and B. Pasternack. 1974. "On the Development of Unilineal Descent." *Journal of Anthropological Research*, 30:69–94.

Ember, Melvin. 1982. "Statistical Evidence for an Ecological Explanation of Warfare." *American Anthropologist*, 84:645–649.

Ember, Melvin and Carol Ember. 1971. "The Conditions Favoring Matrifocal Versus Patrifocal Residence." *American Anthropologist*, 73:571–594.

Errington, Fredrick and Deborah Gewertz. 1987. *Cultural Alternatives and a Feminist Anthropology.* New York: Cambridge University Press.

Evans-Pritchard, E. E. 1940. *The Nuer, A Description of the Modes of Livelihood and Political Institutions of a Nilotic People.* Oxford: Clarendon Press.

———. 1970. "Sexual Inversion Among the Azande." *American Anthropologist*, 72:1428–1433.

Exter, Thomas. 1991. "The Cost of Growing Up." *American Demographics*, 13(8):59ff.

Fausto-Sterling, Ann. 1993. *The Sciences*, March/April:20–24.

Fei, Hsiao-T'ung, and Chang Chih-I. 1947. *Earthbound China: A Study of Rural Economy in Yunnan.* Chicago: University of Chicago Press.

Feil, Daryl. 1987. *The Evolution of Highland Papua New Guinea Societies.* New York: Cambridge University Press.

Feinman, G., and J. Neitzel. 1984. "Too Many Types: An Overview of Sedentary Prestate Societies in the Americas." In *Advances in Archaeological Method and Theory*, M. B. Schiffer, ed., pp. 39–102. New York: Academic Press.

Feraca, Stephen. 1984. Personal Communication. (See Pl. 97–403, 97th Congress, Second Session, 1982.)

Ferguson, Brian R. 1984. "Introduction: Studying War." In *Warfare, Culture and Environment*, Brian Ferguson, ed., pp. 1–61. Orlando, Florida: Academic Press.

———. 1989a. "Game Wars? Ecology and Conflict in Amazonia." *Journal of Anthropological Research*, 45:179–206.

———. 1989b. "Ecological Consequences of Amazonian Warfare." *Ethnology*, 27:249–264.

———. 1992. "A Savage Encounter: Western Contact and the Yanomami War Complex." In *War in the Tribal Zone: Expanding States and Indigenous Warfare*, R. Brian Ferguson and Neil Whitehead, eds., pp. 199–227. Santa Fe: School of American Research Press.

———. 1995. *Yanomami Warfare: A Political History.* Santa Fe: School of American Research.

Fittkau, E. J. and H. Klinge. 1973. "On Biomass and Trophic Structure of the Central Amazon Rain Forest Ecosystem." *Biotropica*, 5:1–14.

Folbre, Nancy. 1991. *Women on Their Own: Global Patterns of Female Headship.* Washington, D. C.: International Center for Research on Women.

Fortune, Reo. 1965. *Manus Religion.* Lincoln: University of Nebraska Press.

Foster, George M. 1967. *Tzintzuntzan: Mexican Peasants in a Changing World.* Boston: Little, Brown.

———. 1974. "Limited Good or Limited Goods: Observations on Acheson." *American Anthropologist*, 76:53–57.

Foster, George and Barbara Anderson. 1978. *Medical Anthropology.* New York: Wiley.

Fouts, Roger S. and Deborah H. Fouts. 1985. "Signs of Conversation in Chimpanzees." Paper given at meeting of AAAS, Los Angeles, May 28–31.

———. 1989. "Loulis in Conversation with the Cross-Fostered Chimpanzees." In *Teaching Sign Language to Chimpanzees*, R. Allen Gardner, Beatrix T. Gardner, and Thomas E. Van Cantfort, eds., pp. 293–307. Albany: State University of New York Press.

Franke, Richard W. 1974. "Miracle Seeds and Shattered Dreams." *Natural History*, 83(1):10ff.

Frayer, David, et al. 1993. "Theories of Modern Human Origins: The Paleontological Test." *American Anthropologist*, 95:14–50.

Frayser, Suzanne. 1985. *Varieties of Sexual Experience: An Anthropological Perspective on Human Sexuality.* New Haven: Human Relations Area Files.

Freedman, Robert. 1977. "Nutritional Anthropology: An Overview." In *Nutrition and Anthropology in Action*, Thomas Fitzgerald, ed., pp. 1–23. Amsterdam: Van Gorcum.

Fried, Morton, H. 1978. "The State, the Chicken, and the Egg; or What Came First?" In *Origins of the State*, Ronald Cohen and Elman Service, eds., pp. 35–47. Philadelphia: Institute for the Study of Human Issues.

Frisch, R. 1984. "Body Fat, Puberty and Fertility." *Science*, 199:22–30.

Fulton, Robert and Steven Anderson. 1992. "The Amerindian 'Man-Woman': Gender, Liminality, and Cultural Continuity." *Current Anthropology*, 33:603–609.

Gajdusek, D. C. 1977. "Unconventional Viruses and the Origin and Disappearance of Kuru." *Science*, 197:943–960.

Gal, S. 1989. "Language and Political Economy." *Annual Review of Anthropology*, 18:345–367.

Galaty, John G. and Douglas L. Johnson. 1990. *The World of Pastoralism: Herding Systems in Comparative Perspective.* London: Belhaven Press.

Gandhi, Mohandas K. 1954. *How to Serve the Cow.* Ahmedabad: Navajivan Publishing House.

Gardner, B. T. and R. A. Gardner. 1971. "Two-Way Communication with a Chimpanzee." In *Behavior of Non-Human Primates*, A. Schrier and F. Stollnitz, eds., vol. 4, pp. 117–184. New York: Academic Press.

———. 1975. "Early Signs of Language in Child and Chimpanzee." *Science*, 187:752–753.

Garon, Sheldon M. 1987. *The State and Labor in Modern Japan.* Berkeley: University of California Press.

Gaulin, Stephen and James S. Boster. 1990. "Dowery as Female Competition." *American Anthropologist,* 92:994–1005.

Gay, Judith. 1986. "'Mummies and Babies' and Friends and Lovers in Lesotho." In *Anthropology and Homosexual Behavior,* Evelyn Blackwood, ed., pp. 97–116. New York: Haworth Press.

George, Sabu, R. Abel, and B. Miller. 1992. "Female Infanticide in Rural South India." *Economic and Political Weekly,* 30:1153–1156.

Gibbons, Ann. 1991. "Deja Vue All Over Again: Chimp Language Wars." *Science,* 251:1561–1562.

Gilmore, David. 1990. *Manhood in the Making: Cultural Concepts of Masculinity.* New Haven: Yale University Press.

Givens, David and Susan Skomal. 1993. "The Four Fields: Myth and Reality." *Anthropology Newsletter,* 34, May:1-ff.

Glaser, Danya and S. Frosh. 1988. *Child and Sexual Abuse.* Chicago: Dorsey Press.

Glasser, Ira. 1989. "How Long America?" *Civil Liberties,* Summer: 12ff.

Glover, G., et al. 1984. "Making Quality Count: Boca Raton's Approach to Quality Assurance." *The Cornell Hotel and Restaurant Administration Quarterly,* November: 39–45.

Gluckman, Max. 1955. *Custom and Conflict in Africa.* Oxford: Blackwell.

Good, Kenneth. 1987. "Limiting Factors in Amazonian Ecology." In *Food and Evolution: Toward a Theory of Human Food Habits,* M. Harris and E. Ross, eds., pp. 407–426. Philadelphia: Temple University Press.

———. 1989. Yanomami Hunting Patterns: Trekking and Garden Relocation as an Adaptation to Game Availability in Amazonia, Venuzuela. Ph.D. dissertation, University of Florida.

Goodale, Jane. 1971. *Tiwi Wives.* Seattle: University of Washington Press.

Goodall, Jane. See Van Lawick-Goodall, Jane.

Goody, Jack. 1976. *Production and Reproduction.* New York: Cambridge University Press.

Gordon, Andrew. 1987. "The Right to Work in Japan: Labor and State in the Depression." *Social Research,* 54(2):247–272.

Gough, E. Kathleen. 1959. "Criterion of Castle Ranking in South India." *Man in India,* 39:115–126.

———. 1968. "The Nayars and the Definition of Marriage." In *Marriage Family and Residence,* Paul Bohannon and J. Middleton, eds., pp. 49–71. Garden City, New York: Natural History Press.

Gould, Richard. 1982. "To Have and Not to Have: The Ecology of Sharing Among Hunter-Gatherers." In *Resource Managers: North American and Australian Hunter-Gatherers,* Nancy Williams and Eugene Hunn, eds., pp. 69–91. Boulder, Colorado: Westview Press.

Graber, Robert. 1992. "Population Pressure, Agricultural Origins, and Global Theory: Comment on McCorriston and Hole." *American Anthropologist,* 94:443–445.

———. 1991. "Population Pressure, Agricultural Origins, And Cultural Evolution: Constrained Mobility or Inhibited Expansion?" *American Anthropologist,* 93:692–697.

Gramby, Richard. 1977. "Deerskins and Hunting Territories: Competition for a Scarce Resource of the Northeastern Woodlands." *American Antiquity,* 42:601–605.

Gray, Patrick and Linda Wolfe. 1980. "Height and Sexual Dimorphism and Stature Among Human Societies." *American Journal of Physical Anthropology,* 53:441–456.

Greenberg, Joseph. 1968. *Anthropological Linguistics: An Introduction.* New York: Random House.

Gregerson, Edgar. 1982. *Sexual Practices: The Story of Human Sexuality.* London: Mitchell Beazley.

———. 1986. "Human Sexuality in Cross Cultural Perspective". In *Alternative Approaches to the Study of Sexual Behavior,* Donn Byrne and Kathryn Kelley, eds., pp. 87–102. Hillsdale, New Jersey: Lawrence Erlbaum Associates.

Gregor, Thomas. 1985. *Anxious Pleasure: The Sexual Lives of an Amazonian Peoples.* Chicago: University of Chicago Press.

———. 1977 *Mehinacu.* Chicago: University of Chicago Press.

Gross, Daniel R. 1975. "Protein Capture and Cultural Development in the Amazon Basin." *American Anthropologist,* 77:526–549.

———. 1984. "Time Allocation: A Tool for the Study of Cultural Behavior." *Annual Review of Anthropology,* 13:519–558.

Gruenbaum, Ellen. 1988. "Reproductive Ritual and Social Reproduction: Female Circumcision and the Subordination of Women in the Sudan." In *Economy and Class in Sudan,* Norman O'Neil and Jay O'Brien, eds., pp. 308–322. Brookfield, Vermont: Gower.

Gumbel, Peter. 1988. "Down on the Farm: Soviets Try Once More to Straighten Out Old Agricultural Mess." *The Wall Street Journal,* December 2.

Goudsblom, Johan. 1982. *Fire and Civilization.* New York: Penguin.

Haas, Jonathan. 1982. *The Evolution of the Prehistoric State.* New York: Columbia University Press.

Hacker, Andrew. 1989. "Affirmative Action: The New Look." *The New York Review of Books,* October 12, pp. 63–68.

———. 1992. *Two Nations: Black and White, Separate, Hostile, Unequal.* New York: Scribner's.

Hadley, Arthur. 1978. *The Empty Polling Booth.* Englewood Cliffs, New Jersey: Prentice-Hall.

Hamilton, Sahni, B. Popkin, and D. Spice. 1984. *Women and Nutrition in Third World Countries.* South Hadley, Massachusetts: Bergin Garvey.

Handwerker, W. P. 1983. "The First Demographic Transition: An Analysis of Subsistence Choices and Reproductive Consequences." *American Anthropologist,* 85:5–27.

Haraway, Donna. 1989. *Primate Visions: Gender, Race, and Nature in the World of Modern Science.* New York: Routledge.

Harner, Michael J. 1970. "Population Pressure and the Social Evolution of Agriculturalists." *Southwestern Journal of Anthropology,* 26:67–86.

———. 1972. *The Jivaro: People of the Sacred Waterfalls.* Garden City, New York: Natural History Press.

———. 1977. "The Ecological Basis for Aztec Sacrifice." *American Ethnologist,* 4:117–135.

———. 1982. *The Way of the Shaman: A Guide to Power and Healing.* New York: Bantam.

———. 1984. *The Jivaro: People of the Sacred Waterfall.* Berkeley: University of California Press.

Harrington, Charles and J. Whiting. 1972. "Socialization Process and Personality." In *Psychological Anthropology,* Francis Hsu, ed., pp. 469–507. Cambridge, Massachusetts: Schenkman.

Harris, David. 1987. "Aboriginal Subsistence in a Tropical Rain

Forest Environment: Food Procurement, Cannibalism and Population Regulation in Northeastern Australia." In *Food and Evolution: Toward a Theory of Human Food Habits*, Marvin Harris and Eric Ross, eds., pp. 357–385. Philadelphia: Temple University Press.

Harris, Marvin. 1977. *Cannibals and Kings: The Origins of Cultures*. New York: Random House.

———. 1979a. "Comments on Simoons' Questions in the Sacred Cow Controversy." *Current Anthropology*, 20:479–482.

———. 1979b. "Reply to Sahlins." *The New York Review of Books*, June 28, pp. 52–53.

———. 1984. "Animal Capture and Yanomam Warfare: Retrospective and New Evidence." *Journal of Anthropological Research*, 40:183–201.

———. 1985. *Good to Eat: Riddles of Food and Culture*. New York: Simon & Schuster.

———. 1989. *Our Kind: Who We Are, Where We Came From, Where We Are Going*. New York: Harper & Row.

Harris, M., J. Gomes Consorte, J. Lang, and B. Byrne. 1993. "Who Are the Whites? Imposed Census Categories and the Racial Demography of Brazil." *Social Forces*, 72:451–462.

Harris, Marvin and Eric Ross, eds. 1987a. *Food and Evolution: Toward a Theory of Human Food Habits*. Philadelphia: Temple University Press.

———. 1987b. *Death, Sex, and Fertility*. New York: Columbia University Press.

Hart, C. W. M. and A. R. Pilling. 1960. *The Tiwi of North Australia*. New York: Holt, Rinehart and Winston.

Hart, Keith. 1985. "The Social Anthropology of West Africa." *Annual Review of Anthropology*, 14:243–272.

Hartung, John. 1985. "Review of Incest: A Bisocial View, by J. Sheper." *American Journal of Physical Anthropology*, 67:169–171.

Hassig, Ross. 1988. *Aztec Warfare: Imperial Expansion and Political Control*. Norman: University of Oklahoma Press.

Hassan, Fekri. 1978. "Demographic Archaeology." In *Advances in Archaeological Method and Theory*, Michael Schiffer, ed., pp. 49–103. New York: Academic Press.

Hawkes, Kristen. 1993. "Why Hunter-Gatherers Work: An Ancient Version of the Problem of Public Goods." *Current Anthropology*, 34:341–361.

Hawkes, Kristen, Kim Hill, and J. O'Connell. 1982. "Why Hunters Gather: Optimal Foraging and the Ache of Eastern Paraguay." *American Ethnologist*, 9:379–398.

Hayden, Brian. 1987. "Alliances and Ritual Ecstasy: Human Responses to Resource Stress." *Journal for the Scientific Study of Religion*, 26:81–91.

———. 1992. "Conclusions: Ecology and Complex Hunter/Gatherers." In *A Complex Culture of the British Columbia Plateau*, Brian Hayden, ed., pp. 525–559. Vancouver: University of British Columbia Press.

———. 1993a. *Archaeology: The Science of Once and Future Things*. New York: W. H. Freeman

———. 1993b. "The Dynamics of Emerging Inequality." Paper Read at the Annual Meetings of the Society for American Archaeology, St. Louis.

Hayden, Brian, M. Deal, A. Cannon, and J. Casey. 1986. "Ecological Determinants of Women's Status Among Hunter/Gatherers." *Human Evolution*, 1(5):449–474.

Hays, Terence E. 1988. "'Myths of Matriarchy' and the Sacred Flute Complex of the Papua New Guinea Highlands." In *Myths of Matriarchy Reconsidered*, Deborah Gewertz, ed., pp. 98–120. Sydney, Australia: University of Sydney.

Headland, Thomas N., Kenneth L. Pike, and Marvin Harris. 1990. *Emics and Etics: The Insider/Outsider Debate*. Newbury Park, California: Sage.

Heider, Karl G. 1972. *The Dani of West Irian*. Reading, Massachusetts: Addison-Wesley.

Herbers, J. 1985. "Non-Relatives and Solitary People Make Up Half of New Households." *The New York Times*, November 20, p. 1.

Herdt, Gilbert. 1984a. "Semen Transactions in Sambia Cultures." In *Ritualized Homosexuality in Melanesia*, Gilbert Herdt, ed., pp. 167–210. Berkeley: University of California Press.

———. 1984b. "Ritualized Homosexuality Behavior in the Male Cults of Melanesia 1862–1983: An Introduction." In *Ritualized Homosexuality in Melanesia*, Gilbert Herdt, ed., pp. 1–81. Berkeley: University of California Press.

———. 1987. *The Sambia: Ritual and Custom in New Guinea*. New York: Holt, Rinehart and Winston.

Herman, Edward S. and Noam Chomsky. 1988. *Manufacturing Consent: The Political Economy of the Mass Media*. New York: Pantheon Books.

Hern, Warren. 1992. "Shipibo Polygyny and Patrilocality." *American Ethnologist*, 19:501–522.

Herskovitz, M. 1938. *The Dahomey*. New York: J. J. Augustin.

Hewes, Gordon. 1992. "Comment on McCauly." *Current Anthropology*, 33:162.

Hewlett, Barry S. 1991. "Demography and Child Care in Preindustrial Societies." *Journal of Anthropological Research*, 47(1):1–37.

Hicks, Esther. 1993. *Infibulation: Female Mutilation in Islamic Northeastern Africa*. New Brunswick, New Jersey: Transaction Publishers.

Hill, Jane. 1978. "Apes and Language." *Annual Review of Anthropology*, 7:89–112.

Hill, Jane and Bruce Mannheim. 1992. "Language and World View." *Annual Review of Anthropology* 21:381–406.

Hirsch, Jerry. 1981. "To Unfrock the Charlatans." *Sage Race Relations Abstracts*, 6:1–67.

Hirschfeld, Lawrence, J. Howe, and B. Levin. 1978. "Warfare, Infanticide and Statistical Inference: A Comment on Divale and Harris." *American Anthropologist*, 80:110–115.

Hogbin, H. Ian. 1964. *Guadacanal Society: The Koaka Speakers*. New York: Holt, Rinehart and Winston.

Holland, Dorothy. 1992. "The Woman Who Climbed Up The House." In *New Directions in Psychological Anthropology*, pp. 68–79. New York: Cambridge University Press.

Hommon, Robert. 1986. "Social Evolution in Ancient Hawaii." In *Island Societies: Archaeological Approaches to Evolution and Transformation*, Patrick Kirch, ed., pp. 55–69. New York: Cambridge University Press.

Hopkins, Keith. 1980. "Brother–Sister Marriage in Ancient Egypt." *Comparative Studies in Society and History*, 22:303–354.

Horgan, John. 1993. "Eugenics Revisited". *Scientific American*, June:123–131.

Howe, W. and William Parks. 1989. "Labor Market Completes

Sixth Year of Expansion in 1988." *Monthly Labor Review,* 112:3–12.

Hunt, Robert. 1988. "Size and Structure of Authority in Canal Irrigation Systems." *Journal of Anthropological Research,* 44:335–355.

Husain, Tariq. 1976. "The Use of Anthropologists in Project Appraisal by the World Bank." In *Development from Below: Anthropologists and Development Situations,* David Pitt, ed., pp. 71–81. The Hague: Mouton.

Irwin, Geoffrey. 1983. "Chieftanship, Kula and Trade in Massim Prehistory." In *The Kula: New Perspectives on Massim Exchange,* J. Leach and E. Leach, eds., pp. 29–72. Cambridge: Cambridge University Press.

Isaac, Barry. 1988. "Introduction." In *Prehistoric Economies of the Pacific Northwest Coast,* Barry Isaac, ed., pp. 1–16. Greenwich, Connecticut: JAI Press.

———. 1992. "Discussion." *Research in Economic Anthropology, Supplement,* 6:441–442.

Itani, Jun'ichiro. 1961. "The Society of Japanese Monkeys." *Japan Quarterly,* 8:421–430.

Itani, Jun'ichiro and A. Nishimura. 1973. "The Study of Infra-Human Culture in Japan." In *Precultural Primate Behavior,* E. W. Menzell, ed., pp. 26–50. Basel: S. Karger.

Jacobs, Sue. 1978. "Top-down Planning: Analysis of Obstacles to Community Development in an Economically Poor Region of the Southwestern United States." *Human Organization,* 37(3):246–256.

Jacobs, Sue and C. Roberts. 1989. "Sex, Sexuality, Gender, and Gender Variance." In *Gender and Anthropology,* Sandra Morgan, ed., pp. 438–462. Washington, D.C.: American Anthropological Association.

Jensen, Neal. 1978. "Limits to Growth in World Food Production." *Science,* 201:317–320.

Joans, Barbara. 1984. "Problems in Pocatello in Linguistic Misunderstanding." *Practicing Anthropology,* 6(3,4):6ff.

Johnson, Allen and Timothy Earle. 1987. *The Evolution of Human Societies from Foraging Groups to Agrarian States.* Stanford, California: Stanford University Press.

Johnason, Donald. 1993. "A Skull to Chew On." *Natural History,* May:52–53.

Johnson, Donald and James Shreeve. 1989. *Lucy's Child: The Discovery of a Human Ancestor.* New York: Morrow.

Jonaitis, Aldona. 1991. *Chiefly Feasts: The Enduring Kwakiutl Potlatch.* Seattle: University of Washington Press.

Jones, Delmos. 1976. "Applied Anthropology and the Application of Anthropological Knowledge." *Human Organization,* 35:221–229.

Joseph, Suad. 1978. "Muslim-Christian Conflicts in Lebanon: A Perspective on the Evolution of Sectarianism." In *Muslim-Christian Conflicts: Economic, Political and Social Origins,* S. Joseph and B. Pillsbury, eds., pp. 63–98. Boulder, Colorado: Westview Press.

Josephides, Lisette. 1985. *The Production of Inequality: Gender and Exchange Among the Kewa.* New York: Tavistock.

Josephy, Alvin. 1982. *Now That the Buffalo's Gone: A Study of Today's American Indians.* New York: Knopf.

Kaberry, Phyllis, 1970(1939). *Aboriginal Woman, Sacred and Profane.* London: Routledge.

Kaeppler, Adrienne. 1978. "Dance in Anthropological Perspective." *Annual Review of Anthropology,* 7:31–49.

Kang, Elizabeth. 1979. "Exogamy and Peace Relations of Social Units: A Cross-Cultural Test." *Ethnology,* 18:85–99.

Katz, Phyllis and S. A. Taylor. 1988. *Eliminating Racism: Profiles in a Controversy.* New York: Plenum.

Kay, Paul and W. Kempton. 1984. "What Is the Sapir—Whorf Hypothesis?" *American Anthropologist,* 86:65–79.

Keegan, William F. and Morgan D. MacLachlan. 1989. "The Evolution of Avunculocal Chiefdoms: A Reconstruction of Taino Kinship and Politics." *American Anthropologist,* 91:613–630.

Keeley, Lawrence. 1988. "Hunter-Gatherer Economic Complexity and 'Population Pressure': A Cross-Cultural Analysis." *Journal of Anthropological Archaeology,* 7:373–411.

Keller, Janet. 1992. "Schemes for Schemata". In *New Directions in Psychological Anthropology* Tim Schwartz, G. White, and C. Lutz, eds., pp. 59–67. New York: Cambridge University Press.

Kelly, Raymond. 1976. "Witchcraft and Sexual Relations." In *Man and Woman in the New Guinea Highlands,* P. Brown and G. Buchbinder, eds., pp. 36–53. Washington, D.C.: Special Publication No. 8, American Anthropological Association.

Kendall, Carl. 1984. "Ethnomedicine and Oral Rehydration Therapy: A Case Study of Ethnomedical Investigation and Program Planning." *Social Science and Medicine,* 19(3):253–260.

Kertzer, David. 1978. "Theoretical Developments in the Study of Age Group Systems." *American Ethnologist,* 5(2):368–374.

———. 1993. *Sacrificed for Honor: Italian Infant Abandonment and the Politics of Reproductive Control.* Boston: Beacon.

Khare, Ravindra. 1984. *The Untouchable as Himself: Identity and Pragmatism Among the Lucknow Chamars.* New York: Cambridge University Press.

Khazanov, K. M. 1984. *Nomads and the Outside World.* Cambridge: Cambridge University Press.

Kinneckell, Arthur and R. L. Woodburn. 1992. "Technical Working Paper." Washington, D.C.: Federal Reserve.

Kirch, Patrick. 1984. *The Evolution of Polynesian Chiefdoms.* New York: Cambridge University Press.

Kivisto, Peter, ed. 1989. *The Ethnic Enigma: The Salience of Ethnicity for European-Origin Groups.* Philadelphia: Balch Institute Press.

Klass, Morton. 1979. *Caste: The Emergence of the South Asian Social System.* Philadelphia: ISHI.

Kleugel, James and E. R. Smith. 1981. "Beliefs About Stratification." *Annual Review of Sociology,* 7:29–56.

Knaupft, Bruce. 1990. "Melanesian Warfare: A Theoretical History." *Oceania,* 60:250–311.

Konner, Melvin. 1991. "The Promise of Medical Anthropology: An Invited Commentary." *Medical Anthropology Quarterly,* 5:78–82.

Kottak, Conrad. 1990. *Prime-time Society: An Anthropological Analysis of Television and Culture.* Ann Arbor: University of Michigan Press.

Kroeber, Alfred L. 1948. *Anthropology.* New York: Harcourt Brace.

Kumagai, Hisa and Arno Kumagai. 1986. "The Hidden 'I' in Amae: Passive Love and Japanese Social Perception." *Ethos,* 14:305–320.

Kusin, Jane, S. Kardjati, and H. Renqvist. 1993. "Chronic Undernutrition in Pregnancy and Lactation." *Proceedings of the Nutrition Society,* 52:19–28.

Labov, William. 1972. *Language in the Inner City.* Philadelphia: University of Pennsylvania Press.

Ladd, Everett, Jr. 1978. *Where Have All the Voters Gone?* New York: Norton.

Lakoff, R.T. 1990. *The Politics of Language in Our Lives.* New York: Basic Books.

Landy, David. 1985. "Pibloktok and in Nutrition: Possible Implications of Hypervitaminosis A." *Social Science and Medicine,* 21:173–185.

Lang, H. and R. G. 1985. "Completed Fertility of the Hutterites: A Revision." *Current Anthropology,* 26(3):395.

Langdon, Steve. 1979. "Comparative Tlingit and Haida Adaptation to the West Coast of the Prince of Wales Archipelago." *Ethnology,* 18:101–119.

Lauman, Edward. 1994. *The Social Organization of Sexuality.* Chicago: University of Chicago Press.

Lawrence, Peter. 1964. *Road Belong Cargo: A Study of the Cargo Movement in the Southern Madang District, New Guinea.* Manchester, England: University of Manchester Press.

Leacock, Eleanor Burke. 1978. "Women's Status in Egalitarian Society: Implication for Social Evolution." *Current Anthropology,* 19:247–275.

———. 1983. "Ideologies of Male Dominance as Divide and Rule Politics:AnAnthropologist'sView."In*Women'sNature*,MarianLowe and Ruth Hubbard, eds., pp. 111–121. New York: Pergamon Press.

Leakey, Richard and Roger Lewin. 1993. *Origins Reconsidered: In Search of What Makes Us Human.* New York: Doubleday

Leavitt, Gregory. 1989. "Disappearance of the Incest Taboo." *American Anthropologist,* 91:116–131.

———. 1990. "Sociobiological Explanations of Incest Avoidance: A Critical Review of Evidential Claims." *American Anthropologist,* 91:971–993.

———. 1992. "Inbreeding Fitness: A Reply to Uhlman". *American Anthropologist,* 94:448–449.

Lee, Richard. 1968. "What Do Hunters Do for a Living, or How to Make Out on Scarce Resources." In *Man the Hunter,* R. B. Lee and I. DeVore, eds., pp. 30–43. Chicago: Aldine.

———. 1979. *The !Kung San: Men and Women in a Foraging Society.* Cambridge: Cambridge University Press.

———. 1990. "Primitive Communism and the Origin of Social Inequality." In *The Evolution of Political Systems: Sociopolitics of Small-Scale Sedentary Societies,* Steadman Upham, ed., pp. 225–246. New York: Cambridge University Press.

Lee, Richard and Mathias Guenther. 1991. "Oxen or Onions? The Search for Trade and the Truth in the Kalahari." *Current Anthropology,* 32:593–601.

Leo, John 1993. "The Melting Pot Is Cooking." *U.S. News & World Report,* July 5: p. 15.

Lesser, Alexander. 1968. "War and the State." In *War: The Anthropology of Armed Conflict and Aggression,* M. Fried, M. Harris, and R. Murphy, eds., pp. 92–96. Garden City, New York: Natural History Press.

Lett, James. 1991. "Interpretive Anthropology, Metaphysics, and the Paranormal." *Journal of Anthropological Research,* 47:305-329.

Lewis, Michael. 1990. *Rioters and Citizens: Mass Protest in Imperial Japan.* Berkeley: University of California Press.

Lewis, Oscar. 1966. *La Vida: A Puerto Rican Family in the Culture of Poverty—San Juan and New York.* New York: Random House.

Lewontin, R., S. Rose, and L. Kamin. 1984. *Not in Our Genes: Biology, Ideology, and Human Nature.* New York: Pantheon.

Lieberman, Philip. 1991. *The Evolution of Speech, Thought, and Selfless Behavior.* Cambridge, Massachusetts: Harvard University Press.

Lightfoot-Klein, Hanny. 1989. *Prisoners of Ritual: An Odyssey into Female Genital Circumcision in Africa.* New York: Harrington Park Press.

Lindebaum, Shirley. 1975. "The Last Course: Nutrition and Anthropology in Asia." In *Nutrition and Anthropology in Action,* Thomas Fitzgerald, ed., pp. 141–155. Atlantic Highlands, New Jersey: Humanities Press.

———. 1979. *Kuru Society.* Palo Alto, California: Mayfield.

Lindsey, Robert. 1985. "Official Challenges Outlets that Offer Explicit Videotapes." *The New York Times,* June 3, pp. 1, 9.

Linton, Ralph. 1959. "The Natural History of the Family." In *The Family: Its Function and Destiny,* R. Anshen, ed., pp. 30–52. New York: Harper & Row.

Livingstone, Frank B. 1969. "Genetics, Ecology, and the Origins of Incest and Exogamy." *Current Anthropology,* 10:45–62.

———. 1982. "Comment on Littlefield, Lieberman, and Reynolds." *Current Anthropology,* 23:651.

Lizot, Jacques. 1977. "Population, Resources and Warfare Among the Yanoman." *Man,* 12:497–517.

———. 1979. "On Food Taboos and Amazon Cultural Ecology." *Current Anthropology,* 20:150–151.

Lockard, Denyse. 1986. "The Lesbian Community: An Anthropological Approach." In *Anthropology and Homosexual Behavior,* Evelyn Blackwood, ed., pp. 83–96. New York: Haworth Press.

Lomax, Alan, ed. 1968. *Folksong Style and Culture.* Washington, D.C.: American Association for the Advancement of Science, Publication No. 88.

Lomax, Alan and Conrad Arensberg. 1977. "A Worldwide Evolutionary Classification of Cultures by Subsistence Systems." *Current Anthropology,* 18:659–708.

Long, Bruce. 1987. "Reincarnation." In *Encyclopedia of Religion,* Vol. 12, pp. 265–269. New York: Macmillan.

Lowie, Robert. 1948(1924). *Primitive Religion.* New York: Liveright.

Lunn, P.G. 1988. "Malnutrition and Fertility." In *Natural Human Fertility: Social And Biological Mechanisms,* P. Diggory, et al., eds. pp. 135–152. New York: MacMillan.

McCall, Daniel. 1980. "The Dominant Dyad: Mother-Right and the Iroquois Case." In *Theory and Practice,* Stanley Diamond, ed., pp. 221–261. The Hague: Mouton.

MacCormack, Carol P. 1982. "Adaptation in Human Fertility and Birth." *Ethnography of Fertility and Birth,* Carol P. MacCormack, ed., pp. 1–23. New York: Academic Press.

MacLachlan, Morgan. 1983. *Why They Did Not Starve: Biocultural Adaptation in a South Indian Village.* Philadelphia: Institute for the Study of Human Issues.

MacLaury, Robert E. 1992. "From Brightness to Hue: An Explanatory Model of Color-Category Evolution." *Current Anthropology,* 33:137–186.

MacLeish, Kenneth. 1972. "The Tasadays: The Stone Age Cavemen of Mindanao." *National Geographic,* 142:219–248.

MacNeish, Richard. 1981. "The Transition to Statehood as Seen from the Mouth of a Cave." In *The Transition to Statehood in the*

New World, Grant Jones and Paul Kautz, eds., pp. 123–154. New York: Cambridge University Press.

McGrath, Janet, et al. 1992. "Cultural Determinants of Sexual Risk Behavior for AIDS among Baganda Women." *Medical Anthropology Quarterly*, 6:153–161.

McGrew, W. C. 1977. "Socialization and Object Manipulation of Wild Chimpanzees." In *Primate Bio Social Development*, Susan Chevalier-Skolinkoff and Frank Poirier, eds., pp. 261–288. New York: Garland.

———. 1992. *Chimpanzee Material Culture: Implications for Human Evolution*. Cambridge: Cambridge University Press.

McGurk, F. C. J. 1975. "Race Differences Twenty Years Later." *Homo*, 26:219–239.

Mair, Lucy. 1969. *Witchcraft*. New York: McGraw-Hill.

Malinowski, Bronislaw. 1920. "War and Weapons Among the Natives of the Trobriand Islands." *Man*, 20:10–12.

———. 1927. *Sex and Repression in Savage Society*. London: Routledge & Kegan Paul.

———. 1929. *The Sexual Life of Savages in North-Western Melanesia*. New York: Harcourt, Brace & World, Inc.

———. 1935. *Coral Gardens and Their Magic* (2 vols.). London: Allen and Unwin.

Maloney, William. 1987a. "Dharma." *Encyclopedia of Religion*, Vol. 4, pp. 239–332. New York: Macmillan.

———. 1987b. "Karma." *Encyclopedia of Religion*, Vol. 8, pp. 261–266. New York: Macmillan.

Mamdani, Mahmood. 1973. *The Myth of Population Control: Family, Caste, and Class in an Indian Village*. New York: Monthly Review Press.

Marano, Lou. 1982. "Windigo Psychosis: The Anatomy of an Emic-Etic Confusion." *Current Anthropology*, 23:385–412.

Marett, Robert. 1914. *The Threshold of Religion*. London: Methuen.

Margolis, Maxine. 1984. *Mothers and Such*. Berkeley: University of California Press.

———. 1994. *Little Brazil: An Ethnography of Brazilian Immigrants in New York City*. Princeton: Princeton University Press.

Marshall, Donald. 1971. "Sexual Behavior on Mangaia." In *Human Sexual Behavior*, D. Marshall and R. Suggs, eds., pp. 103–162. Englewood Cliffs, New Jersey: Prentice-Hall.

Marx, Karl. 1970(1859). *A Contribution to the Critique of Political Economy*. New York: International Publishers.

Mason, J. Alden. 1957. *The Ancient Civilizations of Peru*. Harmondsworth, England: Penguin.

Massing, Michael. 1989. "Crack's Destructive Sprint Across America." *The New York Times Magazine*, October 1, pp. 38ff.

Mathews, Holly. 1985. "We Are Mayordomo: A Reinterpretation of Women's Roles in the Mexican Cargo System." *American Ethnologist*, 12:285–301.

Mead, Margaret. 1970. *Culture and Commitment*. Garden City, New York: Natural History Press.

Meggitt, Mervyn. 1977. *Blood Is Their Argument: Warfare Among the Mae Enga Tribesmen of the New Guinea Highlands*. Palo Alto: Mayfield Publishing Company.

Mencher, Joan. 1974. "The Caste System Upside Down: Or, the Not So Mysterious East." *Current Anthropology*, 15:469–478.

Mencher, Joan and Anne Okongwu. 1993. "Conclusion." In *Where Did All the Men Go?*, Joan Mencher and Anne Okongwu, eds., pp. 272–280. Boulder: Westview.

Merson, Michael. 1993. "Slowing the Spread of HIV: Agenda for the 1990's." *Science*, 260:1266–1268.

Messenger, J.C. 1971. "Sex and Repression in an Irish Folk Community." In *Human Sexual Behavior: Variations in the Ethnographic Spectrum*, D. S. Marshall and R. C. Suggs, eds. New York: Basic Books.

Miller, Barbara. 1981. *The Endangered Sex: Neglect of Female Children in Rural North India*. Ithaca, New York: Cornell University Press.

———. 1987a. "Wife-beating in India: Variations on a Theme." Paper read at the annual meetings of the American Anthropological Association, November.

———. 1987b. "Female Infanticide and Child Neglect in Rural North India." In *Child Survival*, Nancy Scheper-Hughes, ed., pp. 95–112. Boston: D. Redidel.

———. 1992. "Wife Beating in India: Variations on a Theme." In *Sanctions and Sanctuary: Cultural Perspectives on the Beating of Wives*, Dorothy Counts, Judith Brown, and J. C. Campbell, eds., pp. 173–184. Boulder, Colorado: Westview.

Millett, Kate. 1970. *Sexual Politics*. Garden City, New York: Doubleday.

Minturn, Leigh and John T. Hitchcock. 1963. "The Rajputs of Khalapur, India." In *Six Cultures, Studies of Child Rearing*. B. B. Whiting, ed., pp. 203–361. New York: Wiley.

Minturn, L. and J. Stashak. 1982. "Infanticide as a Terminal Abortion Procedure." *Behavior Science Research* 17:70–90.

Mishel, Lawrence and David Frankel. 1990. "The State of Working America." A report released by the Economic Policy Institute, Washington, D.C.

Mitchell, D. and L. Donald. 1988. "Archaeology and the Study of Northwest Coast Economies." In *Prehistoric Economies of the Pacific Northwest Coast*, Barry Isaac, ed., pp. 293–351. Greewich, Connecticut: JAI Press.

Miyadi, D. 1967. "Differences in Social Behavior Among Japanese Macaque Troops." In *Progress in Primatology*, D. Starck, R. Schneider, and H. Kuhn, eds., pp. 228–231. Stuttgart: Gustav Fischer.

Mooney, James. 1965(1896). *The Ghost Dance Religion*. Chicago: University of Chicago Press.

Moore, John. 1990. "The Reproductive Success of Cheyenne War Chiefs: A Contrary Case to Chagnon's Yanomamo." *Current Anthropology*, 31:322–330.

Moran, Emilio. 1982. *Human Adaptability: An Introduction to Ecological Anthropology*. Boulder, Colorado: Westview Press.

Morehouse, Ward and David Dembo. 1988. *Background Paper. Joblessness and the Pauperization of Work in America*. New York: Council on International and Public Affairs.

Morren, George. 1984. "Warfare in the Highland Fringe of New Guinea: The Case of the Mountain Ok." In *Warfare, Culture and Environment*, Brian Ferguson, ed., pp. 169–208. Orlando, Florida: Academic Press.

Morris, C. 1976. "The Master Design of the Inca." *Natural History*, 85(10):58–87.

Moser, Mary. 1982. "Seri: From Conception Through Infancy." In *Anthropology of Human Birth*, Margarita Kay, ed., pp. 221 ff. Philadelphia: F. A. Davis.

Mouer, Ross E. and Yoshio Sugimoto. 1986. *Images of Japanese Society: A Study in the Structure of Social Reality*. London: Kegan Paul.

Moynihan, Daniel P. 1965. *The Negro Family, the Case for National Action.* Washington, D.C.: U.S. Department of Labor.

Murdock, George P. 1949. *Social Structure.* New York: Macmillan.

———. 1967. *Ethnographic Atlas.* Pittsburgh: University of Pittsburgh Press.

Murdock, George and C. Provost. 1973. "Factors in the Division of Labor by Sex." *Ethnology,* 12:203–225.

Murphy, Robert. 1956. "Matrilocality and Patrilineality in Mundurucu Society." *American Anthropologist,* 58:414–434.

———. 1976. "Man's Culture and Women's Nature." *Annals of the New York Academy of Sciences,* 293:15–24.

Murray, Charles. 1984. *Losing Ground: American Social Policy 1950–1980.* New York: Basic Books.

Murray, Gerald. 1984. "The Wood Tree as a Peasant Cash Crop: An Anthropological Strategy for the Domestication of Energy." In *Haiti—Today and Tomorrow: An Interdisciplinary Study,* Charles Fost and A. Valdman, eds., pp. 141–160. Lanham, Maryland: University Press of America.

Nadel, S. F. 1952. "Witchcraft in Four African Societies." *American Anthropologist,* 54(1):18–29.

Nader, Laura. 1972. "Up the Anthropologist—Perspectives Gained from Studying Up." In *Reinventing Anthropology,* Dell Hymes, ed., pp. 284–311. New York: Random House.

———. 1980. *No Access to Law.* New York: Academic Press.

Nag, Moni. 1972. "Sex, Culture, and Human Fertility: India and the United States." *Current Anthropology,* 13:231–238.

———. 1983. "The Impact of Sociocultural Factors on Breastfeeding and Social Behavior." In *Determinants of Fertility in Developing Countries,* Rodolfo A. Bulatao, Ronald D. Lee, with Paula E. Hollerbach and John Bongaarts, eds., pp. 163–198. New York: Academic Press.

Nag, Moni and N. Kak. 1984. "Demographic Transition in the Punjab Village." *Population and Development Review,* 10:661–678.

Nag, Moni, Benjamin White, and Robert Peet. 1978. "An Anthropological Approach to the Study of the Economic Value of Children in Java and Nepal." *Current Anthropology,* pp. 239–306.

Nardi, Bonnie. 1983. "Reply to Harbison's Comments on Nardi's Modes of Explanation in Anthropological Population Theory." *American Anthropologist,* 85:662–664.

Naroll, Raul. 1973. "Introduction." In *Main Currents in Anthropology,* R. Naroll and F. Naroll, eds., pp. 1–23. Englewood Cliffs, New Jersey: Prentice-Hall.

Nash, Jill. 1974. "Matriliny and Modernization: The Nagovisi of South Bougainville." *New Guinea Research Bulletin,* No. 55. Canberra, Australia.

National Research Council. 1992. *Sustainable Agriculture and the Environment in the Humid Tropics.* Washington, D.C.: National Academy Press.

National Urban League. 1990. State of Black America.

Nelson, Sarah. 1993. "Gender Hierarchy and the Queens of Silla" In *Sex and Gender Hierarchies,* Barbara Miller, ed., pp. 297–315. New York: Cambridge University Press.

Nelson, Kristen. 1986. "Labor Demand, Labor Supply, and the Suburbanization of Low-Wage Office Work." In *Production, Work, Territory: The Geographical Anatomy of Industrial Capitalism,* A. Scott and M. Storper, eds., pp. 149–171. Boston: Allen and Unwin.

Netting, Robert M. C. C. 1993. *Smallholders, Householders: Farm Families and the Ecology of Intensive, Sustainable Agriculture.* Stanford: Stanford University Press.

Netting, Robert M. C. C., Richard R. Wilk, and Eric J. Arnould. 1984. *Households: Comparative and Historical Studies of the Domestic Group.* Berkeley: University of California Press.

Neville, Gwen. 1979. "Community Form and Ceremonial Life in Three Regions of Scotland." *American Ethnologist,* 6:93–109.

Newitt, Jane. 1985. "How to Forecast Births." *American Demographics,* January: 30–33, 51.

Newman, Philip L. 1965. *Knowing the Gururumba.* New York: Holt, Rinehart and Winston.

Nishida, T. 1987. "Learning and Cultural Transmission in Nonhuman Primates." In *Primate Societies,* B.B. Smuts, et al., eds., pp. 462–474. Chicago: University of Chicago Press.

Noah, Timothy. 1991. "Number of Poor Americans Is Up." *Wall Street Journal,* September 27, p. A2.

Numbers, Ronald. 1992. *The Creationists.* New York: Knopf.

Oakley, A. 1985. *Sex, Gender, and Society.* London: Gower/Maurice Temple Smith.

Odend'hal, Stuart. 1972. "Energetics of Indian Cattle in Their Environment." *Journal of Human Ecology,* 1:3–22.

Oliver, Douglas. 1955. *A Solomon Island Society: Kinship and Leadership Among the Siuai of Bougainville.* Cambridge, Massachusetts: Harvard University Press.

Opler, Morris. 1968. "The Themal Approach in Cultural Anthropology and Its Application to North Indian Data." *Southwestern Journal of Anthropology,* 24:215–227.

Oppenheimer, Vallery. 1982. *Work and the Family: A Study in Social Demography.* New York: Academic Press.

Orans, Martin. 1968. "Maximizing in Jajmaniland: A Model of Caste Relations." *American Anthropologist,* 70:875–897.

Ortiz de Montellano, B. R. 1978. "Aztec Cannibalism: An Economic Necessity?" *Science,* 200:611–617.

———. 1983. "Counting Skulls: Comments on the Aztec Cannibalism Theory of Harner-Harris." *American Anthropologist,* 85:403–406.

———. 1993. "Melanin, Afrocentricity, and Pseudoscience." *Yearbook of Physical Anthropology,* 36:33–58.

Ortner, Sherry and H. Whiteheads, eds. 1981. *The Cultural Construction of Gender and Sexuality.* Cambridge: Cambridge University Press.

Ottenheimer, Martin. 1984. "Some Problems and Prospects in Residence and Marriage." *American Anthropologist,* 86:351–358.

Otterbein, Keith. 1994. *Feuding and Warfare.* Amsterdam: Gordon and Breach.

Pandian, Jacob. 1992. *Culture, Religion and the Sacred Self: A Critical Introduction to the Anthropological Study of Religion.* Englewood Cliffs, New Jersey: Prentice Hall

Parenti, Michael. 1986. *Inventing Reality: The Politics of Mass Media.* New York: St. Martin's Press.

Parker, Sue. 1985. "A Social-Technological Model for the Evolution of Languages." *Current Anthropology,* 26:617–639.

Pasternak, Burton, Carol Ember, and Melvin Ember. 1976. "On the Conditions Favoring Extended Family Households." *Journal of Anthropological Research,* 32(2):109–123.

Paztory, Esther. 1984. "The Function of Art in Mesoamerica." *Archeology,* January–February: 18–25.

Peletz, Michael G. 1987. "Female Heirship and the Autonomy of Women in Negeri Sembilan, West Malaysia." In *Research in Economic Anthropology: A Research Annual*, Vol. 8, Barry L. Isaac, ed., pp. 61–101. Greenwich, Connecticut: JAI Press.

Pelto, Pertti and Gretel Pelto. 1976. *The Human Adventure: An Introduction to Anthropology*. New York: Macmillan.

Percival, L. and K. Quinkert. 1987. "Anthropometric Factors." In *Sex Differences in Human Performance*, Mary Baker, ed., pp. 121–139. New York: Wiley.

Peterson, J. T. 1978. *The Ecology of Social Boundaries: Agta Foragers of the Philippines*. Urbana: University of Illinois Press.

Peterson, Nicholas. 1993. "Demand Sharing and the Pressure for Generosity Among Foragers." *American Anthropologist*, 95:860–874.

Pfaffenberger, Bryan. 1992. "Social Anthropology of Technology." *Annual Review of Anthropology*, 21:491–516.

Pimentel, David, L. E. Hurd, A. C. Bellotti, et al. 1973. "Food Production and Energy Crisis." *Science*, 182:443–449.

Pimentel, D. and M. Pimentel. 1985. "Energy Use for Food Processing for Nutrition and Development." *Food and Nutrition Bulletin*, 7(2):36–45.

Pimentel, David, et al. 1975. "Energy and Land Constraints in Food Protein Production." *Science*, 190:754–761.

Pivnik, Anitra, et al. 1991. "Reproductive Decisions Among HIV-Infected, Drug-Using Women: The Importance of Mother-Child Co-Residence." *Medical Anthropology Quarterly*, 5:153–169.

Plath, David, ed. 1983. *Work and Life Course in Japan*. Albany: State University of New York Press.

Plattner, Stuart. 1989. "Introduction." In *Economic Anthropology*, Stuart Plattner, ed., pp. 1–20. Stanford, California: Stanford University Press.

Podolefsky, Aaron. 1984. "Contemporary Warfare in the New Guinea Highlands." *Ethnology*, 23:73–87.

Pospisil, Leopold, 1963. *The Kapauku Papuans of West New Guinea*. New York: Holt, Rinehart and Winston.

Post, John. 1985. *Food Shortage, Climatic Variability, and Epidemic Disease in Pre-Industrial Europe*. Ithaca, New York: Cornell University Press.

Price, David. 1993. The Evolution of Irrigation in Egypt's Fayoum Oasis: State, Village and Conveyance Loss. Ph.D. Dissertation, University of Florida.

Price, John. 1980. "On Silent Trade." *Research in Economic Anthropology*, 3:75–96.

Ramirez, F. and J. Meyer. 1980. "Comparative Education: The Social Construction of the Modern World System." *Annual Review of Sociology*, 6:369–399.

Rappaport, Roy. 1968. *Pigs for the Ancestors: Ritual in the Ecology of a New Guinea People*. New Haven: Yale University Press.

———. 1984. *Pigs for the Ancestors: Ritual in the Ecology of a Papuan New Guinea People*, 2nd edition. New Haven: Yale University Press.

Rasmussen, Knud. 1929. *The Intellectual Culture of the Iglulik Eskimos*. Report of the 5th Thule Expedition, 1921–1924, vol. 7, no.1. Translated by W. Worster. Copenhagen: Glydendal.

Reed, C. M. 1984. "Maritime Traders in the Archaic Greek World." *The Ancient World*, 10:31–43.

Renfrew, Colin. 1994. "World Linguistic Diversity." *Scientific American*, (January):116–123.

Reyna, S. P. 1989. "Grudge Matching and War: Considerations of the Nature and Universality of War." Paper presented at the American Anthropological Association annual meeting, Washington, D.C., November 15.

Rhoades, Robert. 1984. *Breaking New Ground: Agricultural Anthropology*. Lima, Peru: International Potato Center.

Riddle, J. and J. W. Estes. 1992. "Oral Contraceptives in Ancient and Medieval Times." *American Scientist*, 80: 226–233.

Rifkind, Jeremy and Ted Howard. 1979. *The Emerging Order: God in the Age of Scarcity*. New York: Putnam.

Riviere, C. 1987. "Soul: Concepts in Primitive Religions." In *The Encyclopedia of Religion*, pp. 426–430. New York: Macmillan and Free Press.

Roberts, Ron and D. Brintnall. 1982. *Reinventing Inequality*. Boston: Schenkman.

Roberts, Sam. 1993. "Fighting the Tide of Bloodshed on Streets Resembling a War Zone." *The New York Times*, Nov. 15, p. B12.

Rohner, Ronald. 1969. *The Ethnography of Franz Boas*. Chicago: University of Chicago Press.

Rohrlich-Leavitt, Ruby. 1977. "Women in Transition: Crete and Sumer." In *Becoming Visible: Women in European History*, Renate Bridenthal and C. Koonz, eds., pp. 38–59. Boston: Houghton Mifflin.

Roosens, Eugene. 1989. *Creating Ethnicity: The Process of Ethnogenesis*. Newbury Park, California: Sage.

Root, Marla, ed. 1992. *Racially Mixed People in America*. Newbury Park, California: Sage.

Rosaldo, Michelle and Louise Lamphere, eds. 1974. *Women, Culture, and Society*. Stanford, California: Stanford University Press.

Ross, Eric. 1979. "Reply to Lizot." *Current Anthropology* 20:151–155.

Ross, Phillip. 1991. "Hard Words." *Scientific American*, April: 137–147.

Roth, Eric. 1985. "A Note on the Demographic Concommitants of Sedentism." *American Anthropologist*, 87:380–381.

Royce, W. F. 1987. *Fishery Development*. New York: Academic Press.

Sabato, Larry. 1989. *Paying for Elections: The Campaign Finance Thicket*. New York: Priority Press.

Sacks, Karen B. 1971. Economic Bases of Sexual Equality: A Comparative Study of Four African Societies. Ph.D. dissertation, University of Michigan.

Safa, Helen I. 1986. "Economic Autonomy and Sexual Equality in Caribbean Society." *Social and Economic Studies*, 35(3):1–20.

Sahagun, Bernardino de. 1951. "Book 2—The Ceremonies." In *General History of the Things of New Spain*, Florentine Codex, A. J. O. Anderson and C. E. Dibble, trans. (from Aztec). In Thirteen Parts, Part III. Santa Fe, New Mexico: School of American Research, and Salt Lake City: University of Utah.

Sahlins, Marshall. 1978. "Culture as Protein and Profit." *The New York Review of Books*, November 23, pp. 45–53.

Sanday, Peggy. 1981. *Female Power and Male Dominance: On the Origins of Sexual Inequality*. New York: Cambridge University Press.

Sanderson, Stephen. 1988. *Macrosociology: An Introduction to Human Societies*. New York: Harper & Row.

Sanjek, Roger. 1972. Ghanian Networks: An Analysis of Interethnic Relations in Urban Situations. Ph.D. dissertation, Columbia University.

———. 1977. "Cognitive Maps of the Ethnic Domain in Urban Ghana: Reflections on Variability and Change." *American Ethnologist*, 4:603–622.

Sanjek, Roger, ed. 1990. *Fieldnotes: The Making of Anthropology*. Ithaca, New York: Cornell University Press.

Sankar, Andrea. 1986. "Sisters and Brothers, Lovers and Enemies: Marriage Resistance in Southern Kuangtung." In *Anthropology and Homosexual Behavior*, Evelyn Blackwood, ed., pp. 69–81. New York: Haworth Press.

Sapir, Edward. 1921. *Language: An Introduction to the Study of Speech*. New York: Harcourt, Brace.

Sakar, Jayanta. 1993. "Till Death Do Us Part: Dowries Contribute to a Rise in Violence Against Indian Women." *Far Eastern Economic Review*, Oct. 28, pp. 40–41.

Savage-Rumbaugh, Sue. 1987. "Communication, Symbolic Communication, and Language: Reply to Seidenberg and Petitto." *Journal of Experimental Psychology: General*, 116: 288–292.

Savage-Rumbaugh, Sue, et al. 1990. "Symbols: Their Communicative Use, Comprehension, and Combination by Bonobos (Pan paniscus)." In *Advances in Infancy Research*, Vol. 6, Carolyn Rovee-Collier and Lewis P. Lipsitt, eds., pp. 222–254. Norwood, New Jersey: ABLEX.

———. 1993. *Language Comprehension in Ape and Child*. Chicago: University of Chicago Press.

Scarr, S. and R. A. Weinberg. 1976. "I.Q. Test Performance of Black Children Adopted by White Families." *American Psychologist*, 31:726–739.

Scheffler, Harold. 1973. "Kinship, Descent, and Alliance." In *Handbook of Social and Cultural Anthropology*, J. Honigman, ed., pp. 747–793. Chicago: Rand McNally.

Scheper-Hughes, Nancy. 1984. "Infant Mortality and Infant Care: Cultural and Economic Constraints on Nuturing in Northeast Brazil." *Social Science and Medicine*, 19(5):535–546.

———. 1992. *Death Without Weeping: The Violence of Every Day Life in Brazil*. Berkeley: University of California Press.

Schlegel, Alice, ed. 1972. *Male Dominance and Female Autonomy*. New Haven: Human Relations Area Files.

Schlegel, Alice and H. Barry. 1979. "Adolescent Initiation Ceremonies: A Cross-Cultural Code." *Ethnology*, 18:199–210.

———. 1986. "The Cultural Consequences of Female Contributions to Subsistence." *American Anthropologist*, 88:142–150.

Schlegel, Alice and R. Eloul. 1988. "Marriage Transactions: Labor, Property and Status." *American Anthropologist*, 90:291–309.

Schields, N.M. 1993. "The Natural and Unnatural History of Inbreeding and Outbreeding." In *The Natural History of Inbreeding and Outbreeding*, N. W. Thornhill, ed., pp. 143–169. Chicago: University of Chicago Press.

Scoditti, G. 1983. "Kula on Kitava." In *The Kula: New Perspectives in Massim Exchange*, J. Leach and E. Leach, eds., pp. 249–273. New York: Cambridge University Press.

Scrimshaw, Susan. 1983. "Infanticide as Deliberate Fertility Regulation." In *Determinants of Fertility in Developing Nations: Supply and Demand for Children*, R. Bulatao and R. Lee, eds. New York: Academic Press.

Serrin, William. 1984. "Experts Say Job Bias Against Women Persists." *The New York Times*, November 25, pp. 1, 18.

Service, Elman R. 1975. *Origins of the State and Civilization: The Processes of Cultural Evolution*. New York: Norton.

Shankman, Paul. 1991. "Culture Contact, Cultural Ecology, and Dani Warfare." *Man*, 26:299–321.

Sharff, Jagna. 1981. "Free Enterprise and the Ghetto Family." *Psychology Today*, March.

Sharma, Ursula. 1983. "Dowry in North India: Its Consequences for Women." In *Women and Property*, Renee Hirschon, ed., pp. 62–74. London: Croom Helm.

Sharma, Rita and T. P. Poleman. 1993. *The New Economics of India's Green Revolution*. Ithaca: Cornell University Press.

Shepher, Joseph. 1983. *Incest: A Biosocial Point of View*. New York: Academic Press.

Short, Richard. 1984. "On Placing the Child Before Marriage, Reply to Birdsell." *Population and Development Review*, 9:124–135.

Shostak, Marjorie. 1981. *Nisa, The Life and Words of a !Kung Woman*. Cambridge, Massachusetts: Harvard University Press.

Shuey, Audrey M. 1966. *The Testing of Negro Intelligence*. New York: Social Science Press.

Silk, Joan and Richard Boyd. 1989. "Anthropology: Human Evolution." U.C.L.A. Lecture Notes.

Silk, Leonard. 1985. "The Peril Behind the Takeover Boom." *The New York Times*, December 29, Sec. 3, p. 1.

Simmons, R.C. and C.C. Hughes, eds. 1985. *The Culture-Bound Syndromes*. Dordrecht: D. Reidl.

Simoons, Frederick. 1979. "Questions in the Sacred Cow Controversy." *Current Anthropology*, 20:467–493.

Skinner, G. William. 1993. "Conjugal Power in Tokugawa Japanese Families: A Matter of Life or Death." In *Sex and Gender Hierarchies*, Barbara Miller, ed., pp. 236–270. New York: Cambridge University Press.

Smith, Eric and Bruce Winterhalder. 1992. *Evolutionary Ecology and Human Behavior*. Hawthorne, New York: Aldine de Gruter.

Smith, M. G. 1968. "Secondary Marriage Among Kadera and Kagoro." In *Marriage, Family, and Residence*, P. Bohannan and J. Middleton, eds., pp. 109–130. Garden City, New York: Natural History Press.

Smith, Raymond T. 1988. "Kinship and Class in the West Indies: Genealogical Study of Jamaica and Guyana." *Cambridge Studies in Social and Cultural Anthropology*, 65. New York: Cambridge University Press.

Snowden, Charles T. 1990. "Language Capacities of Nonhuman Animals." *Yearbook of Physical Anthropology*, 33:215–243.

Soloway, Jaqueline S. and Richard B. Lee. 1990. "Foragers, Genuine or Spurious?" *Current Anthropology*, 31(2):109–146.

Sorenson, Richard. 1972. "Socio-Ecological Change Among the Fore' of New Guinea." *Current Anthropology*, 13:349–383.

Sorenson, Richard, and P. E. Kenmore. 1974. "Proto-Agricultural Movement in the Eastern Highlands of New Guinea." *Current Anthropology*, 15:67–72.

Soustelle, Jacques. 1970. *Daily Life of the Aztecs*. Stanford, California: Stanford University Press.

Spencer, P. 1965. *The Samburu: A Study of Gerontocracy in a Nomadic Tribe*. Berkeley: University of California Press.

Spengler, Joseph. 1974. *Population Change, Modernization, and Welfare*. Englewood Cliffs, New Jersey: Prentice-Hall.

Spickard, Paul. 1992. "The Illogic of American Racial Categories". In *Racially Mixed People in America*, Marla Root, ed., pp. 12–23. Newburry Park, California: Sage

Spiro, Melford. 1954. "Is the Family Universal?" *American Anthropologist,* 56:839–846.

———. 1982. *Oedipus in the Trobriands.* Chicago: University of Chicago Press.

Spuhler, James. 1985. "Anthropology, Evolution, and Scientific Creationism." *Annual Review of Anthropology,* 14:103–133.

Srinivas, M. N. 1955. "The Social System of a Mysore Village." In *Village India: Studies in the Little Community,* M. Marriot, ed., pp. 1–35. Memoir 83. Washington, D.C.: American Anthropological Association.

Stacey, Judith. 1990. *Brave New Families: Stories of Domestic Upheaval in Late Twentieth Century America.* New York: Basic Books.

Stack, Carol. 1974. *All Our Kin: Strategies for Survival in a Black Community.* New York: Harper & Row.

Steadman, Lyle and C. Merbs. 1982. "Kuru: Early Letters and Field-Notes from the Collection of D. Carleton Gajdusek." *American Anthropologist,* 84:611–627.

Stearman, Allyn. 1994. "Losing Game." *Natural History,* (January):6–10.

Stein, Howard and R. F. Hill. 1977. *The Ethnic Imperative: Examining the New White Ethnic Movement.* University Park: Pennsylvania State University Press.

Steinhart, John and Carol Steinhart. 1974. "Energy Use in the U.S. Food System." *Science,* 184:307–317.

Stern, Steve J. 1988. "Feudalism, Capitalism, and the World System in the Perspective of Latin America and the Carribean." *American Historical Review,* 93:829–897.

Stewart, Omer. 1987. *Peyote Religion: A History.* Norman: University of Oklahoma Press.

Strauss, Claudia. 1992. "What Makes Tony Run: Schemas As Motives Reconsidered." In *Human Motives and Cultural Models,* Roy D'Andradade and Claudia Strauss, eds., pp. 197–224. New York: Cambridge University Press.

Strehlow, T. 1947. *Aranda Traditions.* Melbourne: Melbourne University Press.

Stringer, C. B. 1992. "Replacement, Continuity, and the Origin of Modern Homo Sapiens." In *Continuity or Replacement? Controversies in Homo Sapiens Evolution,* G. Brauer and F. H. Smith, eds., pp. 9–24. Rotterdam: Balkema.

Swisher, C. C., et al. 1994. "Age of the Earliest Known Hominids in Java, Indonesia." *Science,* 263:1118–1121.

Sudarkasa, N. 1973. *Where Women Work: A Study of Yoruba Women in the Marketplace and in the Home.* Ann Arbor: University of Michigan Museum.

Suggs, David and A. Miracle, eds. 1993. *Culture and Human Sexuality.* Pacific Grove; California: Brooks/Cole.

Sugimoto, Y. and R. Mouer. 1983. *Japanese Society: A Study in Social Reconstruction.* London: Kegan Paul.

Sullivan, Lawrence. 1987. "Supreme Beings." In *The Encyclopedia of Religion,* M. Eliade, ed. New York: Macmillan and Free Press.

Swanson, Guy E. 1960. *The Birth of the Gods: The Origin of Primitive Beliefs.* Ann Arbor: University of Michigan Press.

Tefft, Stanton. 1975. "Warfare Regulation: A Cross-Cultural Test of Hypotheses." In *War: Its Causes and Correlates,* Martin Nettleship, et al., eds., pp. 693–712. Chicago: Aldine.

Terrace, Herbert. 1979. "Is Problem Solving Language?" *Journal of the Experimental Analysis of Behavior,* 31:161–175.

Testart, Alain. 1982. "The Significance of Food-Storage Among Hunter-Gatherers: Residence Patterns, Population Densities and Social Inequalities." *Current Anthropology,* 23(3):523–537.

Thomas, Lewis. 1986. "Peddling Influence." *Time,* March 3, pp. 26–36.

Thurston, Robert. 1939. *A History of the Growth of the Steam Engine.* Ithaca, New York: Cornell University Press.

Tilakaratne, M. W. 1978. "Economic Change, Social Differentiation, and Fertility: Aluthgana." In *Population and Development: High and Low Fertility in Poorer Countries,* G. Hawthorn, ed., pp. 186–197. London: Frank Cass.

Titon, J. T., et al. 1984. *Worlds of Music: An Introduction to the Musics of the World's Peoples.* New York: Schirmer Books.

Torrey, E. F. 1980. *Schizophrenia and Civilization.* New York: Jason Aronson.

Trevor-Roper, H. 1983. "The Invention of Tradition: The Highland Tradition of Scotland". In *The Invention of Tradition,* Eric Hobsbawm and Terrance Ranger, eds., pp. 15–41. New York: Cambridge University Press.

Trigger, Bruce. 1978. "Iroquois Matriliny." *Pennsylvania Archaeologist,* 48:55–65.

Tronick, E. Z., G. A. Morelli, and S. Winn. 1987. "Multiple Caretaking of Efe (Pygmy) Infants." *American Anthropologist,* 89:96–106.

Turnbull, Colin M. 1978. "The Politics of Non-Aggression." In *Learning Non-Aggression,* Ashley Montagu, ed. Oxford: Oxford University Press.

———. 1982. "The Ritualization of Potential Conflict Between the Sexes Among the Mbuti." In *Politics and History in Band Societies,* Eleanor Leacock and Richard Lee, eds., pp. 133–155. Cambridge: Cambridge University Press.

Turner, Terrence. 1991. "Report of the Special Commission to Investigate the Situation of the Brazilian Yanomami." Washington, D.C.: American Anthropological Association.

Tylor, Edward B. 1871. *Primitive Culture.* London: J. Murray.

Uhlman, Allon. 1992. "A Critique of Leavitt's Review of Sociobiological Explanations of Incest Avoidance." *American Anthropologist,* 94:446–448.

UNDP (United Nations Development Programme). 1993. *Human Development Report.* New York: Oxford University Press.

U. S. Bureau of the Census. 1990. Statistical Abstract of the United States. Washington, D.C.

———. 1994. Statistical Abstract of the United States. Washington, D.C.

Upham, Steadman. 1990. *The Evolution of Political Systems: Sociopolitics in Small-Scale Sedentary Societies.* New York: Cambridge University Press.

Vaidyanathan, A., N. Nair, and M. Harris. 1982. "Bovine Sex and Age Ratios in India." *Current Anthropology,* 23:365–383.

Vaillant, George C. 1966(1941). *The Aztecs of Mexico.* Baltimore: Penguin.

Van Allen, J. 1972. "Sitting on a Man: Colonialism and the Lost Political Institutions of Igbo Women." *Canadian Journal of African Studies,* 6(2):165–182.

Van Beek, W. E. A. 1991. "Dogon Restudies: A Field Evaluation of the Work of Marcel Griaule." *Current Anthropology,* 12:139–167.

Vandiver, Pamela B., et al. 1989. "The Origins of Ceramic Technology at Dolni Vestonice, Czechoslovakia." *Science,* 246:1002–1008.

Van Lawick-Goodall, Jane. 1986. *The Chimpanzees of Gombe.* Cambridge, Massachusetts: Harvard University Press.

Wagley, Charles. 1943. "Tapirap Shamanism." *Boletim Do Museu Nacional (Rio de Janeiro) Anthropologia,* 3:1–94.

———. 1977. *Welcome of Tears.* New York: Oxford University Press.

Walker, Deward. 1972. *The Emergent Native Americans.* Boston: Little, Brown.

Walker, Phillip L. 1988. "Cranial Injuries as Evidence of Violence in Prehistoric California." *American Journal of Physical Anthropology,* 80:313–323.

Wallace, Anthony F. C. 1966. *Religion: An Anthropological View.* New York: Random House.

———. 1970. *Cultural and Personality,* 2nd edition. New York: Random House.

———. 1972. "Mental Illness, Biology and Culture." In *Psychological Anthropology,* Francis Hsu, ed., pp. 363–402. Cambridge, Massachusetts: Schenkman.

Walsh, John. 1991. "The Greening of the Green Revolution." *Science,* 252:26.

Warner, Richard. 1985. *Recovery from Schizophrenia: Psychiatry and Political Economy.* London: Routledge and Kegan Paul.

Warner, W. Lloyd. 1958. *A Black Civilization.* New York: Harper & Row.

Watson, James. 1977. "Pigs, Fodder, and the Jones Effect in Postipomean New Guinea." *Ethnology,* 16:57–70.

Watson, Richard. 1990. "Ozymandius, King of Kings: Postprocessual Radical Archaeology as Critique." *American Antiquity,* 55:673–689.

Weatherford, Jack. 1988. *Indian Givers: How the Indians of the Americas Transformed the World.* New York: Crown.

Weber, Peter. 1994. "Safeguarding Oceans." In *State of the World,* Lester Brown, ed. pp. 41–59. New York: W. W. Norton.

Weidman, Helen. 1983. "Research, Service, and Training Aspects of Clinical Anthropology." In *Clinical Anthropology,* D. Shimkin and P. Golde, eds., pp. 119–153. Washington, D.C.: University Press of America.

Weil, Peter. 1986. "Agricultural Intensification and Fertility in the Gambia (West Africa)." In *Culture and Reproduction: An Anthropological Critique of Demographic Transition Theory,* W. P. Handwerker, ed., pp. 294–320. Boulder, Colorado: Westview Press.

Weiner, Annette. 1976. *Women of Value, Men of Renown.* Austin: University of Texas Press.

Weisman, Steven. 1978. "City Constructs Statistical Profile in Looting Cases." *The New York Times,* August 14, p. 1.

Weismantel, Mary. 1989. "Making Breakfast and Raising Babies." In *The Household Economy: Reconsidering the Domestic Mode of Production,* Richard Wilk, ed., pp. 55–72. Boulder: Westview.

Weisner, Thomas and Ronald Gilmore. 1977. "My Brother's Keeper: Child and Sibling Caretaking." *Current Anthropology* 18:169–190.

Weiss, Gerald. 1977. "Rhetoric in Campa Narrative." *Journal of Latin American Lore,* 3:169–182.

Weitzman, Lenore. 1985. *The Divorce Revolution: Consequences for Women and Children in America.* New York: Free Press.

Welsing, Francis. 1991. *The Isis (Yssis) Papers.* Chicago: Third World Press.

Werge, R. 1979. "Potato Processing in the Central Highlands of Peru." *Ecology of Food and Nutrition,* 7:229–234.

Werner, Dennis. 1979. "A Cross-Cultural Perspective on Theory and Research on Male Homosexuality." *Journal of Homosexuality,* 4:345–362.

Westermark, E. 1894. *The History of Human Marriage.* New York: Macmillan.

Westoff, Charles. 1986. "Fertility in the United States." *Science,* 234:544–559.

Weyer, E. 1932. *The Eskimos.* New Haven: Yale University Press.

White, Benjamin. 1982. "Child Labour and Population Growth in Rural Asia." *Development and Change,* 13:587–610.

White, Leslie. 1949. *The Science of Culture.* New York: Grove Press.

Whitesides, George. 1985. "Nut Cracking by Wild Chimpanzees in Sierra Leone, West Africa." *Primates,* 26:91–94.

Whiting, John, ed. 1969. "Effects of Climate on Certain Cultural Practices." In *Environmental and Cultural Behavior: Ecological Studies in Cultural Anthropology,* A. P. Vayda, ed., pp. 416–455. Garden City, New York: Natural History Press.

Whiting, John. 1993. "The Effect of Polygyny on Sex Ratio at Birth." *American Anthropologist,* 95:435–442.

Whiting, John and Beatrice Whiting. 1978. "A Strategy for Psychocultural Research." In *The Making of Psychological Anthropology,* George Spindler, ed., pp. 41–61. Berkeley: University of California Press.

Whorf, Benjamin. 1956. *Language, Thought, and Reality.* New York: Wiley.

Williams, Terry. 1989. *The Cocaine Kids: The Inside Story of a Teenage Drug Ring.* Reading, Massachusetts: Addison-Wesley.

Williams, Walter. 1986. *The Spirit and the Flesh: Sexual Diversity in American Indian Culture.* Boston: Beacon Press.

Willigen, John Van. 1986. *Applied Anthropology: An Introduction.* South Hadley, Massachusetts: Bergin and Garvey.

Willmsen, Edwin N. 1982. "Biological Variables in Forager Fertility Performance: A Critique of Bongaart's Model." Working Paper No. 60, African Studies Center. Boston University.

Wilmsen, Edwin and James Denbow. 1990. "Paradigmatic History of San-speaking Peoples and Current Attempts at Revision." *Current Anthropology,* 31:489–524.

Wilson, E. O. 1975. *Sociobiology: The New Synthesis.* Cambridge, Massachusetts: Harvard University Press.

———. 1978. *Human Nature.* Cambridge, Massachusetts: Harvard University Press.

Wilson, Monica. 1963. *Good Company: A Study of Nyakyusa Age-Villages.* Boston: Little, Brown.

Winkelman, Michael. 1990. "Shamans and Other 'Magico-Religious' Healers." *Ethos,* 18:308–351.

Witowski, Stanley and Cecil A. Brown. 1978. "Lexical Universals." *Annual Review of Anthropology,* 7:427–451.

———. 1985. "Climate, Clothing, and Body-Part Nomenclature." *Ethnology,* 24:197–214.

Wolf, A. P. and C. S. Huang. 1980. *Marriage and Adoption in China, 1845–1945.* Stanford, California: Stanford University Press.

Wolf, Eric. 1994. "Perilous Ideas: Race, Culture, People." *Current Anthropology,* 35:1–12.

Wood, James. 1990. "Fertility in Anthropological Populations." *Annual Review of Anthropology*, 19:211–242.

Woodburn, James. 1982a. "Egalitarian Societies." *Man*, 17:431–451.

————. 1982b. "Social Dimension of Death in Four African Hunting and Gathering Societies." In *Death and the Regeneration of Life*, Maurice Block and Jonathan Parry, eds., pp. 187–210. New York: Cambridge University Press.

Worsley, Peter. 1968. *The Trumpet Shall Sound: A Study of "Cargo" Cults in Melanesia*. New York: Schocken.

Yates, Robin D. S. 1990. "War, Food Shortages, and Relief Measures in Early China." In *Hunger in History: Food Shortage, Poverty, and Deprivation*, Lucile F. Newman, et al., eds., pp. 147–176. Cambridge, Massachusetts: Basil Blackwell.

NAME INDEX

SUBJECT INDEX

CREDITS

❦

Cain "The Economic Activities of Children in a Village in Bangladesh." *Population and Development Review*, 3:3 (September 1977), p. 225; p. 77 Table 7.1: Donald S. Marshal, "Sexual Behavior in Mangaia" p. 123 in *Human Sexual Behavior*, Donald S, Marshal and Robert Suggs, eds. Copyright 1971 by The Institute for Sex Research, Inc. Reprinted by permission of the publisher, Prentice Hall/ a division of Simon & Schuster, Englewood Cliffs, NJ.; p. 89: Excerpts from *The Semai A Non-violent People of Malaya*, Fieldwork Edition by Robert K. Dentan, copyright 1979 by Holt, Rhinehart and Winston, Inc., reprinted by permission of the publisher.; p. 97: Excerpt from *The Kapauku Papuans of West New Guinea: Case Studies in Cultural Anthropology* by Leopold Pospisil, copyright 1963 by Holt, Rhinehart and Winston Inc. and renewed 1991 by Leopold Pospisil, reprinted by permission of the publisher.; p. 139 Box 11.4: Evans-Pritchard, *The Neur, A Description of the Modes of Livelihood and political Institutions of a Nitotic People*, pp. 181-182. Published 1940 by Clarendon Press, Oxford. Reprinted with permission.; p. 145: Brian R. Ferguson, "A Savage Encounter: Western Contact and the Yanoman War Complex." p. 209 in *War in the Tribal Zone: Expanding States and Indigenous Warfare*, Brian Ferguson and Niel Whitehead eds. Copyright 1992 by School of American research Press. Reprinted by permission.; p. 151: Bartram in Collin Renfrew, *Before Civilization: The Radiocarbon Revolution and Prehistoric Europe*, p. 234. Published 1973 by Alfred A. Knopf. Reprinted by permission.; p. 165: Oscar Lewis, *La Vida: A Puerto Rican Family in the Culture of Poverty - San Jaun and New York*, p. 21. Published 1966 by Random House, Inc. Reprinted with permission of the author.; p. 167 Box 13.2: Thomas Belmonte, *The Broken Fountain 2/e*. p. 144 Copyright 1989 Columbia University Press. Used by permission.; p. 175 Box 14.1: H. Trevor Roper, "The Invention of Tradition: The Highland Tradition of Scotland." in *The Invention of Tradition*, Eric Hobsbawm and Terrance Ranger eds. Copyright 1983 Reprinted with the permission of Cambridge University Press.; p. 195: Shirley Lindenbaum, *Kuru Society*, p. 129. published 1979 by Mayfield, Mountain View, California. Reprinted by permission.; p. 193: Annettee Weiner, *Women of Value, Men of Renown*, pp. 118 and 228. Copyright 1976 by The University of Texas Press. Reprinted by permission.; p. 199 Table 15.1: Reprinted with permission from *The World Almanac and Book of Facts 1994*. Copyright 1993 by funk & Wagnalls Corporation. All Rights Reserved.; p. 198: Darly Feil, *The Evolution of Highland Papua New Guinea Societies*, pp. 69, 203. Copyright 1987. Reprinted with the permission of Cambridge University Press.; p. 223: Excerpt from *Knowing the Gururumba* by Philip L. Newman, Copyright 1965 by Holt, Rhinehart and Winston, Inc. and renewed 1993 by Philip L. Newman, reprinted by permission of the publisher.; p. 226 Box 17.1: Charles Wagley, "Tapirape Shamanism" in Boletin Do Museu Nacional Anthropologia, 3 (1943), 73-74. Reprinted by Permission of Meseu Nacional, Rio de Janiero.; p. 265 Box 19.3: Gerald Murray, "The Wood Tree As Peasant Cash Crop: An Anthropological Strategy for the Domestication of Energy," p. 147 in *Haiti - Today and Tomorrow: An Interdisciplinary Study*, Charles Frost and A. Valdman eds. Published 1984 by University Press of America. Reprinted by permission.